MARY STUART AT THE AGE OF SEVENTEEN

Mary Queen of Scotland and the Isles

MARY
QUEEN OF SCOTLAND AND THE ISLES

By

Stefan Zweig

Translated by Eden and Cedar Paul

ISHI PRESS
INTERNATIONAL

Mary Queen of Scotland and the Isles

by Stefan Zweig

Translated by Eden and Cedar Paul

First published in 1935 in Germany as
Maria Stuart

This Printing in May, 2010
by Ishi Press in New York and Tokyo

with a new foreword by Sam Sloan

Copyright © 1935 by Stefan Zweig
Copyright © 2010 by Sam Sloan

All rights reserved according to International Law. No part of this book may be reproduced by for public or private use without the written permission of the publisher.

ISBN 4-87187-858-9
978-4-87187-858-6

Ishi Press International
1664 Davidson Avenue, Suite 1B
Bronx NY 10453-7877
1-917-507-7226

Printed in the United States of America

Mary Queen of Scotland and the Isles
by Stefan Zweig
Foreword by Sam Sloan

She was born to be Queen of Scotland, she was briefly the Queen of France and she had a claim to being Queen of England, which resulted in her having her head chopped off.

They chopped off her head after she was found guilty of conspiring to have **Queen Elizabeth (1533-1603)** assassinated so that she could take power. Had she not been executed, she would eventually have become Queen of England when Elizabeth died.

That was only one of the many controversies in which she was involved. Her first husband, who became the King of France, making her the Queen, died shortly thereafter and her second husband was found murdered, apparently strangled. Mary Queen of Scots (1542-1587) was believed to have been complicit in that murder. Her Father, King James V of Scotland (1512-1542), had many, many mistresses and possibly as many as twenty illegitimate children. His father too, King James IV of Scotland (1473-1513), had a similar number of mistresses and a similar number of illegitimate children. This has left, to this day, the problem genealogists have in sorting out all of these bastard kids.

I have this problem in my own family too. I have a presumed ancestor named Mary Stuart, born 1729 in Gabinheough, Tyrone, Ireland. She was said to have been descended from one of the bastard offspring of King James IV or King James V of Scotland, but nobody has found evidence for this relationship, and many have searched.

Foreword by Sam Sloan

When father of Mary Queen of Scots, King James V of Scotland (1512-1542), died just after a battle when Mary was only six days old, Mary became Queen, not by being the eldest child but by being the only legitimate child, as her mother, *Marie de Guise* (1515-1560) was the only legal wife of the King. The bastard children of King James V, although older, did not get to rule.

Later, her only son, who became King James I of England as well as King James VI of Scotland (1566-1625), thereby uniting England and Scotland into one kingdom, was taken away from her shortly after his birth and she never saw him again.

This widely acclaimed biography by Stefan Zweig is regarded as the best of the many biographies of this famous woman.

The great thing about the author, Stefan Zweig, is that his biographies are smooth and easy to read. By contrast, there is a weighty tome with exactly the same title but 880 pages long. Here in 386 easy to read pages you can learn everything about Mary Queen of Scots that you will probably ever want to know.

The way I remember the confusing but important facts of this tumultuous period is that I remember that King James I was a Protestant, because under him the **King James Version of the Bible** was authorized and composed. The King James Version is a Protestant Bible. The Catholics have a different Bible. Therefore, King James I must have been a Protestant. I remember his era because Jamestown, the First Permanent Settlement in North America, was established during his rule.

His mother, Mary Queen of Scots, was a Catholic. Since Catholics do not recognize divorce, she was the rightful Queen of England under the Catholic System of counting. Therefore, her rival, **Queen Elizabeth**, had to be Protestant if she wanted to remain Queen. The mother of Elizabeth, **Anne Boleyn (1501-1536)**, had her head chopped off because her husband, **King Henry VIII (1491-1547)**, wanted another wife. However, when he again tired of the next wife too, he decided that it would be bloody inconvenient to chop her head off too, so he changed the Religion of England, abolishing Catholicism and establishing the Church of England in its place. This change in religion enabled King Henry VIII simply to divorce his next wife. He did not have to kill that one.

The author, **Stefan Zweig** (born **November 28, 1881, Vienna, Austria – died February 22, 1942, Petrópolis, Brazil**), was an Austrian novelist, playwright, journalist and biographer was one of the most successful and popular authors of the 20th Century. Although he wrote in German, his works were translated into English and several other languages. Zweig was a prolific writer. In the 1930s he was one of the most widely translated authors in the world. His extensive travels led him to India, Africa, North and Central America, and Russia.

This book was first published in 1935 in Frankfurt, Germany in German as **Maria Stuart**.

There is a tragedy associated with this book, because the author and his wife died by suicide. He left a suicide note stating that he and his wife were killing themselves because he was in despair because his native country, Austria, had been overrun by the Nazis.

However, that was not a good reason for suicide, as he was safely in Brazil and Austria had been taken by the Nazis years earlier.

Perhaps another reason for his suicide was he had lost his royalty income due to the "Trading with the Enemies Act". His books were all first published in Germany. Under the Trading with the Enemies Act, it was illegal for any US company to pay money to any German company. Austria had by then been annexed by Germany and was therefore part of Germany. Therefore, the distributors of his books were prohibited from paying money to his publishers who, in turn, could not pay him.

This seems monumentally unfair to Zweig, as Zweig was Jewish. Life is unfair.

Although one can sort-of understand why Stefan Zweig might commit suicide, one cannot understand why he entered into a suicide pact with his new wife so that they would both die together. She was only 33 years old and had everything to live for. He was 27 years older. They had a nice apartment and a good life in Brazil. They took poison together and dead bodies were found by a housekeeper with their arms wrapped around each other.

Strangely, at the peak of his popularity and having just completed his autobiography while still working on four other books, Zweig **committed suicide** in **Brazil** with his new wife by them both taking poison. In **1939**, he had married **Charlotte Altmann**, his secretary from **1933**. She was twenty-seven years his junior.

Zweig left a suicide note stating that he had done so because of the **Nazi** takeover of his country of **Austria** and because Europe was **destroying itself** with **World War II** that was taking place.

This does not seem like a good reason for suicide and why did he take his new wife, **aged only 33**, with him?

Sam Sloan
New York NY
May 21, 2010

STEFAN ZWEIG, WIFE END LIVES IN BRAZIL

Austrian-Born Author Left a Note Saying He Lacked the Strength to Go On

By The United Press.

RIO DE JANEIRO, Brazil, Feb. 23—Stefan Zweig, noted Austrian-born author who became a man without a country because of the spread of nazism in Europe, and his wife, Elizabeth, said to have been about 30 years old, committed suicide today. They took poison at their home near Petropolis, Brazilian Summer capital.

The author left a letter explaining the suicide pact, addressed to Claudio de Souza, president of the P. E. N. Club of Brazil. The letter said:

"Before I depart from life by my own free will, I want to do my last duty, which is to thank this marvelous country—Brazil—which so hospitably received me. Each day I spent here I loved this country

Continued on Page Twenty-three

The New York Times
Published: February 24, 1942
Copyright © The New York Times

AUTHOR AND WIFE DIE IN COMPACT

Mr. and Mrs. Stefan Zweig — The New York Times

ZWEIG AND WIFE COMMIT SUICIDE

Continued From Page One

more, and in no other could I have had such hopes of reconstructing my life.

"Europe Destroying Itself"

"After I saw the country of my own language fall, and my spiritual land—Europe—destroying itself, and I have reached the age of 60, it would require immense strength to reconstruct my life, and my energy is exhausted by long years of peregrination as one without a country.

"Therefore, I believe it is time to end a life that was dedicated only to spiritual work, considering human liberty and my own as the greatest wealth in the world.

"I leave an affectionate good-bye to all my friends."

The Zweigs were found dead shortly after 4 P. M. The police said a servant knocked on their bedroom door at 8 A. M., but went away upon getting no answer. The servant knocked at noon without reply and again at 4 P. M. Neighbors then were summoned, and they broke down the door.

The bodies were on the bed. The couple had died with their arms around each other. Two empty glasses from which the poison had been drunk were on a bedside table.

The room was in perfect order. Besides the letter addressed to Senhor de Souza there was a letter addressed to Zweig's first wife, Mrs. Frederike Zweig, said to reside in Sheridan Square, New York City. Other letters were addressed to a friend, Alfred Schaeffer of New York, and a friend in Rio de Janeiro, Abraham Kogan. Zweig had bequeathed his unfinished manuscripts, papers and books to the latter.

President Getulio Vargas ordered that burial expenses be paid by the Brazilian Government. The Chief Executive is staying now in Petropolis, and he was one of hundreds who visited the home to view the bodies. President Vargas ordered that autopsies be performed at the home rather than at the morgue as a mark of respect.

Funeral services will be at 3 P. M. tomorrow.

Reviled and Uprooted

When Stefan Zweig left his native Austria at the approach of the Nazi hordes that later burned some of his greatest works at a public pyre in the square of Salzburg, he left behind him much more than some of his personal belongings. He left the only world he had ever known — the world of Vienna, where culture, gaiety and the humanities gave freedom added zest.

At first his exile seemed to have no effect on Zweig. He continued his writing and lecturing and did everything within his power to aid his fellow émigrés, particularly his writing colleagues. But within the last two years a note of despair could be found in some of his public statements. When the war started he said it seemed frivolous to represent the private fate of imaginary persons.

"The artist has been wounded in his concentration," Zweig told Robert Van Gelder of THE NEW YORK TIMES in July, 1940. "The last months have been fatal for the European literary production. The basic law of all creative work remains invariably concentration, and never has this been so difficult for the artists in Europe. How should complete concentration be possible in the midst of a moral earthquake."

He was later quoted as saying that the "continuous war fear of the creative mind is as bad as war itself."

It was perhaps in one of these moods that Zweig, one of the ablest writers of our times, decided that suicide was a way out.

Born of Jewish parents in Vienna on Nov. 28, 1881, Zweig received an excellent education. He had published two volumes of verse before his university career was completed. For the next decade he wandered around the world. The shock of the first World War changed all this. Zweig sought new values. Deserting his beloved Vienna, he settled in Salzburg and began a serious literary career. He was often referred to as "the most translated author in the world."

His major works included numerous biographies—"Mary Queen of Scotland and the Isles," "Erasmus of Rotterdam," "Marie Antoinette," "Romain Rolland," "Joseph Fouche," "Mental Healers: Franz Mesmer, Mary Baker Eddy, Sigmund Freud," "Master Builders," studies of genius in various guises; "The Tide of Fortune," twelve historical miniatures; "Conqueror of the Seas," the story of Magellan, and "Kaleidoscope."

His American publisher, Viking Press, published his latest book yesterday. It is "Amerigo: A Comedy of Errors in History," his investigation of the facts and fictions of Vespucci's "discovery" of America. B. W. Huebsch, director of Viking Press, said last night that Zweig completed a few weeks ago an autobiography he had been working on for many years. At the time of his death he was working on four new books, according to Mr. Huebsch, including a novel and a biography of Balzac.

Two of Zweig's plays were produced in New York by the Theatre Guild. The first was "Volpone," which had been a great success in Europe. In February, 1939, the Theatre Guild produced his "Jeremiah," a dramatization of the theme that a prophet is never so thoroughly wanting in honor in his own country as when a war is brewing.

His other works included "Adepts in Self-Portraiture," a series of biographical studies; "Amok," a short novel; "The Right of Heresy: Castellio Against Calvin," "Letter From an Unknown Woman," a novelette; "The Buried Candelabrum," a story of Jewish folklore; "Brazil: Land of the Future," and his only full-length novel, "Beware of Pity," published in March. 1939.

The New York Times
Published: February 24, 1942
Copyright © The New York Times

Original Back Cover and Flaps Blurb

Stefan Zweig

MARY

Queen of Scotland and the Isles

STEFAN ZWEIG says of his heroine: "The subject of Mary will always be fascinating because of a certain quality of mystery and secrecy about her. As so often happens in life, this woman had one great moment of passion. All the tragedy of Mary's life was packed into two years of her forty-four--the two years of her-great passion with Bothwell."

THE CRITICS hail this superb biography as the outstanding achievement of a master biographer:

"Zweig's most dramatic and poignant work"' ' Peter Munro Jack, N. Y. Times.

"At once the most readable and the most reliable of the lives of the Scottish queen." May Lamberton Becker, NY Herald Tribune

"The whole book goes with the swing of a novel" J. E. Neale, Saturday Review of Literature

"It ought to be sufficient to say that he has once more handled a romantic subject as it deserved to be handled" Herschel Brickell, N. Y. Post

"Freshness and spontaneity mark every page of a book that cannot fail to be extremely important in any future study of the unhappy Queen. It is probably the fairest biography of her ever written" Muriel Fuller, N. Y. World-Telegram.

Original Back Cover and Flaps Blurb

“Astir with the atmosphere of courts, the gestures of royalty, and -the whispers of court intrigue” The New Yorker

“A really notable achievement in historic biography-one that likely to stand for a long time to come." S. Morgan Powell, Montreal Star.

“It is all-embracing and satisfying a re-appraisal of a life and character as was Zweig's Marie Antoinette” Elrick B. Davis, Cleveland Press'

The .Harrowing life of Superb Woman

Of Mary Queen of Scotland a great historian has written -.The passion of love, after very sufficient experience, she apparently and naturally outlived; the passion of hatred and revenge was as inextinguishable in her inmost nature as the emotion of loyalty and gratitude. Of repentance it would seem that she knew as little as of fear.”

From the moment of her birth, Mary became a pawn in the hands of scheming statesmen. As an infant in arms, she was betrothed to King Henry VIII's heir, but the people of Scotland denounced the match and she was sent to France and married while still a child to the French dauphin, the first of her three marriages. Her husband lived long enough to make her Queen of France and on his early death Mary returned to strife-torn Scotland to plunge into a bitter struggle with the mighty Queen Elizabeth, a struggle in which love and ambition, vile treachery and magnificent courage, violence and subterfuge, all played I part, a struggle which in the end brought Mary, proud and unyielding to the last, to the executioners block.

To all the admirers of Stefan Zweig's brilliant biographical skill, to the thousands of readers of his internationally

Original Back Cover and Flaps Blurb

famous MARIE ANTOINETTE, it must be an occasion for rejoicing that this author has chosen to write the life of Scotland's fascinating headstrong queen in a work which he describes as a "sister book" to his superb portrait of the tragic Queen of France.

An idea of the enthusiastic reception accorded to Mary Queen of Scotland and The Isles may be gained from glancing at the extracts from the comments of distinguished critics which appear on the back of this wrapper.

With diabolical cunning, history began by making Marie Antoinette a spoiled darling, wearing a crown while she was still in her teens, endowed with charm, grace and wealth as a young wife, and dowered with a light heart that never troubled to ask the cost of her gifts. Then destiny, having raised her to the pinnacle, dragged her down again. She was torn from her 100-room palace and thrust into a common jail, was hurried from jail to scaffold, from golden coach to tumbril, from luxury to privation and a cruel death.

To read the story of Marie Antoinette is to experience the terror-filled days of the French Revolution. Days when in their determination to overthrow the old regime the people of France sent a woman of heroic character to the guillotine, a queen accused of every form of moral corruption and perversion.

Here is her story, and well does Stefan Zweig's superb book merit Alexander Woollcott's tribute - "The best book on the Revolution I ever read."

Foreword

The clear, the manifest, is self-explanatory; but mystery is a spur to creative imagination. Always, therefore, figures and events that are shrouded in mystery demand elucidation and stimulate the ingenuity of the artistic mind. Among historical problems that call unceasingly for solution, the tragedy of Mary Stuart ranks as a crucial instance. Surely of all the women who have made their mark in the world, no other has been the theme of so many dramas, novels, biographies, and discussions. Throughout four centuries she has allured poets and tormented the fancy of men of learning. Still, today, her story has again and again to be retold. Because that which is confused craves for clarity, that which is in darkness strains towards the light.

The answers to the riddle of Mary's life and character are almost as contradictory as they are manifold. Some regard her as a murderess, others as a martyr; some as an intriguer, others as a saint. The diversity of opinions about this woman is due, not to a shortage of material, but to the perplexing superabundance of contemporary records. In the thousands upon thousands of documents, reports, records of trials, letters, etc., relating to her, the question of her guilt or innocence is continually being re-examined, and the re-trial has continued for three centuries. The more meticulously we scrutinize the documents, the more painfully do we become aware how dubious is the authenticity of historical evidence, and how untrustworthy therefore the conclusions of historians. For no matter how incontestably genuine an ancient document may be, this genuineness does not provide any guarantee as to the human validity of its contents. In the case of Mary Queen of Scots more plainly perhaps than in any other do we become aware how diversely two or more observers may describe an incident which they have witnessed simultaneously. Every well-attested

"Yes" is countered by an equally well-attested "No"; every charge by a rebuttal. Falsehood and truth, fact and fiction, are so confusingly mingled, that every possible view as to her guilt or innocence where this or that matter is concerned (and especially as to her complicity in Darnley's murder), seems equally supported by reliable testimony. When, over and above this conflict of evidence, we have to allow for the partisanship of politicians and patriots, our dubiety as to the value of the picture that emerges is yet further increased.

In any case it is but natural for people to take sides where characters, ideas, and outlooks are contrasted one with another; so that few, if any, can avoid the temptation of calling one right and the other wrong, one guilty and the other innocent. If, as in the present instance, the witnesses belong to one or other of the contending parties, religions, or philosophies, we may take bias to be a matter of course. Speaking generally, we find that Protestant writers ascribe the blame to Mary, and Catholic ones the blame to Elizabeth; that English historians tend to describe the former unhesitatingly as a murderess, whilst Scottish authorities incline to exonerate her and to speak of her as a victim of calumny. The members of one faction describe the Casket Letters (the thorniest problem of the period) as genuine; the members of the other faction are no less firmly convinced that these epistles must have been forgeries. The rivalry of interpretation extends into the most trivial details of the Scottish Queen's life. It is perhaps easier for one who is neither an Englishman nor a Scot to form an unbiased judgment upon these issues than for one whose national blood begins to course more swiftly when they come up for consideration—easier for him to contemplate them with that artistic interest which is at one and the same time passionate and dispassionate.

True, it would be over-bold even for a foreigner to presume that he was capable of learning the truth, the whole truth, and nothing but the truth about Mary Stuart's life. He can hope to achieve no more than an approximation to the truth, to arrive at "extremely probable" conclusions; and however objectively he may strive to consider the facts, he will still be bound by the limitations of his own subjectivity. When the sources do not run clear, he will endeavour to clarify; when contemporary reports give one another the lie, he will, despite himself, assume the attitude of counsel for the defence or counsel for the prosecution.

He will choose between accusations and exonerations. However carefully he may choose, he will often find his canons of personal honesty best satisfied by leaving questions open instead of deciding them one way or the other, and by frankly admitting that, with regard to one or another of Mary's actions or alleged actions, he cannot ascertain the truth, which is likely to remain for ever undiscoverable.

In the present study the author has scrupulously abstained from relying upon evidence obtained by torture, force, or fear. He has also been extremely cautious in the use of the reports of spies or ambassadors (the terms in those days were almost synonymous). Where there is a conflict of testimony, the possible political motives that might lead to distortion have been carefully weighed. In embracing the view that the sonnets and, for the most part, the Casket Letters, are genuine, the author has only done so after the most exhaustive study and in the light of internal evidence which seems to him to warrant his conviction. When a decision between two divergent accounts has been requisite in the absence of corroborative evidence on one side or the other, judgment has been guided by the reflection which of the two versions is more conformable, psychologically, with the general picture of Mary's character. That character, that personality, was by no means abstruse; on the contrary, it was lucid. Mary Stuart was one of those rare and interesting women whose period of supreme activity is comparatively restricted in duration; one of those who have a brief though vigorous blossoming; one of those whose life is mainly lived during the short and glowing phase of a great passion, instead of being spread equably throughout the normal span of existence. Until her twenty-third year, her affective life was almost quiescent; so was it again after her twenty-fifth. During the two years that intervened, passion flamed up in her with elemental force, and what might have seemed an average destiny assumed the lineaments of a Greek tragedy as formidable as that of Orestes. It was only during these two years that Mary underwent the supreme experiences which led in the end to her destruction, and thanks to which, likewise, her memory has become so noteworthy—for what destroyed her made her immortal in song and story.

This peculiar compression of the main happenings of her career into, as it were, one explosive surge of feeling, dictates the form and rhythm of her biography. The reader, therefore, must not feel a sense of disproportion because, in the chronological assignment of space in this book, the twenty-three opening years of Mary's life and the nineteen years of her imprisonment occupy fewer pages than do the two years of her tragical passions. Only in semblance are the outward and inward seasons of a life identical; in verity, wealth of experience is the sole measure of living, and the spirit is timed by another clock than that of the calendar. Under the intoxication of destiny, the mind may traverse lengthy periods in a few days; whereas long years may count for nothing when life is void of momentous spiritual happenings. Just as the historian pays little heed to slow and stagnant epochs, and his interest is focused upon a few and scattered but dramatic and decisive moments—so, for the biographer, who is concerned with the inmost story of a life, only the pulses of passion count. A human being is not fully alive except when his best energies are at work; and when feeling is active, time moves swiftly though the clock-hands circle at their customary pace. Then, as in dreams, one under stress of powerful affects lives through measureless epochs between two ticks of the pendulum; and with each of us it is as with the enchanted man in the folk-tale who fancied that he had spent a thousand years in the interval between two heart-beats.

Contents

CHIEF PERSONS OF THE DRAMA

First Act:	Scotland, 1542–1548
Second Act:	France, 1548–1561
Third Act:	Scotland, 1561–1568
Fourth Act:	England, 1568–1587

SCOTLAND

James V (1512–1542), Mary Stuart's father.

Marie de Guise-Lorraine (1515–1560), James V's wife and Mary Stuart's mother.

Mary Stuart, Queen of Scotland and the Isles (1542–1587).

James Stuart, Earl of Moray (1533–1570), illegitimate son of James V by Margaret Douglas, daughter of Lord Erskine; half-brother to Mary Queen of Scots; Regent of Scotland before and after Mary's queenship.

Henry Stuart, Lord Darnley (1546–1567), great-grandson of Henry VII through his mother Lady Lennox, who was niece of Henry VIII; second husband of Mary Queen of Scots, and titular King of Scotland.

James VI (1566–1625), son of Mary Stuart and Darnley; became King of Scotland on his mother's forced abdication on July 24, 1567, and, on Elizabeth's death (March 24, 1603), succeeded to the throne of England as James I.

James Hepburn, Earl of Bothwell (1536–1578), later Duke of Orkney; third husband of Mary Queen of Scots.

William Maitland of Lethington (1528–1573), secretary of State to Mary Queen of Scots.

Sir James Melville (1535–1617), Mary Stuart's most trusty diplomatist.

James Douglas, Earl of Morton (1530–1581), Regent of Scotland after Moray's murder, executed for complicity in the murder of Darnley.

Matthew Stuart, Earl of Lennox, father of Darnley and chief accuser of Mary Stuart after Darnley's murder; Regent of Scotland 1570, murdered 1571.

ARGYLL, ARRAN, ERSKINE, GORDON, HERRIES, HUNTLY, KIRKCALDY OF GRANGE, LINDSAY, MAR, MORTON, RUTHVEN — Scottish lords and lairds who sometimes supported Queen Mary, sometimes rebelled against her; were now in league, now at odds; and almost all died by violence.

MARY BEATON, MARY FLEMING, MARY LIVINGSTONE, MARY SETON — "the Queen's Marys"

JOHN KNOX (1505–1572), Calvinist minister, fierce adversary of Mary Stuart.

DAVID RIZZIO, musician and secretary at Mary's Scottish court; murdered in 1566.

PIERRE DE CHASTELARD, French poet at Mary's Scottish court, executed 1563.

GEORGE BUCHANAN (1506–1582), Latin master to Queen Mary, author of the *Detection,* tutor to King James VI.

FRANCE

HENRY II (1518–1559), King of France 1547–1559.

CATHERINE DE' MEDICI (1519–1589), his wife.

FRANCIS II (1544–1560), their eldest son, Mary Stuart's first husband.

CHARLES IX (1550–1574), their second son.

HENRY III (1551–1589), their third son.

THE CARDINAL OF LORRAINE, CLAUDE DE GUISE, FRANÇOIS DE GUISE, HENRI DE GUISE — the four Guises

RONSARD, DU BELLAY, BRANTÔME — poets who eulogized Mary Stuart

ENGLAND

HENRY VII (1457–1509), King of England from 1485, grandfather of Elizabeth, great-grandfather of Mary Stuart and Darnley.

HENRY VIII (1491–1547), son of above, King of England from 1509.

ANNE BOLEYN (1507–1536), Henry VIII's second wife, executed as an adulteress.

MARY I (1516–1558), commonly known as "Bloody Mary," daughter of Henry VIII by his first marriage to Catherine of Aragon, became Queen of England on the death of her brother Edward in 1553.

ELIZABETH (1533–1603), daughter of Henry VIII by his second marriage to Anne Boleyn, declared a bastard during her father's lifetime, and imprisoned by her half-sister Mary, on whose death in 1558 she became Queen of England.

EDWARD VI (1537–1553), son of Henry VIII by his third marriage with Jane Seymour, succeeded Henry on the latter's death in 1547, betrothed in early childhood to Mary Stuart.

JAMES I OF ENGLAND AND VI OF SCOTLAND, Mary Stuart's son and Elizabeth Tudor's successor on the English throne (see above).

WILLIAM CECIL, LORD BURLEIGH (1520–1598), held office successively under Protector Somerset, Edward VI, Mary I, and Elizabeth. The last-named's lord high treasurer and chief minister from 1572 to 1598.

SIR FRANCIS WALSINGHAM (1536–1590), Elizabeth's secretary of State and director of espionage from 1573 onwards.

WILLIAM DAVISON (1541 ? –1608), secretary to Queen Elizabeth.

ROBERT DUDLEY, EARL OF LEICESTER (1532–1588), for many years Elizabeth's closest intimate, proposed by the latter as husband of Mary Stuart.

THOMAS HOWARD, DUKE OF NORFOLK (1536–1572), premier peer of England, a suitor for Mary Stuart's hand, and joined in a conspiracy for her liberation, consequently executed.

GEORGE TALBOT, EARL OF SHREWSBURY (1528 ? –1590), for fifteen years Mary Stuart's "guardian," i.e., jailer.

ELIZABETH, COUNTESS OF SHREWSBURY (BESS OF HARDWICK, 1518–1608), married the foregoing as her fourth husband.

Sir Amyas Paulet (1536?–1588), Mary Stuart's jailer during the last years, and present at her execution.

Anthony Babington, Ballard, Savage, and others executed for Babington's (or Walsingham's) conspiracy.

Bulle, the London executioner.

Mary Queen of Scotland and the Isles

CHAPTER ONE

Queen in the Cradle

(1542-1548)

MARY STUART was but six days old when she became Queen of Scotland, thus obeying in spite of herself what appears to have been the law of her life: to receive too soon and without conscious joy what Fate had to give her. On the same dreary December day in 1542 that Mary was born at Linlithgow Castle, her father, James V, was breathing his last in the royal palace at Falkland, little more than twenty miles away. Although he had hardly reached the age of thirty-one, he was broken on the wheel of life, tired of his crown, and wearied of perpetual warfare. He had proved a brave and chivalrous man, fundamentally cheerful by disposition, a passionate friend of the arts and of women, trusted by his people. Many a time would he put on a disguise in order to participate unrecognized at village merry-makings, dancing and joking with the peasant folk. But this unlucky scion of an unlucky house had been born into a wild epoch and within the borders of an intractable land. From the outset he seemed foredoomed to a tragical destiny.

A self-willed and inconsiderate neighbour, Henry VIII, tried to force the Scottish king to introduce the Reformation into the northern realm. But James V remained a faithful son of the old Church. The lords and nobles gleefully took every opportunity to create trouble for their sovereign, stirring up contention and misunderstanding, and involving the studious and pacific James in further turmoil and war. Four years earlier, when he was suing for Mary of Guise's hand in marriage, he made clear in a letter to the lady how heavy a task it was to act as king to the rebellious and rapacious clans. "Madam," he wrote in this moving epistle (penned in French), "I am no more than seven-and-twenty years of age, and life is already crushing me as heavily as does my crown. . . . An Orphan from my earliest childhood, I fell a prey to ambitious noblemen; the powerful House of Douglas kept me prisoner for many years, and I have come to hate the name of my persecutors and any references to the sad days of my captivity. Archibald, Earl of Angus, George his brother, together with their exiled relatives, are untiring in their endeavours to rouse the King of England against me and mine. There is not a nobleman in my realm who has not been seduced from his allegiance by promises and bribes. Even my person is not safe; there is no guarantee that my wishes will be carried out, or that existing laws will be obeyed. All these things alarm me, Madam, and I expect to receive from you both strength and counsel. I have no money, save that which comes to me from France's generosity and through the thrift of my wealthier clergy; and it is with these scanty funds that I try to adorn my palaces, maintain my fortresses, and build my ships. Unfortunately, my barons look upon a king who would act the king in very deed as an insufferable rival. In spite of the friendship shown me by the King of France, in spite of the support I receive from his armies, in spite of the attachment of my people to their monarch, I fear that I shall never be able to achieve a decisive victory over my unruly nobles. I would fain put every obstacle out of the path in order to bring justice and tranquillity to my people. Peradventure I might achieve this aim if my nobles were the only impediment. But the King of England never wearies of sowing discord between them and me; and the heresies he has introduced into the land are not only devouring my people as a whole, but have penetrated even into ecclesiastical circles. My power, as did that of my ancestors, rests solely upon the burgesses of my towns and upon the fidelity of my clergy, and I cannot but ask myself whether this power will long endure. . . ."

All the disasters foretold by the king in this letter took place, and even worse things befell the writer. The two sons Mary of Guise brought into the world died in the cradle, so that James, in the flower of his manhood, had no heir growing up beside him, an heir who should relieve him of the crown which, as the years passed, pressed more heavily on his brow. In despite of his own will and better judgment, he was pressed by his nobles to enter the field against England, a mighty enemy, only to be deserted by them in the eleventh hour. At Solway Moss, Scotland lost not only the battle but likewise her honour. Forsaken by the chieftains of the clans, the troops hardly put up even the semblance of a fight, but ran leaderless hither and thither. James, too, a man usually so acutely aware of his knightly duty, when the decisive hour came was no longer in a position to strike down the hereditary foe, for he was already wounded unto death. They bore him away, feverish and weary, and laid him to bed in his palace at Falkland. He had had his fill of the senseless struggle and of a life which had become nothing but a burden to him.

Mist-wreaths darkened the window-panes on December 9, 1542, when there came a messenger knocking at the door. He announced to the sick king that a daughter had been born to the House of Stuart—an heiress to the throne. But James V was by that time so near his end that he lacked the strength to feel happy at the tidings or to harbour any hope as to the issue. Why was he not granted a son, a male heir? The dying man could see nothing but disaster in every event, nothing but tragedy and defeat. In a resigned voice, he answered the messenger: "Farewell, it came with ane lass and it will pass with ane lass." This dismal prophecy proved to be the last words he was destined to utter. With a sigh, he turned his face to the wall and, heeding nobody, refused to answer any questions. A few days later he was buried, and Mary Stuart, before she had been given time to open her baby eyes and look around her, became Queen of the Scottish realm.

To be a Stuart and at the same time to be Queen of Scotland was to be placed indeed under an evil star and to be exposed to a twofold doom, for no Stuart had so far been happy on the Scottish throne, nor had any occupied it for long. James I and James III were murdered; James II and James IV perished on the battlefield; while for two of their descendants, the unwitting infant Mary and her grandchild Charles I, an even crueller end was in prospect, for they both died on the scaffold. Not one of this Atrides-race ever reached the zenith of life's course, not one was born under a happy star. The Stuarts were always to be at war with enemies without, with enemies within the frontiers of their homeland, with themselves; they were surrounded by unrest, and unrest raged perpetually in their hearts. Just as they could find no peace for their own turbulent spirits, so they could not safeguard peace for their country. Those who should have proved the most loyal of their subjects were the least to be depended upon—lords and barons of the dark, strong land, the whole knighthood, inconstant and headstrong, wild and unbridled, rapacious and rejoicing in the fight, constantly betraying and betrayed. As Ronsard sighed during his enforced stay in this fog-bound region, "c'est ung pays barbare et un gent brutelle." Themselves acting the king on their estates, behind the massive walls of their strongholds they would herd the clansmen, who were their ploughmen and shepherds, into vast armies so as to carry on their endless feuds and forays—for these autocrats of the clans knew only one genuine pleasure, and that pleasure was war. "A bonnie fecht" was their delight; they were goaded on by jealousy; their one thought was to have power and ever more power. The French ambassador wrote: "Money and personal advantage are the only Sirens to whose voices the Scottish lords will lend an ear. To try and bring them to a sense of their devoir towards their prince, to talk to them of honour, justice, virtue, decent and reliable negotiations, merely incites them to laughter." In their amoral combativeness and cupidity they resembled the Italian condottieri, though lacking their culture, and being even more unbridled in their instincts. Thus they were ceaselessly battling for precedence; and the ancient and powerful clans of the Gordons, the Hamiltons, the Arrans, the Maitlands, the Crawfords, the Lindsays, the Lennoxes, the Argylls, were unendingly at one another's throats. During certain periods they would be fighting their age-long feuds; during others, swearing a pact—which was never of long duration!—that they might outwit and overthrow a third party; though they were never tired of forming cliques and factions, none of these minor leagues ever possessed any internal cohesion; and no bond of blood or of kinship by marriage was able to break down the relentless feeling of envy and enmity that existed among them. A vestige of the heathen barbarian lived on in their wild souls, whether they called themselves Protestants or Catholics; and they took up with either faith according to which would be most profitable to their ambitions. They were genuine descendants of Macbeth and Macduff, the fierce thanes of Shakespearian drama.

One cause only was capable of bringing this envious rabble to act in concert: to attack their liege lord, their king; for they knew neither what loyalty meant nor obedience. If, in actual fact, this "pack of rascals" (as Burns, that true son of his native soil, nicknamed them) tolerated a shadow king to rule over their castles and estates, this was made possible solely through the jealousies entertained by one clan against another. The Gordons helped to keep the crown on the Stuarts' heads merely that it might not fall to the Hamiltons; whereas the Hamiltons swore fealty to the king to keep the Gordons out. But woe to him who should try to act as a genuine king in Scotland, should endeavour to introduce discipline and order into the realm, should, in a fit of youthful enthusiasm, set his will up against the arrogance and greed of his nobles! In such circumstances, they would join forces to frustrate the designs of the sovereign, and if the issue could not be solved on the battlefield, it could easily be dealt with through the assassin's dirk.

This last outpost of Europe towards the northern seas that lash its rugged coasts was indeed a tragic land, perpetually rent in sunder by antagonistic passions, dark and romantic as a saga, a poverty-stricken land to boot, since unremitting warfare crushed every effort to make it prosperous. The few towns, which hardly deserved the name seeing that they consisted of a huddle of wretched hovels clustering for protection around a stronghold, were eternally being plundered and destroyed by fire, so that it was impossible for them to acquire wealth or to bring the semblance of wellbeing to a settled burgherdom. We may still behold today the ruins of the gloomy and domineering castles wherein the nobles dwelt, castles by courtesy, for these buildings show none of the ornate brilliance we are accustomed to find in such edifices, nor is it easy to imagine any courtly state possible within those austere walls. Their uses were purely for war, and there had been no scope in their construction for the gentler arts of entertainment and hospitality. Between this handful of nobles and their serfs there existed no middle estate of the realm which could serve as an efficient pillar for the maintenance of the State authority. The most populous district, that situated between Tweed and Forth, was never given a chance to prosper, for it was always being invaded by the English from over the border, its people killed and the fruits of their industry destroyed. In the northern half of the country a man could walk for hours by lonely lake-shores over boundless heaths, through mysterious forests and woodlands, without spying a village, a castle, a town. Here the hamlets did not press one upon the other as they did on the over-populated continent of

Europe; here were no broad highways serving as channels for intercourse and commerce; not here, as in Holland and England, did one see the ships sail forth out of busy harbours, making for far-off strands, and bringing back gold and spices. Sheep-herding, fishing, hunting—such constituted the patriarchal occupations of the folk in northern Scotland at that date. Their customs, their laws, their wealth, and their culture lay a hundred years in arrear of England and the rest of Europe. Whereas, with the advent of new times in the coast towns elsewhere banks and exchanges were beginning to flourish, in Scotland, as in biblical days, wealth was calculated by the amount of land and the number of sheep a man owned. James V, Mary's father, possessed ten thousand head, and that was the whole of his fortune. He had no crown treasure; nor had he an army, or a body-guard wherewith to strengthen his authority, for he could not have paid for their services. Nor would his parliament, where the decisive word belonged to his lords, ever consent to vote him supplies. Everything this king needed over and above the barest necessities of life was provided by wealthy allies, France and the Pope for instance, either as a loan or as a gift, so that every carpet, every Gobelin, every chandelier to be found in his palaces, was bought with fresh humiliation.

Poverty—such was the purulent ulcer which sapped the strength from political life in this fair and hardy land. Because of the poverty and the voracity of its kings, its soldiers, and its lords, this realm was ever the gruesome plaything of foreign powers. Those who fought against the king and in the cause of Protestantism were in the pay of London; those who championed the Catholic side received their emoluments from Paris, Madrid, and Rome. Outsiders gladly put their hands into their pockets for the spilling of Scottish blood. A final decision had yet to be come to between England and France after perennial strife, and Scotland furnished France with a trump card in her contest with the mighty rival across the Channel. Each time the English armies set foot in Normandy, France hastened to stab England in the back. At the first summons, the Scots, who were by nature a war-lusty people, would be over the border, prepared for the enjoyment of a bonnie fecht with the "auld enemies." Even in times of peace they were a perpetual menace to the southern realm. It became, therefore, a recognized feature of French policy to strengthen Scotland from the military point of view. What could be more natural, in the circumstances, than that England should seek to consolidate her own position by sowing discord and encouraging rebellion among the Scottish nobles? Thus the unhappy country was the cockpit of centenarian wars, of which Mary's fate was at length to mark the close.

With her incurable delight in racy and paradoxical symbolism, Dame History decreed that this decisive struggle should begin while Mary Stuart was an infant in the cradle. The wee lassie can neither speak nor think as yet, hardly is she sentient and conscious, her tiny hands are scarcely strong enough to move, yet already the world of politics thrusts relentlessly into her innocent life, seizing upon her immature body and grasping at her unsuspecting soul. For it was Mary's doom to be under the spell of this dicers' game of politics. Never was she allowed to develop her ego unhindered. All her life long she would be the pawn of policy; be queen or heiress, ally or foe, never simply child or girl or woman. The messenger bearing the twin tidings of James V's death and the birth of his daughter as Queen of Scotland and the Isles had barely time to convey his news to the King of England when the latter determined to sue for her hand in favour of his little son Edward. A bride worth the wooing from every point of view, Henry VIII considered. So it was that this girl's body with its yet unawakened soul became an object of haggling from the outset. But politics is impervious to the feelings of mankind; what it is interested in are crowns, countries, heritages. The individual man or woman simply does not exist when politics is in the ascendant; such things are of no value as compared with tangible and practical values to be won in the world-game.

In the present instance, however, Henry VIII's desire to bring about a matrimonial union between the heiress to Scotland's throne and the heir to the throne of England was reasonable and humane. For the sempiternal warfare between the neighbouring nations had long since become a senseless iniquity. England and Scotland, forming as they do one island in the northern seas, their shores washed by the waters of the selfsame oceans, their peoples so closely akin, and their mode of life so similar, could have but one common duty to perform: come together in unity and concord. Nature in this case could not have made her wishes plainer. There was nothing to hinder unification except the jealous rivalries which existed between the two dynasties of the Tudors and of the Stuarts. But if a marriage between the children of the contending dynasts could be successfully arranged, then the differences might be amicably smoothed out and the Stuarts and Tudors would achieve simultaneously kingship of England, Scotland, and Ireland. Thus the contentious parties would become friends; no more blood need be spilled in fratricidal strife; and a powerful, united Great Britain could take the place that was due to her among the nations in their struggle for dominion over the world.

When, quite exceptionally, a clear and logical idea comes to light up the political arena, it is invariably ruined by the idiotic way men have of putting it into execution. At the start the suggestion of this marriage seemed to strike the precise note that was required to establish harmony. The Scottish lords, whose pockets were quickly and amply filled with moneys from England, gladly agreed to the proposal. But Henry VIII was astute enough not to be satisfied with a mere piece of parchment. Too often had he suffered from the double-dealing and greed of these honourable gentlemen not to know that such shifty wights can never be bound by a treaty, and that should a higher bidder present himself—should, let us say, the French king offer his son and heir as aspirant for Mary's hand—they would snap their fingers at the first proposal in order to reap what advantage they might from the second. He therefore demanded of the negotiators that Mary should immediately be sent to England. But if the Tudors were suspicious of the Stuarts, the latter whole-heartedly reciprocated the sentiment. The Queen Mother, in especial, opposed the treaty. A Guise and a strict Catholic, she had no wish to see her daughter brought up by heretics. Moreover, in the treaty itself she was not slow to detect a trap which might prove highly injurious to her child's welfare. In a clause that had been kept secret Henry VIII bribed the Scottish nobles to agree that if the little girl died before her majority the whole of her rights and ownership in the Scottish crown should pass to him. The clause was undoubtedly suspect, especially when associated with the fact that its inventor had already done away with two wives. What more natural than to suppose that a child might die prematurely and not altogether by natural means in order that he might come into the heritage the sooner? Mary of Guise, in her role of prudent and loving mother, rejected the proposal of sending her infant daughter to London. Thereupon the proxy wooing was upon the verge of being converted into a war, for Henry VIII, overbearing as was his wont, dispatched his troops across the border that they might seize the coveted prize by force of arms. The army orders disclose the brutality of those days: "It is His Majesty's will that all be laid waste with fire and sword. Burn Edinburgh and raze the city to the ground, as soon as you have seized whatever is worth taking. Plunder Holyrood and as many towns and villages as you can; ravage, burn, and destroy Leith; and the same whithersoever you go, exterminating men, women, and children without mercy, wherever resistance is shown." At the decisive hour, however, mother and child were safely conducted to Stirling and placed within the shelter of its fortified castle. Henry VIII had to rest content with a treaty wherein Scotland was committed to send Mary to England on the day she reached the tenth year of her life—again she was treated as an object of chaffering and purchase.

Now all was happily settled. Another crown had fallen into the cradle of the Scottish infant queen. By her future marriage with young Edward of England the kingdoms of Scotland and England would become united. But politics has always been a science of contradiction. It is for ever in conflict with simple, natural, sensible solutions; difficulties are its greatest joy, and it feels thoroughly in its element when dissension is abroad. The Catholic party soon set to work intriguing against the compact, wondering whether it would not be preferable to barter the girl elsewhere and offer her as a bride for the French king's son; and, by the time Henry VIII came to die, there was scant inclination anywhere to hold to the bond. Protector Somerset, acting on behalf of Edward, who was still in his minority, demanded that the child-bride should be sent to London. Since Scotland refused to obey, an English army was dispatched over the border. This was the only language the Scottish lords properly understood. On September 10, 1547, at the battle, or, rather, the massacre, of Pinkie, the Scots were crushed, leaving more than ten thousand dead on the field. Mary Stuart was not yet five years old when blood in gallons flowed in her cause.

Scotland now lay open to any incursion England chose to make. But there was nothing left worth the plundering; the countryside was empty, was cleaned out. One single treasure remained so far as the House of Tudor was concerned: a little girl in whose person was incorporated a crown and the rights this crown commanded. It was essential, therefore, to place the treasure where covetous hands could not reach it. To the despair of the English spies the child suddenly vanished from Stirling Castle. None, not even those in the Queen Mother's confidence, knew whither Mary had been spirited away. The hiding-place was admirably chosen. One night, in the custody of a trustworthy servant, the girl had been smuggled into the Priory of Inchmahome. This is situated on a speck of an island in the Lake of Menteith, "dans le pays des sauvages," as the French envoy reports, very remote from the world of men. Not even a path led to this romantic spot. The precious freight was conveyed to its destination in a boat. Here the child dwelt, hidden and removed from the turmoil of events, while over lands and seas diplomacy continued to weave the tissue of her fate.

Meanwhile France had entered the lists, menacing and determined, resolved that Scotland should not become subject to England. Henry II, son of Francis I, sent a strong fleet to the northern realm and, through the lieutenant-general of the auxiliary army, sued the hand of Mary Stuart for his young son and heir, Francis. In a night-time, Mary's destiny changed its course owing to the set of the political wind which swept in mighty war-engendering gusts over the Channel. Instead of becoming Queen of England the little daughter of the House of Stuart was now fated to become Queen of France. Hardly had the new and advantageous bargain been struck when, on August 7, 1548, the costly merchandise (Mary was then five years and eight months old) was shipped from Dumbarton for a French port. Once more she had been sold to an unknown bridegroom, and committed to a marriage which might have lasted for decades. Again, and not for the last time, alien hands were moulding her destiny.

Trustfulness is a distinctive quality of childhood. What does a toddler of two, three, or even four years old know of war and of peace, of battles and of treaties? What can such words as England or France, Edward or Francis, mean to it? A fair-haired girl ran gleefully in and out the dark or the brightly lighted rooms of a palace, with four other girls of the same age at her heels. A charming thought had been allowed to blossom in the bleak atmosphere of a barbaric age. From the earliest days of her life Mary Stuart had been given four companions, all of them born at the same time as herself, chosen from among the most distinguished Scottish families, the lucky clover-leaf of the four Marys: Mary Fleming, Mary Beaton, Mary Livingstone, and Mary Seton. In early years these namesakes of the queen were her gay playmates; later they were her classmates in a foreign land so that she did not feel her novel surroundings to be unbearably strange; still later they were to become her maids of honour. In a moment of unusual affection, they took a vow not to enter the married state before Mary herself had found a spouse. Even after three of them had forsaken the queen in the days when misfortune befell her, the fourth of the Marys followed her mistress, clave to her in adversity, shared in her exile and her prisons, waited upon her when she died on the scaffold, and never left her until her body had been consigned to the grave. Thus, to the very end of her life, Mary was accompanied by a touch of childhood. But at the time she sailed for France as a small child, these sad and darkened days lay far ahead.

At Holyrood or at Stirling, the palace and the castle rang with peals of laughter and the patter of small feet, as the five Marys ran from room to room, untiringly, from morning till nightfall. Little did they care for high estate, for dignities, for kingdoms; nothing did they know of the pride and danger encompassing a crown. One night, Mary the Queen was roused from her baby sleep, lifted from her crib; a boat was waiting in readiness on a lake that was hardly bigger than a pond; someone rowed her across, and they landed on an island. How quiet and pleasant the place! Inchmahome, the isle of peace. Strange men stooped to welcome her; some of these men were robed more like women, and had peaked hoods to their black gowns. They were gentle and kind, they sang beautifully in a high-ceilinged hall with stained-glass windows. Mary soon grew accustomed to her new home. But all too soon another evening came when once more she was taken in a boat across the waters. Fate had decreed that Mary Stuart was constantly to be making such night flittings from one destiny to another. On this occasion she awoke to find herself on a ship with high masts and milk-white sails, surrounded by unknown, rugged soldiers and hirsute sailors. What need was there for Mary to be frightened? Everyone aboard was kind and friendly to her; her seventeen-year-old half-brother James was gently stroking her silky hair. This youngster was one of her father's innumerable bastards, born in the decade before he married Mary of Guise. There, too, were the four Marys, her beloved playfellows. Delighted and happy in their novel environment, the five little girls frolicked about the vessel, dodging in and out among the cannons of the French man-of-war, laughing madly and joyously. Above these innocents, at the mast-head, was a man whose vigilance never relaxed. Anxiously he spied in every direction, for he knew that the English fleet was cruising about in those waters and only awaited an auspicious moment to pounce upon the precious freight and make her England's queen before she had been given a chance to become Queen of France. But what should she know of crowns and the ways of men, of trouble and danger, of England and France? The seas were blue, the people around her were amiable and strong, and the great vessel swam onward like some huge bird, speeding over the waves.

On August 13, the galleon dropped anchor in the small harbour of Roscoff near Brest. A boat was lowered, and conveyed the queen to the landing-place. Enchanted with her voyage by land and by sea, Mary sprang lightheartedly from the gangway on to French soil. She was not yet six years old; but with this landing, the Queen of Scotland left her childhood behind.

CHAPTER TWO

Youth in France

(1548-1559)

THE FRENCH court excelled in the courtly accomplishments of the day, and was practised in the mysterious science of etiquette. Henry II, a prince of the House of Valois, knew what was proper to the reception of a dauphin's bride. Before her arrival he issued a decree that "la reinette," the little Queen of Scotland, was to be welcomed by every town and village through which she might pass with as much ceremony as if she had been his own daughter. In Nantes, therefore, Mary Stuart was received with almost overwhelming pomp. At the street-corners there had been erected galleries adorned with classical emblems, goddesses, nymphs, and sirens; to put the escort in a good humour, barrels of costly wine were broached; salvos of artillery and a firework-display greeted the newcomer; furthermore, a lilliputian body-guard had been enrolled, consisting of one hundred and fifty youngsters under eight years of age, dressed in white uniforms, and marching in front of the child-queen, playing drums and fifes, armed with miniature pikes and halberds, shouting acclamations. Everywhere the same sort of reception had been prepared, so that it was through an uninterrupted series of festivities that Mary at length reached Saint-Germain. There she, not yet six years of age, had the first glimpse of her husband-to-be, four and a half years old, weakly, pale, rachitic, a boy whose poisoned blood foredoomed him to illness and premature death, and who now greeted his "bride" shyly. All the heartier, however, was the welcome accorded her by the other members of the royal family, who were greatly impressed by her youthful charm; and Henry II described her enthusiastically in a letter as "la plus parfayt enfant que je vys jamès."

At that time, the French court was one of the most resplendent in the world. A gleam of dying chivalry illumined this transitional generation, which belonged in a certain measure to the gloomier period of the Middle Ages. Hardihood and courage were still displayed in the chase, in tilting at the ring, and in tourneys; the old harsh and virile spirit was manifested in adventure and in war; but more spiritual outlooks had already come into their own amid the ruling circles, and humanistic culture, which had before conquered the cloisters and the universities, was now supreme in the palaces of kings. From Italy the papal love of display, the joie de vivre of the Renaissance (a joy that was both mental and physical), and delight in the fine arts had made their triumphal entry into France; the result being, at this juncture, an almost unique welding of strength with beauty, of high spirits with recklessness—the supreme faculty of having no fear of death while loving life with the full passion of the senses. More naturally and more easily than anywhere else temperament was, among the French, associated with frivolity, Gallic chevalerie being extraordinarily akin to the classical culture of the Renaissance. It was expected of a French nobleman that he should be equally competent in full panoply to charge his adversary in the lists, and gracefully and correctly to tread the mazes of the dance; he must at one and the same time be a past master of the science of war, and proficient in the manners and practices of courts. The hand which could wield the broadsword in a life-or-death struggle must be able to strum the lute tunefully and to indite sonnets to a fair mistress. To be simultaneously strong and tender, rough and cultured, skilled in battle and skilled in the fine arts, was the ideal of the time. In the daylight hours, the king and his nobles, attended by a pack of baying hounds, hunted the stag or the boar, while spears were broken and lances splintered; but when night fell there assembled in the halls of the splendidly renovated palaces of the Louvre or of Saint-Germain, of Blois or Amboise, lords and ladies eager to participate in witty conversation. Poems were read aloud, musical instruments were played, madrigals were sung, and in masques the spirit of classical literature was revived. The presence of numerous lovely and tastefully dressed women, the work of such poets and painters as Ronsard, du Bellay, and Clouet, gave the French royal court a colour and a verve which found lavish expression in every form of art and of life. As elsewhere in Europe before the unhappy outbreak of the wars of religion, in the France of that epoch a wonderful surge of civilization was in progress.

One who was to live at such a court, and, above all, one who might be expected in due time to rule there, must become adapted to the new cultural demands. He must strive to perfect himself in the arts and sciences, must develop his mind no less carefully than his body. It will be an everlasting glory of the movement we call humanism that its apostles insisted upon familiarity with the arts even among those whose mission it was to move in the highest circles. We can hardly think of any other period in history than the epoch then dawning, in which not only men of station, but noblewomen as well, were expected to be highly educated. Like Mary of England and her half-sister Elizabeth, Mary Stuart had to become familiar with Greek and Latin, and, in addition, with modern tongues, with French, Italian, English, and Spanish. Having a clear intelligence and a ready wit coupled with an inherited delight in learning, these things came easily to the gifted child. When she was no more than thirteen (having been taught her Latin from Erasmus's *Colloquies*) she recited, in the great gallery of the Louvre, before the assembled court and the foreign ambassadors, a Latin oration of her own composition, and did this so ably, with so much ease and grace, that her uncle the Cardinal of Lorraine was able to write to Mary of Guise: "Your daughter is improving, and increasing day by day in stature, goodness, beauty, wisdom, and worth. She is so perfect and accomplished in all things, honourable and virtuous, that like of her is not to be seen in this realm, whether among noble damsels, maidens of low degree, or in middle station. The king has taken so great a liking to her that he spends much of his time chatting with her, sometimes by the hour together; and she knows as well how to entertain him, with pleasant and sensible subjects of conversation, as if she were a woman of five-and-twenty."

In very truth Mary's mental development was no less speedy than it was thorough. Soon she had acquired so perfect a command of French that she could venture to express herself in verse, vying with Ronsard and du Bellay in her answers to their adulatory poems. In days to come, when most sorely distressed, or when the fires of passion must find vent, she would by choice use the metrical form; and down to her last hour she remained true to poesy as the most loyal of her friends. In the other arts she could express herself with extraordinarily good taste: she sang charmingly to the accompaniment of the lute; her dancing was acclaimed as bewitching; her embroideries were those of a hand gifted no less than trained; her dress was always discreet and becomingly chosen, since she had no love for the huge hooped skirts in which Elizabeth delighted to strut; her maidenly figure looked equally well whether she was clad in Highland dress or in silken robes of State. Tact and a fine discrimination were inseparable from her nature; and this daughter of the Stuarts would preserve even in her darkest hours, as the priceless heritage of her royal blood and courtly training, an exalted but nowise theatrical demeanour which will for all time endow her with a halo of romance. Even in matters of sport she was wellnigh the equal of the most skilful at this court where sport was a cult. An indefatigable horsewoman, an ardent huntress, agile at the game of pall-mall, tall, slender, and graceful though she was, she knew nothing of fatigue. Bright and cheerful, care-free and joyous, she drained the delights of youth out of every goblet that offered, never guessing that this was to be the only happy period of her life. Mary Queen of Scots at the French court comes down to us as an unfading and unique picture. There is scarcely another woman in whom the chivalrous ideal of the French Renaissance found so entrancing and maidenly an expression as in this merry and ardent daughter of a royal race.

She had barely left childhood when, as a maid in her teens and later as a woman, the poets of the day sang her praises. "In her fifteenth year her beauty began to radiate from her like the sun in a noontide sky," wrote Brantôme. Du Bellay was even more passionate in his admiration:

En votre esprit le ciel s'est surmonté.
Nature et art ont en votre beauté
Mis tout le beau dont la beauté s'assemble.

Lope de Vega exclaimed: "From her eyes the stars borrow their brilliancy, and from her features the colours which make them so wonderful." Ronsard attributes the following words to a brother of Charles IX:

Avoir joui d'une telle beauté,
Sein contre sein, valoit ta royauté.

Again, du Bellay sums up all the praise of all the poets in the couplet:

Contentez-vous, mes yeux!
Vous ne verrez jamais une chose pareille. . . .

Poets are prone to let their feelings run away with them; especially is this so in the case of court poets when they wish to sing the merits of their ruler. With the greater curiosity do we turn to the portraits left to us by such a master as Clouet. Here we suffer no disappointment, indeed, and yet we cannot altogether agree with the pæans of the poets. No radiant beauty shines down from the canvas, but, rather, a piquant little visage, a delicate and attractive oval, a slightly pointed nose, giving the features that charming irregularity which invariably renders a woman's face so attractive. The dark eyes are gentle, mysterious, veiled; the mouth closed and calm. It must be admitted that each feature is finely moulded, and that nature had made use of her best materials when she was fashioning this daughter of many kings. The skin is wonderfully white and smooth, shimmering like nacre; the hair is abundant and of a chestnut colour, its beauty of texture being enhanced by the pearls entwined in its strands; the hands are long and slim, pale as snow; the body tall and straight; "the corselet so cut as to give but a glimpse of the snowy texture of her breast; and the collar raised, thus revealing the exquisite modelling of her shoulders." No flaw is to be found in this face and figure. But precisely because it is so cool and flawless, so smooth and pretty, the face is lacking in expression. It seems to be a fair, clean page on which nothing personal, nothing characteristic of the young woman herself, has yet been inscribed. There is something indecisive and vague in the lineaments; something that has not yet blossomed, is awaiting the moment of awakening. Every portrait produces an impression of flatness and debility. Here, one feels, the nature of the real woman has still to be revealed; perhaps the true character of the sitter has never been given the chance to develop along its own lines. The visage is that of one whose spirit and senses lie dormant; the woman within has yet to find expression without. What we see is the portrait of an attractive schoolgirl.

Verbal accounts of the young queen serve only to confirm the impression of unawakened and incomplete maidenhood, for everyone seems agreed to affirm Mary's perfection, to praise her deportment, her industry and earnest endeavour, just as if she were the top girl of her class. We are told that she was studious, amiable and pleasantly sociable, pretty-mannered and pious, that she excelled in the practice of the arts and sports of the day and yet showed no predilection for any art or sport in particular, nor any special talent one way or the other. Good, obedient, she was a model of the virtues expected of a king's bride in the making. Always it is her social and courtly virtues that her contemporaries belaud, which seems to point to the fact that the queenly characteristics were developed in Mary before the womanly ones. Her true personality was, for the moment, eclipsed behind a façade of decorum, merely because, so far, it had not been allowed to blossom. For many years to come her dignified behaviour and general culture successfully hid the passionate nature of this lovely princess; no one could guess what the soul of the woman was capable of; it lay quiet and untroubled within her, unmoved and untouched. Smooth and mute is the brow, friendly and sweet the mouth; the dark eyes are pensive, sly, and searching, eyes that have looked forth into the world but have not yet looked deep into her own heart. Her contemporaries and Mary herself have no inkling of what is in store for her; they know nothing of the heritage in her own blood. She who was life's spoiled darling, who had experienced nothing but happiness, could not foresee the dangers lying in the path of her career. Passion is needed in order that a woman may discover herself, in order that her character may expand to its true proportions; love and sorrow are needed for it to find its own magnitude.

Mary Stuart had created so powerful an impression upon all who came in contact with her, and was so universal a favourite at court, that it was agreed to celebrate her nuptials earlier than had been anticipated. Throughout her life Mary's hour seemed always to be in advance of the solar time, and she invariably was called upon to do things earlier than any others of her own age. The dauphin, her future husband as by treaty arranged, was barely fourteen, and in addition he suffered from all-round debility. But politics cannot afford to wait upon nature. The French court was suspiciously eager to get on with the job, to celebrate the marriage, especially since it knew from the royal physicians that young Francis's health was undermined, that, indeed, the boy was dangerously ill. The important thing for France, however, was to make sure of the Scottish crown, and this could be accomplished only if the wedding took place. With all possible speed, therefore, the two children were brought to the altar. In the marriage procuration, which was drawn up by the French and the Scottish parliamentary envoys acting in concert, the dauphin was to receive the "crown matrimonial." Simultaneously with the signing of the public marriage contract, Mary's relatives, the Guises, made the fifteen-year-old girl sign three other, separate and secret, deeds which rendered the public guarantees worthless, and which remained hidden from the Scottish parliament. Herein she pledged herself, in the event of her premature death, or if she died without issue, to bequeath her country as a free gift to France—as if it were her own private estate—and to hand over to the reigning House of Valois her rights of succession to the thrones of England and Ireland.

The secrecy wherein the signing of these documents was shrouded was in itself a proof that the bargain was a dishonourable one. Mary Stuart had no right to change the course of succession in so arbitrary a manner, and to hand over her kingdom to a foreign power as if it were a cloak or other personal belonging. But her uncles brought pressure to bear, and the unsuspecting hand of an innocent girl duly signed the instrument. Tragical obedience! The first time Mary Stuart put her signature to a political document brought dishonour upon her fair head, and forced an otherwise straightforward, trustful, and candid creature to acquiesce in a lie. If she was to become a queen and remain a queen in actual fact, she could never again follow the dictates of her own will, could never again be genuinely true to herself. One who has vowed himself to politics is no longer a free agent.

These secret machinations were, however, hidden away behind the magnificence of the wedding festivities. It was now more than two hundred years since a dauphin of France had been married within the frontiers of his homeland, and for that reason the Valois court was disposed to provide the French people (who were not, in general, cosseted) with a spectacle of unexampled splendour. Catherine de' Medici had witnessed festivals in Italy designed by the leading artists of the Renaissance, and it became a point of pride with her to excel these wonders when her eldest son was married. On April 24, 1558, Paris held high revel such as had not before been witnessed. In the large square before Notre Dame there had been erected an open pavilion in which there was a "ciel royal" of blue Cyprus silk bespangled with golden fleur-de-lis; and a huge blue carpet, stamped likewise with golden lilies, covered the ground. Musicians led the way, clad in red and yellow, playing manifold instruments. Then came the royal procession, sumptuously attired and enthusiastically acclaimed. The rite was solemnized under the eyes of the populace, assembled in thousands to gloat over the bride and the sickly boy-bridegroom, who seemed overwhelmed by the pomp and circumstance. The court poets, on this occasion, again vied with one another in ecstatic descriptions of Mary's beauty. "She appeared," wrote Brantôme (whose pen was better accustomed to the writing of salacious anecdotes), "a hundred times more beautiful than a goddess." Indeed, in that momentous hour, a glow of happiness and a sense of good fortune may have equipped this ambitious girl with a peculiar aureole. As she smiled upon all and sundry, and acknowledged the acclamations, she had arrived in truth—though so early—at the climax of her life. Never again would Mary Stuart be the central figure in such a galaxy of wealth, approval, and jubilation as now when, at the side of the most distinguished crown prince in Europe and at the head of a troop of gaily dressed cavaliers, she passed through the streets to the accompaniment of thunderous applause. In the evening there was a banquet at the Palais de Justice, and all Paris thronged to gape through the open windows at the royal family, gleaming with gold, silver, and precious stones, paying honour to the young woman who was adding a new crown to the crown of France. The celebrations ended in a ball, for which artists who had studied the achievements of the Italian Renaissance had prepared marvellous surprises. Among these there was a pageant of six ships decked with gold, having masts of silver and sails of gauze, which were propelled into the hall by an unseen and cunning mechanism. They rolled and pitched as if on a stormy sea and made their mimic voyage round the hall. In each of these miniature ships was sitting, apparelled in gold and wearing a damask mask, a prince who, rising with a deferent gesture, led one of the ladies of the court to his vessel: Catherine de' Medici, Mary Queen of Scots and heiress to the throne of France, the Queen of Navarre, and the Princesses Elizabeth, Margaret, and Claude. This was intended to symbolize a happy voyage through life, amid a flourish of pageantry. But fate is not subject to human wishes, and from this dazzling moment the life-ship of Mary Stuart was to be steered towards other and more perilous shores.

The first danger arose unexpectedly in her path. Mary was Queen of Scotland in her own right, by birth and heritage, whereas the "roi-dauphin," the crown prince of France, had raised her to a further high estate by marriage. But hardly had the marriage ceremony terminated when a third and more advantageous crown began to shimmer vaguely before the girl's eyes; and her young hands, inexperienced and ill advised, grasped at this treasure and its treacherous brilliance. In the year of the Scottish queen's marriage to Francis, Mary Tudor, Queen of England, died. Elizabeth, her half-sister, succeeded to the crown. But had she any legal right to ascend the throne? Henry VIII, a veritable Bluebeard with his many wives, had left only three children behind him, Edward and two daughters. Mary, the eldest of the three, issued from his lawful union with Catherine of Aragon; Elizabeth, seventeen years younger than Mary, was the child of his marriage with Anne Boleyn. Edward, four years junior to Elizabeth, was the son of Henry's third wife, Jane Seymour, and, as the only male heir, being then only ten years of age, immediately succeeded his father. On Edward's premature demise, there was no question as to the legality of Mary's accession. She left no children, and Elizabeth's right was of a dubious nature. The English crown lawyers contended that, since Henry's marriage with Anne had been sanctioned by an ecclesiastical court's pronouncement and the previous marriage to Catherine of Aragon had been annulled, Elizabeth was a legitimate child of the union. She was his direct descendant, and was a legal claimant to the throne. The French crown jurists, on the other hand, recalled the fact that Henry VIII had himself declared his marriage to Anne Boleyn a union with no legal foundation, and had insisted upon his parliament's proclaiming Elizabeth a bastard. The whole of the Catholic world held the opinion that Elizabeth was born out of lawful wedlock and was, therefore, cut off from the succession. If this view was a true one, then the next legitimate claimant could be no other than Mary Queen of Scots, the great-granddaughter of Henry VII.

Young Mary was faced with a decision of worldwide importance.

Two alternatives presented themselves. She could be diplomatic and yielding, could maintain friendly relations by recognizing her cousin as the rightful Queen of England, thus putting aside her own claim which in any case could not be pushed except by the use of arms. Or she could boldly and resolutely declare Elizabeth to be a usurper, and thereupon gather together an army of French and Scottish supporters to enforce her claim and deprive Elizabeth of a usurper's crown. Unfortunately, Mary and her counsellors chose a third way out of the dilemma, a way which is invariably beset with difficulties, especially in the realm of politics. They elected to take a middle course. Instead of marching forth in full strength and with determination against Elizabeth, the French royal house made an absurd and vainglorious gesture. Henry II commanded that the bridal pair should have the royal arms of England and Scotland surmounted by the crown of France painted and engraved on blason, shield, and seal, and, moreover, that Mary Stuart, in all public announcements and proclamations, henceforward should style herself: "Regina Franciae, Scotiae, Angliae, et Hiberniae." The claim was thus maintained but was left undefended. War was not declared against Elizabeth; she was merely fretted and annoyed. Instead of enforcing a right at the point of the sword, the claim was asserted by a mere painting on a piece of wood and a style at the foot of a sheet of paper. Misunderstanding and ambiguity were thus created, for Mary Stuart's claim to the English throne remained a fact which at the same time was no tangible fact. According to the prevailing mood, the claim was trotted out into the light of day or kept hidden in the background. When, acting upon the clauses of a well-known treaty, Elizabeth demanded the return of Calais to the English crown, Henry II answered: "Calais ought to be surrendered to the dauphin's consort, the Queen of Scotland, whom we take to be the Queen of England." Nevertheless, Henry made no move to enforce his daughter-in-law's claim, and continued to deal on equal terms with the English monarch as if there were no question of her being a usurper.

This foolish and vain gesture, this childish and idiotic painting of the coat of arms of England and Scotland upon a single escutcheon, brought absolutely no advantage to Mary Stuart. On the contrary it ruined her cause. In this instance Mary Stuart had to suffer throughout life for an act committed in her behalf when she was hardly more than a child, an act which was a gross political blunder performed as a salve to aggressiveness and vanity. This petty mortification of Elizabeth's pride converted the most powerful woman of Europe into Mary's irreconcilable foe. A genuine ruler, to the manner born, can tolerate and permit everything except that another should put his dominion in doubt and make a counter-claim to that same dominion. Elizabeth, therefore, in spite of apparently friendly and even tender letters, always looked upon Mary Stuart as a spectre casting a shadow over her throne, invariably held her young cousin to be an enemy, an opponent, a rival. Mary, on the other hand, was too proud to acknowledge herself in the wrong once the claim had publicly been made, and never could she consent unconditionally to recognize a "concubine's" bastard as the legitimate Queen of England. Relations between the two women could not be any other than a pretence and a subterfuge, beneath which the cleavage remained. Half-measures and dishonourable deeds, whether in the world of politics or in private life, invariably bring more damage in their train than energetic and free-handed decisions. The painting-in of the English coat of arms on to the dauphin's and Mary's blason made more blood to flow than a real war could have done, for open warfare in the end must decide the issue one way or another, whereas the ambiguous method adopted by Henry II proved to be a constant and ever-recurring pin-prick which estranged the two women for a lifetime and played havoc with their rule as monarchs.

The coat of arms incorporating the English heraldic emblems was, in July 1559, publicly displayed by the "roi-dauphin" and the "reine-dauphine" when they were on their way to a tournament which was to take place in Paris. On that occasion they were borne to the arena in a triumphal car emblazoned with the fatal escutcheon. The car was preceded by two Scottish heralds, apparelled with the arms of England and Scotland, and crying for all men to hear: "Make place! Make place, for the Queen of England!" This festivity had been arranged to celebrate the Peace of Cateau-Cambrésis (April 1559). King Henry II, ever the chivalrous knight, did not feel it beneath his dignity to splinter a lance or two "pour l'amour des dames," and everyone knew which lady was in his mind. Diane de Poitiers, proud and beautiful as ever, sat in her box and looked down leniently upon her royal lover. On a sudden, however, what had been a joyous sport became deadly earnest. The tourney proved to be a pivot of world history. The Comte de Montgomery, a French knight and officer in the Scottish lifeguard of the king, entered the lists at the latter's command as the opponent of his royal master. Having broken his lance, he galloped to the attack once more with the stump of his weapon. The onslaught was so energetic that a splinter of Montgomery's lance penetrated the king's eye through the visor. The monarch fell from his horse in a faint. At first the wound was considered trifling, but the king never regained consciousness. Around his bed the family gathered, appalled and horrified. Valois's sturdy frame fought valiantly for a few days, but on July 10 he gave up the ghost.

Even when plunged into the deepest grief, the French never forgot the dictates of etiquette. As the royal family was leaving the palace, Catherine de' Medici, Henry II's wife, held back at the door. From the hour when she became a widow she had no longer any right to take precedence at court. This right now fell to a girl who had automatically become Queen of France as the last breath went out of the erstwhile king's body. Mary Stuart, the spouse of France's new king, a chit of sixteen, had to go before, and in this moment Mary rose to the highest peak life had reserved for her.

CHAPTER THREE

Queen, Widow, and Still Queen

(1560-1561)

NOTHING CONTRIBUTED so greatly to render Mary Stuart's fate tragic as that at the outset of her career earthly honours fell deceptively to her lot without her lifting a finger to attain them. Her rise to power was like a rocket for swiftness: six days after birth she was already Queen of Scotland; at six years of age she became the betrothed of one of the most powerful princes in Europe; at fifteen she was his wife; at sixteen, Queen of France. She reached the zenith of her public career before she had had time to develop her inner life. Things dropped into her lap as if out of a horn of plenty; never did she fight in her own behalf for a desired object, or reap any advantage through the exercise of personal endeavour. Not through trial and merit did this princess attain a goal; everything flowed towards her by inheritance, or grace, or gift. As in a dream, wherein happenings fly past in ephemeral and multicoloured precipitancy, she lived through the wedding ceremony and the coronation. Before her senses could begin to grasp the significance of this precocious springtime, the blossoms were already withered and dead, the season of flowering was over, and Mary awoke disappointed, disillusioned, plundered of her hopes, fleeced as it were, bewildered to distraction. At an age when other maids are beginning to form wishes, are beginning to hope for and to hanker after they hardly know what, Mary experienced in profusion the possibilities of a triumphant progress without being granted time or leisure to grasp their spiritual significance. This premature coming to grips with destiny explains her subsequent restlessness and voracity. One who has so early been the outstanding figure in a country, indeed in the world, will never again be content with a less exalted position. It was in the stubborn fight to maintain herself at the centre of the stage that her real greatness was developed. Renunciation and forgetfulness are permissible to the weak; strong natures, on the other hand, are not in the habit of resigning themselves, but challenge even the mightiest destiny to a trial at arms.

In truth this brief period of royalty in France passed for Mary like a dream—a poignant, uneasy, and anxious dream. The ceremony at the cathedral at Rheims—where the archbishop crowned the sickly youth, and where the lovely girl-queen, bedecked with the jewels appropriate to her position, shone forth from among the nobles like a slender white lily not yet in full bloom—was an isolated occasion of splendour. Except for this the chronicles have nothing to tell of festivals or merry-making. Fate left Mary Stuart no time to found the troubadour's court of the arts and poesy for which she yearned; left the painters no time to finish portraits of the monarch and his lovely wife in the panoply of royal robes; no time for historians to describe their respective characters; no time for the populace to make close acquaintance with its new rulers or learn to love them. In the long procession of kings and queens of France, the figures of these two children are driven onward like mist-wreaths before the wind.

Francis II, a tainted tree in the forest, was doomed to premature death. In a round and bloated face, timid eyes, weary, and reminding us of those of one who has been startled out of sleep, give the dominant expression to his countenance. His strength was further undermined by a sudden and extensive growth in stature such as often occurs at his age. Physicians watched over him sedulously and urgently advised him to take care of himself. But the boy was animated by a foolish dread lest he should be outdone by his willowy, untiring wife, who was passionately devoted to outdoor sports. That he might seem hale and manly, he rode hell-for-leather and engaged in other exhausting bodily exercises. But nature could not be cheated. His blood was incurably sluggish, was poisoned by an evil heritage from his grandfather Francis I. Again and again he was laid low by paroxysms of fever. When the weather was inclement, he had to keep indoors, restive and bored, a pitiful shade, surrounded by his train of doctors. So weakly a king aroused more pity than respect among his courtiers; among the common people, on the other hand, it was soon bruited abroad that he was smitten with leprosy, and that he bathed in the blood of freshly killed children in the hope of regaining health. The peasants regarded the stricken lad menacingly when he went out riding. At court, those with an eye to the future were beginning to throng round Catherine de' Medici and Charles, the next heir to the throne. Hands so weak as Francis's could not long nor firmly grip the reins of power. Now and again, in stiff, awkward writing, the boy would pen his "François" at the foot of decrees; but the real rulers were the Guises, the kin of Mary Stuart, in place of one whose energies must be devoted to keeping his vital spark aglow as long as possible. Such a sick-room companionship, with its perpetual watchfulness over failing health, can scarcely be spoken of as a happy marriage, even if we suppose it to have been a marriage in any true sense of the term. Yet there is nothing to justify the supposition that the union of these youngsters was an unhappy one, for even at this malicious court where gossip was rife, at this court where every amourette was recorded by Brantôme in his *Vie des dames galantes,* no suspicion seems to have been aroused by Mary Stuart's behaviour. Long before they were dragged to the altar, Francis of Valois and Mary Stuart had been playmates, and it seems unlikely that the erotic element can have had much part in their companionship after the wedding. Years were still to pass before there was to develop in Mary Queen of Scots the capacity for passionate self-surrender to a lover; and Francis, an ailing boy, was not the type of male to arouse the passion hidden so deep in the enigmatic nature of his wife. Tenderness and clemency of character prompted Mary to care for her husband to the best of her ability. Even if she had not been moved to this by feeling, her reason would have informed her that power and position depended upon the breathing and the heart-beats of this poor, sick body, to safeguard which would be to defend her own happiness. But for real happiness, during her brief span of queenship in France, there was no scope. The storms aroused by the Huguenot movement were causing widespread agitation. After the conspiracy of Amboise, in which the royal pair were personally endangered, Mary had to pay one of the painful tributes called for by her position as ruler. She had to witness the execution of the rebels, and we may well suppose that the sight was deeply graven in her memory, forgotten then, maybe, for decades, to leap back again into vivid reality when the hour of her own doom struck. Now she watched the awesome sight of a human being, hands tied behind the back, kneeling with head on the block and awaiting the fall of the executioner's axe. She heard for the first time the curiously muffled and dull tone of steel that severs living flesh, she saw the blood squirt and the head rolling away from the body into the sand. A picture gruesome enough to blot out from the remembrance of a sensitive soul the splendid scenes so recently enacted at Rheims when her young head was crowned.

Now evil tidings followed quickly one upon the other. Mary's mother, Mary of Guise, who had been acting as regent in Scotland during her daughter's minority, had reached her end and, surrounded by enemies, breathed her last in June 1560. She left the country embroiled in religious strife and in full rebellion, with war raging along the border and English armies occupying the Lowlands. Mary Stuart had to exchange her festal attire for mourning. For the time being she was to hear no more music; her feet were for a while no longer to tread the mazes of the dance. Then Death's bony knuckle came knocking at the door of her heart and home. Francis II grew weaker and weaker; the envenomed blood usually flowing so sluggishly through his veins now beat a tattoo in his temples and his ears. No more could he even walk or ride, but had to be carried in a litter from place to place. At length the gathering pus burst the ear-drum; but it was too late, for the inflammation had already spread inwards to the brain, and the sufferer was beyond reach of medical aid. His heart ceased to beat on December 6, 1560.

Once more a tragical scene between two women was played to the finish beside this second deathbed. Hardly was the breath out of Francis's frail body when Mary Stuart, no longer Queen of France, had to yield precedence to Catherine de' Medici; the younger of the royal widows had to draw back at the door in order to allow the elder one to go first. Mary was no longer the first lady in the realm, but again, as before, the second. One short year sufficed to bring Mary Stuart's dream to an end. She would never again be reigning Queen of France, but must henceforth remain till the hour of her death what she had always been from birth: Mary Queen of Scotland and the Isles.

The rigours of regal etiquette in France decreed that a king's widow should pass forty days in strict seclusion during which she might not for a moment leave her private apartments, or admit the daylight into her rooms. In the first two weeks of mourning she was forbidden to receive any visitors except the new king and his next of kin, and these she entertained in her retreat which, gloomy as it was and lighted only by candles, resembled a living tomb. Nor might a royal widow wear the regulation black adopted almost universally by commoners as a sign of bereavement. The widow of a French monarch had to don the "deuil blanc" prescribed by the law of the land. A white coif framed the pale face, a white brocade dress covered body and limbs, the shoes and stockings were white. Ample folds of white fell from head to waist. This is how Janet depicts Mary Stuart in the days of her mourning; this is how Ronsard portrays her in words:

Un crespe long, subtil et délié
Ply contre ply, retors et replié
Habit de deuil, vous sert de couvertuire,
Depuis le chef jusques à la ceinture,
Qui s'enfle ainsi qu'un voile quand le vent
Soufle la barque et la cingle en avant.
De tel habit vous étiez accoutrée
Partant, hélas! de la belle contrée
Dont aviez eu le sceptre dans la main,
Lorsque, pensive et baignant votre sein
Du beau cristal de vos larmes coulées
Triste marchiez par les longues allées
Du grand jardin de ce royal château
Qui prend son nom de la beauté des eaux.

Never before had this young and sympathetic and gentle creature been more successfully painted than at this time of her first grief and her first disappointment. Her roving and restless eyes had become steadfast and earnest in expression; the dignity of her bearing is more obvious in the modest and simple garb of mourning than in the portraits which show her bedecked with gems and the insignia of power.

The same dignified melancholy speaks to us from the lines she herself composed as a lament for her dead husband. These verses are not unworthy of the young queen's master, Ronsard. Even if it had not been penned by a queen, the tender elegy would appeal to any heart through the simplicity of its tone and its touching candour. Here we find no passionate regret for the young dead king, since Mary Stuart was always truthful and candid where poetry was concerned, though not invariably so in the world of politics. But we are given a picture of her utter loneliness, and the feeling that she was lost and forsaken.

Sans cesse mon cœur sent
Le regret d'un absent.
Si parfois vers les cieux
Viens à dresser ma veue
Le doux traict de ses yeux
Je vois dans une nue;
Soudain je vois dans l'eau
Comme dans un tombeau.
Si je suis en repos
Someillant sur ma couche,
Je le sens qu'il me touche:
En labeur, en recoy
Toujour est près de moy.

Mary Stuart's sorrow at the loss of her husband, Francis II, was undeniably genuine, and not merely a poetical fiction. For in losing Francis, Mary not only lost a pleasant and docile companion and an affectionate friend, but at the same time her position among European potentates, her power, and her security. This woman, who was still half a child, soon felt how much it signified to her stability and gratification to be the first lady in a great kingdom, and how paltry it was to have to be content with playing second fiddle. Indeed, for proud natures, this is even more galling than to be nobody at all. Mary's situation was rendered if anything bitterer by Catherine de' Medici's open hostility now that that haughtiest member of a haughty house had resumed her old place at Court. It would appear that Mary, in an unwitting moment, goaded by the inconsiderate rashness of youth, had incurred the elder lady's undying displeasure by hazarding an observation on the commercial origins of the wealthy family of Medici, and referring to the upstart ancestors of this merchant's daughter, thus making a derogatory comparison with her own long line of kingly forefathers. Such scatter-brained utterances—heedless and ill-advised, she was at a future date to let her tongue run away with her in regard to Elizabeth of England as well—when spoken by one woman to the detriment of another, are more devastating in their consequences than open invectives. Catherine's ambitions had already been thwarted during two long decades through the power wielded by Diane de Poitiers; then came Mary Stuart's rise. Hardly, therefore, had she at length entered into her own and taken her place in the political arena when she allowed her detestation of these two rivals to find challenging and dictatorial vent.

But in Mary Stuart's case, pride, which was an essential trait in her make-up, prevented her from accepting a minor part. High-hearted and passionate by nature, she refused half-glories and petty positions. Better to be accounted nothing, better to be dead, than to be an underling. For a space she thought seriously of retiring to a nunnery, of eschewing worldly prerogatives, of forfeiting her rights and privileges, since she could not be the leading lady of her court. But life was still too seductive a business for a girl of eighteen to go against the dictates of her innermost being and give up its allurements for ever. Besides, it was possible that the lost crown might yet be compensated for by the acquisition of another, and no less resplendent, one. The Spanish ambassador was even now suing for Mary on behalf of Don Carlos, the heir to two worlds; the court of Austria was simultaneously undertaking secret negotiations; the Kings of Sweden and of Denmark were offering her throne and hand. And was she not, as ever, a queen in her own right; was she not Queen of Scotland and the Isles? Then there was the neighbour crown of England which might fall to her at any moment. Incalculable possibilities lay around the girl-widow now ripening to the full beauty of womanhood—though henceforward she would have to grab what she could get. Gone for ever the days when treasures dropped into her lap like gifts from the gods. Henceforward she would have to fight a lone hand, would have to seize what she wanted by the manipulation of the arts of diplomacy, using her utmost skill, exercising patience. But with such an abundance of courage, with so much loveliness at her command, with youth to warm her blossoming body, why should she not venture on the boldest game? Resolute and greatly daring, Mary Stuart marched forth to battle.

Granted, it would be hard to bid farewell to France. She had lived twelve years at this royal court, in this beautiful, wealthy, happy land that seemed more like home to her than Scotland, which had by now become no more than a vague memory of childhood. Here, in France, dwelt her mother's relatives, who cherished and guarded her; here were the many palaces and castles wherein she had passed any number of cheerful hours; here lived the poets who had sung her praises and who had so well understood her; here she was surrounded by the knightly courtesies which rendered life so charming, the gallant chivalry which suited her taste so admirably. She put off her departure from month to month, hesitant in spite of urgent messages from her homeland. She visited her relatives in Joinville and in Nancy, was present at the coronation of her ten-year-old brother-in-law, Charles IX, in Rheims cathedral. Perpetually she found fresh excuses for postponing the journey, as though she harboured a premonition of its finality. It was as if she were waiting for some sign that would spare her the dreaded separation from France and the voyage home.

For no matter how inexperienced a girl of eighteen may be in affairs of State, it is undeniable that Mary Stuart must have been convinced that a very hard test was awaiting her so soon as she set foot on her native soil. Since her mother's death, the Protestant Lords of the Congregation, her fiercest enemies, had gained the upper hand, and they were at no pains to hide the fact that they did not want a Catholic, a believer in the Mass and other idolatrous practices, to return to the land. They brazenly declared (and the English ambassador eagerly conveyed the news to London) that the queen's journey to Scotland must be postponed for a few months longer, and, were it not that it was their duty to obey, they would not be much put out if they never saw her again. They had, as a matter of fact, been intriguing on the quiet, proposing that the Queen of England should marry the Protestant James Hamilton, Earl of Arran, who was the next heir to the Scottish throne, thus bartering the crown to Mary's rival, a crown that was unquestionably Mary Stuart's by right of succession. Nor could she place any greater confidence in her own half-brother James Stuart, who, as envoy from the Scottish parliament, sought Mary out in France "to know her mind." His relations with Elizabeth were dubious, and some even suspected that he was in the English queen's pay. The only way for Mary to put an end to these intrigues was to be on the spot herself, and with proverbial Stuart courage defend and maintain her rights to the Stuart throne. Determined not to lose a second crown within a year of losing the other, full of dreary foreboding and heavy at heart, Mary Stuart obeyed a summons which had not proceeded from loyal hearts and which she obeyed while half doubtful as to its honesty.

Before returning to her native land, Mary Stuart could not but be aware that Elizabeth had no reason and still less any inclination to make things easy and smooth for a rival who was only awaiting her death to step into her shoes and mount the English throne. With cynical candour, Elizabeth's minister, Cecil, supported every aggressive act on the part of his sovereign, saying: "The longer the Scottish queen's affairs remain in disorder, the better for Your Majesty's cause." The animus aroused by that painted claim to the throne of England was still fresh and vigorous. True, the Scottish estates and lords in Edinburgh had drawn up a treaty with England wherein it was clearly stated that Mary Stuart "for all times coming" undertook to recognize Elizabeth as the rightful tenant of the English throne. But when the document reached Paris and was placed before Mary for signature, she and young Francis refused to ratify it or to have anything to do with it. Renunciation was not in Mary's blood, especially since her claim had officially been incorporated in her husband's coat of arms. Never would she be able to lower the standard once it had been raised. For political reasons she might consent to not making a display of her pretensions, but in the innermost sanctum of her heart Mary Stuart had an iron determination never to yield in this matter.

Elizabeth could not tolerate such ambiguity; for her the question must be settled with an outright Yes or No. Acting on behalf of Mary, the Scottish queen's representatives in Edinburgh, said Elizabeth, had already signed the treaty, thus committing their sovereign to the undertaking, and compelling her to acquiesce. The English monarch would not be satisfied with a secret agreement; what she needed was a public and binding pronouncement, a document which should leave no door open for misinterpretation. Every refusal on Mary's part suggested that she still laid claim to Elizabeth's possessions; that, in addition to the Scottish throne, she felt herself entitled to ascend the English. Elizabeth, whose sympathies lay more in the direction of the Protestant cause, knew only too well that half her realm was still passionately Catholic in sentiment. A Catholic pretender to her throne meant, therefore, not merely a danger to her public office, but likewise a menace to her private life. For safety's sake she must have Mary's signature to the before-mentioned treaty, and it was sound policy on her part that she should not relax in open hostility to the Scottish queen so long as the latter refused to sign. She felt her position insecure, felt that she was no true queen, until her rival had made public acknowledgment and had abdicated all immediate claims to the English crown.

None would venture to deny that right was on Elizabeth's side in the quarrel. Unfortunately she put herself in the wrong by trying to settle a political conflict of such magnitude by adopting petty and unworthy methods. When women enter the field of politics, they are often tempted to wound opponents with pin-pricks and to envenom rivalries by the use of personal invective. In this instance Elizabeth, despite the width of her political vision, fell into the fault peculiar to her sex when faced by such circumstances. Mary was proposing to travel home by sea, but asked for a "safe-conduct" should sickness or rough weather make a landing on English soil desirable. Was not this demand a fairly plain proffer of a desire for a friendly personal talk with her cousin—a talk which might smooth away their differences? To grant the safe-conduct would have been no more than a formal act of courtesy, since anyhow the sea route was open. Elizabeth's response was to say that she would grant no safe-conduct so long as Mary had not placed her signature at the foot of the Edinburgh treaty. In the hope of coercing the queen she thus wounded the woman. Instead of making a magnanimous gesture or if necessary going to war, she had recourse to a personal affront.

So far the conflict between the two cousins had been more or less masked; now all veils were wrenched aside, and with hard, hot eyes one proud woman confronted the other. Mary Stuart summoned the English ambassador to audience, and addressed him with passionate disdain: "There is nothing that doth more grieve me than that I did so forget myself as to require of the Queen your mistress that favour which I had no need to ask. I needed no more to have made her privy to my journey than she doth me of hers. I may pass well enough home into my own realm, I think, without her passport or licence, for though the late King your master used all the impeachment he could both to stay me, and to catch me when I came hither, yet you know, Monsieur l'Ambassadeur, I came hither safely: and I may have as good means to help me home again as I had to come hither, if I would employ my friends.... You have, Monsieur l'Ambassadeur, oftentimes told me that the amity between the Queen your mistress and me was very necessary and profitable for us both. I have some reason now to think that the Queen your mistress is not of that mind; for I am sure, if she were, she would not have refused me thus unkindly. It seemeth she maketh more account of the amity of my disobedient subjects than she doth of me their sovereign, who am her equal in degree, though inferior in wisdom and experience, her nighest kinswoman, and her next neighbour.... I ask nothing but her friendship; I do not trouble her State, nor practise with her subjects: and yet I know there be in her realm those that be inclined enough to hear offers."

This was a threat in good earnest, strong rather than wise, for, before ever setting foot in Scotland, Mary Stuart already allowed it to be known that, if constrained to fight Elizabeth, she would carry the war over the border and on to English soil. In courtly words the ambassador drew Mary's attention to the fact that these many difficulties and misunderstandings had arisen because she bore the arms of England diversely quartered with her own and used notoriously the style and title of the Queen his mistress. To which Mary answered in spirited protest:

"Monsieur l'Ambassadeur, I was then under the command of King Henry my father, and of the King my lord and husband; and whatsoever was done then by their order and commandments, the same was in like manner continued until both their deaths; since which time, you know I have neither borne the arms, nor used the title of England. Methinks these my doings might ascertain the Queen your mistress that that which was done before, was done by commandment of them that had the power over me; and also in reason she ought to be satisfied, seeing I order my doings as I tell you. It were no great dishonour to the Queen my cousin . . . though I, as Queen also, did bear the Arms of England; for, I am sure, some, inferior to me, and that be not on every side so well apparented as I am, do bear the Arms of England. You cannot deny but that my grandmother was the King her father's sister, and, I trow, the eldest sister he had. . . ."

Though the method of expression was quite friendly, beneath the outer semblance of amiability the ambassador detected another threat. When, wishing to smooth matters over, he urged Mary to clear unpleasantness out of the way by fulfilling her representatives' pledge and signing the Edinburgh protocol, Mary was evasive, as always when this thorny point came up for discussion. She did not actually decline to sign the treaty, but promised to consult her estates after her arrival in Scotland. The English ambassador, however, paid her back in her own coin, and remained as evasive as she, refusing to commit himself or his mistress in the matter of the succession. Whenever negotiations took a critical turn, and it became evident that one queen or the other would have to cede a particle of her rights, both women became insincere. Each hung on to her trump card, grimly and resolutely. Thus the game was protracted indefinitely, and must inevitably lead to a tragical issue. Of a sudden Mary broke off the discussion concerning her safe-conduct; it was as if a cloth had been torn across, producing a harsh and rasping hiss. "If my preparations were not so much advanced as they are, peradventure the Queen your mistress's unkindness might stay my voyage; but now I am determined to adventure the matter, whatsoever come of it; I trust the wind will be so favourable that I shall not need to come on the coast of England; for if I do, then, Monsieur l'Ambassadeur, the Queen your mistress shall have me in her hands to do her will of me; and if she be so hardhearted as to desire my end, she may then do her pleasure and make sacrifice of me. Peradventure that casualty might be better for me than to live. In this matter, God's will be fulfilled."

For the first time in her life Mary Stuart put force, self-determination, and resoluteness into the words she spoke. As a rule she had proved herself to be of an affable, easy-going, frivolous, and laughter-loving nature, more enthralled with enjoyment and the beauty of life than with a fight; but now she showed herself to be hard as iron, defiant, daring, for she was faced by an issue involving her personal pride, while her rights as queen were likewise being questioned. Better by far to die than bend to another's will. Better royal folly than pitiful weakness. One who challenged her queenly dignity touched the very nerve of her life. In moments like this she became truly great and, woman though she was, she showed a man's knightly strength. The ambassador sent an express to London, reporting that his mission had not met with success. Elizabeth thereupon, with her usual suppleness and shrewdness where politics were concerned, yielded the point, and dispatched a passport to Calais forthwith. It arrived two days behind time, for Mary had meanwhile decided to undertake the voyage even though this might mean an encounter with English privateers in the Channel. She infinitely preferred running a risk and experiencing grave discomfort to accepting a favour at the price of humiliation. Elizabeth had missed a splendid opportunity. Had she, on this occasion, acted with magnanimity, had she welcomed as an honoured guest the young woman whom she had reason to fear as a rival, she might have swept the whole of this dangerous conflict out of her path. Alas that reason and politics so seldom can step hand in hand along the same road! May it not be that the dramatic events in the history of mankind arise solely from a failure to seize possibilities?

The sun in its setting often illuminates the countryside with a red and golden glory, giving to the landscape a false aspect of life and vitality. Such a deceptive aureole surrounded Mary Stuart as she took her final leave of France, for the French made a point of carrying out in her honour a full ceremonial in all its magnificent ostentation. She, who had been a French king's bride, who had fallen from her high estate through no fault of her own, and who had been deprived of her position as France's ruler by a mishap, could not be allowed to leave the land of her adoption unaccompanied and unsung. It must be made abundantly clear to everyone that Mary was not sailing forth under a cloud, as the unhappy widow of a French monarch or as a weak and helpless woman whom her friends had left in the lurch. No, the Queen of Scotland was going home, backed by French honour and French arms. Setting out from Saint-Germain, she made her way to Calais in the company of a vast procession, a cavalcade whose horses were caparisoned with the most elaborate and beautiful harness, trappings inlaid with gold and other precious metals, and whose riders were dressed in the full splendour of which the French Renaissance was capable. The highway leading to the little port was made gay with colour, bright with the polished steel of weapons, loud with the voices of the flower of the French nobility. At the head of the brilliant retinue was a State carriage conveying the queen's uncles, the Duke of Guise and the Cardinals of Lorraine and of Guise. Mary herself was surrounded by the four girls who had never left her, by noblewomen, by pages, poets, and musicians. The days of romance and chivalry seemed to be living a second springtime. The train was followed by a succession of chariots bearing costly furniture and other objects that had gone to the making of her homes in France. The crown jewels were transported in a closed shrine. As she had come a queen, welcomed with a pageantry and honour worthy of her rank, so, too, did she leave the country of her adoption, the country which had won the love of her heart. But on this occasion joy was lacking, that innocent joy which had lighted up the eyes of an astonished child; this was the fading afterglow of sunset and not the radiance of dawn.

The main body of the princely cortège stayed ashore in Calais. Then the cavalcade dispersed, each rider seeking his own home. Away in Paris, sheltered behind the walls of the Louvre, another monarch was awaiting the return of these nobles who were henceforth to serve him, for courtiers may not live in the pomp of yesterday, it being their business to think only of the present and the future. Dignities and position, not the human being who has to shoulder them, are the only things that count so far as a courtier is concerned.

These fine fellows will forget Mary Stuart as soon as the wind has filled the sails of her galleon; they will expunge her image from their hearts. The parting was no more to them than a pathetic ritual, belonging to the same category of public pageantry as a coronation or a funeral. Genuine sorrow at Mary Stuart's melancholy pilgrimage was felt only by the poets, for poets are endowed with keener perceptions and with the twofold gifts of prophecy and remembrance. Those who wept over Mary's going knew only too acutely that with this young woman, who had wished to create a court of cheerfulness and beauty, the Muses would disappear likewise from French territory; they foresaw days filled with vicissitude and uncertainty for themselves and the French people; they sensed the advent of political and religious disputes and contentions, the struggle with the Huguenots, the disastrous St. Bartholomew's night, squabbles with zealots and quibblers. Gone were the days of chivalry, gone romance, as the maidenly figure disappeared over the waters. The star of poesy, the star of the "Pléiade," was about to set in a murky sky rendered the gloomier by the prospect of war. Spiritual happiness, pure and unsullied, sailed away with Mary Stuart. As Ronsard put it, in his elegy "Au Départ":

Le jour que votre voile aux vents se recourba,
Et de nos yeux pleurants les vostres déroba,
Ce jour la même voile emporta loin de France
Les Muses, qui songeoient y faire demourance.

In this same poem the writer, with a heart ever responsive to all that was young and charming, wished to celebrate in the written word that which his ardent eyes would never again behold in the quick, warm flesh. The genuine grief which pulled at his heart-strings inspired him to pen a dirge which alone would make him rank high among the poets of his day.

Comment pourroient chanter les bouches des poètes,
Quand par vostre départ les Muses sont muettes?
Tout ce qu'il est de beau ne se garde longtemps,
Les roses et les lys ne règnent qu'un printemps.
Ainsi votre beauté, seulement apparue
Quinze ans en notre France, est soudain disparue,

Comme on voit d'un éclair s'évanouir le trait,
Et d'elle n'a laissé sinon le regret,
Sinon le déplaisir qui me remet sans cesse
Au cœur le souvenir d'une telle princesse.

Whereas by the court and nobles and gentry of France the absent queen was soon to be forgotten, the poets of that fair realm were to remain for long her faithful servitors; for to the poetic imagination misfortune invests the sufferer with fresh nobility, and she whom the poets had sung on account of her beauty would henceforward be doubly loved because of the evils which befell her. To the end of her days Mary Stuart kept their faithful homage, and their tuneful lyrics accompanied her even as she mounted the scaffold. When a person of intrinsic worth lives a life that is a genuine poem, a true drama, a beautiful saga and ballad, poets will never be lacking to clothe it anew and to breathe into it the fresh and vibrant imagery of inspiration.

A splendid white galleon was riding at anchor in Calais roads. She was a French flag-ship, flying the Scottish colours as well. Here, on August 14, 1561, Mary Stuart went aboard, accompanied by three of her uncles, a few of the most distinguished noblemen, and the four Marys, her inseparable companions. Two other vessels formed an escort. But the ship had not left the inner harbour, her sails had not been fully unfurled, when a portent cast a shadow on this voyage into the unknown. A vessel entering the port the queen had barely left, struck the bar, foundered, and sank. Mary, greatly agitated, called upon her captain to save the drowning mariners. But the accident had occurred too suddenly for human aid to be of any avail. This catastrophe was, indeed, a bad omen for the young and inexperienced woman who was leaving the protection of a land she loved to take up her duties as queen and ruler in a country that was strange and foreign to her.

Was it a secret dread of what fate held in store for her, was it a keen sense of loss as she left what had hitherto been her homeland, was it a feeling that she would not return to these shores, which brought the tears to eyes whose gaze never for a moment left the retreating landscape, the country where she had spent her care-free girlhood, where she had been so happy because no worries had been allowed to approach her? Her passionate grief on bidding farewell to France has been touchingly described for us by Brantôme: "So soon as the ship had steered clear of the harbour and the wind rose a little, the crew began to hoist the sails. Standing in the stern, close to the rudder, and leaning with both arms on the taffrail, Queen Mary wept as she looked at the harbour and the country from which she was departing. There she remained, again and again mournfully repeating: 'Farewell, France,' until night fell. Her companions urged her to retire to her cabin and rest, but she refused, so a couch was improvised for her on the poop. Before lying down she told the pilot to awaken her at dawn if the coast of France were still visible. He was not to be afraid, even if he had to shout at her. Fortune favoured her wishes. Since the wind had dropped, it was necessary to have recourse to the oars, and the galleon made little progress. At daybreak France was still in the offing. Directly the pilot spoke to her, she rose and continued to gaze at the coasts so long as they were in sight, again and again repeating plaintively: 'Farewell, France! Farewell, France! I fear I shall never see you more.'"

CHAPTER FOUR

Return to Scotland

(AUGUST 1561)

A FOG, THICKER than is usual in summer even in a northerly clime, shrouded sea and land when, on August 19, 1561, Mary stepped out of the boat which put her ashore at Leith. What a contrast was this arrival in Scotland as compared with the magnificent send-off she had been accorded when bidding adieu to la douce France! Then she had been escorted by the bravest and noblest gentlemen of the land; princes and counts, poets and musicians, had graced her passage along the roads and at the port, coining courtly phrases and composing rapturous songs in her honour. In Scotland, no one was expecting her, and it was not until she was handed out of the boat and stepped along on firm ground that a few commoners gathered to gape open-mouthed at the dainty apparition. A fisherman or two in their rough working clothes, a handful of loitering soldiers, some shopkeepers, and peasants who had come to sell their sheep in the town looked at her and her suite shyly rather than with enthusiasm. They seemed to be asking themselves who these fine folk could be with their sumptuous clothing and display of jewels. Strangers gazed into the eyes of strangers. A rude welcome, hard and austere as are the souls of these northern people. From the first hour of her landing, Mary Stuart was made to see the appalling poverty of her native country, to realize that during the few days of her voyage she had travelled backward in history at least one hundred years, that she had left behind her a great civilization, rich and luxurious, wasteful and sensuous, had exchanged the refined and open-handed culture of France for something narrow, dark, and fraught with tragedy. A dozen times and more, the town had been ravaged and plundered by the English, and by Scottish rebels, so that it could boast of no palace or baronial hall wherein Mary might be received with a dignity worthy of her rank.

This night, therefore, she was put up in a burgher's house; simple quarters it is true, but at least the Queen of Scotland had a roof over her head.

First impressions make a distinctive mark on the mind; they are stamped in deeply, and much of subsequent happenings depends upon whether they are good or bad. Perhaps Mary herself scarcely understood what moved her so profoundly when, after an absence of thirteen years, she returned to her kingdom as a stranger. Could it be homesickness, an unconscious longing for a warm, sweet existence which had taught her to love the French soil? Was it perhaps the shadow cast upon her high spirits by the grey skies of an unknown land? May it not have been a premonition of coming disaster? Whatever the emotion was, Brantôme tells us that hardly did she find herself alone in the room allotted her when she burst into tears. It was not like William the Conqueror, strong in the consciousness of his power, that this poor girl set foot on British earth. Her feeling was one of constraint and perplexity mingled with gloomy forebodings.

Meanwhile, her half-brother, Lord James Stuart (better known to history by his later title, the Earl of Moray, or as the Regent Moray in subsequent years), had been informed of Mary's arrival, and he in company with some of his fellow-noblemen rode with all haste to Leith in order to provide a worthy escort to accompany her on her entry into Edinburgh. But the cavalcade did not cut much of a figure. Under the very transparent pretext of a search for pirates, the English had waylaid one of Mary's ships. This happened to be the one conveying the favourite palfrey that she used on State occasions, together with the whole of the royal stud. Since the queen rode well, she would not have been loath to display her equestrian skill to the crowds assembled to see her pass. But being deprived of her own mount, she had to ride into her kingdom sitting the best horse the town of Leith could provide. A sorry nag, indeed, but serviceable. The mortification was no small thing for a girl of eighteen to face. Her suite fared worse, having to be content with what the stables and stalls of the neighbouring countryside could produce. Again tears suffused Mary's eyes, tears of wounded pride and regret, for suddenly there was borne in on her the magnitude of her loss the day her husband, Francis II, was taken from her. Also she realized that to be Queen of Scotland was a poor, mean thing when compared with the glory of being Queen of France. Her national pride was piqued at having to cut so wretched a figure before the French gentlemen who accompanied her, and she felt personally affronted at having to present herself for the first time to her new subjects in so pitiable a plight. Instead, therefore, of making a "joyeuse entrée" through the main streets of Edinburgh, Mary decided to stop at Holyrood, which was outside the city walls. Her father had built this palace; its crenellated battlements dominated the landscape, dark and defiant; at first sight it created a formidable impression, with its menacing towers, its clear-cut lines, its square-shaped majesty. But how chill, empty, and dismal must it have appeared to a child who had lived amid the voluptuous refinement of the French Renaissance. Here were no Gobelins to cheer and refresh the eyes, no chandeliers reflecting their lustrous illumination in Italian mirrors from wall to wall, no costly hangings, no sheen of gold and silver. Many years had gone by since the place had been used; no laughter re-echoed from its forlorn walls, no kingly hand had cared for or renovated the building since her father's death. Poverty, the age-long curse of her kingdom, stared down at her from every nook.

But, night though it was, the inhabitants of Edinburgh had no sooner learned that their queen had come than they issued from their houses, determined to give her a suitable welcome. It is not to be wondered at that this welcome seemed uncouth and boorish to Mary and her entourage, used as they were to French brilliancy and polish. Edinburgh's townsfolk had no festive attire to grace the ceremony, nor did they know how to set up triumphal arches in honour of their young queen. Here were no "musiciens de la cour" to enchant the ears of Ronsard's pupil with sweet madrigals and smoothly flowing canzoni. They could only follow the traditional customs such occasions demanded. The country was rich in wood, so what more natural than to construct huge bonfires in the public squares, and by their glare change night into day? They gathered beneath her window and serenaded her with the wild skirling of bagpipes and other outlandish instruments, a sound they called music, but which to her trained ears was nothing but an ugly noise. In addition they raised their rough, manly voices in song; and since they were forbidden by their Calvinistic pastors to sing profane melodies, they filled the air with the lilt of psalms and hymns. With the best will in the world, they were incapable of producing a more soothing lullaby. Nevertheless, Mary Stuart's heart warmed with the honest love which breathed through these rustic endeavours; the reception was instinct with friendliness towards herself and pleasure at her advent. For decades such harmony had not existed between the sovereign and the people of this distraught and tragical land.

Neither the queen, young and politically inexperienced as she was, nor her chief advisers, blinked the fact that unusually difficult tasks lay ahead. Maitland of Lethington, who had one of the shrewdest brains of his day in Scotland, wrote prophetically before Mary returned to her native heath: "It could not fail to raise wonderful tragedies." Even an energetic man, a man with an iron fist and resolute mind, could not for long impose peace on this unmanageable environment with its chaos of contradictions making for perpetual unrest. How, then, could so joyous and ethereal a young queen, a stranger in these parts, unaccustomed to rule, how could Mary be expected to fare better? A poverty-stricken country, a corrupt nobility that seized upon any and every occasion to rise in arms, a countless number of contending clans on the look-out for a pretext to engage in civil strife, a clergy that was half Catholic and half Protestant fighting for precedence, an alert and dangerous neighbour profiting by fratricidal disputes over the border to feather her own nest, antagonism on the part of the big powers ruthlessly making use of Scotland as catspaw in their bloody game—such was the situation by which Mary Stuart was faced.

At the time of Mary's return, dissension and discord were at their height. Instead of leaving the treasury full, Mary of Guise had left a veritable "damnosa hereditas": no money, and a war of religions which was to become, perhaps, more bitter on this soil than anywhere else in the world. During the years Mary had spent so happily in France, the Reformation had struck deep roots in the Scottish earth, and was almost universally victorious. The cleavage was felt at court and in the home, in villages and towns, throughout whole kinships and families—one half of the nobility and gentry Catholic whilst the other half was Protestant, the towns advocating the new faith, the countryside the old, clan opposed to clan, family opposed to family, and all parties stimulated in their hatred by fanatical priests and by the political ambitions of foreign powers. What constituted the gravest danger so far as Mary was concerned was that the most powerful and influential of her nobles had gone over to the Calvinistic camp; they had made the best of their opportunities, and had seized the lands and properties of the old Church while simultaneously weakening the power of the crown, two achievements which made a special and quasi-magical appeal to this rout of ambitious and greedy rebels. They found a specious and ostensibly moral pretext, as protectors of the true faith, as Lords of the Congregation, to set themselves up in opposition to their ruler, and England as usual was not tardy in giving them a helping hand in this endeavour. Though Elizabeth was by nature of a thrifty disposition, she had not grudged spending more than two hundred thousand pounds sterling in financing these traitors, in fomenting rebellion and civil war to undermine the throne of the Catholic Stuarts. Even now, when a truce had been signed, a goodly number of Mary's subjects were in the secret pay of the English queen. Of course equilibrium could easily be restored if Mary should consent to embrace the new faith, and some of her advisers urged her to do so. But Mary was not only a Stuart, she was also a Guise. She was a child of the most ardent champions of the Catholic cause and, though not fanatically pious, she was true to the beliefs of her forebears. Never was she to stray from the path of her convictions, no matter the dangers that encompassed her; and, loyal to her own nature, she chose rather perpetual warfare than, in a moment of cowardly weakness, to run counter to the dictates of her conscience.

Unfortunately this meant that the cleavage between herself and her nobles was irremediable. It is always a fatal thing when a ruler belongs to a different religion from that of the majority of his subjects. The scales cannot vacillate for ever, but must incline definitely in one direction or the other. Thus in the end Mary Stuart was compelled either to make herself mistress of the Reformation or else to bow her head beneath its superior force. The inevitable settlement of accounts as between Luther, Calvin, and Rome was, by an extraordinary coincidence, to find a dramatic decision in the fate that awaited her. For the personal struggle between Mary and Elizabeth, between Scotland and England, was decisive also—and this is what makes the struggle so important historically—for the struggle between England and Spain, between the Reformation and the Counter-Reformation.

The ominousness of the situation was aggravated by the fact that the religious dissensions above described extended into Mary's family, her palace, and her council chamber. The most powerful man in Scotland, her half-brother James Stuart, whom she found it expedient to appoint prime minister, was an ardent Protestant and protector of that Kirk which she, being a good Catholic, could not but regard as heretical. Four years earlier he had been the first to append his signature beneath the joint pledge of the Lords of the Congregation "to forsake and renounce the Congregation of Satan, with all superstitions, abominations, and idolatry thereof, and moreover to declare themselves manifestly enemies thereto." What was here called the "Congregation of Satan" was nothing other than the Holy Catholic Church of which his half-sister Queen Mary was a devoted adherent. Thus from the start there was a profound cleavage of convictions between the monarch and her chief minister. Such a state of affairs does not make for peace. For, at the bottom of her heart, the queen had but one thought, to repress the Reformation in Scotland; whereas James, her brother, had but one desire, to make Protestantism the only religion in Scotland.

James Stuart was to be one of the most notable figures in the life drama of Mary Queen of Scots. Fate had allotted him a leading role which he was destined to play in masterly fashion. A natural son of James V, the fruit of an enduring liaison with Margaret Erskine, who belonged to one of the best families in Scotland, he seemed, no less by his royal blood than by his iron energy, to be the most suitable heir to the throne. Nothing but the political weakness of James V's position had forced that monarch to refrain from legal marriage with the woman he deeply loved, and (that he might increase his power and fill his purse) to contract a marriage with the French princess who became the mother of Mary Queen of Scots. Thus the stigma of illegitimacy debarred the ambitious youth from the throne. Even though, at the urgent request of James V, the Pope had officially acknowledged James Stuart and five other love-children of his father to be of the blood royal, young James was still legally a bastard.

Innumerable times have history and her greatest imaginative exponent, Shakespeare, disclosed the spiritual tragedy of the bastard who is a son and yet not a son, of one whom laws spiritual and laws temporal unfeelingly deprive of a right which nature has stamped on his character and countenance. Condemned by prejudice—the harshest, the most unbending of judges—are these illegitimates, those who have not been procreated in the royal bed, who are treated as inferior to the lawful heirs, though the latter are as a rule weaklings in comparison, because engendered, not out of love, but out of political calculation. They are eternally rejected and thrust out, condemned to beg where they should command and possess. But if the brand of inferiority is visibly placed on a man, the permanent sense of inferiority will either weaken or strengthen him decisively. Such a pressure can break a character or can consolidate it amazingly. Those who are cowardly and half-hearted will be rendered even more so by humiliations of the kind; they will become beggars and flatterers, accepting favours and employment from their officially acknowledged rivals. But in the strong, enforced inferiority will arouse and liberate latent and leashed energies. For the very reason that the direct path to power is not freely opened to them, they will learn to draw power from within their own souls.

James Stuart was a man of strong character. The fierce resolution of his royal ancestors, their pride, and their sense of mastery were continually at work in the hidden recesses of his being. In shrewdness and determination, no less than in clarity of thought, he was head and shoulders above the rufflers who comprised the bulk of the Scottish nobility. His aims were far-reaching, his plans the fruit of profound political thought. No less able than his sister, he, a man of thirty, was enormously in advance of her, thanks to cool-headedness and masculine experience. He looked down upon her as no more than a sportive child who might go on playing so long as her games did not disturb his circles. A man fully grown, he was not, like his sister, a prey to violent, neurotic, or romantic impulses; he was not a heroic ruler, but he had the virtue of patience, which gives better assurance of success than can passionate impetus.

Nothing bears stronger witness to a statesman's political ability and clear-mindedness than his refusal to strive after the unattainable. In Lord James Stuart's case the unattainable was the kingly crown, since he had been born out of lawful wedlock. He knew only too well that the title "James VI" would never be his, and from the outset he renounced any pretensions he might have to ascending the throne of Scotland. But this initial abnegation made his position, as effective ruler over the realm, all the more secure. Giving up any idea of being invested with the insignia of power or of assuming the title of king, he could henceforward wield real power unmolested. As quite a young man he saw to it that he was well furnished with that tangible form of power: wealth. His father had left him handsomely provided for; he never lost countenance when the question of a gift was raised; he made good use of the wars to fill his pockets; and when the monasteries were dissolved, he saw to it that he was always present at the distribution of the prize morsels. Nor was he reluctant to accept subsidies from Elizabeth. When Mary got back to Scotland, it did not take her long to discover that her half-brother was the wealthiest and most powerful man in the realm, so secure that none could oust him from his position, so mighty that he would constitute one of the most solid pillars of her dominion if she acquiesced in his remaining at the helm, and would be her most dangerous enemy if she ran counter to his will.

Mary Stuart, in her wisdom and necessity, chose to place him on a footing of friendship. Wishing above all to secure her own dominion, she was keen-sighted enough to give him, for the time being, whatever he coveted, and fed his insatiable cupidity for riches and power. It was Mary's good fortune that her brother's hands were both strong and supple, for he knew when to hold firm and when to give way. True statesman that he was, James Stuart chose a middle course in his undertakings: a Protestant but no iconoclast, a Scottish patriot and yet keeping in Elizabeth's good graces, ostensibly a friend of his peers but well aware of the exact minute when they needed to be threatened with the mailed fist, a cool-headed, clear-sighted, calculating individual, with no unruly nerves, incapable of being blinded by the glitter of power, and content only when wielding power.

A personage of such outstanding qualities was an inestimable boon to Mary Stuart so long as he remained in her faction, and a colossal danger so soon as he should become her adversary. Bound to her by the ties of blood, our cheerfully egoistical Stuart had every reason to maintain his sister's authority so long as it suited his personal interests, for, were a Hamilton or a Gordon to step into her shoes, he would never be given such a free hand and such unlimited influence over administrative affairs. He could look on calmly while she was ceremoniously presented with crown and sceptre, for real government was in his safe-keeping. But if she should ever try to rule in her own right, if she should ever question his authority, then one form of Stuart pride would rise in revolt against the other form of Stuart pride, and no enmity is more to be dreaded than when similar is confronted with similar, and when both make use of the same weapons against one another.

Maitland of Lethington, Mary's secretary of State, next only to her half-brother in importance at her court, was also a Protestant. To begin with, nevertheless, he was on her side. Maitland was extremely able, had a supple and cultivated mind, and was (as Elizabeth called him) "the flower of the wits of Scotland." He had not, like James Stuart, a masterful pride, nor any keen love for power. It was diplomacy that interested him, the confused and confusing intricacies of politics, the art of combination. He took artistic pleasure in these, which mattered more to him than rigid principles, creed and country, the queen, and the Scottish realm. He was personally attached to his sovereign, and Mary Fleming, one of the four Marys, became his wife. To Mary Stuart herself he was neither positively loyal nor positively disloyal. He would serve her as long as chance favoured her, and abandon her in times of peril. From him, as from a weathercock, she could judge whether the wind was fair or foul. A typical politician, he would devote himself, not to her, but to bettering his own fortunes.

Thus, on her return home, Mary Stuart could find no thoroughly dependable friend, whether she sought to right or to left, in the city or among the members of her own household. She had to be content with the services of a James Stuart or a Maitland, to allow herself to be guided by them, and to make the best terms with them. On the other hand, from the moment of her landing, John Knox made no secret of his merciless antagonism. He was the great demagogic leader in religious affairs, the organizer and master of the Scottish Kirk, the most popular preacher in Edinburgh. The struggle with him was one of life or death.

For the shape Calvinism had assumed under John Knox's inspiration was no longer a purely reformative renovation of the Church, but a brand-new doctrinal system, a kind of superlative Protestantism. Domineering and authoritarian, Knox, the zealot, claimed that even kings must slavishly obey his theocratic laws. Mary Stuart, since she was of a mild and yielding disposition, might have come to a compromise with a High Church, with a Lutheran Church, or with any other less virulent form of Reformation. But Calvinism was so dictatorial a faith that from the outset it rendered any kind of mutual understanding impracticable. Even Elizabeth, who favoured Knox because he was her rival's enemy, detested him for his arrogance. Much more vexatious, of course, were the zealot's bluster and harshness to Mary, who was in close contact with them, and had so recently returned from the freedom and cheerfulness of France. Nothing could have been more revolting to Mary's joyous and voluptuous nature and to her delight in the Muses than the austere severity, the hatred of everything that made life pleasant, the iconoclastic antagonism to the arts, the dislike of merriment and laughter, incorporated in the Genevese doctrines; nothing more repulsive than the stubborn treatment of jollity and beauty as sin, than the bigotry which aimed at overthrowing all that she held dear, which banned good spirits and urbane manners and customs, music, poetry, and dancing, and which cast a still gloomier mantle over a land already condemned by nature to gloom and sadness.

Under Master John's ægis, the Kirk in Edinburgh assumed a hard, Old Testament character, for Knox was one of the most iron-willed, most zealous, most mercilessly fanatical of reformers, exceeding even his master, Calvin, in venom and intolerance. He had taken orders as a Roman Catholic priest, and had in the sequel hurled himself with the full ardour of his disputatious soul into the ranks of the reformers, becoming a pupil of George Wishart, who was burned alive for heresy during the regency of Mary of Guise, at the instigation of Cardinal Beaton. The flames which destroyed his teacher were henceforward to consume Knox's own heart. As one of the leaders in the rebellion against the queen-regent, he was made a prisoner of the French forces and consigned to the galleys. For eighteen months he remained chained to his forced labour, and some of the iron of his chains bit into his soul. On being released through the intervention of Edward VI, he sought out Calvin, from whom he learned the power enchased in the spoken word, from whom he likewise learned to hate everything that was bright, cheerful, and Hellenic. Within a few years of his return to Scotland his genius for violence enabled him to force acceptance of the Reformation upon lords and commons.

John Knox is perhaps the most finished example of the religious fanatic. He was of harder metal than Luther, who was not free from occasional gleams of jovial humour; and he was yet more rigid than Savonarola, because he lacked the Italian's brilliancy and faculty for mystically illuminated discourse. Though he was fundamentally honest and straightforward, the blinkers that he wore made him one of those cruel and narrow-minded persons for whom only their own truth is true, only their own virtue virtuous, only their own Christianity Christian. To differ from him was criminal; to refuse compliance with every letter of his demands was to show oneself to be Satan's spawn. Knox had the dour courage of the self-possessed (in the demoniacal sense of the word possession), the passion of the ecstatic bigot, and the detestable pride of the self-righteous. His acerbity was also tinged by a dangerous pleasure in its exercise, while his impatience manifested a gloomily voluptuous joy in his own infallibility. Jehovah-like, with flowing beard, Hebrew prophet in complete perfection, he took his stand Sunday after Sunday in the pulpit of St. Giles's, thundering invectives and maledictions against those who differed from him in the minutest of details. A born kill-joy, he railed against the "Devil's brood" of the happy-go-lucky, of those who did not serve God precisely in the way which seemed best to him. This cold-hearted fanatic knew no other gratification than the triumph of his dogmas, no other justice than the victory of his cause. He frankly rejoiced if a Catholic, or any other whom he regarded as a heretic, was slain or humiliated. Publicly would he thank God when the assassin's dagger had swept an adversary of the Kirk out of the way. To him it was self-evident that God must have willed and furthered the deed. He vociferated his rejoicings from the pulpit when the news came that pus had burst through one of poor little Francis II's ear-drums, and that the French king was at the point of death. When Mary of Guise died, he did not hesitate to pray for the death of Mary Queen of Scots: "God, for his great mercy's sake, rid us from the rest of the Guisian brood. Amen, amen." In his sermons, there was no trace of the suavity and divine goodness characteristic of the Gospels; his discourses swished like a scourge. His God was the vengeful, bloody, and inexorable Yahveh of the Old Testament, which, with its barbarous threats, was for him the real Bible. References to Moab, Amalek, all the enemies of the People of Israel who must be annihilated with fire and sword, were continually in his mouth as he voiced threats against the enemies of the true faith—by which he meant his own. When he volleyed abuse at Queen Jezebel, the congregation knew that it was another queen he had in mind. Calvinism, with Knox as its chief exponent, loured over Scotland like a thunderstorm that at any moment might burst.

No compromise is possible with a person thus impeccable and incorruptible, a man whose only thought is to command and who expects instant and unreflecting obedience. Attempts to placate him or smooth him down could only intensify his exactions, make him harsher and more scornful. Always those who regard themselves as God's doughtiest warriors are the unkindliest men in the world. Believing themselves the vehicles of heavenly messages, they have their ears closed to whatever is humane.

A bare week sufficed to make Mary Stuart aware of the presence of so fanatical an opponent. Before her return she had promised her subjects absolute freedom of belief—a promise which to a woman of her tolerant disposition demanded no sacrifices on her part. In addition she had recognized the law which prohibited any public celebration of the Mass in Scotland. This was a painful concession to John Knox and his followers, but one they insisted upon winning, for, as the divine once said, "one Mass is more fearful to me than if ten thousand armed enemies were to land and suppress the whole religion." But Mary was a devout Catholic, a daughter of the Guises, and she insisted upon practising her own religion in the privacy of her chapel whenever and however she pleased. Not stopping to reflect upon the possible consequences, the Scottish parliament granted her request. But on the first

Sunday after her arrival, when the preparations for celebrating Mass in the Chapel Royal at Holyrood had been made, an excited crowd gathered round the entries, and when the queen's almoner was carrying the candles to light upon the altar, he was waylaid, and the candles were wrenched from his hands and smashed. A loud murmur arose which reduced itself to a demand that the "idolatrous priest" should be slain; more and more excited grew the cries against this "Satan worship"; at any moment it seemed that the queen's private chapel might be stormed by the mob. Lord James Stuart, however, saved the situation. Although himself a staunch champion of the Kirk, he confronted the fanatical rout and defended the main entry while the queen was engaged in her devotions. After saying Mass in fear and trembling, the unhappy priest was brought safely back to his quarters. Open revolt was thus avoided, and the queen's authority had been kept intact, though with difficulty. But the gay festivities that had been organized to greet her arrival, the "joyousities" as Knox mockingly called them, were broken off, much to his grim delight. The young and romantic queen was made to feel how genuine and strong were the antagonisms extant in the realm she had come over the seas to rule.

Mary Stuart's reaction to the slight found vent in a storm of rage. Tears and harsh words welled up from within her to express the depth of her mortification. A clear ray of light was thus shed upon a character which hitherto had lacked precision. The spoiled darling of fate ever since birth, Mary had always shown the tender and gentle aspects of her nature, for she was fundamentally of a pliant and accommodating disposition. All who came in contact with her, from the highest court official down to the humblest maid, extolled her friendliness, her lack of arrogance, her affectionate and endearing ways. She won hearts because she never harshly or haughtily reminded people of her majesty. But this gentleness was counterbalanced by an insuperable consciousness of what she really was, a consciousness that was latent so long as nothing came to disturb it, but which broke forth in violent storms of weeping and vituperation so soon as she met with contradiction or resistance. This wonderful woman was often known to forgive a personal affront, but a belittling of her queenly estate never.

She was, therefore, determined not to pass over this initial outrage to her dignity as Scotland's ruler. Such presumption must, in her view, be stamped upon from the first. Only too well did she know with whom she had to deal, never doubting for a moment that it was the bearded heretic preaching from his parochial pulpit who had incited the rabble against her. She would take the man personally to task, and that without delay. Mary Stuart, accustomed to instant obedience on the part of the subjects of a French monarch, all-powerful ruler by divine grace, never imagined for a moment that she would meet with contradiction from one of her own subjects, an ordinary burgher living in the capital of her realm. She was prepared for everything in the world but that anyone should openly and boldly venture to oppose her will. John Knox, however, was not only prepared to do so, but eager and joyfully prepared. "Why should the pleasing face of a gentlewoman frighten me? I have looked in the faces of many angry men, and yet have not been afraid above measure." His heart bounded within him as with rapid strides he made his way to the palace for this private colloquy. A fight—and in Knox's opinion, such a fight was in God's behalf—is the greatest delight the soul of a fanatic can experience. If God Almighty had given crowns to kings, He had endowed His priests and representatives here below with the gift of uttering fiery words and, in addition, the divine right of speaking them. His duty was to defend God's reign upon earth; nor must he hesitate to use the flail of his wrath to chastise the insubordinate as of yore did Samuel and the judges described in Holy Writ. The scene that ensued was like one taken out of the Old Testament: regal pride confronted sacerdotal pride; it was not one woman fighting one man to gain the upper hand, but two age-old ideas which were engaged for the thousand thousandth time in bitter strife.

Mary Stuart endeavoured to retain her usually unruffled sweetness and to be forbearing. Sincerely wishful to bring about an understanding, she concealed her mortification, for she had at heart to preserve peace in her realm. It was, therefore, with courteous words that she opened the conversation. John Knox, for his part, was resolved to be as implacable as he pleased and to show the "idolatress" that he was not inclined to bow down an inch before the mighty of this world. Silent and gloomy, not as accused but as accuser, he listened to the counts the queen had against him. Among other items "she charged me with my book" (*The First Blast of the Trumpet against the Monstrous Regi-*

ment of Women) wherein he challenged a woman's right to wield authority. This same work had got him into trouble with Elizabeth, the Protestant sovereign, before whose reproaches he had bowed his head with due meekness; now, in the encounter with his own "unpersuaded princess," he obstinately maintained his privilege to express such opinions as he honestly held. As had been feared, his intolerance seemed bound to mar all, for gradually the conversation took a more caustic turn. Mary showed a "shrewdness beyond her years," and there was no little acuteness in her reasoning. She asked him point-blank: "Think you that subjects . . . should resist their princes?" Instead of giving the negative answer she had expected, Knox, a born tactician, evaded the crucial point by lapsing into parable: "A father may be struck with a frenzy, in which he would slay his children. Now, Madam, if the children arise, join together, apprehend the father, take the sword from him, bind his hands, and keep him in prison till the frenzy be over, think you, Madam, that the children do any harm? Even so is it with princes who would murder the children of God that are subject unto them. . . ."

The queen was nonplussed by so bold an answer, feeling that by such provisos Knox, the theologian, was for countenancing a revolt against her just rights as sovereign. "Well then," she retorted briskly, "I perceive that my subjects shall obey you and not me, and will do what they list, and not what I command, and so maun I be subject to them, and not they to me!" This was precisely what Knox had meant, but he was too cautious to say so outright, seeing that Lord James Stuart was present at the interview. Evasively he replied: "God forbid that ever I take upon me to command any to obey me, or set subjects at liberty to do what pleaseth them. My travail is that both princes and subjects may obey God. . . . He craves of kings that they be as foster-fathers and queens as nursing-mothers to his Church." The queen, sorely vexed by the reformer's persistent ambiguity, made sharp rejoinder: "But ye are not the Church that I will nourish. I will defend the Church of Rome, for I think it is the true Church of God."

Blow swiftly followed upon blow. The point had been reached where understanding between a zealous Catholic and a fanatical Protestant, one who "ruleth the roost" and of whom "all men stand in fear," was impossible. With the rough manners begotten of unceasing controversy and polemic, he retorted: "Your will, Madam, is no reason; neither doth your thought make that Roman harlot to be the true and immaculate spouse of Jesus Christ." And when Mary rebuked him for the use of such words, and pleaded conscience, Master John retaliated provocatively: "Conscience, Madam, requires knowledge, and I fear that right knowledge ye have none." Thus the first interview, instead of bringing reconciliation, only served to make the antagonism between the two more pronounced. "In communication with her I espied such craft as I have not found in such age. Since, hath the court been dead to me and I to it." Mary had been made to realize that there were limits to her royal power. With head erect, Knox left the audience chamber, proud and pleased at having defied majesty. The young queen, on the contrary, felt discomfited, knowing that her overtures had received a rebuff. She recognized her own impotence, and gave way to her bitterness of soul in a passion of tears. Nor were these the last she was to weep. Soon she was forced to recognize that power was not a thing inherited once and for all, but had to be fought for in persistent struggle and amid constantly renewed humiliations.

CHAPTER FIVE

The Stone Begins to Roll

(1561-1563)

FOR THREE years after assuming the reins of government Mary's life was fairly quiet and uneventful. Fate had decreed from the outset that the great happenings of her life were to be concentrated into swift, short episodes, and it is this peculiarity which has always made such appeal to the dramatic instincts of playwrights. Lord James Stuart, now Earl of Moray, and Maitland of Lethington were the real rulers, while Mary acted as figure-head; and this division of forces proved of the utmost advantage to all concerned. Both Moray and Lethington governed wisely and prudently. Mary, too, admirably played the part assigned her. Endowed by nature with beauty and charm, a mistress of the arts of chivalry, virile in her audacity, intrepid as a horsewoman, dextrous in archery and pall-mall, an ardent lover of fowling and the chase, she won all hearts by the grace of her appearance. The commonalty of Edinburgh gazed fondly and proudly on this daughter of the Stuarts when, of a morning, she rode forth with a falcon perched upon her uplifted wrist, surrounded by her gaily dressed court, and returning each salutation with a friendly and joyous smile. Something limpid, something cheerful, something touching and romantic, a ray of youth and beauty, had come like sunshine into this austere and gloomy land with the advent of its girlish queen. A nation's love is quickly captured by a ruler who is both young and handsome. The lords were more beguiled by what was manly in her composition; she would gallop for hours at a stretch without showing undue fatigue, far in advance of her followers. Just as her gentleness and her kindhearted ways were backed by a latent and invincible pride, so did the lithe, slim, soft, thistle-down body, though feminine in its curves, mask a frame of iron, incapable of weariness. No exercise seemed too hard for her endurance; and once, as she rode in a foray, the swordsmen beside her overheard their lady wishing she were a man "to know what life it was to lie all night in the fields." When Moray marched against the clan of the Huntlys in the north, she declared it her will to go with him, sword at her side and pistols in her belt. She gloried in risk and adventure, and whatever she undertook to do she entered into with her whole soul and body, brought to it all the passion her resolute nature was capable of feeling. But in spite of her manlike courage, her huntsman's simplicity, her warlike valiance and hardihood, when closeted in the apartments of her palace she showed herself a ruler both astute and cool-headed; in the midst of her gay court she would be the gayest of the party, pleasant and familiar in her small world. In her juvenile person the ideals of her epoch seemed to be conjoined—courage with light-heartedness, strength with gentleness. A last ray of the setting sun from the days of troubadour and knight illuminated the misty chill of this northern clime as Mary moved sprightly and gay among its shadows made all the deeper by the gloomy teachings of the Reformation.

Never had the romantic figure of this girl-wife and girl-widow shone more radiantly than in the first years of her third decade; but here, likewise, her triumphs came too early, for she did not understand that they were indeed triumphs, and she therefore failed to make the best use of her advantage. Her inner life had not yet been fully awakened; the woman in her did not yet know what were the claims her blood might make on her; her proper, her deepest self was still unformed and undeveloped. Not until roused by excitement and passion would it reveal its true essence. But the first years of her sojourn in Scotland were a period of indifference and waiting, an aimless, happy-go-lucky passage of time, a preparation for eventualities, without the inner will guessing what it was awaiting or whom. Resembling as it did the taking of a deep breath before great exertion, it was a moment of stagnation, a dead-point in her life. For Mary Stuart, having as a maid experienced what it was like to be queen of one of the mightiest realms in Europe, was not concerned about remaining the ruler of so poor, so small, so out-of-the-way a land as Scotland. Not for this had she returned. Wider ambitions floated before her mind. The crown of Scotland was nothing better than a makeshift which might lead to the winning of a more dazzling one. They err vastly who maintain that

Mary Stuart's highest aim was to rule over the heritage her father had left her, in tranquillity and peace and wisdom. To equip her with so small an ambition is to minimize her spiritual and intellectual greatness; for, young though she was, she was already dominated by an untamable and unbridled will-to-power. She who at seventeen had been wedded to a king of France in the cathedral of Notre Dame in Paris, who in the Louvre had been acclaimed as the sovereign lady of millions of subjects, could not rest content with governing a few dozen unruly clodhoppers going by the title of earl or laird, together with a few hundred thousand worthy shepherds and fisherfolk. It is fallacious to ascribe patriotic and nationalistic feelings to a woman who had no such feelings at all. Indeed, these sentiments were only unearthed some centuries after Mary's death! The princes of the fifteenth and sixteenth centuries—with the possible exception of Mary's great rival Elizabeth—were not in the habit of considering their peoples, but aimed solely at acquiring personal power. Kingdoms were stitched together and rent asunder as though they had been clothes; States were formed by wars and marriages, and not by any self-determination on the part of the nations concerned. No sentimental motive influenced the creation of such realms. Mary in her day was quite prepared to exchange Scotland's crown for a Spanish, an English, a French, or any other available one; no qualm would have assailed her conscience as to the honourability of her conduct in the matter, no tear would have dimmed her eye as she bade farewell to the woods and lakes and romantic castles of her homeland, for her impassioned ambition had led her invariably to look upon her Scottish throne as no more than a jumping-off place to higher and better awards. She knew that by inheritance she had been called to the position of ruler, that her beauty and breeding and culture made her worthy to occupy any throne in Europe; and just as other women of her tender years are wont to dream of immeasurable love, so did she dream but one dream—the dream of immeasurable power.

It was for these reasons that she left the responsibility of government in Moray's and in Lethington's hands, without feeling any jealousy or resentment, and without any interested participation. She allowed the two men to do what they thought wise and advantageous for the country without let or hindrance from her. What did she care about the destinies of this pitiful little realm, she who had so long worn a crown and had so early learned to expect the acknowledgment of her royal majesty? Among the hundreds of letters she left behind we hardly find a reference to the welfare of her subjects, nor a mention of Scotland's rise to a higher position among the world powers. In this she differed notably from her neighbour Elizabeth, who was constantly and earnestly occupied with ways and means for raising her beloved England's status. The administration of her possessions, their aggrandizement, their improvement (one of the most important points in the sphere of politics), did not occupy Mary Stuart's mind. She could defend what was hers, but she could not make it secure. Only when her rights were threatened, when her pride was challenged, only when an alien will set itself up in opposition to her own, would she awaken, combative and irate. Only in supreme moments did this woman prove great and dangerous; at other times she remained an average woman, showing nothing but indifference to what went on around her.

During this comparatively peaceful time, the enmity of her English rival was in abeyance; for whenever the impetuous heart of Mary Queen of Scots was beating tranquilly for a space, Elizabeth, too, was quiescent. One of the most conspicuous political merits of the daughter of the Tudors was her realism, her willingness to face facts, her disinclination to resist the inevitable. She had done everything in her power to prevent the return of Mary Stuart to Scotland. Now, when the return had taken place, Elizabeth would not waste energy in fighting against actualities, preferring to live on amicable terms so long as she could not sweep her cousin out of her path. One of the strongest positive qualities of Elizabeth's wayward and arbitrary character was that, from motives of prudence and economy, she had a dislike for war, was averse to forcible measures and irrevocable decisions. Her calculating mind made her seek to gain her ends by negotiation. As soon as it was certain that Mary would return to Scotland, James Stuart urged Elizabeth, in moving terms, to enter into an honest friendship with her cousin. "You be . . . both Queens in the flower of your ages. . . . Your sex will not permit you to advance your glory by war and bloodshed, but in that of a peaceful reign. Neither of you is ignorant from what root the contrary affection proceeds. . . . I wish to God the Queen my sovereign lady had never by any advice taken in head to pretend interest or acclaim any title to Your Majesty's realm, for then I am fully persuaded you would have been and continued as dear friends as you be tender cousins—but now since on her part something hath been thought of it . . . I fear that unless the root may be removed, it shall ever breed unkindness betwixt you. Your Majesty cannot yield, and she may on the other part think of it hard, being so nigh of the blood of England, to be made a stranger from it! If any mid way could be picked out to remove this difference to both your contentments, then it is like we could have a perpetual quietness. . . ."

Elizabeth was not slow to take the hint. As nothing more than Queen of Scotland, and under the guidance of the Queen of England's pensioner James Stuart, Mary was for the time being less dangerous than she would have been as Queen of both France and Scotland. Why not swear a truce although in her heart she remained hostile? A brisk correspondence between the pair was soon in progress, in which each of the "dear sisters" expressed the most cordial sentiments upon sheets of long-suffering paper. One who reads these epistles today might well believe that nowhere in the world can there have been more affectionate kinswomen than the two cousins. Mary sent Elizabeth a diamond ring; the English queen reciprocated with a still more valuable trinket; before the world, and before the audience of their own selves, they played the comedy of family love. Mary wrote: "Above all things I desire to see my good sister," and declared her determination to break the alliance with France, for she appreciated Elizabeth's goodwill "more than all the uncles in the world." In response, Elizabeth, in the large, formal handwriting which she kept in reserve for important occasions, gave Mary extravagantly worded assurances of fondness and fidelity. But as soon as the question of a binding agreement arose, and a personal meeting loomed nigh, both the correspondents grew cautious and evasive. The negotiations which had been proceeding so long were still at a deadlock. Mary Stuart would not sign the treaty of Edinburgh recognizing Elizabeth's position until Elizabeth had accorded the succession to Mary—but to Elizabeth, this would have been tantamount (so she thought) to signing her own death-warrant. Neither would waive a particle of the rights they severally claimed; so, in the long run, the flowery phrases they interchanged barely concealed the unbridgeable chasm. As Genghis Khan resolutely declared: "There cannot be two suns in the sky or two Khans on the earth." One of the women must give way, Elizabeth Tudor or Mary Stuart. Both realized this, and both were awaiting the appointed hour. But since the hour had not yet struck, why should they not enjoy a period of truce? The truce would be brief. When mistrust is ineradicable, a reason will soon be found for giving it vent in action.

In these years the young queen had many minor troubles: she was often bored by affairs of State, more and more did she feel out of her element among these hard-fisted and quarrelsome nobles, and she was continually harassed by implacable churchmen and wily intriguers. At such hours she took refuge, imaginatively, in France, which she continued to regard as her true home. Since she could not leave Scotland, she had established a Little France for herself in the palace of Holyrood, a tiny corner of the world where, withdrawn from inquisitive eyes, she could follow her most heartfelt inclinations. It was her Trianon. In the round tower of Holyrood she had her rooms equipped after the French model, with Gobelins brought from Paris, Turkey carpets, ornate beds and other furnishings, pictures in gilt frames, her finely bound books—Erasmus, Rabelais, Ariosto, Ronsard. Here they talked French and lived French. In the evening, by the light of flickering candles, music was performed, round games were played, verses were read aloud, and madrigals were sung. For the first time, at this miniature court, were staged on the western side of the North Sea and the Channel those masques which were subsequently to attain their highest blossoming in the English theatre. Dancing would continue till long after midnight. In one of the masques, *The Purpose,* Mary appeared as a young man, wearing black silk breeches, while Chastelard wore a woman's gown—a sight which would certainly have aroused the fury of John Knox!

Puritans, zealots, and mutinous warriors had not the entry to these scenes of merriment. Vainly did the Calvinist preacher, his beard swinging like a pendulum, rail in St. Giles's pulpit against these "souparis" and "dansaris." Here is an extract from one of his sermons:

"Princes are more exercised in fiddling and flinging than in reading or hearing of God's most blessed Word.... Musicians and flatterers, these corrupters of youth, please them better than do men old and wise" (of whom is our self-righteous friend thinking?) "who desire with their salutary exhortations to tame some of that pride which is our common and sinful heritage." But the members of this young and gay circle had little desire for the "salutary exhortations" of the "kill-joy." The four Marys, and a few noblemen whose tastes had been moulded in the French court, found it agreeable, in rooms which (for the day) were well warmed and well lighted, to forget the gloom of this austere and tragical country. More than all was Queen Mary herself gladdened at being able to lay aside the cloak of majesty, and to become a cheerful young woman among companions of her own age and her own way of thinking.

Her desire was natural enough. But it was always dangerous for Mary Stuart to give way to indolence. Sham and hypocrisy crushed her; prudence, in the long run, exasperated her. She herself once wrote: "Je ne sais point déguiser mes sentiments." And it was precisely an innate lack of reticence on her part which caused her more political trouble and unpleasantness than if she had been guilty of the vilest deceit and the most ruthless severity. For the familiarity the queen permitted herself among this jocund company, the warmth with which she accepted their homage, the smile with which all unconsciously she beguiled them, could not but arouse in these unruly natures a spirit of camaraderie which for those of a passionate disposition must have constituted a serious temptation. There must have been something in Mary, whose beauty is not shown to us on any of the canvases that portray her, which made a sensual appeal. Maybe a few of the men who were brought into contact with her and who came to their conclusions on the strength of certain almost imperceptible signs had a premonition that under the sensibility, the exquisite grace of manner, and apparently perfect self-possession of the maidenly woman there lurked an infinite capacity for amorous passion, hidden as might be a quiescent volcano beneath a pleasant landscape. Did they not, perhaps, discover her secret long before she herself was aware of its existence; did not their virile instinct guess at the presence in her of an abandon, a power to allure men's senses even more indubitably than their romantic love? Her very innocence, her unawakened condition, may have led her to make use of those delicate physical endearments —a touch of the hand, a gossamer-like kiss, an invitation of the eyes— which a woman of experience knows to be dangerous. Be this as it may, it is indisputable that Mary allowed the men in her circle of intimates to forget that a queen must be kept unsullied by any daring thought where the fleshly woman was concerned. Once a young Scottish captain named Hepburn got himself into trouble by delivering to Mary—in the presence of the English ambassador—an obscene missive. Hepburn was probably no more than a featherbrained intermediary, but he escaped condign punishment only through flight. The incident had been quickly forgiven, and the queen's forbearance encouraged another member of her small circle to make further advances.

The affair was to remain in the realm of romance and, like almost every episode which took place in this Scottish land, was more like a ballad, a beautiful poem, than a historical fact. Mary's first admirer at the French court was Monsieur d'Anville, and he had confided his passion to his friend, the poet Chastelard. Anville, together with a number of other gentlemen of France, had accompanied Mary on the journey to Scotland. Now he had to return to his country, his wife, and his official duties. Chastelard, however, regarding himself in some sort as the representative of foreign culture in a barbarous land, remained behind in Scotland. He indited tender verses to his lovely mistress, for poems are not in themselves dangerous things, though amorous sport may at any time change into reality. Unheeding what it might imply, Mary accepted the poetical homage paid to her by the stripling, a Huguenot, versed in the arts of chivalry. Indeed, she went so far as to answer in verses of her own composition. How could a sensitive and artistically endowed girl, forced to live in a rough and backward country, cut off from nearly all those she had known and loved—how could she fail to sun herself in the flattery that underlay such inspired strophes as the following?

O Déesse immortelle,
Escoute donc ma voix,
Toi qui tiens en tutelle
Mon pouvoir sous les loix,

Afin que si ma vie
Se voit en bref ravie
Ta cruauté
La confesse périe
Par ta seule beauté.

Moreover, she was quite unaware that there was anything serious behind the young man's protestations. She may have enjoyed the game, but she certainly did not return the passion. Chastelard himself mournfully regretted her coldness when he wrote:

Et néanmoins la flâme
Qui me brûle et enflâme
De passion
N'émeut jamais ton âme
D'aucune affection.

Mary Stuart probably looked upon these adulatory screeds as part of the complimentary exaggeration inseparable from court life. She herself, being a writer in the lyrical vein, knew very well that the Muse of Poetry delighted in hyperboles of the sort, and it was in a playful humour that she countenanced gallantries which did not strike a false note in the romantic glamour which surrounded the court of a young and captivating woman. In her guileless way she jested and played with Chastelard, just as she was wont to do with her Marys. She would single him out by harmless acts of special favour and esteem, would (though her rank made such approaches on his part impossible) choose him as partner for a dance; once, during the fashionable *Talking Dance* or *The Purpose,* Mary leaned on Chastelard's breast; she allowed him certain freedoms of speech which were looked on askance in Scotland, and especially by John Knox, whose pulpit was only a few streets distant from the "wanton orgies" of which he said that such fashions were "more lyke to the bordell than to the comeliness of honest women"; at a masked ball or during a game of forfeits Mary may even have permitted the young Frenchman to snatch a kiss. Though these familiarities were not in themselves of any grave import, they were dire in their effect on a lad of his years and ardent disposition, so that, like Torquato Tasso, his contemporary, he forgot the barriers separating a lady of high estate from her servitor, overstepped the limits that respect imposes upon camaraderie, that decorum enforces upon gallantry, that seriousness imposes upon jest, and, hotheaded, he followed the dictates of his own feelings.

This led to a most disastrous adventure. One evening the gentlewomen who were in attendance on Mary Stuart discovered Chastelard hiding in the queen's bedchamber. They did not suspect him of improper designs, merely looking upon the escapade as a practical joke not in very good taste. Laughing merrily, and with the pretence of being extremely angry, they chased the jackanapes from the room. Mary Stuart, too, took a lenient view of his misbehaviour. The prank was sedulously kept from the ears of Moray, however; and though the enormity of the crime was not to be denied, the question of meting out suitable punishment was soon dropped. This consideration was unfortunately not appreciated at its full value by the delinquent. For either the young spark was encouraged by such leniency to have another try, or his love for Mary was so violent as to rob him of any capacity for self-discipline he may hitherto have possessed. He secretly followed the queen on her journey to Fife, and no one suspected his presence in her vicinity until, at bedtime, when Mary was already half-undressed, her attendants again discovered him in her bedchamber. Considerably alarmed, Mary uttered so wild a cry that it was heard all over the house. Moray, hastening from a neighbouring room, rushed in to see what could be amiss. Now every chance of forgiving and forgetting was out of the question. Certain chroniclers maintain that the queen urged her brother forthwith to slay the presumptuous youth, but this does not seem likely. Moray, whose cool-headedness contrasted greatly with his sister's passionate nature, quickly foresaw and shrewdly calculated the consequences. He realized at once that the slaying of a man in the queen's private apartment would besprinkle her with some of the blood. Circumstances such as these demanded the utmost publicity if Mary's character was to be cleared and her virtue remain unsullied in the eyes of her people and of the world.

A few days later Chastelard was led to public execution. His audacity had been condemned as a crime, and his frivolity was deemed an "evil design" by those who sat in judgment upon him. With one voice they allotted him the severest penalty: execution. Even had she wished to deal clemently, the possibility of so doing had been taken out of Mary Stuart's hands. The ambassadors had already sent in their reports of the matter, and censorious eyes at the French and English courts would watch her behaviour. A word in favour of the offender would instantly be interpreted as meaning that she, too, was culpable. She had to put a harder face upon the affair than she probably felt was demanded by the occasion, and thus leave the companion of so many cheerful and amusing hours in the lurch, without hope and without help in this his cruellest hour.

As became one who had been an intimate at the court of a queen of faëry and romance, Chastelard perished with the radiance of romance about him. Refusing the comforts of priest and religion, he went to his death hand in hand with the poetic Muse, murmuring:

Mon malheur déplorable
Soit sur moy immortel.

Straight as a wand, the troubadour bravely mounted the scaffold and, instead of singing psalms and saying prayers, he intoned his friend Ronsard's celebrated "Hymn to Death":

Je te salue, heureuse et profitable Mort,
Des extrêmes douleurs médecin et confort.

His last words, uttered more as a sigh than as an accusation, were: "O cruelle dame." Then he quietly submitted to the executioner's ministrations. His death was like a ballad, like a beautiful poem.

But this unhappy Chastelard was no more than the first of the macabre procession of those who were to die for Mary Stuart. Many, how many, of Mary's associates and adherents were to perish on the scaffold, caught up in the eddies of her fate. They came from all lands. As in Holbein's celebrated "Alphabet of the Dance of Death," they trailed along in the wake of a black and bony drummer; step by step, year after year, monarchs and regents, earls and other men of birth and station, priests and warriors, striplings and elders, all sacrificing themselves for her, all sacrificed for her who, though innocent, was yet guilty of their drear fate and had to atone for it with hers. Seldom has it been decreed that one woman should have so many deaths woven into the magic tapestry of her life. Like some dark magnet, she lured the men who came into contact with her to enter the spellbound circle of her personal doom. He who crossed her path, whether as friend or foe, was condemned to mischance and to violent death. No luck ever blessed him who hated Mary Stuart, and those who loved her were consigned to an even more terrible end.

Only to outward seeming, therefore, was the Chastelard affair a chance matter, an episode or an interlude. Though she did not yet realize as much, it disclosed itself as the law of her being that she would always have to pay when she allowed herself to be light-hearted, easy-going, and trustful. Destiny had willed that, from the outset, she must be in the limelight, must remain queen and never be anything more than queen, a public character, a pawn in the world's great game of chess. What at first had seemed a signal mark of favour, her early crowning, her birth into the highest rank, was really a curse. The Chastelard affair was merely an initial warning. Having spent her childhood under conditions which deprived her of childhood, during the brief interval before she gave her body to a second man or a third, before her life was, for purposes of State, to become coupled with that of another, she had tried for a few months to be young and care-free—to enjoy, only to enjoy. But harsh hands were speedily to pluck her out of this merry sport. Rendered uneasy by the incident, Moray, parliament, the Scottish lords, urged her to wed without delay. She must choose a husband, not the man after her heart, but the one whose acceptance as consort would redound most to the power and safety of her realm. Negotiations were opened or speeded up, for the responsible persons in her entourage had become alarmed lest this heedless young woman might commit some folly which would shatter her reputation. Chaffering in the marriage market was resumed; Mary Stuart was forced back into the evil circle of politics within which she was prisoned for almost the whole of her life. Whenever she tried to escape from the chill environment, to break down the barriers and relish for a moment, for a breathing-space, a warm life of her own, she would do irreparable harm to others and to her personal fortunes.

CHAPTER SIX

Political Marriage Mart

(1563-1565)

ELIZABETH OF ENGLAND and Mary of Scotland were probably the most courted damsels of their day. Whoever in Europe happened to be heir to a throne, or king and unwedded, sent an official wooer to these unmated queens. The Houses of Habsburg and Bourbon, Philip II of Spain, his son Don Carlos, the Archduke of Austria, together with the Kings of Sweden and of Denmark, old men and young, dotards and striplings, became aspirants for one or the other of these two fair hands. Never had the political marriage market been so glutted with suitors. The reason was a good one, for by wedding a lady of royal birth and lineage, who was in addition queen in her own right, a man might extend his power and his lands in a perfectly legitimate manner. For, during the hey-day of absolutist rule, it was easier to build up a nicely rounded-off kingdom by way of marriage than through war. By such means had France become a united whole; Spain, a worldwide empire; the dominion of the Habsburgs, an enlarged and consolidated realm. Unexpectedly now England and Scotland, the last precious and unannexed crown-jewels of Europe, offered themselves as alluring prizes. Elizabeth Tudor and Mary Stuart were unwedded. Whoever could win either southern or northern Britain by a lucky conjugal deal would become winner in the game of world politics and, concomitantly with success in the struggle of the nations, would gain a prize helping to decide the great religious issues of the epoch.

This was an important point at the time; for if either queen were to wed a Catholic, the British Isles, influenced by the religious faith of such a royal consort, would load the scales in favour of Rome, so that the struggle raging between Protestantism and the old belief might very well be settled to the advantage of the "ecclesia universalis."

Thus the mad chase that presently ensued was of far wider import than a mere pleasant opportunity for securing conjugal bliss; the future of the western world was at stake.

For the two young queens, however, it was in addition a matter which concerned them personally to the end of their days, since a decision one way or the other would necessarily seal their fate. Should one of the ladies make a better match than the other, the balance of power would turn in her favour and her rival's throne lose in value and prestige. An appearance of friendship between Elizabeth and Mary was possible only so long as both were single; the former must remain Queen of England and Ireland, while the latter must remain Queen of Scotland and the Isles, if an equable poise were to be maintained. In the event of the scales being loaded to the profit of one or the other, the successful princess would become the more powerful of the two, and thus she would become the victor. The two queens pitted pride against pride, neither wishing to yield ground to the other. A life-or-death struggle, therefore, took place between them; and death alone was able to unravel the terrible entanglement.

As stage-manager for this superb drama Dame History selected herself, and she chose for her star performers two women of outstanding talent and personality. Both Mary Stuart and Elizabeth Tudor were exceptionally gifted for the parts they were allotted. Their energy and vitality were in crass contrast with the ineptitude of the other reigning monarchs of the period: Philip of Spain was monkish and bigoted; Charles IX of France was a mere boy, extremely weak, and possessing queer tastes; Ferdinand of Austria was utterly insignificant—none of those kings attained the high stage of intellectual development which these women reached. Both were shrewd, though their shrewdness was often hampered by passion or by feminine caprice; both were inordinately ambitious; both, from earliest childhood, had been trained and educated for the great roles they were destined to play. Their outward decorum was exemplary; and they were cultured ladies, their minds having absorbed all the humanities of the day.

In addition to the mother tongue, they conversed fluently in Latin, French, and Italian. Elizabeth, moreover, had a fair command of

Greek. So far as the art of letter-writing was concerned, their style greatly excelled that of their best ministers in flexibility and freshness of expression, Elizabeth's being more full of colour and more picturesque and metaphorical than that of Cecil, her secretary of State, whereas Mary's was more polished and showed greater originality of thought and choice of words than that of Maitland of Lethington or Moray. The intelligent interest they took in the arts, the beautiful ordering of their courtly lives, have stood the test of centuries; Elizabeth had her Shakespeare and Ben Jonson, while Mary encouraged and admired Ronsard and du Bellay. But once having enumerated these manifold outward resemblances between the two women, we have to realize that the list is exhausted. Inwardly they were totally unlike. Their spiritual and temperamental contrast has at all times lured dramatic authors into the endeavour to portray them.

The aforesaid contrast made itself felt throughout their respective careers. It was one of circumstance as well as of character. Here is a first and notable difference: Elizabeth had a hard time of it at the opening of her life, whereas Mary's closing years were heavy with disaster and shrouded in gloom. Mary Stuart rose to power and good fortune lightly, brilliantly, and quickly like the morning star in a clear sky; a queen already in the cradle, when hardly more than a child she was anointed a second time as aspirant to a second throne. But her fall was as precipitate as her ascent. Her destiny became concentrated in three or four catastrophic happenings, genuine drama which has for ever made of her the quintessential heroine of tragedy. Elizabeth Tudor, on the other hand, rose to greatness slowly and with difficulty. Her career, therefore, takes, rather, an epic form. No spontaneous gifts were conceded her. As a child she was declared a bastard; she was confined to the Tower by her sister's orders; she was threatened with execution; by cunning and precociously developed diplomatic arts, she succeeded in procuring a bare living for herself and at least a tolerant outlook on her mere existence as a human being. Whereas Mary had from the outset dignities and honours showered upon her, Elizabeth was compelled to fight her way upward and to mould her life for herself.

Two such fundamentally diverse characters were fated to lead their possessors in the long run down utterly divergent paths. At times these paths might intersect, might cross one another, but they could never pursue the same direction, so that the two women were prohibited from ever bearing one another company and becoming true friends. The contrasts between them bored deep down into essentials: one was born with a crown as she was born with her own hair; the other had slowly and patiently to work her way upward and was hard pressed to retain power when achieved. From these contrasted origins the queens as they passed from childhood to girlhood and thence to womanhood were compelled to cultivate their own, individual strength and qualities. Mary Stuart had versatility, attained her goal without effort, possessed a certain light-hearted frivolity of mind, and almost an overplus of self-confidence, so that she adventured much—and this made her great though it brought about her undoing. With head erect and proudly, she stepped forward to meet what life had to offer, feeling her position to be impregnable. God Almighty had bestowed a throne upon her, and no one could snatch the gift out of her hands. She was born to command, the rest of mankind had to obey; even if the whole world doubted her regal rights, she felt that these were ineradicably planted in her blood and bone. Life meant to dare much and to enjoy everything to the full, to go forth in search of a unique and passionate hazard. She would allow herself to be suggested into enthusiasms, thoughtlessly, quickly, and would make up her mind with the fiery intensity of a man affronted who seizes upon his sword. Just as, dauntless horsewoman that she was, she would urge her steed over hedges and ditches, risking life and limb, so in the sport of politics she imagined she could ride roughshod over every obstacle and difficulty. What Elizabeth looked upon as a carefully thought-out game of chess, a diplomatic issue demanding the utmost intellectual exertion, was for Mary a delightful entertainment, an enhancement of joy in life, a chivalric tourney. The Pope once said of her that she had a man's soul in a woman's body. Her daring frivolity and egotism—characteristics which make excellent material for poesy and ballad, and feed the tragic muse—doomed the young sovereign to an early fall.

Now Elizabeth was a practical realist through and through; her knowledge of what was feasible amounted almost to genius. She won her victories by way of a shrewd utilization of thoughts she had long digested in her mind, and by turning the vagaries of her rival to good account. With her clear, sharp, and birdlike eyes—one needs but glance at her portraits to realize how bright and penetrating they were—she looked with mistrust upon the universe of men and things around her, for she recognized the dangers which beset her, and her heart was filled with fear. Early in life she had passed through the school of adversity, and had learned caution and the art of moderation. Statesmanship could never be practised extempore—that she had been taught well—it needed prolonged calculation and immense patience. Nothing lay further from her purpose than the bold, the over-bold feeling of security which was a virtue in Mary, but a virtue that led to her ruin.

As a child Elizabeth had witnessed the rise and fall of Fortune's ball; she had seen how short a step was needed to bear a queen from throne to scaffold; she had seen that one day a person might be languishing in the Tower of London—that antechamber of so many deaths—and the next would be making a royal progress to Westminster. Power seemed to her a fluid substance in the hands of a ruler; it might slip unawares through the fingers, and a position of security would thereby be endangered. The crown and sceptre appeared to her made of fragile glass, and consequently she held them in her grasp with the utmost precaution and anxiety. Her whole life was filled with care and irresoluteness.

All the portraits of the queen confirm the traditional descriptions of her aspect and character. None of them show her to have been lucid, free, and proud, like a born ruler of men. She always looks timid and anxious, with strained eyes, as if watching and waiting for something untoward. We never see a smile of glad self-confidence on her lips. Simultaneously shy and vain, the wan countenance peeps forth from behind the make-up and from among the glittering jewels. We feel that whenever she was alone, having doffed her robes of State and wiped the rouge from her wasted cheeks, there could have been no royal dignity left—nothing but a poor, solitary, uneasy, prematurely aged woman, the tragical figure of one who, far from being competent to govern a world, was unable to master even her own urgent distresses.

The attitude she assumed lacked any vestige of the heroic, and her everlasting hesitation, postponement, and want of determination robbed her of much of her queenly dignity. Nevertheless, Elizabeth's indubitably great capacity for statesmanship lifted her to a higher plane than that of romantic heroism. Her power resided, not in venturesome plans and decisions, but, rather, in a tough and circumspect persistence for obtaining the utmost that was compatible with security, with scraping and pinching where State expenses were concerned, and in the cultivation of such virtues as are habitually ascribed to burgesses and housewives worthy of their salt. Her very faults—timidity, excess of caution—bore fruit in the political field.

Mary lived for herself; Elizabeth lived for her country, contemplating her position as ruler through the spectacles of a realist and looking upon it as a profession. Mary's mind was stuffed with romance, and she accepted her queenly estate as a gift from God and as exacting no duties on her part. Both women were strong and both were weak, but their strength and their weakness assumed different aspects. Whereas Mary's madly heroic self-confidence led her to her doom, Elizabeth's weakness, her lack of decision, led her in the end to victory. For in the world of politics persistence invariably gains the day over undisciplined strength, carefully prepared plans triumph over improvisations, practical realism gets the better of unpractical romanticism.

But the antithesis went even deeper. Elizabeth and Mary were not only poles apart as queens; they were equally different in feminine qualities. It was with them as if Nature had set about deliberately to create two figures whose make-up was diametrically opposed, down to the smallest details.

Mary Stuart as woman was wholly woman, first and last and for always, so that the greatest decisions forced upon her during her brief span took their shape from this deepest spring-head of her being. Yet it would be far from true to say that impulse invariably governed her reason, or that she allowed herself to be driven unresistingly hither and thither by her passions. Quite otherwise. In early youth Mary proved amazingly reserved in all that appertained to the exercise of feminine charm. Year followed upon year, and the life of feeling still slumbered quietly within her. What portraits have come down to us show a friendly, gentle, rather weak and indolent face, a slightly disdainful pair of eyes, an almost childishly smiling mouth. Indeed, this countenance is that of an undifferentiated being, an immature woman. Essentially sensitive, she would blush on the slightest provocation, or she would turn pale with emotion, and tears came readily to her eyes. Thus the abysses of her nature lay undisturbed until her time was ripe; in a few words, she was a thoroughly normal and genuine woman, and it was not until a later date that she herself, Mary Stuart, was to discover her real depths, her real strength, in a passion of love that was to be the only true passion of a lifetime. But this merely serves to prove how feminine was her character, how much a thing of impulse and instinct, how firmly it was chained to her sex. For in her brief moment of ecstasy all her higher cultural attainments seemed to vanish as a dream; all the dams of courtly training, of morals, and of royal dignity were broken down, and when she saw herself confronted by a choice between passion and honour, her queenship was set aside to give place to the woman who chanced to sit upon a throne. The regal mantle slipped easily from her shoulders, and she stood naked and unashamed as do so many other women who yield to the ardours of love, who allow themselves to be swept off their feet, and swallowed up in their desire. This is it, perhaps, which lends so much splendour to her story: for the sake of one rich moment of passionate accomplishment she was capable of risking kingdom, power, and sovereign dignity.

Elizabeth, however, was quite incapable of yielding to such a complete abandonment of herself. The reason for this was a physiological one: she was "not like other women." Nature had not only debarred her from motherhood, but had further deprived her of the possibilities for enjoying the emotions and resulting acts of a woman in love. This secret organic inferiority lay at the root of all the strange evolutions and spasmodicities of her temperament. Not voluntarily, as she pretended, but perforce, did she remain a "virgin queen." Even though some of the statements, such as Ben Jonson's, that have come down to us regarding her physical malformation are open to question, there can be no doubt that passionate fruition was for her rendered impossible by bodily or mental hindrances. Obviously such circumstances must profoundly affect a woman's character. The scintillations, the vacillations, the moodiness of her nerves; her weathercock behaviour, which frequently assumed the aspect of hysteria; her lack of balance and the incalculability of her resolves; her unceasing swing from hot to cold, from Yes to No; the comedies she played, her finesse and her reserve, and (not least) that coquetry which wrought such tricks with her statesmanlike dignity—one and all, these things are hardly explicable except as the outcome of bodily defect. Wounded as she was by it to the core of her being as woman, she could neither feel, nor think, nor act unambiguously and naturally; no one could count upon her, and even less could she count upon herself. Nothing could be more wrong-headed, superficial, and commonplace than the customary view (to which Schiller gives the weight of his authority) that Elizabeth played a cat-and-mouse game with the gentle and defenceless Mary. Though mutilated in spirit because abnormal in body, though her nerves were always on edge, though an unscrupulous intriguer, Elizabeth was neither cruel, inhuman, cold, nor hard. One with insight can discern in this woman, freezing on her solitary throne, hidden sources of warmth. Though her relations with her half-lovers were a torment to her, because to none of them could she give herself wholly, we can see behind her whimsies and outbursts of temper an earnest wish to be magnanimous and kind. She detested bloodshed. The signing of a death-warrant was a misery to her. She took no pleasure in the murderous chances of war. One of her amiable vanities was a desire to be regarded by the world as the noblest, the most glorious, the humanest of monarchs, and to astonish her adversaries by unexpected clemency. Violence was foreign to her timid disposition. She loved the petty, pin-prick arts of diplomacy, and to act irresponsibly behind the scenes. When she had to declare war, she hesitated and shuddered. Any strenuous resolve cost her sleepless nights, and she devoted her best energies to maintaining peace for her country. If she showed enmity to Mary Stuart, it was only because she felt the latter's existence to be a menace to her own life and authority; yet she avoided open conflict, being by nature a trickster rather than a fighter. Both the cousins, Mary Stuart from indifference, Elizabeth Tudor from timidity, would have preferred the maintenance of a spurious peace. But the stars in their courses were set against the untroubled existence of this pair side by side in the same firmament. The stronger will of history is regardless of the innermost longings of individuals, often involving persons and powers, despite themselves, in her murderous game.

For behind these personal differences of character and disposition there loured, like huge and menacing spectres casting their shadows over the destiny of the British queens, the gigantic opposing forces of the epoch. Mary Stuart was the champion of the old Catholic faith; Elizabeth Tudor constituted herself the defender of the Reformation. The two queens symbolized two antagonistic eras, two antagonistic outlooks upon the universe; Mary incorporating that which was dying out, the Middle Ages, the days of chivalry; Elizabeth being the embodiment of the new, the coming time. Thus the birth-pangs of a fresh turn in history came to be suffered in the struggle that ensued between these cousins.

What imparted so much picturesqueness and romance to Mary Stuart was that she stood or fell with the past, that she was a last and dauntless paladin of a cause that lay already in the death agony. She was merely obeying the directive will of history when she rallied to the side of those who still had their gaze fixed upon the past, when she made political pacts with those powers which had already declined from the zenith of their influence, when she allied herself with Spain and the papacy. Elizabeth looked ahead; she was far-sighted, sending her envoys into distant lands, into Russia and Persia for example, encouraging her subjects to explore oceans and continents, just as if she foresaw that on a day to come the foundations of the new world that was in the making must be laid in other continents than Europe. Mary was perfectly happy to remain fixed in what had come to her by inheritance, and she could not disentangle her mind from the dynastic conception of sovereignty. God had given power and dominion to potentates that they might reign supreme at the apex of an earthly hierarchy. What could terrestrial justice do against so divine an ordinance? There was no room for criticism, for resistance; a king's subjects and his territories were his private possessions. It is an actual fact that Mary Stuart twice tried to transfer her royal inheritance, once to France and the second time to Spain. She considered that the territory of Scotland and the Isles belonged to her as ruler, but she failed to recognize that such a relationship is mutual—that a sovereign belongs to the country over which he or she rules. During all the years of her reign, Mary was nothing but Queen of Scotland, she never acted as queen for Scotland's benefit. From the hundreds of letters which issued from her pen we learn only that she desired to consolidate and extend her personal rights, never that she had the folk-wishes at heart, or envisaged some betterment in commerce, in navigation, or even in the armed forces of the crown. Just as, when she wrote poetry or entered into an interesting conversation, she invariably lapsed into a foreign idiom, the courtly French she had been taught in childhood and youth, so did her thoughts and feelings never clothe themselves in the Scottish, the national phraseology. She did not live and, ultimately, die for Scotland; all her thoughts were concentrated on remaining Queen of Scotland. Mary Stuart never gave anything creative to the land of her birth except the saga of her life.

So strong a sentiment of being above everyone and everything necessarily created a solitude around Mary. Though she far exceeded Elizabeth in courage and determination, her cousin gained daily in strength during the struggle because of wider vision and more disciplined shrewdness. The English queen surrounded herself with quiet and clear-thinking personalities, a kind of general staff of able advisers from whom she learned the arts of strategy and tactics, thus protecting herself from herself, where great decisions were concerned, against her own fitfulness and caprice. So splendid an organization did she create around her that even to this day it is wellnigh impossible to disentangle her personal achievements from those of the collectivity of statesmen who served during the "Elizabethan epoch"; moreover the immeasurable renown which haloes her name includes the lives of her helpers. Mary Stuart was Mary Stuart, and nothing more; whereas Elizabeth was Elizabeth plus Cecil, plus Leicester, plus Walsingham, plus the superlative energies of all her subjects. It is hard to distinguish how far she was personally responsible for the rise of the English nation, and how far the nation itself worked its way to so vast a predominance, bearing the Virgin Queen aloft on its sturdy shoulders. England and Elizabeth formed one united whole. Elizabeth set an example to the monarchs of her day and of subsequent epochs, in that she never arrogated to herself the position of ruler of England, but assumed the more modest role of administrator, of carrier-out of the folk-will, of servitor to the national mission; she understood the trends of the epoch that was emerging from an autocratic regime into a constitutional regime. Honestly and voluntarily, she recognized the new forces that were at work transforming the estates of the realm, and widening the world frontiers by far-flung geographical discoveries; she knew how to encourage the guilds, the merchants, the financiers, and even the privateers and filibusters of her day, to superhuman efforts on behalf of England, so that England might become Queen of the Seas. Repeatedly did she renounce her personal wishes (a thing Mary Stuart could never bring herself to do) in order to serve the general desires of the nation she was called to govern.

To save herself from spiritual shipwreck, Elizabeth had to find an outlet in creative endeavour. Because as a woman she was frustrated, she sublimated her feminine inferiority into the happiness and welfare of her people. Her egoism, her passionate desire for power, her realization that never could she become a mother or the dearly beloved of a man, were transfigured into a national ambition, a longing to see her country great. Her lack of personal triumph could be compensated for by England's victory. The sublimest of her vanities was to be made great in the eyes of posterity through England's greatness, in which she would posthumously live. Whereas Mary would have gladly exchanged her throne for a better one, Elizabeth had no longing for any other crown than that of England. Mary Stuart wanted to be resplendent here and now; Elizabeth Tudor, the thrifty, the far-sighted, devoted her best powers to the future of her nation.

It was natural, therefore, that the favour of war should fall to the woman who was in advance of her time, who possessed a talent for looking ahead, while Mary Stuart, the queen who still believed in the moribund days of chivalry and romance, was left in the lurch. In the person of Elizabeth the will of history found expression, for the will of history is always straining forward, leaving the empty shells of outlived forms behind, and seeking renewed strength in other creative activities. The whole energy of a nation was incorporated in Elizabeth's person, for the nation behind the queen wished to become conqueror of the globe. With Mary Stuart the past died a chivalrous, a magnificent, a heroic death. Thus both women remained victors in the field of their choice: Elizabeth, the realist, conquered in the realm of history; whereas Mary, the romanticist, has conquered in the realm of poetry and legend.

The choice of figurantes was indeed majestic both in space and time; unfortunately the manner in which the tragedy was fought to a finish was petty and mean. In spite of their superlative traits these two women remained women throughout, and were unable to overcome the weaknesses inherent in their sex. Thus, instead of dealing honestly with one another, they entered into paltry intrigues, and by their lack of frankness fostered enmities. If, instead of Mary and Elizabeth, two kings had been faced by the same circumstances, they would have come to a firmer decision, declared war, countered one dark threat by another, set courage against courage. The struggle between Mary and Elizabeth, however, never came to a stout and clear issue; it was "catty," each lying in wait for the other with claws covered but ready for use; it was a thoroughly unloyal and dishonest game.

For a quarter of a century these two women consistently lied to one another and betrayed one another, without for a moment either of them being effectively humbugged. They had no illusions about one another. Their correspondence, in which each of the "dear sisters" bespatters the other with asseverations of inviolable affection, makes one's gorge rise by its hypocrisy. While the two sovereigns are smiling graciously at one another and exchanging congratulations, each is secretly sharpening a knife to slit the other's weasand. They never look one another candidly in the eyes, never engage in bold and open struggle. The story of the duel between Elizabeth Tudor and Mary Stuart contains no word about Homeric combats or glorious situations. We seem to be reading a chapter from Machiavelli, an account of clever and even dazzling manœuvres and counter-manœuvres, psychologically most exciting, but morally repulsive because it was always malice confronting malice and never courage confronting courage.

This mutual hanky-panky began with the negotiations for Mary's second marriage. Royal suitors appeared upon the scene, and one was as good as another to Mary, for the woman in her was not yet awakened and she was not fastidious. Don Carlos, a lad of fifteen, would do well enough, although rumour described him as an ill-natured madcap. Nothing amiss with Charles IX of France, another minor. Young or old, attractive or repulsive, their personalities were of no moment to her provided the marriage would obviously give her a higher standing than her Tudor cousin. Being thus dispassionate, Mary was content to leave the bargainings to James Stuart, who proved a selfishly zealous go-between, for if his half-sister could be married, and then dispatched to wear a crown in Paris, Vienna, or Madrid, he would be quit of her, and once more become uncrowned king of Scotland.

Elizabeth, however, being well served by her spies across the border, was promptly informed about these various suitors, and hastened to interpose a veto. She wrote in plain terms to her ambassador in Edinburgh to the effect that, should Mary accept a husband of royal blood from Austria, France, or Spain, she (Elizabeth) would regard this as an unfriendly act. Yet the same courier carried the most affectionate letters to "my dear cousin," who is to trust Elizabeth alone, "no matter what mountains of happiness and earthly splendour others may promise you." Of course Elizabeth had not the slightest objection to a Protestant prince, to the King of Denmark or the Duke of Ferrara. In plain English, she had no objection to a suitor who would be valueless, and therefore not dangerous. The best thing would be, however, for Mary to look "at home" for a husband, to wed some member of the Scottish or English aristocracy; in that case she could rely on Elizabeth's friendship, be certain of her help.

Elizabeth was obviously playing foul. What the unwillingly "virgin queen" wanted was to spoil her rival's chances of a good match. Mary returned the ball no less adroitly. Of course she did not admit for an instant Elizabeth's overlordship, Elizabeth's right of veto in this matter of marriage. But before saying as much in plain terms, she wanted to make sure of a bridegroom of her own choice, and Don Carlos, the leading candidate, still hung in the wind. To gain time, Mary therefore feigned heartfelt thanks for Elizabeth's kindly interest. "Not for all the uncles in the world" would she risk losing the English queen's valuable friendship by precipitate and headstrong action. She was honestly desirous of following her dear cousin's advice. Elizabeth need only tell her explicitly which suitors were to be regarded as "allowed." This pliability was most touching, but in the midst of declarations of confidence Mary interspersed a timid inquiry as to how Elizabeth proposed to compensate her for being so docile. Well and good, she writes (substantially), I shall be guided by your wishes, and shall be careful not to marry any man of so high a rank that my position, well-beloved sister, will overshadow yours. But, in return, please be good enough to let me know how things stand with regard to my right of succession to the English crown!

Therewith the conflict had got back to the old dead-point. As soon as Elizabeth was asked to say a plain word about the succession, no god was mighty enough to wring a plain word from her. She resorted to circumlocutions. "Being wholly devoted to the interests" of her dear sister, she would work on behalf of Mary as on behalf of her own daughter. The mellifluous words streamed on for page after page; but the one, the clear, the decisive utterance that was wanted was not forthcoming. Like two Levantine merchants, each waited for the other to make a move; neither wanted to be the first to open the hand. "Marry the suitor I propose to you," said Elizabeth in effect, "and I shall appoint you my successor." "Appoint me your successor, and I will marry whomsoever you please," rejoined Mary. But because each of them wished to over-reach the other, neither would trust the other.

The negotiations concerning the marriage, the suitors, and the right of succession dragged on for two years. Strangely enough, these women, who were both, so to say, cheating at cards, unconsciously played into one another's hands. Elizabeth's supreme purpose was to restrain Mary from marriage; and Mary, unfortunately, was mainly bargaining with the most slow-moving of the monarchs of his day, Philip II Cunctator. Not until there seemed to be an insuperable hitch in the chafferings with Spain, and one of the other conjugal possibilities had to be seriously considered, did Mary deem it expedient to make an end of her own policy of procrastination and to put a pistol to her dear sister's head. She bluntly asked Elizabeth which member of the English aristocracy the latter had in mind for her as a husband.

Elizabeth never liked a plain question demanding a plain answer, and such a proceeding was particularly uncongenial in this instance. She had long been holding counsel within herself as to which among her nobles would be best suited for Mary, and she had ambiguously declared her determination to give her cousin someone whom none could expect. The Scottish court, however, said that these dark hints were incomprehensible, and pressed for a positive proposal, a specific name. With her back against the wall, Elizabeth could no longer evade the issue by unintelligible allusions. Through clenched teeth she allowed the name to escape her—Robert Dudley.

Now the diplomatic comedy seemed, for a moment, to be degenerating into farce. Elizabeth's proposal must be regarded either as a monstrous affront or else as a stupendous bluff. According to the notions of the day, it was almost an outrage to ask the Queen of Scotland, who was also Queen-Dowager of France, to wed the subject of a sister queen, a man without a drop of royal blood in his veins. Still more preposterous was the actual personality of the chosen suitor, since it was common talk throughout Europe that for years Robert Dudley had been as near to becoming Elizabeth's lover as was physically possible, so that now the Queen of England was suggesting as consort for the Queen of Scotland a man who was tantamount to a cast-off article of clothing for which Elizabeth had no further use. Earlier, no doubt, in the days of her liveliest passion for him, she had thought of marrying Dudley herself. She was bound by extremely intimate ties, half of friendship and half of love, to him who had been the companion of her youth during those fateful days in the Tower. Year after year she had irresolutely toyed with the notion (it was her way with notions); but when Dudley's wife, Amy Robsart, died by an accident under highly suspicious circumstances, Elizabeth hastily withdrew from the scene in order to escape inculpation in the affair. Thus Dudley was compromised, first by the inexplicable strangeness of his wife's death, and secondly by his notorious erotic relationship with Elizabeth, whose proposal of this cast-off lover as husband for

Mary was, perhaps, the most amazing of all the amazing deeds of the English queen during her long reign.

It is not likely that we shall ever know every thought in Elizabeth's mind when she brought forward this perplexing scheme. Who can fathom the wish-dreams of a woman of hysterical temperament, or formulate them in logical terms? Was she still honestly in love with Dudley, and did she wish (since she did not dare to marry him herself) to bestow upon him, as the most precious of possible gifts, the succession to her realm? Or did she merely want to rid herself of a gallant who had become a nuisance? Or did she fancy that by palming off a confidant on her ambitious rival she could keep Mary's actions the better under control? Was she simply putting Dudley's fidelity to the test? Did she entertain dreams of a persistent triangle, a ménage à trois? Or was the absurd suggestion made only in the firm conviction that Mary would refuse, and would, thereby, put herself in the wrong? All these possibilities are conceivable, and it seems even more probable that this capricious woman did not herself know what she wanted. It is likely enough that she was toying with the idea, just as she loved to toy with persons and with resolves. Futile to discuss might-have-beens, or to inquire, in this instance, what would have happened if Mary had seriously considered the acceptance of Elizabeth's discarded lover. Perhaps, in that event, Elizabeth would have taken a sharp curve, would have forbidden Robert Dudley to marry the Queen of Scots, and thus would have heaped upon her rival the shame of a rejection following upon the shame of such a proposal.

To Mary the idea that she should wed anyone who was not of the blood royal seemed little short of blasphemous. In the first flush of anger she scornfully asked the English ambassador whether his sovereign lady could be in earnest when she put forward "Lord Robert" as suitor. Speedily, however, she mastered her indignation and assumed a friendly aspect, for it would be inexpedient to offend her dangerous adversary by a blunt refusal. If she could secure the heir to the Spanish or to the French throne as husband, this would be vengeance enough for Elizabeth's insult. In Edinburgh, therefore, Dudley was not rejected as a possible suitor. Mary entered into the spirit of the farce, supplying to it an admirable second act. Sir James

Melville was thereupon sent to London, ostensibly to negotiate about the Leicester marriage, but really that he might involve the complicated issues in a further tangle of lies and misrepresentations.

Melville, the most loyal and trustworthy of Mary's courtiers, was a skilful diplomatist. He also wielded a facile and descriptive pen, for which posterity owes him thanks. His account of his visit to London has handed down to us the most vivid picture we possess of Elizabeth's personality, and is at the same time an extraordinarily amusing historical comedy. Elizabeth was well aware that Sir James, a highly educated man, had lived for years at French and German courts, and she therefore set great store on making a good impression upon him, never suspecting that his infallible memory would enable him to set on record all her weaknesses and coquetries. In the case of Elizabeth Tudor, feminine vanity often played havoc with her royal dignity. So was it now when the Queen of England, instead of trying to produce a political effect upon the ambassador of the Queen of Scots, was mainly concerned to show off her airs and graces before the man. She strutted forth one antic after another. From her extensive wardrobe (after her death it was found to contain three thousand dresses) she selected the most expensive gowns, attiring herself by turns in the English, the Italian, and the French fashions of the day; some of these costumes were cut so low in the neck as to effect an extremely liberal display; at the same time she showed off by turns her Latin, her French, and her Italian, luxuriating in the courteous admiration of the ambassador. Still, none of his superlatives satisfied her conceit. It was not enough for Melville to assure her that she was beautiful, clever, and well informed. In the spirit of the question, "Mirror, mirror on the wall, Who is loveliest of us all?" she was eager to hear from Melville that he found her more admirable than his own sovereign lady, handsomer, abler, more cultured than even Mary Stuart. Pointing to her wealth of naturally curling red-gold hair, she asked him whether Mary's locks were as splendid—a thorny question to put to a queen's envoy! Sir James was equal to the occasion, declaring with the wisdom of Solon that Elizabeth "was the fairest queen in England" and Mary "the fairest in Scotland." But such praise was too half-hearted to gratify her foolish vanity. Again and again she paraded her charms, playing on the virginals and singing to the lute. At length Melville, whose business it was to lead his hostess by the nose in political matters, thought it expedient to admit "that the Queen of England was whiter," that he "gave her the praise as the better performer on the lute and virginals," and that his "queen danced not so high and disposedly" as Elizabeth did.

Amid this peacocking, Elizabeth had forgotten the matter in hand. When, at length, Melville broached the thorny topic, the queen, now wholly the comédienne, took a miniature of Mary out of a drawer and kissed it affectionately. With a thrill in her voice, she assured him how much she longed to become personally acquainted with Mary, her beloved sister (although in reality she had done everything in her power to hinder such an encounter); and anyone who was swept off his feet by this bold actress could not fail to believe that Elizabeth's chief desire on earth was to make her Scottish neighbour happy. But Melville had a cool head and a clear vision; he was not taken in by these languishings and prevarications, for on his return to Edinburgh he reported: "Ther was neither plain dealing nor upricht meaning, but great dissimulation, and emulation, and fear." When Elizabeth asked him point-blank what Mary thought of the Dudley proposition, the trained diplomat was equally careful to avoid a decisive No or an irrevocable Yes. He talked round the subject, saying that Mary had not yet given full attention to the possibility. But the more evasive the envoy, the more insistent the queen, who remarked that Melville "appeared to make small account of my Lord Robert . . . but ere it were long she would make him Earl of Leicester and Baron of Denbigh," and that Melville "should see it done before his returning home; for she esteemed the Lord Robert as her brother and best friend, whom she would have married herself if she had been minded to take a husband; but being determined to end her days in virginity, she wished that the queen her sister should marry him, as meetest of all other, and with whom she might rather find it in her heart to declare her next in succession to her realm than with any other person; for, being matched with him, she would not then fear any attempts at usurpation during her own life."

Actually, a few days later (third act of the farce), the promotion of Dudley thus announced took place with great pomp and ceremony. Lord Robert, under the eyes of the court, knelt before his sovereign and lady-friend, to be created Earl of Leicester. Once more, however, Elizabeth's feelings ran away with her, and the woman in her played the queen a prank, for, says Melville, while she was "herself helping to put on his ceremonials . . . she could not refrain from putting her hand in his neck to kittle him, smilingly, the French ambassador and I standing beside her." What an amusing detail to report when he returned from his embassy!

Melville had not come to London in order to divert himself as chronicler of a royal comedy; he played an independent role. His diplomatic portfolio had some secret compartments whose contents he was by no means inclined to disclose to Elizabeth, and his civil chatter with Her Majesty about the Earl of Leicester was only intended to camouflage the real objects of his journey south. The most important of these was to convince the Spanish ambassador that Mary Queen of Scots would not wait any longer for a decision in the matter of Don Carlos's suit. Was it or was it not proposed that King Philip's heir should marry her? Next, Melville was, with due discretion, to get into touch with a candidate of the second class, with Henry Darnley.

This stripling stood, for the moment, upon a loop-line. Mary wished to hold him in reserve in case her chances of a better marriage should be frustrated. For Darnley was neither king nor prince, while his father, the Earl of Lennox, had been banished from Scotland as an enemy of the Stuarts, and the family estates had been sequestrated. On the maternal side, however, this young man of eighteen was of high descent, for he was of Tudor stock. As great-grandson of Henry VII, he was the first "prince of the blood" at the English court, and therefore of suitable rank to become consort of any queen in Christendom. As possible husband for Mary, he had the further advantage of being a Roman Catholic. Unquestionably, then, Darnley could be considered third, fourth, or fifth iron in the fire; and Melville had a number of non-committal talks with Margaret Countess of Lennox, who was an extremely ambitious woman.

Now it is an attribute of genuine comedy that, though all the participants must best one another, they should not be wholly deceived, since from time to time each will get a momentary glimpse of the cards of one of the other players. Elizabeth, being no fool, never imagined that Melville had come to London solely in order to compliment her upon her hair and upon her touch on the virginals. She knew that the suitorship of her own cast-off lover was not likely to commend itself to Mary, and she was also acquainted with the ambitious designs of her dear cousin, Lady Lennox. No doubt, as usual, there were spies at work. During the ceremony at Westminster, when Robert Dudley was invested as Earl of Leicester, Elizabeth asked Melville what he thought of the newly created earl. Melville replied: "As he is a worthy subject, so he is happy in a princess that can discern and reward merit." In his *Memoirs,* Melville continues: "'Yet,' said she, 'ye like better of yonder long lad,' pointing towards my Lord Darnley who, as nearest prince of the blood, bore the sword of honour that day before her." Melville did not lose his nerve at this sudden invasion of one of the secret compartments of his portfolio. He would have been unworthy of his reputation as diplomatist had he not known how, on occasion, to lie like a trooper. Wrinkling his brows, and glancing contemptuously at the man with whom the day before he had been bargaining as Mary's potential husband, he replied that "no woman of spirit would make choice of such a man that was liker a woman than a man, for he is lovely, beardless, and lady-faced." Sir James adds as comment: "I had no will she should think that I liked him, or had any eye that way."

Was Elizabeth deceived by this feigned contempt? Did Melville's adroit parry lull her suspicions to sleep? Or was she, throughout, playing a double game which to this day remains impenetrable? However this may be, the improbable happened. First the Earl of Lennox was granted leave to go to Scotland, and then, in January 1565, his son Henry Darnley. Strangely enough the go-between in securing these permits was none other than the Earl of Leicester, who had his own ends to serve, wishing to escape from the conjugal noose his royal mistress had spun for him. Now the fourth act of the farce could proceed merrily in Scotland, where, however, chance took a leading hand in the sport. The threads of the tangle were abruptly snapped, so that the comedy of the suitors was ended in a remarkable fashion which none of those concerned had expected.

For politics, a mortal and artificial power, was overridden, on this January day of 1565, by an eternal and elemental force. The suitor who had come to woo a queen to his surprise found, in Mary Stuart—a woman. After years of patient waiting, she at length became aware of her own self. Hitherto she had been no more than a king's daughter, a king's wife, a queen, and a queen-dowager: the sport of alien wills, a pawn in the game of diplomacy. At length, passion surged up from within. Ambition was discarded like a constricting garment. The awakened woman found herself confronted by a man. Therewith opened the history of her inner life.

CHAPTER SEVEN

Passion Decides

(1565)

NOW THE unexpected happened, and yet, though unexpected, it was one of the most ordinary things on earth—a young woman fell in love with a young man. In the long run Nature cannot be repressed. Mary, a woman with warm blood and healthy senses, was at this momentous period in her destiny on the threshold of her twenty-third year, the most appropriate age for an ardent passion. She had now been four years a widow, and fully abstinent, for her conduct in sexual matters was irreproachable. The time had come when feeling was to have its way with her, when the woman in the queen was to demand her most sacred right, the right to love and to be loved.

The object of her first passion was, strangely enough, no other than the man who was a suitor for political reasons; no other than Darnley, whom his mother had sent to Scotland in this month of January 1565. Mary had already made the young man's acquaintance. Four years earlier, when he was a lad of fifteen, he had come to France in order to bring his mother's condolences to the widow of Francis II. At that time, however, Mary had been in a mournful mood; and in any case she would have been unlikely to regard this hobbledehoy as a possible future wooer. Since then, Darnley had grown into a tall and vigorous young fellow. He was (as Melville has told us) fair-haired, beardless, with a pretty, womanish face, from which two large, round eyes looked forth somewhat uncertainly into the world. "Il n'est possible de voir un plus beau prince" was the description given of him by the French ambassador Mauvissière; and the young queen herself speaks of him as "the handsomest and best-proportioned long man" she has ever seen. Proneness to illusion was part of the fiery and impatient temperament of Mary Stuart. As with all who are romantically inclined, she had little knowledge either of the world or of men. Day-dreamers such as she rarely see things in their true light; facile enthusiasms making them discern, rather, what they want to discern. Sobriety is foreign to such unteachables, who vacillate between the extremes of delight and disappointment; and, on awakening from one illusion, they do so only to become victims of a new one—since illusion, not reality, is for them the real world! Thus it came to pass that Mary, in her quickly kindled liking for the tall, smooth-chinned young Darnley, failed to perceive that beneath the comely surface there was no depth, that there was no moral strength in this man of powerful muscles, no intellectual culture to back up his courtly manners. Unaffected by her puritan environment, she could see no more than that the young prince had a good seat on horseback, danced gracefully, was fond of music and of cheerful conversation, and could, on occasion, write pretty verses. Such artistic accomplishments always made a strong appeal to her. She was delighted to find in Darnley an agreeable comrade in the ballroom, at the chase, and in her other amusements. His coming was a refreshment, since he brought an aroma of youth into this tedious court. Others besides the queen took a liking to Darnley, who, acting on his mother's shrewd advice, behaved modestly. Soon he had become a welcome guest throughout Edinburgh, "well liked for his personage," as Randolph, Elizabeth's spy, reported to the latter. He played his part of wooer adroitly, courting the favour, not only of Mary Stuart, but of all and sundry. He struck up a close friendship with David Rizzio, the queen's new private secretary and an initiate of the Counter-Reformation. Day after day Darnley and Rizzio played tennis together; at night they slept in the same bed. But while Darnley thus got into close contact with the Catholic party, at the same time he wanted to stand well with the Protestants. On Sundays he accompanied Prime Minister James Stuart to kirk, where he listened with well-simulated attention to the sermons of John Knox. To avert suspicion, he often took his midday meals with the English ambassador, and was careful to say soft things of Queen Elizabeth. In the evening he danced by turns with the five Marys. In a word, his obedience to his mother's instructions making up for his lack of intelligence, he got on well at the

Scottish court, and, for the very reason that he was personally insignificant, it was easy for him to avoid suspicion.

Suddenly, however, a spark kindled in the queen's heart. Mary Stuart, who had famous kings and princes as wooers, herself began to woo this foolish stripling of nineteen. Passion flamed up in her, as it is apt to do in those who have not prematurely frittered away their feelings in petty love-adventures. For Mary, Darnley was the object of her first great passion. Her child-marriage to Francis II had made of her little more than the young king's playmate. Since Francis's death, the woman in her had remained in abeyance. Now she had come into contact with a man upon whom her affection could discharge itself like a torrent. Unreflectingly, in the happy intoxication of self-forgetfulness, she gave herself up to the rush of feeling, in the belief that Darnley was all she could have dreamed of, was to be the one and only love of her life.

To expect reasonableness from a young woman in love is to look for the sun at midnight. It is of the essence of the love-passion to be unanalysable and irrational. Always it is outside the range of mathematical calculations. Beyond question Mary Stuart's choice of Darnley conflicted sharply with the general excellence of her understanding. The young man was crude, vain, with nothing to commend him but good looks. Like countless other men who have been passionately loved by women of outstanding intelligence, Darney's only merit, his only magic, was that he chanced to be the man who, at the decisive hour, presented himself to a young woman whose will-to-love had long been pent up.

Long, too long, had been the pause before the amatory passions of this proud daughter of the Stuarts were aroused. Now, after this time of waiting, she was impatient, was twitching with eagerness. When Mary Stuart wanted anything, she was not inclined to wait and to consider; as soon as she had made up her mind, her impulses urged her to action. The woman forgot the queen; political considerations did not weigh with her for a moment. What mattered England or France or Spain, what mattered the future, as compared with the entrancing present? She would no longer trifle with Elizabeth's proposal of Leicester as husband, nor would she await the slothful wooer from Madrid even though he was to bring her the crown of two worlds. Here, ready to her hand, was the bright-visaged, gentle, and voluptuous youth, with his full, red lips, his childlike eyes, his cautious advances! A speedy alliance, that she might give herself to him unrestrainedly—such was the unquestioning impulse of her happily awakened senses. At first, however, she confided her intention to only one person at court, David Rizzio, who did his utmost, like a skilful smuggler, to guide the lovers' ship past all rocks into the harbour of Cythera. A confidant of the Pope, Rizzio believed that Mary's marriage to the Catholic Darnley would ensure the re-establishment of the old Church in Scotland. His zeal for the union was the outcome, not so much of a desire for Mary's happiness or for Henry's, as of the political scheming of a champion of the Counter-Reformation. Before James Stuart or Maitland of Lethington, the effective rulers of Scotland, had any notion of Mary's intentions, the young Italian had written to the Pope for the dispensation requisite to the marriage, since Henry Stuart, Lord Darnley, was Mary's cousin. Foreseeing every possible difficulty, Rizzio likewise wrote to Philip II to ask whether Mary could count upon the King of Spain's help should Elizabeth make trouble about the marriage. Both by day and by night this confidential agent was hard at work, for Rizzio believed that the rising of the two stars would promote his own ascent in the courtly heaven as well as the triumph of Catholicism. But for all that he drove his mines so busily, he worked too slowly and too cautiously for Mary's impatience. She would not be stayed for weeks and weeks while the letters took their tedious course across seas and lands. There would not be any hitch in the negotiations for the Holy Father's dispensation. Why should she wait for a piece of parchment before having her desires gratified? As if to cut off the possibility of retreat (had she an inkling that her passion would be inconstant?), she wanted to give herself wholly to her lover without delay. Always in her resolves Mary showed this same blind disregard of consequences, this charming and foolish exaggeration. The faithful and adroit Rizzio soon found a way of gratifying the wishes of his royal mistress. He arranged for a Catholic priest to come to his room. Even though irrefutable evidence of a premature wedding be undiscoverable (as for all the details of Mary's life, there is a conflict of testimony here), some sort of formal betrothal must have taken place. Why, otherwise, should the trusty henchman have exclaimed: "Laudate sia Dio"? Why should he have declared that no one could now "disturbare le nozze"? Long before any at court except Rizzio had taken Darnley's wooing seriously, Mary's cousin had become lord of her life and perhaps also of her body.

This "matrimonio segreto" remained secret for a time because the pair chiefly concerned and also Rizzio and the priest knew how to hold their tongues. Still, the lovers' manner betrayed them, as the heat of a hidden fire can be felt. It was not long before the court began to watch Mary Stuart and Darnley more closely. At this juncture the poor young fellow fell sick of measles—a distressingly childish ailment for a bridegroom. The anxious Mary watched day after day at his bedside and, when he was convalescent, continued to spend her time with him. The first among Mary's statesmen and advisers to become seriously uneasy was James Stuart, Earl of Moray. Doubtless with a keen eye to his own advantage, he had honestly done his best to promote a good marriage for his sister; and, although he was a strict Protestant, he had urged her to wed Don Carlos, scion of the Spanish Habsburgs, and therefore one of the leading figures in Catholic Christendom. But a wedding with Darnley ran athwart his plans and interests. Moray was clear-sighted enough to know that, should the conceited, soft-headed Darnley become prince consort, he would at once wish to wrest the royal authority into his own hands, and would never be content to let James Stuart rule. Besides, Moray had sufficient political flair to guess whither the intrigues of Rizzio, Italian secretary and papal agent, were tending—namely, towards the re-establishment of Catholicism and the downfall of the Reformation in Scotland. In his resolute mind personal ambition joined forces with religious conviction, the will-to-power with patriotic anxiety. He therefore urgently warned his sister against a marriage which would lead to disastrous conflict in a land that was just beginning to quiet down. When he saw that his warnings were unheeded, he abruptly left the court.

Lethington, the other trustworthy adviser, likewise offered resistance. He, too, saw that his position and the religious peace of Scotland were endangered. By degrees there assembled round the two Protestant statesmen the whole body of Scottish nobles that supported the Reformed Church. At length even Randolph, the English ambassador, began to notice what was going on at court. Afraid lest he should have been nodding at the decisive hour, in his report to Elizabeth he described handsome young Darnley's influence with the queen as the outcome of "witchcraft," and began to drum lustily for aid. But the discontent and murmurings of these lesser folks were as nothing in comparison with the fury of Elizabeth when she learned of Mary's choice of husband. Now, indeed, she was distressingly repaid for the dubious game she had been playing; she had actually been made a fool of. While Mary was pretending to negotiate with her for her favourite Leicester, the real wooer had been smuggled out of her hands and across the border into Scotland; she was left stranded in London to reap the fruit of excess of diplomatic craft. In the first outburst of her anger, regarding Lady Lennox, Darnley's mother, as at the bottom of the whole business, she caused the countess to be arrested and confined in the Tower. Threateningly she commanded Darnley, as one of her "subjects," to return instantly to England; she alarmed his father with the threat of confiscating his estates; she summoned the Privy Council, which, acting on her instructions, declared the marriage of Mary to Darnley "unmeet, unprofitable, and perilous to the sincere amity between the queens and their realms"; she uttered veiled menaces of war. Substantially, however, she was so greatly alarmed and perplexed that simultaneously she tried chaffering. To save her own face, she played her last trump, the card which she had hitherto been careful to keep out of sight.

Now, when Elizabeth (though she does not yet know it) is too late in the field, for the first time she makes Mary an open and firm offer of succession to the English crown. Being in a great hurry, she sends a special envoy to convey the following declaration: "If the Queen of Scots would accept Leicester, she would be accounted and allowed next heir to the crown as though she were her own born daughter." Here we have a signal instance of the futility of diplomacy. What Mary Stuart has for years been striving to attain with skill, urgency, and cunning, that her rival should grant this right of succession to the English crown, is now put almost within her reach—would have been within her reach, had she not gone too far—by the most foolish action of her life.

It is part of the nature of political concessions that they come too late. Yesterday Mary Queen of Scots was still playing the political game; today she is only a woman, only a woman in love. Her leading ambition was, until a few weeks ago, to become acknowledged heiress to the throne of England. Now this desire for an enhanced royal state has been forgotten because of the woman's impulsive longing to surrender her body to the embrace of a handsome young man. Even if she wanted to draw back, to secure the coveted prize in England, the secret marriage has made withdrawal out of the question. She and Darnley are man and wife, or at least formally betrothed. Too late come Elizabeth's menaces; too late her offer of the English succession; too late, likewise, are the warnings of sincere friends, such as the Duke of Lorraine, her uncle, who urges Mary to have nothing more to do with that "joli hutaudeau"—that popinjay. Intelligence and reasons of State no longer weigh with the impetuous young woman.

Sarcastically she replied to the angry Elizabeth, who had been caught in her own net: "I am truly amazed at my good sister's dissatisfaction, for the choice which she now blames was made in accordance with her wishes. I have rejected all foreign suitors, and have chosen an Englishman who is of the royal blood of both kingdoms, and, as far as England is concerned, is, on his mother's side, the eldest male descendant from the royal House of Tudor." Elizabeth could not say a word to the contrary, for it was literally true that Mary had fulfilled her wishes, although after Mary's own fashion! Mary had wedded an English nobleman, and one sent to her by Elizabeth, although the latter had an ambiguous intent. Elizabeth Tudor, her nerves distraught, nevertheless continued to overwhelm Mary Stuart with offers and threats. Thereupon Mary grew blunt. She denied any right on Elizabeth's part to exercise "overlordship," any grounds for interference. She herself, said Mary, had so long been "trayned with fayre speeches and beguyled in her expectations," that she had at length made her own choice, with the full consent of her estates. Regardless of missives from London, whether sweet or sour, in Edinburgh Mary made speedy arrangements for a public marriage. Darnley was knighted, made Earl of Ross, and granted other honours. The English envoy, who galloped up at the last minute carrying a pack of protests from England, arrived just in time to hear the proclamation that Henry Darnley was henceforward to be "namit and stylit king."

Being already Duke of Albany, Darnley was proclaimed King of Scotland by Mary's authority. On July 29, 1565, the nuptials of the pair were publicly celebrated in the Catholic chapel at Holyrood. To the general surprise, Mary Stuart, who always had an inventive turn where ceremonial was concerned, appeared in mourning dress, the robe she had worn at the interment of her first husband the King of France. She designed to show that she had not frivolously forgotten her first spouse, and now appeared a second time before the altar as wife in order to fulfil the wishes of her country. Not until after she had heard Mass and had withdrawn to her room did she allow herself to be persuaded by Darnley (though really all had been prearranged, and the festal robes were laid out ready) to doff her mourning and put on gay attire suitable to a bride. The palace was surrounded by a jubilant crowd. Largesse was freely scattered, and the populace gave itself up to rejoicing—greatly to the annoyance of John Knox, who had himself just married a girl of eighteen as his second wife, but wished no one except himself to find enjoyment. In Knox's despite, the rejoicings went on for four days and four nights, as though gloom were for ever to be dispelled from Scotland, and that misty land were to become a happy realm of youth.

Measureless was Elizabeth's despair when she, unmarried and never to marry, learned that Mary had for the second time become a wife. Her most artful manœuvres had brought her only slaps in the face. She had offered the Queen of Scotland her own favourite as husband, and Leicester had been publicly refused. She had vetoed the wedding with Darnley, and her veto had been openly disregarded. She had dispatched a special envoy with a last warning, and he had been kept waiting outside barred gates until the marriage ceremony was over. It was essential for her now to do something to regain prestige. She must either break off diplomatic relations or declare war. But what pretext could she find for either step? Obviously Mary Stuart had the right to choose a husband for herself; she had complied with Elizabeth's wish, since Elizabeth had disapproved of her wedding a foreign prince. There was no flaw in the marriage. Henry Darnley, great-grandson of Henry VII and chief male descendant of the House of Tudor, was worthy husband to a queen. He was co-heir presumptive to the English crown, and Mary's marriage to him greatly strengthened her claim to the English succession. Any further protest on Elizabeth's part would only make her private spleen manifest to the world.

Throughout Elizabeth's life, however, ambiguity remained one of her chief characteristics. Although in this instance its result had been so unfortunate, she could not desist from it. Naturally she did not declare war on Mary Stuart; she did not recall her ambassador; but, by underground ways, she did everything she could to make things uncomfortable for those whom she did not wish to be a happy wedded pair. Too timid, too cautious, to come into the open against Darnley and Mary Stuart, she intrigued against them behind the scenes. Rebels and malcontents were never difficult to find in the Scotland of those days when it was a question of running counter to the established authorities, and on this occasion there was forthcoming a man who stood head and shoulders in energy and wrath above all the petty rabble of the disgruntled. Moray had been conspicuous by his absence from his sister's wedding, and his non-attendance was regarded as an evil omen. For Moray (this is what makes his figure so mysteriously attractive) had an extraordinary instinct for detecting the onset of changes in the political weather and an incredibly keen capacity at forecasting; he always knew where the danger-points were to be found, and on this occasion he did the cleverest thing a politician of his stamp can do—he vanished. Having dropped the helm of State, he became invisible and undiscoverable. Like the drying-up of springs, the failure of rivers to flow, great natural catastrophes, the disappearance of Moray—as we shall see again and again in the history of Mary Stuart—always foreboded political disaster. For the time, however, he remained passive. During the days when the wedding was being celebrated, he stayed at his castle, having quietly withdrawn from the court, wishing to show in a loyal and yet unmistakable manner that, as first minister of State and protector of Protestantism, he disapproved of the choice of Henry Darnley as King of Scotland. Elizabeth, however, wanted something more than this passive protest against the new royal pair. She desired open rebellion, was eager that Mary Stuart should pay for her private happiness with political trouble; and, keeping this end in view, the Queen of England sought the favour of Moray and of the no less discontented Hamiltons. She herself must, on no account, be compromised. "In the most secret way," therefore, she commissioned Bedford, one of her agents, to support Moray and Hamilton with troops and money "as if from himself," and with the implication that Elizabeth knew nothing of the matter. The money fell into the clutching hands of the Scottish lords like dew upon a parched meadow; they rallied their courage, and the pledges of military aid soon brought about the rebellion England desired.

It was, perhaps, the only mistake made by the shrewd and far-seeing Moray that he should rely upon the English queen, who was so utterly unreliable, and should put himself at the head of this insurrection. Being cautious, indeed, he did not start proceedings at once, and was content for the time being to find secret confederates, for he really wanted to wait until Elizabeth would openly espouse the cause of the Protestant lords, so that he could take the field against his sister, not as an ordinary rebel, but as defender of the threatened Church. Mary, on the other hand, disquieted by her brother's ambiguous conduct, and rightly unwilling to tolerate a holding aloof that was manifestly hostile, formally summoned him to appear before parliament and justify his conduct. Moray, however, as proud as his sister, would not present himself in the character of an accused person. He haughtily refused to comply, with the result that he and his adherents were "put to the horn" in Edinburgh market-place, that is, they were publicly declared outlaws. Once more, arms were to decide instead of reason.

On this occasion, however, the temperamental difference between Mary Stuart and Elizabeth Tudor was signally disclosed once more. Mary showed herself prompter to act and far more resolute, her courage being always impatient, swift, and impetuous. Elizabeth, on the other hand, acting timidly as was her wont, hesitated too long. Before she had made up her mind to instruct her treasurer to equip an army and openly to support the insurgents, Mary had taken action. She issued a proclamation in which she dealt roundly with the rebels. "You are not satisfied to heap wealth upon wealth, honours upon honours, you want to have ourselves and our kingdom altogether in your hands that you may deal with them as you will, and compel them to act wholly in accordance with your desire—in a word, you want to be kings yourselves, and leave us nothing more than the nominal title of ruler of the kingdom." Without losing an hour, the intrepid woman mounted her horse, and, armed with pistols, her young husband wearing gilt armour riding by her side, surrounded by those of the nobles who had remained true to her, she set forth against the rebels at the head of a quickly assembled army. The wedding march had become a war march. This resoluteness was justified by the result. Most of the opposing barons were daunted by the display of royal energy; all the more seeing that the promised aid from England was not forthcoming, and Elizabeth continued to send dubious words instead of an army. One after another, with hanging heads, they returned to pay allegiance to their rightful ruler. Moray alone remained stout-hearted, but before he, forsaken by his allies, could gather a new army, he was a defeated man and had to flee. The victorious royal pair followed him hot-foot, so that it was only by the skin of his teeth that he saved himself on October 14, 1565, through crossing the border on to English soil.

Mary's victory was complete. All the peers of the Scottish realm now formed a solid front round Mary Stuart; once more Scotland was in the hands of a king and a queen. For a moment Mary's confidence was so overwhelming that she was minded to take the offensive and cross the border into England, where she knew that the Catholic minority would welcome her as a deliverer. The more prudent among her advisers were able, with some difficulty, to hold this impulse in check. In any case, now that Elizabeth had put her cards on the table, the days of an exchange of courtesies between the cousins were over. The independent choice of a husband had been Mary's first triumph over Elizabeth; the crushing of the rebellion was the second; henceforward she could look freely and proudly across the border and stare her "good sister" out of countenance.

Before these troubles had arisen, Elizabeth's position had been far from enviable. Now, after the defeat of the Scottish rebels whose movement she had fomented, that position became alarming. Doubtless it has at all times been an international custom for rulers who have secretly instigated revolts in neighbouring lands to disavow the rebels when these are conquered. But since misfortunes never come singly, one of Elizabeth's consignments of money to the Scottish lords had chanced to fall into the hands of Bothwell, Moray's deadly enemy, when making a raid, so that plain proofs of the complicity of the Queen of England had been secured. A second grave inconvenience was caused by the fact that Moray, almost as a matter of course, had taken refuge in England, the country which had given him both open and tacit support. Nay, more, the defeated man actually put in an appearance in London. This was most embarrassing for the English ruler, accustomed though she was to play a double game! If she received Moray, the rebel, at court, this would imply that she approved or at least condoned his rebellion against Mary. If, on the other hand, she were to shame her secret ally by refusing him an audience, the affront might lead him to let the cat out of the bag, to explain to foreign courts that he had been Elizabeth's pensioner. Scarcely on any other occasion did Elizabeth's habit of playing double put her in a tighter place than this.

Fortunately, however, the sixteenth century was one when many notable comedies were composed. Elizabeth had the advantage of breathing the same vital atmosphere that Shakespeare and Ben Jonson were to breathe. A born actress, she could play her part as well as any queen of the stage; so that high comedy was already as much in vogue at Hampton Court and Westminster as later in the Globe or the Fortune Theatre. Hardly had she been informed of the arrival of her inconvenient ally, when she arranged for Cecil, the same evening, to put Moray through a sort of dress-rehearsal of the part it would be incumbent upon him to play in order to save Queen Elizabeth's honour.

It would be hard for a dramatist to imagine anything more impudent than the comedy that was staged next morning. The French ambassador came to pay his respects, talking of this, that, and the other, for how could he dream that he had been summoned to look on at an impudent farce? While he was discussing the political situation, a lackey entered and announced the Earl of Moray. The queen knitted her brows. Who? Had she not misheard the name? Really, the Earl of Moray? How could this base rebel against her "good sister" have made his way to London? What unheard-of insolence for him to demand audience of her, whom all the world knew to be devoted to her Scottish cousin! Poor Elizabeth! At first, she could hardly contain her astonishment and indignation. Still, after brief and gloomy reflection, she made up her mind to receive the "scoundrel"; but, God be praised, she need not see him alone! She begged the French ambassador to be good enough to remain as witness of her "honest" indignation.

Now it was Moray's turn to play up. He did so with all due seriousness. His aspect as he entered was designed to show contrition and a sense of guilt. Humbly and timidly, with a mien altogether different from his customary stride, did he enter the room. He was clad in black, kneeled before Elizabeth, and began to address her in his native Doric. The queen promptly interrupted him, commanding him to speak French, so that the ambassador could follow their conversation and no one would be able to say she had talked secrets with so opprobrious a rebel. Moray stammered a little, in assumed embarrassment, but Elizabeth went on, taking a high tone. She could not understand how he, a refugee who had been rebelling against her cousin and friend, dared to enter her court uninvited. There had, no doubt, been various misunderstandings between herself and Mary Stuart, but none of them had been serious. She, Elizabeth, had always regarded the Queen of Scotland as her good sister, and hoped that the pair of them would ever remain upon such excellent terms. Unless Moray satisfactorily proved that only in a moment of folly or in self-defence had he taken up arms against his lawful sovereign, Elizabeth would have him arrested, and would call him to account for his rebellious behaviour. Moray would do well to excuse himself as best he could.

Moray, having been carefully drilled by Cecil, knew that now he might say anything in the world except the truth. He knew that he must take all the blame upon himself, in order to exonerate Elizabeth in the ambassador's eyes. Instead, therefore, of stating his grievances against Mary Stuart, he praised his half-sister to the skies. She had bestowed upon him lands, titles of honour, and other rewards far beyond his merits; he had, for that reason, served her faithfully; and nothing but the dread of a conspiracy against his own person, nothing but the fear of assassination, had led him to behave as foolishly, as recklessly, as he had done. He had only come to Elizabeth hoping for her gracious help to induce the Queen of Scotland to forgive him.

This seemed already to exculpate very efficiently the woman who had fomented the whole affair. But Elizabeth needed more. The comedy had been staged, not merely that Moray, before the French ambassador, should take the blame on his own shoulders, but that, as witness for the crown, he might declare that Elizabeth had had nothing whatever to do with the affair. A thumping lie never means any more to a politician than empty breath, so Moray solemnly assured the ambassador that Queen Elizabeth "had known nothing whatever about the conspiracy, and had never encouraged him or his friends to disobey the orders of their lawful sovereign."

Elizabeth had got what she wanted. She had been solemnly whitewashed, and was able, with theatrical emotion, to rail at her fellow-conspirator in front of the ambassador. "Now," she exclaimed, "ye have told the truth; for neither did I, nor any in my name, stir ye up against your queen, for your abominable treason might serve for example to move my own subjects to rebel against me; therefore pack you out of my presence, ye are but an unworthy traitor." Moray bowed his head, perhaps to conceal a smile. He had not forgotten the many thousand pounds which, in the queen's name, had been handed to Lady Moray for him, and to some of the other rebel lords; nor had he forgotten Randolph's imploring letters, nor yet the pledges of English military aid. He knew, moreover, that if, for the time being, he were prepared to accept the role of scapegoat, Elizabeth would not chase him forth into the desert. The French ambassador, meanwhile, stood respectfully listening and watching, for, being a man of education, he could enjoy a good comedy. Not until he got back to the embassy would he allow himself to smile, when sitting alone at his desk, and writing a report to his royal master. Elizabeth, one may suppose, was not altogether happy in her mind, for she can hardly have believed that anyone could have taken these assurances at their face value. Still, no one had ventured to smile openly. Appearances had been kept up, and what did truth matter? Without a word more, sustained by the dignity of her voluminous skirts, she rustled out.

Nothing can show better how great, for the time, had become the power of Mary Stuart, than that her English cousin and adversary should, after losing the battle, have been driven to such petty subterfuges in order to make a seemly retreat. The Queen of Scotland could raise her head proudly, for everything had happened as she had willed. The man of her choice wore the Scottish crown; the barons who had risen against her had returned to their allegiance or were outlawed in foreign lands. All the omens were favourable, and when she now bore a son to her young husband, the last and greatest of her dreams was fulfilled. This Stuart boy would be king of the united thrones of Scotland and England.

The omens were favourable. Fortunate stars shed their light like a silent blessing over the land. Now, one might suppose, Mary Stuart could rest in the enjoyment of the happiness she had harvested. But the law of her unruly nature was to suffer storm or to raise it. One whose heart is untamed cannot rest content when the outer world proffers happiness and peace. Impetuously this disorderly heart continued, from within, to create fresh disasters and new perils.

CHAPTER EIGHT

The Fatal Night in Holyrood

(MARCH 9, 1566)

IT IS part of the nature of every true passion neither to count nor to save, neither to hesitate nor to question. When one of a regal type of character loves, this implies unrestricted self-surrender and expenditure without thrift. During the first weeks of her marriage, Mary found it impossible to do enough to show her fondness for her young husband. Every day she surprised Darnley with some new gift: now a horse, now a suit of clothes; a hundred small and tender things, to follow up the bestowal of the greatest things in her power to bestow—the royal title and the warmth of her heart. Reporting to London, Randolph, the English ambassador, wrote: "All honour that may be attributed unto any man by a wife, he hath it wholly and fully. All praise that may be spoken of him, he lacketh not from herself. All dignities that she can indue him with are already given and granted. No man pleaseth her that contenteth not him; and what may I say more? She hath given over unto him her whole will, to be ruled and guided as himself best liketh." Mary Stuart was not one to do things by halves; she gave with both hands. Now that she was passionately in love, she was wholly obedient and ecstatically humble.

Great gifts, however, are advantageous only to one who is worthy of them; for others, they are dangerous. Strong characters become yet stronger through a sudden accession of power, since power is their natural element; weak characters, on the other hand, are ruined by unmerited good fortune. Triumph, instead of teaching them humility, makes them arrogant; and, childish in their folly, they believe that the favour of fortune is a testimony to their own worth.

It was not long before Mary's unrestrained and voluptuous delight in giving proved disastrous to this narrow-minded and vain youth, who still stood in need of a tutor instead of becoming the master and lord of a generous and high-spirited queen. For as soon as Darnley perceived what power he had gained, he became pretentious and overbearing. He accepted his wife's gifts as nothing more than tributes due to him and took the guerdon of her royal love as something that accrued to him by right as a man. Having become a master, he felt entitled to treat his wife as a slave. A poor creature with a "heart of wax" (to quote Mary's own contemptuous words about him later), the spoiled lad threw off all restraint, suffered from what would nowadays be called "swelled head," and meddled autocratically in affairs of State. The courtliness and modesty that he had assumed in the days of his wooing were now discarded as superfluous. It was no longer necessary for him to write verses to Mary, or to be gentle in his manner. At the council he assumed dictatorial airs, speaking rudely and loudly; he drank deep with his boon companions; and, on one occasion, when the queen tried to withdraw him from unworthy associates, he berated her so shamefully that the poor woman, thus publicly humiliated, burst into tears. Since his wife had granted him the title of king (the title and nothing more), he believed himself to be in very truth a king, and impetuously demanded the "crown matrimonial," that is to say joint powers of rule. Indeed, this beardless lad of nineteen was already dreaming of autocracy, of becoming the sole and irresponsible head of the Scottish realm. Yet everyone knew that his presumption was not backed up by any effective will, that a conceited boy was intoxicating himself with his own rodomontade, and that the braggart believed himself to be a man because he displayed the arrogance of an upstart. Inevitably, before long, Mary herself came to recognize, with shame, that her first and most devoted love had been squandered upon one who was both ungrateful and unworthy.

Now, in a woman's life, there can be no worse humiliation than to discover she has given herself to one who does not deserve or appreciate the gift; and never will a true woman pardon either herself or the man for so gross a mistake. When the love passion has once flamed high between a man and a woman, it would be unnatural were it to lapse into mere coolness and smooth civility; love, in cases of bitter disappointment, is speedily metamorphosed into hatred and contempt. Thus Mary Stuart, who was never one to show moderation in her feelings, having recognized Darnley to be a pitiful specimen of mankind, withdrew her favour from him more suddenly and swiftly than a thoughtful and calculating woman would have done. She swung from one extreme to the other. Piece by piece, she took away from Darnley what she had unreflectingly, uncalculatingly, given him in the first flush of passion. There was no more talk of his being effective joint ruler, of the "crown matrimonial" which in former days she had conceded to her sixteen-year-old husband Francis II. Wrathfully, Darnley became aware that he was no longer summoned to important sittings of the council, and he was enraged when he was forbidden to include the royal emblem in his coat of arms. Instead of becoming the autocrat he had hoped to be, he found that he had been degraded to the position of prince consort, and that, instead of, as he had dreamed, playing the chief part, he was, at court, barely allowed a consultative voice. Soon his wife's contemptuous treatment of him was copied by the courtiers. Rizzio no longer showed him State documents and, without consulting him, signed the queen's letters with the "iron stamp." The English ambassador refused to address him as "Your Majesty." At Christmas, only six months after the honeymoon, Randolph reported "strange alterations" at the Scottish court. "Until recently it was the custom here to speak of the King and the Queen, but of late Darnley has only been spoken of as the Queen's husband. He had grown accustomed to see his name put first beneath all edicts, but now it occupies the second place. Not long ago, coins were struck bearing the joint heads of 'Henricus et Maria'; but they have been withdrawn from circulation and new ones have been issued. . . . Some private disorders there are among themselves, but because they may be but amantium irae or household words as poor men speak, it maketh no matter if it grow no farther."

But it did grow farther. To the slights which the paper king had to suffer in his own court were now superadded the more grievous slights of a husband who believes himself betrayed. For years past, Mary, upright though she was by nature, had had to learn that lying is needful in politics; but she remained unable to counterfeit where her personal feelings were involved. As wife, she must give herself wholly or not at all. Lukewarm emotions and half-heartedness were impossible to her. As soon as it had become clear to her that she had given the treasure of her love to a worthless wight, directly the fancied

Darnley of the honeymoon had been replaced by a foolish, vain, impudent, and ungrateful youth such as Mary's husband actually was, physical attraction was replaced by physical repulsion. It was now intolerable to her to go on surrendering her body to this man from whom her heart had been estranged. The instant she was aware of being with child, she began to shun Darnley's embraces on any and every pretext. She was ailing, she was tired; she could always find some such reason for refusing herself to him; and whereas, during the first months of their married life (Darnley, in his anger, revealed these connubial privacies), Mary had been the more forthcoming of the two, she now shamed her husband by frequently rejecting his advances. Even in this most intimate sphere, where he had first won power over her, Darnley, to his profound mortification, found himself deprived of the ordinary privileges of a husband.

He lacked the moral strength to keep his frustration to himself. He shouted it from the house-tops, chattered about it in every tavern, raged and threatened, talked fatuously of revenge. But the more bombastic his language, the more absurd an impression did he produce, until, within a few months, the royal title notwithstanding, he was regarded as nothing better than a tiresome and capricious outsider to whom the courtiers showed the broad of their backs. No longer did people incline their heads reverentially; they merely smiled when Henricus rex Scotiae voiced his demands. To one who is or would be a ruler, however, universal contempt is more dangerous than universal hatred.

Mary's disappointment in Darnley was political as well as the disappointment of a loving woman. She had hoped that, with the aid of a husband who would be devoted to her body and soul, she would at length be able to shake off the tutelage of Moray, Lethington, and the Scottish lords in general; she had dreamed of ruling Scotland jointly with her beloved. But these illusions, likewise, had vanished with the honeymoon. For Darnley's sake, she had estranged Moray and Lethington, with the result that she was now utterly alone. But a woman of such a nature as hers, however profoundly her hopes have been belied, cannot live without a confidant, so she was continually looking round her for someone upon whom she could unconditionally rely.

Better, she thought, that it should be a man of low rank, lacking the prestige of a Moray or a Lethington, but having, in place thereof, a virtue which was more essential to her at the court of Scotland—absolute loyalty, the trustworthiness which is the most precious of boons in a servitor.

Chance had brought such a man to Scotland. When Marchese Moreta, the Savoyard ambassador, visited Scotland, there came in his train a young Piedmontese, David Rizzio by name, "in visage very black," about twenty-eight years of age, with round, alert eyes and a lively mouth—that of a good singer. ("Particolarmente era buon musico.") Poets and musicians were always welcome guests at Mary's court. Both her father and her mother had transmitted to her a passion for the fine arts. Nothing could better relieve the gloom of her environment than the strains of the lute or the violin, as accompaniment of a good voice. It happened, at the moment, that she was short of a basso, and since "Seigneur Davie" (as he came to be called by his intimates at the Scottish court) was not only a competent bass, but a fairly skilled composer, the queen begged Moreta to allow the "buon musico" to remain behind in her personal service. Moreta had no objection, so Rizzio was appointed, at a salary of sixty-five pounds. In the palace account-books is inscribed "David le Chantre," but among the domestic staff he was known as "valet de chambre"—groom of the chamber. In those days there was nothing degrading in such a designation for a musician, seeing that down till Beethoven's time the greatest of musicians were at court accounted as no more than members of the domestic staff. Even Wolfgang Amadeus Mozart and the old white-haired Haydn, though famed throughout Europe, never sat at meals among the nobles and princes, but took their food in the servants' hall.

Rizzio was not merely a young man with a fine voice. He had a shrewd intelligence, a lively wit, and an all-round artistic education. He spoke Latin and French fluently, as well as his native Italian; he wrote a "fair hand" and in a good style; those of his sonnets which have been preserved are tasteful and correct. Soon an opportunity occurred for promoting him from the servile rank. Paulet, Mary's private secretary, had not proved immune to a malady that was endemic at the Scottish court, namely corruption by English gold. The queen was forced to dismiss him at short notice. The vacant place in the queen's study was promptly filled by David Rizzio, who now rose rapidly at court. Soon he was something more than a secretary; he became Her Majesty's adviser. No longer did Mary Stuart dictate her letters to the Piedmontese secretary, for the latter drafted the epistles as he thought best. The precise nature of the diplomatic negotiations in which he became engaged under these circumstances, and whether he worked exclusively in the Scottish interest or also had an eye to the advantage of foreign powers, will probably never be known. This much is certain, that he came to play a more and more important part in State affairs. As we have seen, he had a good deal to do with his royal mistress's marriage to the Catholic prince consort Darnley; and Mary's stubborn refusal to pardon Moray and the other rebel lords was ascribed by the latter, probably with good reason, to Rizzio's influence. Suspicion had been rife that the young Piedmontese was a papal agent at the Scottish court. How much truth there may have been in this idea must remain uncertain. Beyond question, even if Rizzio was devoted to the papal and to the Catholic cause, he served Mary Stuart with a devotion and loyalty that had not been shown by any of her Scottish subjects. Now when Mary was faithfully served, she knew how to reward; and she was wont to give freely to anyone with whom she could converse frankly. She made her favour for Rizzio all too plain, giving him costly apparel, entrusting him with the Great Seal of the realm, and making him acquainted with State secrets. Before long David Rizzio, the sometime servant, rose to be a great gentleman, sitting down at table with the queen and her ladies, helping as "maître de plaisir" like Chastelard before him (an ominous parallel!), organizing musical festivals and other court diversions, and becoming more and more the queen's close friend instead of merely her servitor. Until far on into the night, envied by the domestic staff, this low-born foreigner was closeted with the queen in her private apartment. In princely attire, arrogant and offhand, the man who had arrived in Edinburgh as little better than a lackey and with nothing to recommend him but a fine voice now exercised the highest functions in the realm. He had more influence in such matters than Darnley the queen's husband, more influence than Moray when prime minister—the "buon musico" who was actual chief of the State. Nothing happened without his knowledge and consent, but this knowledge and this consent were honestly subservient to the queen's interests.

As a second sturdy pillar of her independence, the military power as well as the political was now in trustworthy hands. In the former domain, likewise, she had found someone to serve her faithfully, the Earl of Bothwell, who years before, in early youth, had (though a Protestant) espoused the cause of Mary of Guise against the Lords of the Congregation, and had therefore been driven from Scotland by the enmity of James Stuart. Returning to his country after Moray's rebellion and downfall, Bothwell put his powers, which were far from inconsiderable, at the queen's disposal. A bold soldier, prepared for every hazard, a man of iron nature, passionate both in love and in hatred, Bothwell was devotedly served by the border clansmen, whom he had led in many a guerrilla campaign against the English. His person alone was worth an army. Grateful for his support, Mary confirmed him in the hereditary appointment of Lord Admiral of Scotland.

With these two loyal assistants to rely upon, Mary Stuart, at twenty-three, had at length both the chief implements of power, the political and the military, firmly grasped in her hands. For the first time she could venture to rule alone, and she was never a woman to shrink from risk.

Always, however, in Scotland, when the monarch endeavoured to become an effective ruler, the Scottish lords resisted his will. Nothing could be more distasteful to these insurrectionary-minded nobles than a queen who neither wooed their favour nor was afraid of them. From England, Moray and the other outlaws were clamouring for permission to return. They exploded all possible mines, those of silver and gold as well as the others. The discontent of the nobility was concentrated upon Rizzio, and soon their castles were full of the murmur of scandalous tongues. The Protestants in Holyrood were convinced that the Italian was spinning Machiavellian webs. They suspected rather than knew that Scotland was about to be dragged into the secret schemes of the Counter-Reformation; and it is, indeed, possible that Mary had given some such pledge to her relatives the Guises who, a few years later, were to found the Catholic League.

Rizzio, having no longer a friend at the Scottish court, was held responsible for these plots. The shrewdest of mortals often act most imprudently. Rizzio made the usual mistake of upstarts. Instead of modestly concealing his power, he boastfully displayed it. He wore splendid attire, bestowed costly gifts, made those with whom he had as a newcomer sat in the servants' hall feel how high he had risen above them, and he does not seem to have been himself exempt from corruption by presents. What, in any case, could be more insufferable to the Scottish nobles' pride than that an ex-servant, a strolling musician of dubious origin, should spend hour after hour in the queen's private apartments, adjoining her bedchamber, in the most intimate companionship which was denied to them, the bearers of ancient names? Stronger and stronger grew their suspicions that these secret conversations must concern an attempt to make an end of the Protestant power in the country; and, to be beforehand with the queen, a number of the nobles who were devoted to the Reformed religion joined in a conspiracy.

For centuries the Scottish aristocracy had been accustomed to employ one method, and one only, for dealing with their adversaries—murder. Not until the spider which was spinning these secret threads had been crushed, not until the subtle and inscrutable Italian adventurer had been swept out of their path, would the way be opened for rendering Mary Stuart more pliable. The plan for making a violent end of Rizzio must have been conceived some months in advance, at the time when Randolph reported to Elizabeth that the Italian might expect at God's hand either a speedy end or an intolerable life. It was long, however, before the malcontents could summon up courage to begin a definite rising. The speed and firmness with which Mary had suppressed the last rebellion was still fresh in their memories, and they had little inclination to share the fate of Moray and the other exiles. They also dreaded the iron hand of Bothwell, who loved to strike hard, and whose pride, they knew, would keep him from joining in their plot. They could only murmur among themselves, and clench their fists, until at length one of them thought of the brilliant but devilish plan of transforming Rizzio's murder from a rebellious act into a legal and patriotic deed by making Darnley, the titular king of Scotland, head and front and protector of the conspiracy.

At the first glance the notion seems absurd. Involve the king of a country in a conspiracy against his own wife, the king against the queen? But the scheme proved psychologically sound, for in Darnley's case, as in that of all weaklings, the mainspring of his activities was his measureless vanity. Since the "iron stamp," the facsimile of the queen's signature, had been confided to Rizzio's charge, the friendship between the two men had been broken, for the right to sign documents in Mary's name gave Rizzio powers which Darnley coveted on his own account. Was this beggar on horseback to conduct diplomatic negotiations about which Darnley, Henricus Scotiae, was not informed? The secretary was wont to stay in the queen's room until one or two in the morning—to spend there the midnight hours when a husband had the right to demand his wife's company—and the Italian's power grew from day to day as, in the sight of the whole court, Darnley's diminished. It must be Rizzio's fault that the crown matrimonial had been refused him, and that alone would have sufficed to explain the hatred of a man who was no less mean-spirited than mortified. But the Scottish nobles instilled a yet more virulent poison into the open wound of Darnley's vanity, stimulating him where he was most sensitive, in his virile jealousy. By numberless hints they encouraged his suspicion that Rizzio shared, not only the queen's board, but also her bed. Though there was no proof of any such misconduct, Darnley was the readier to believe the tale because his wife had of late refused conjugal embraces. It was a hateful thought that Mary's aloofness must be due to a preference for this black-haired musician. A man whose feelings have been wounded is easy to enrage, and one who does not trust himself is apt to distrust others. Ere long Darnley was convinced "that he had suffered the greatest dishonour which can be inflicted on a man." The incredible became fact; the king assumed the leadership of the conspiracy against the queen.

It has never been proved, nor is ever likely to be proved, that this swarthy little musician David Rizzio was really the queen's lover. The very fact that Mary showed open favour for her private secretary in face of the whole court speaks against the supposition. Even if we admit that there is but a narrow line separating spiritual intimacy between a man and a woman from carnal relationship—a line which can be crossed in any incautious moment or as the outcome of an unconscious gesture—still, as regards Rizzio, Mary Queen of Scots, a woman with child, showed her royal friendship with such confidence and carelessness as would have never been shown in such circumstances by an adulteress. Had the pair really crossed the aforesaid line to become lovers, Mary's first and most natural thought would have been to avoid giving tokens of manifest intimacy; she would not have made music or played cards with her lover until the small hours in her private apartment; nor would she have secluded herself with him in her study when diplomatic correspondence was being indited. But as had already been shown in the case of Chastelard, one of her most gracious qualities was a danger to her: her absolute self-confidence when she knew herself to be blameless, her contempt for what "they say," her sovereign disregard of gossip, her amiable nonchalance. Almost always incaution and courage go together, as virtue and danger, like the obverse and reverse of a coin; it is only cowards and those who are unsure of themselves that dread the semblance of guilt.

But when rumour has once charged a woman with misconduct, however malicious and nonsensical the rumour may be, it continues to spread, being perpetually nourished by malicious curiosity. Forty years later, Henry IV of France was to keep the ball of calumny rolling, for he said mockingly of his fellow-sovereign James I (whom, as a babe, Mary was now bearing in her womb) that he well deserved the name of "Solomon" because, like King Solomon of old, he was a son of David. For the second time Mary's reputation was gravely damaged, not by any fault she had committed, but by her lack of caution.

At the Scottish court, no one took this fable seriously; for afterwards, when the nobles were publicly accusing Mary Stuart of all possible crimes, they simultaneously declared her son James to be the rightful King of Scotland. Hate her though they did, they knew the truth of this matter. Only in Darnley, irritated beyond endurance, his judgment confused by an inferiority complex, did the suspicion take root and grow rankly. Like fire, it coursed through his veins; like a bull, he charged the red cloth waved in front of his eyes, and entered blindly into the plot. Without stopping to reflect, he allowed himself to be entangled in a conspiracy against his own wife, so that within a few days no one thirsted more ragingly than he for the blood of Rizzio, who had been his close friend, who had shared bed and board with him—the insignificant musician from Italy who had helped Henry Stuart, Lord Darnley to a crown.

Among the Scottish nobles of those days, political assassination was a solemn affair. Those who had determined on it did not rush hastily upon their victim in the first blast of anger. The conspirators entered into a formal bargain. Word of honour was not security enough for them, for they knew one another too well. This remarkable scheme of chivalry had to be contracted for with seal and charter, as if it had been a legal undertaking. When the Scots had determined on violence, the details were clearly stipulated on parchment, upon one of the so-called "covenants" or "bonds" in which the princely bandits pledged themselves to abide by one another through weal or woe—for only as a troop, as a clan, did they feel courageous enough to rise against their sovereign lady. This time, as a novelty in Scottish history, the conspirators were honoured by having a king's signature upon their covenant. Between Darnley and the conspirators two bonds were entered into and duly signed, bonds in which the king who had been cold-shouldered and the lords who had been banished reciprocally pledged themselves to overthrow the authority of Mary Stuart. In the first bond Darnley promised to hold the conspirators "shaithless" (unharmed), and to protect and defend them even in the palace and in the presence of the queen. He further agreed to recall the banished lords from outlawry and to overlook their "faults," on condition "that they would procure for him the crown matrimonial of Scotland, and that, in the event of Queen Mary's death, he should be declared her rightful successor, and his father the next heir after himself; and that the lords would pursue, slay, and extirpate all who opposed this resolution." He also promised to defend the Kirk against any diminution of its rights. In the second bond the conspiring lords pledged themselves to procure for Darnley the crown matrimonial, and even (we shall see why this possibility was considered) in the event of the queen's premature death to leave Darnley in possession of the royal rights.

These words, seemingly plain, implied more than Darnley realized. But Randolph, who saw the text of the bonds, understood well enough, reporting to London: "If persuasion to cause the Queen to yield to these matters" (the resignation of the crown) "do no good, they purpose to proceed we know not in what sort." This is a broad hint of the intention of the conspirators to rid themselves of Mary during the chance medley of which Rizzio's assassination was the avowed object.

Hardly was the ink dry upon the signatures to this iniquitous bargain, when messengers galloped off to inform Moray, who was at Newcastle awaiting the issue of the plot, that he might make ready for his return to Scotland, while Randolph, who was likewise across the border, at Berwick, and was actively participating in the conspiracy, hastened to inform Elizabeth of the bloody surprise which was preparing for her royal sister. On February 13, 1566, several weeks before the murder, he wrote to London: "I now know for certain that the Queen regrets her marriage, and hates her husband and all his kin. I know also that he believes he will have a partaker in his play and game, and that certain intrigues have been going on between father and son to seize the crown against her will. I know that if these come to fruition, David, with the king's assent, will have his throat cut within the next ten days." The spy went on to convey fuller knowledge of that at which he had already hinted. "Even worse things than these have come to my ears, actually proposals for attacking her own person."

There can, then, be no doubt that the conspiracy had more extensive aims than those disclosed to the foolish Darnley; that the blow which was ostensibly directed against Rizzio alone was intended to destroy Mary as well, so that her life was just as much in peril as her secretary's. Darnley, however, being cruel, as cowards always are when they win to power, was blindly longing for vengeance upon the man who had wormed his way into Mary's confidence, and who signed documents in her name. He insisted, therefore, wishing to debase his wife as much as possible, that the murder must take place in her presence; being moved by the illusion of a weakling, who hopes that "punishment" will make a strong nature pliable, and believing that a brutal exhibition of force would render once more submissive the wife who had come to despise him. Such crude and vengeful natures as his are capable of the last extremity of baseness. The conspirators acceded to the wretched creature's desire that the slaughter should take place in Mary's apartment, and in her presence, with child though she was. March 9 was chosen for the deed, whose performance was to prove even more abominable than its planning had been.

While Elizabeth and her ministers in London had for weeks been fully informed of the details (though the English queen had no thought of conveying a friendly warning to her cousin and "good sister"), and while Moray was waiting across the border ready to spring into the saddle and John Knox had already prepared the sermon in which he was to extol the murder as "a deed most worthy of all praise"—Mary Stuart, betrayed on every hand, was utterly without forebodings and void of suspicion. During the last few days Darnley, making treachery more hideous by simulated affection, had been kindlier than usual, so that there was nothing to show, at sunset on the appointed day, what a night of horror was awaiting her with its promise of doom that would overshadow her for years to come. Rizzio had received an anonymous warning, to which he paid no heed, for in the afternoon when Darnley came to ask him to play a game of tennis, the musician cheerfully accepted the invitation of his former comrade.

Now it was dark. Mary, following her usual custom at this period, had commanded that supper be served in the turret chamber adjoining her bedroom on the first story of the tower. It was a little cabinet, fitted only for the entertainment of a small company—a few nobles and Mary's half-sister were seated round the heavy oaken table, which was lighted by wax candles in silver candelabra. Opposite the queen sat David Rizzio, dressed as a fine gentleman, his head covered (the French fashion in those days), and wearing a coat trimmed with damask and fur. He was in a cheerful conversational vein, probably expecting that there would be some music after supper, or that in some other way the time would be passed pleasantly. There was no sign of anything unusual—until the tapestry which veiled the queen's bedroom was drawn aside, and Darnley, the king, the husband, entered. Everyone rose to greet him; place was made for the distinguished guest at the crowded table, beside his wife, round whom he put his arm affectionately, kissing her with a Judas kiss. Lively talk was resumed; plates rattled and glasses clinked; then there was some agreeable music.

But again the hangings were drawn aside. Now all were amazed, angered, and startled, for this time the newcomer, looking like a black angel in full armour, naked sword in hand, was one of the conspirators, Patrick, Lord Ruthven, generally dreaded, and believed to be a sorcerer. His face was ghastly pale, for he was dangerously ill, in a high fever, and had only left his bed in order to participate in the night's fell work. His fiery eyes disclosed a fierce determination. The queen, instantly boding ill—for no one except her husband was entitled to use the private spiral staircase, the "limanga," leading from Darnley's ground-floor apartment into her bedroom—asked Ruthven by what right he forced himself unannounced into her presence. Cold-bloodedly and contemptuously he answered: "There is no harm intended to Your Grace, nor to anyone but yonder poltroon, David; it is he with whom I have to speak." Rizzio turned pale beneath his plumed cap, and clasped his hands together beneath the table. He instantly realized what was coming. None but his sovereign, none but Mary, could now protect him, since Darnley made no move to rebuke the presumptuous Ruthven, but sat looking on unconcerned. Now Mary spoke in answer to the intruder:

"What hath he done?" she inquired.

Ruthven shrugged his shoulders and answered:

"Ask the king your husband, Madam."

Mary involuntarily turned to Darnley. But in this decisive hour the weakling, who had for so long been urging others to the deed of murder, lost heart. He had not the courage to take his place by Ruthven's side. Feigning ignorance he said:

"I know nothing of the matter."

Shiftily he turned his eyes away.

Now more heavy footfalls and the clash of weapons were heard behind the tapestry. One after another, the conspirators mounted the spiral staircase, and formed a wall of armed men blocking Rizzio's retreat. Escape this way being impossible, Mary tried to save her faithful servant by a parley. If David had committed any wrong, she said, "I promise to exhibit him before the lords of parliament, that he may be dealt with according to the usual forms of justice." Meanwhile let Ruthven and the others withdraw from her apartment. Rebellion, however, does not know the meaning of obedience.

Ruthven had already advanced towards the trembling Rizzio; another of the conspirators threw a noose over the Italian's shoulders and began to drag him away. Tumult ensued, during which the supper-table was upset and the lights were extinguished. Rizzio, unarmed and a weakling, neither warrior nor hero, clung to the queen's robe, uttering cries of terror. He had caught Mary's last word "justice" and screamed: "Madonna, io sono morto, giustizia, giustizia!" Another of the band pressed the muzzle of a loaded pistol against Mary's side, and would, as the conspirators had intended, have shot her, had not another pulled back his arm, while Darnley himself intervened, holding his wife fast, partly (beyond question) to protect her, while the murderers hurried the shrieking and resisting Rizzio out of the supper-room. As they dragged him through the bedroom, he clung to the bedclothes, still crying to the queen for help; but the ruthless assassins clubbed his fingers to make him let go, and forced him on into the State apartment, where they flung themselves on him with their swords and daggers. Apparently they had intended only to arrest the Italian, and the next day to hang him in due form in the market-place; but their excitement and blood-lust carried them away. So madly and so carelessly did they stab him, that in their savagery they wounded one another. The floor became a pool of blood. Not until their victim had bled to death from fifty wounds did they desist from their brutality. Then the mutilated body of Mary Stuart's most loyal friend was flung through the open casement into the courtyard below.

Crazed with grief, Mary listened to the death-shrieks of her devoted servant. Ailing and pregnant as she was, she lacked strength to drag herself from Darnley's grasp, but with all the energy of her passionate soul she revolted against the humiliation put upon her by these bandits in her own palace. Darnley could press her hand, but not her lips; and she railed at him wildly to show her contempt for the coward. She termed him traitor and son of a traitor; she blamed herself for having raised him from being a nonentity to sit upon a throne. What had, up to now, been nothing more than a wife's dislike for her husband, hardened in this memorable hour to inextinguishable hatred. Vainly did Darnley try to excuse his conduct, reminding her that for some months she had refused to accept his embraces, and that she had long been accustomed to give more time to Rizzio than to himself, her lawful husband. Now Ruthven returned and, exhausted by what he had done, sank into a chair. Mary overwhelmed him with threats and invectives. As a wild beast in a cage will, when infuriated, fling itself against the bars, so did she rage against the pair of them. If Darnley had been able to read the meaning of her looks, he would have shrunk back in horror from the murderous hatred which flamed up against him. Had his mind been more alert, he would have realized the deadly menace of her saying that she no longer regarded herself as his wife, and would never rest "until he had a sorer heart than she had then." Darnley, who was capable of only brief and petty passion, did not realize that she was unconsciously passing a death-sentence upon him. When, worn out by what she had witnessed, she mutely allowed herself to be led to her room, he believed her energy to be broken, and that she would once more become his obedient wife. He was to learn, however, that hatred which knows how to be silent is more dangerous than open threats, and that one who offered a deadly affront to this woman summoned death to touch his own shoulder.

Rizzio's screams, the clash of arms in the royal apartment, had aroused the palace. Sword in hand, those who were faithful to the queen, Bothwell above all and Huntly, rushed out of their rooms. The conspirators, however, had guarded against every possibility. Holyrood was surrounded by armed men; the exits were barred, lest the town should send help to the queen. Bothwell and Huntly, in order to fetch help and save the queen's life, had to jump out of the windows. Hearing from them what had happened and was like to happen, the provost of Edinburgh sounded the tocsin. Five hundred burgesses assembled round Holyrood, demanding sight of the queen and to have speech with her. Instead, however, they were received by Darnley, who falsely declared that nothing serious had happened; only "that the Italian secretary is slain, because he has been detected in an intrigue with the Pope, the King of Spain, and other foreign potentates, for the purpose of destroying the true evangile, and introducing popery again into Scotland." The good people had better go home to their beds. Naturally the provost did not venture to doubt a king's word; the burgesses went home, and Mary, who had vainly tried to get word with her subjects, was kept under guard in her apartment. The court ladies and the servants were debarred from entry; a triple guard was posted at the gates and doors of the palace. This night, for the first time in her life, the Queen of Scotland and the Isles became a prisoner. The conspiracy had been completely successful. In the courtyard lay the mangled corpse of her most trusty henchman; at the head of her enemies was her own husband; his were to be the royal rights, while she herself was not even allowed to leave her room. At one blow she had been dragged down from her high position, was powerless, forsaken, without friends or helpers, an object of scorn. In this dreadful night she seemed to have lost everything, but a strong heart is hardened beneath the hammer of destiny. Always when her liberty, her honour, her queenship, were at stake, Mary Stuart found more vitality within herself than in all her assistants or servitors.

CHAPTER NINE

Traitors Betrayed

(MARCH TO JUNE 1566)

DANGER WAS beneficial to Mary Stuart. Only in decisive moments, when she had to stake everything upon a last hazard, did it become plain that remarkable capacities were hidden away within her: iron resolution, all-embracing insight, fierce and heroic courage. But before the innermost energies could come into action, she needed a hard knock on one of her most sensitive points. Not until then did these otherwise dispersed forces become concentrated. One who tried to humiliate her produced so vigorous a reaction that every severe testing by destiny was advantageous to her.

During this night of her first great humiliation, her character became transformed once and for all. In the fiery forge of a most terrible experience, when she saw that her unduly ready confidence in her husband, her brother, her friends, and her subjects had been misplaced, this otherwise extremely feminine and soft-hearted woman grew as hard as steel, acquiring the resilience and tenacity of metal that has been properly treated in the fire. But, being double-edged like a rapier, her character became ambiguous after that dreadful night, which was the beginning of her disasters. The curtain had risen on the bloody tragedy of her life.

Thoughts of vengeance filled her mind, now she was locked up in her own room, the prisoner of traitorous subjects, as she restlessly paced to and fro, pondering one way and another of breaking the circle of foes who environed her, meditating how she could make them atone for shedding the blood of her faithful servant (the blood which still stood in pools upon the floor)—how she could make them abase themselves before her, or bring them to the block, those who had so impudently forced themselves into her presence and had even laid hands upon her, their anointed sovereign. To her, who had hitherto always been a chivalrous fighter, any means now seemed justifiable in view of the outrage she had suffered. As part of the change which occurred in her, she, who had hitherto been impetuous and incautious, became cautious and reserved; she, who had been too honourable to tell falsehoods, learned how to dissemble; she, whose theory and practice of life had been "fair play," was now prepared to devote her exceptional capacities to the catching of traitors in their own snares.

There are occasions when more can be learned in a day than, at ordinary times, in months or years. Such a decisive lesson had now been taught to Mary Stuart, and would influence her for the rest of her life. The conspirators who, almost under her very eyes, had thrust their daggers into her trusty Rizzio had also stabbed deep into the confidingness and nonchalance of her nature. Henceforward she would not make the mistake of being ready to believe traitors, of being truthful to liars, of frankly disclosing her heart to the heartless! No, henceforward she would be crafty, would wear a mask over her feelings, would conceal her hatred, would seem friendly to her enemies, always awaiting with hidden hatred the hour when she could avenge her favourite's murder! She would devote her powers to the concealment of her true thoughts, would cajole her adversaries while they remained drunken with the triumph of their success, would, for a day or two, seem humble in the presence of miscreants, that thereafter she might humiliate them for ever! Such infamous treason could be avenged only by one who was herself ready to play the traitor more dauntlessly and more cynically than the traitors themselves.

Mary Stuart formed her plans with one of those lightning flashes of genius which, when the danger of death threatens, will often come even to persons of a dull and indifferent temperament. Her situation, as she instantly perceived, was hopeless so long as Darnley and the conspirators hung together. Only one thing could save her—to sow discord among her enemies. Since she could not break her chains by sudden violence, she must cunningly search for the weakest links; she must make one of the traitors betray the others. She knew well enough who was the weakling among these harsh men—had good reason to know. It was Darnley, the man with the "heart of wax" on which every finger could make a dint.

Mary's first artifice was a psychological masterpiece. She declared that she had been seized by the pains of labour. Since she was in the fifth month of pregnancy, the excitement of the preceding night, and the dragging away of her favourite to do him to death in a neighbouring room, were shocks that made a miscarriage likely enough. She feigned violent abdominal cramps, took to her bed; and, in her supposed circumstances, it would have been incredible cruelty to forbid the access of her tire-women and her doctor. That was all she wanted for the moment, since therewith her strict seclusion would be broken. Now she had the chance of communicating with Bothwell and Huntly, and of concerting with them means for her escape. Furthermore, by this assumed illness, she put the conspirators (her husband, above all) in a quandary. For the child in her womb was heir to the throne of Scotland and to the throne of England as well, and an overwhelming responsibility was thrust upon the father before the eyes of the world, since his action overnight had endangered the child's life. Full of concern, Darnley appeared in his wife's apartment.

Now began a dramatic scene, perhaps, in its crowning improbability, comparable only to that scene in Shakespeare when Richard III, before the coffin of a man he has murdered, woos and wins the dead man's widow. At Holyrood, likewise, the murdered man was still unburied; there, likewise, the murderer or one of the confederates was confronted by a person whom he had heinously betrayed; there, likewise, the art of misrepresentation acquired daimonic skill. There was no witness to the scene. We are acquainted only with its opening and its end. Darnley entered his wife's room, the room of the woman on whom, the night before, he had inflicted so gross a humiliation—the woman who, in the first outburst of righteous wrath, had announced her determination to be revenged. Like Kriemhild beside Siegfried's corpse, she had yesterday still clenched her fists against the assassin. But, also like Kriemhild, she had, for the sake of her vengeance, learned during the night to conceal her hatred. Darnley found, not the Mary of yester-eve, the fierce and proud spirit of vengeance personified, but an unhappy, a broken-hearted woman, weary unto death, yielding, ill; a woman who looked submissively and tenderly at the strong, the tyrannical man who had shown himself to be her master. The conceited fool was able to enjoy the triumph that he had dreamed of the day before. At length Mary was wooing him once more. Since she had felt the weight of his iron hand, she, hitherto so arrogant, had become mild and gentle. Now that he had got the Italian rascal out of the way, she was once more ready to serve her true lord and master.

To a man of outstanding intelligence, so rapid a change of front would have appeared suspicious. He would have recalled her outcry of the night before, when, with flashing eyes, she had screamed that he was a traitor and the son of a traitor. He would have borne in mind that, as a daughter of the House of Stuart, she would be most unlikely to forgive a humiliation or to forget an affront. But Darnley was, like most empty-headed persons, exceedingly vain. Like stupids in general, he was blinded by flattery. Then, as a further and remarkable complication, of all the men with whom she had come into contact, this hot-headed youth was the one whose senses had been most effectually roused by Mary Stuart. He craved for the possession of her body, was in this respect her thrall; and nothing had embittered him more than her refusal, of late to accept his embraces. Now, wonder of wonders, the coveted woman declared herself wholly his, asked him to spend the night with her, no longer held aloof. Instantly his forces were undermined; he became once more her affectionate lover, her slave, her servant. No one can tell by what subtle arts of deception Mary effected this conversion which was as wondrous as that of Saul on the road to Damascus. Actually, within twenty-four hours after the murder of Rizzio, Darnley, who had just before betrayed Mary to the Scottish lords, had become her bondsman, willing to fulfil her slightest wish, and prepared to do his utmost to cheat his confederates of yesterday. More easily even than they had won him away from her, did the wife recover the allegiance of her serf. He disclosed to her the names of the conspirators, was ready and willing to flee with Mary, and was weak enough to become her instrument of vengeance in a way which would, in the end, make him betray the traitors. It was as a pliable tool that he left the room he had entered in so masterful a spirit. A few hours after her deepest abasement, Mary thus succeeded in breaking the front of her enemies. Without the conspirators being aware of it, the chief figure among them had entered into a conspiracy against them. Crude betrayal had been vanquished by the treason of genius.

Half the work of liberation had already been achieved when Moray and the other outlawed nobles rode into Edinburgh. In conformity with his temperament as a calculating tactician, the man who had been the soul of the conspiracy had stayed away from its execution, and had been careful to avoid participating in the deed of slaughter. Never would this man of tricks and wiles be found walking along a dangerous path. But, as ever, when others had borne the burden of the day, he turned up with clean hands, tranquil, proud, self-confident, to garner the fruits. On this eleventh day of April, in accordance with his half-sister's original plans, he was to have been publicly declared a traitor by parliament. But, lo and behold, his prisoned sister seemed, all in a moment, to have forgotten her hatred. Despair having made her an admirable actress, she flung herself into his arms, to give him the Judas kiss which yesterday she had received from her husband. Urgently but tenderly she begged the brotherly advice and help of the man whom so recently she had outlawed.

Moray, being a keen psychologist, understood the situation fairly well. Yet his sister outwitted him. There can be no doubt that, in planning and approving the assassination of Rizzio, his aim had been to frustrate Mary's secret aim to restore Catholicism in Scotland. From his point of view, the swarthy Italian intriguer had been a grievous danger to the Protestant, to the Scottish cause, and, furthermore, a serious obstacle in the way of Moray's own will-to-power. Now that Rizzio was dead bones, Moray would have liked the whole unsavoury affair to be speedily forgotten, and he therefore proposed a compromise. The degrading watch kept over the queen by the rebellious lords was to come to an end immediately, and Mary's supreme authority was to be re-established. On her side, she was to let bygones be bygones, and to pardon the patriotic homicides.

It need hardly be said that Mary, who, meanwhile, had planned every detail of her flight with her treacherous spouse, had no intention of forgiving the murderers. Since, however, her supreme object was to lull the rebels' watchfulness to sleep, she declared herself in full agreement with the aforesaid terms. So admirably had she, during that one night of terror, learned the art of deception that her brother, who had known her from earliest childhood, cheerfully believed in her good intentions. Forty-eight hours after Rizzio's assassination, with the burial of his mutilated corpse the incident seemed to have been shovelled away underground. Affairs must go on as if nothing had happened. A strolling musician, a man of no account, had been put out of the way, and that was all that had happened. A strolling musician! The conceited and beggarly fellow would soon be forgotten, and peace would reign once more over Scotland.

The pact was signed. But, strangely enough, the conspirators did not fulfil their side of the bargain and withdraw their sentries from the gates of Holyrood. For one reason or another, they were uneasy. They were too well acquainted with Stuart pride to believe that Mary would forgive and look upon the levelling of a pistol against herself, and the murder of her favourite, as mere trifles. They thought it would be safer for them to keep the unruly woman under watch and ward, and to deprive her of any possibility of taking vengeance. She would be dangerous, they felt, so long as she was left at liberty. Another circumstance that disquieted them was that Darnley was once more on excellent terms with his wife, went often to her apartment, and there held long and private conversations with her. Their own experience had taught them how little pressure was needed to influence this weakling, and they began openly to express their suspicion that Mary was trying to detach him from their cause to her own. They expressly warned Darnley not to trust any of her promises and to keep faith with them, for otherwise, as they said (a true prophecy) "both you and we will have cause to repent." Although, of course, the liar pledged himself to be faithful to them, they thought it would be better to keep their sentries posted round the queen's rooms until she had given them a written promise of impunity. Just as these strange friends of legality had wanted a charter before committing their crime, so now they wanted a charter of absolution.

We see that these tried and trained perjurers knew the emptiness and valuelessness of the spoken word, and would therefore only be satisfied with documentary pledges. Mary, however, was at once too proud and too cautious to bind herself to assassins with a signature.

Not one of the rascals should boast of holding her "bond" in his hand. But precisely because she was determined not to give the conspirators their charter of immunity, she pretended to be perfectly willing to comply with their demand. All she wanted was to gain time until the evening! To Darnley, now thoroughly tamed, she gave the shameful commission (seven times unworthy of a king) of holding his yesterday's comrades in check by fictitious cordiality and of humbugging them about the signature. She sent him as her negotiator to the rebels, and in conjunction with them he drafted a formal charter of impunity to which, then, nothing was lacking but Mary Stuart's signature. Well, it was now too late in the evening to get that. The queen was very tired and had gone to sleep. He promised, however, since one lie more did not matter, to bring back the document to them next morning early, signed and sealed. When a king has given his word, doubt would be a grievous affront. The conspirators, therefore, to fulfil their side of the bargain, withdrew the sentries posted outside the queen's bedchamber. That was what she wanted. The path to flight was open.

Hardly had her doors been freed from the watchers, when Mary rose hastily from what she had pretended to be her sick-bed, and energetically began her preparations. Bothwell and her other friends outside the palace had long since been notified. At midnight saddled horses were waiting in the shadow of the churchyard wall. All that was necessary was to lull the watchfulness of the conspirators; and once more there was assigned to the man whom Mary most despised and whom she now made use of for the last time—to Darnley—the shameful role of numbing their senses with wine and jollity. Such contemptible business was all he was fit for in her estimation. Obedient as a marionette, he asked those who so recently had been his confederates to a mighty carouse. Wine flowed freely, and the boon companions drank to the coming reconciliation. When, at length, with swimming heads and unsteady feet, the members of the company betook themselves to bed, Darnley, wishing to avoid giving rise to suspicion, carefully refrained from betaking himself to the queen's room. But his cronies were no longer troubled about such a trifle. The queen had promised to pardon them, the king had guaranteed their impunity. Rizzio had been buried, and Moray was back in Edinburgh. What further need was there to think or to spy? They retired to their couches and slept soundly after so arduous a day of drunkenness and triumph.

At midnight, when silence had long prevailed in the passages of the sleeping palace, a gate was gently opened. Through the servants' quarters and down the stairs Mary groped her way into the cellarage; then, by a subterranean passage, she went to the churchyard—a gloomy route which led through burial vaults lighted by flickering torches, which fitfully revealed coffins and the bones of the dead in the crypts of the damp and chilly walls. Upstairs, now, to reach, at length, the open air! She had only to cross the churchyard and join her friends, waiting outside with horses. Of a sudden Darnley stumbled over a new-made grave; the queen joined him, and recognized with horror that it was the place of David Rizzio's interment, a little mound over his new-made corpse.

This was a last proof of the hammer of destiny, to harden yet further the injured woman's already hardened heart. She knew what tasks awaited her: to reinstate her royal honour by this flight, and to bring an heir to the throne safely into the world; then to take vengeance upon all who had combined to humiliate her. Vengeance on him, too, who now had become her helper! Without hesitating a moment, the wife, who was well advanced in pregnancy, flung herself astride on horseback behind Arthur Erskine, the faithful captain of the body-guard. She felt safer with her arms round him than she would have if she had been clasping her husband, who indeed, without waiting for her, wishing to make sure of his own skin, had already galloped off. Thus clinging to Erskine, the queen made all possible speed for twenty-one miles to Seton House, where Lord Seton was awaiting her with an escort of two hundred riders. Now, mounted on her own horse and with her attendant train, by daylight the fugitive had once more become the sovereign. Before noon she reached Dunbar. Here, instead of seeking repose, she instantly set to work. It was not enough to call herself queen, for at such times she must fight for the reality of queenship. She wrote dispatches to be sent in every direction, summoning her loyal nobles to form an army against the rebels, who held Holyrood. Her life was saved; now she had to save her crown and her honour. Always this woman, when she became inspired with a thirst for vengeance, or when any of her other passions were strongly aroused, knew how to conquer weakness, to get the better of fatigue. It was in these great and decisive moments that she became equal to her task.

A great shock to the conspirators to discover at Holyrood on the morrow that the royal apartments were empty; that the queen had fled; that Darnley, their confederate and protector, had also disappeared! In the first moments, however, they did not realize the full extent of the disaster. Relying upon Darnley's royal word, they continued to believe in the general amnesty that, in conjunction with him, they had drafted overnight. This, they thought, would hold good, and they could hardly believe that such treachery as his was possible. They refused to accept the notion that they had been humbugged. As envoy, they sent Lord Sempill to Dunbar, with a humble supplication to Her Majesty to sign their securities and perform the other articles, according to her promise. For three days, however, the envoy was kept waiting outside the gates, as Emperor Henry IV was kept waiting by Gregory in the snow at Canossa. She would not treat with rebels—all the less now that Bothwell had assembled his troops. The conspirators became greatly alarmed, and their ranks began to thin. One after another they made their way to Dunbar to sue for pardon; but the ringleaders, such as Ruthven, who had been the first to attack Rizzio, and Andrew Ker of Faudonside, who had threatened the queen with a pistol, knew that for them there could be no pardon. With speed they fled from the country; and even John Knox, who had been too swift and too loud in his approval of the murder, thought it expedient to disappear for a time.

Moved by her desire for revenge, Mary would now have liked to make a signal example of these rebellious nobles, and to show them and the world that no one could conspire against her with impunity. But the situation was already dangerous enough to teach them caution for the future. Moray, though he had certainly been privy to the conspiracy (as was shown by his prompt arrival in Edinburgh after Rizzio's murder), had taken no active part in the affair. Mary perceived that she would be more prudent not to proceed to extremities against this half-brother of hers, who was a man of wide influence. "Not venturing to have so many at once at her hand," as she herself said, "she thought better to close her eyes against some of the offenders." Besides, if she proposed to take extreme measures, was not Darnley, her own husband, the first to be dealt with, since he had led the assassins into her bedroom, and had held her hands while the murder was going on? But since her reputation had previously been injured by the Chastelard scandal, it suited Mary's book better not to show forth Darnley in the light of the suspicious and jealous avenger of his honour. "Throw plenty of mud, for some of it will stick." It would suit both Mary and Darnley better if the tale of recent events were bruited abroad in such a fashion as to show that Darnley, although he had been one of the prime instigators of the disastrous affair, had had neither part nor lot in the murder. This was hard to prove in the case of a man who had signed two bonds guaranteeing in advance impunity to the assassins, and whose own dirk, which he had lent to one of them, had been found sticking in Rizzio's body. Puppets, however, have neither will nor honour, so Darnley danced obediently when Mary pulled the strings. Ceremoniously, staking his "honour" and his "word as a prince," he had the most impudent falsehood of the century announced in Edinburgh market-place, declaring he had had nothing to do with the late "treasonable conspiracy"; that it was calumny to accuse him of anything of the kind; that he had neither "counselled, commanded, consented, or assisted"—though everyone in the capital and throughout the country knew that he had not only done all these things, but had "approved" the murder with seal and charter. If it was possible for a man to act more contemptibly than Darnley during the assassination of his sometime friend, he did so now by having this perjury publicly proclaimed. On all those upon whom she had sworn to be avenged, perhaps Mary Stuart took no more terrible vengeance than that which she took on Darnley when she forced the man, who had long since made himself contemptible, to intensify his disgrace by this outrageous lie.

A white pall of falsehood had now been spread over the murder. The strangely reconciled royal pair made a triumphant entry into Edinburgh. All seemed quiet there. To maintain the semblance of justice without stirring deep waters, a few poor devils were hanged, underlings, clansmen, and private soldiers, who, at the command of their lords, had guarded the doors while these were engaged in the cruel work upstairs; but those of blue blood went unpunished. Rizzio's remains were sumptuously interred in the royal cemetery—as if this could have been any consolation to the dead man! His brother Joseph succeeded David as secretary. With these events, the tragical episode seemed to have been forgotten and forgiven. But the dead are not silent; their blood crieth from the ground against those who have consigned them to it. Persons who have been violently put to rest leave the guilty neither rest nor quiet.

After the dangers and excitement she had traversed, there was one thing essential to Mary if she was to consolidate a position which had been gravely shaken: she must successfully give birth to a healthy heir to the throne. Only as mother of a prospective king would she be safe, with a safety impossible to her as merely the wife of such a king as Darnley, a king of shreds and patches. Uneasily she awaited the difficult hours that lay before her. Gloom and depression overshadowed her during the last weeks before the birth. Was it that Rizzio's death had left a scar in her mind? Was it that with her fortified energies she had an enhanced foreboding of imminent disaster? However that may be, she now made a will in which she bequeathed to Darnley a ring he had given her, "a diamond ring enamelled red." Nor were Joseph Rizzio, Bothwell, or the four Marys forgotten. For the first time in her life this woman, in general so care-free and bold, seemed to be dreading death or peril. Quitting Holyrood, which, as the tragical night of David Rizzio's murder had shown, was not a safe place of residence, she removed to the less comfortable but impregnable Edinburgh Castle to await there the birth of the heir to the Scottish and English crowns.

On the morning of June 19, 1566, a royal salute from the guns of the fortress at length announced to the town the joyful news that a son had been born, a new Stuart king of Scotland. There would be an end to the dangerous "regiment of women." The mother's most ardent wish and the strong desire of the country for a male heir to the House of Stuart had been fulfilled. But hardly had the child been born, when Mary felt it incumbent upon her to safeguard his honour. No doubt rumour had brought to her news of the poisonous suspicion which the conspirators had instilled into Darnley's ears, to the effect that she had had adulterous relations with Rizzio. She knew how glad would be her "dear sister" Elizabeth in London to find any pretext for contesting the paternity of her son, and perhaps subsequently, on that ground, refusing to him the right of succession to the English crown. She therefore determined forthwith and most publicly to nail this lie to the counter. Having summoned Darnley to the lying-in chamber, she presented to him the child before those assembled, saying: "My Lord, God has given you and me a son whose paternity is of none but you."

Darnley was embarrassed, for no one had done more than he, with his jealous loquacity, to spread dishonouring reports about Mary. How was he to respond to his wife's solemn announcement? To hide his shame, he bent over the infant and kissed it.

Mary, fondly taking the baby boy in her arms and uncovering his face, presented him once more to her husband with the words: "My Lord, here I protest to God, and as I shall answer to Him at the great day of judgment, this is your son, and no other man's son; and I am desirous that all here, both ladies and others, bear witness, for he is so much your son that I fear it may be worse for him hereafter."

This was a great and solemn asseveration, and at the same time a strange dread to utter. Even in so weighty an hour, the mortified wife could not conceal her mistrust of Darnley. She could not forget how much he had disappointed and wounded her. After these remarkable words, the queen turned to Sir William Standen, saying: "This is the Prince who I hope shall first unite the two kingdoms of England and Scotland."

With some surprise, Sir William answered: "Why, Madam, shall he succeed before Your Majesty and his father?"

"Alas!" said Mary with a sigh, "his father has broken to me."

Darnley, thus openly shamed, tried to console his wife, and inquired uneasily: "Sweet Madam, is this your promise that you made to forgive and forget all?"

"I have forgiven all," rejoined Mary, "but can never forget."

After a pause she went on: "What if Faudonside's pistol had shot? What would have become of him and me both? Or what estate would you have been in? God only knows, but we may suspect."

"Madam," answered Darnley, "these things are all past."

"Then," said Mary, "let them go."

That was the end of the conversation, in which words like lightning-flashes showed that a storm was brewing. Mary had said no more than half the truth when she declared that she had forgiven though she could not forget. She was not the woman to forgive such an outrage. There would never again be peace in this castle or in this country until blood had atoned for blood, and violence had been requited with violence.

Hardly had the mother been delivered of her babe, between nine and ten in the morning, when Sir James Melville, as always the queen's most faithful emissary, set forth to convey the tidings to London. He received instructions, as he relates in his memoirs, "to post with diligence the 19th day of June, in the year 1566, between ten and eleven before noon. It struck twelve when I took my horse, and I was at Berwick the same night." This was riding post-haste indeed, to cover two days' journey in half a day, for the customary first halt on the way to London was at Dunbar. He continued with the same express speed. "The fourth day after, I was in London." There he was informed that the queer was dancing at Greenwich, so, calling for a fresh horse, he hastened thither in order to convey his great news the same night.

Elizabeth, convalescent from a long and dangerous illness, was rejoicing in the recovery of her strength. Lively, animated, raddled, and powdered, she looked, in her bell-shaped skirt, like a great tulip amid the circle of her admiring courtiers. Secretary Cecil, with Melville at his heels, made his way through the throng of dancers to the queen, and whispered in her ear that Mary Stuart had given birth to a son.

In general, as sovereign, Elizabeth was a skilful diplomatist, self-controlled, practised in the art of hiding her true feelings. But this news struck at the woman in her, pierced her like a dagger. For a moment she lost the mastery over her rebellious nerves. So overwhelming was her consternation that her angry eyes and her tight-pressed lips forgot to dissemble. Her face grew rigid; she flushed beneath her make-up; her hands closed convulsively. She ordered the musicians to cease playing; the dance was suddenly stopped; the queen hurried out of the ballroom. Having reached her bedchamber, when she was surrounded by her agitated ladies-in-waiting, she broke down completely, bursting into tears, collapsing on to a chair, and sobbing out: "The Queen of Scotland is mother of a fair son, whereas I am but a barren stock."

At no moment during the seventy years of her life was the profound tragedy of her unhappy career more plainly revealed; never did she disclose more openly how stricken to the heart she was by her incapacity for love's fruition. The bitter awareness of her infertility found vent in the exclamation that burst from the depths of her heart. One feels that she would have given all the kingdoms of this world for a simple, clear, and natural happiness—for the happiness of being wholly woman, wholly beloved, wife and mother. Despite Elizabeth's jealousy she could have forgiven Mary everything but this. To her, who could be neither wife nor mother, it was unpardonable that Mary should be both.

Next morning, however, she was once more wholly the queen, the politician, the diplomatist. Splendidly did she apply the art in which she was practised, the art of concealing discontent and sorrow behind cold and majestic phrases. When Sir James returned to Greenwich by boat next morning to pay his respects to Her Majesty, he was received by a woman who "had got to show a glad countenance, was clad in her best apparel, and said 'that the joyful news of the Queen her sister's delivery of a fair son, which I had sent unto her by Mr. Cecil, had delivered her out of a heavy sickness which had holden her fifteen days.' Therefore she welcomed me with a merry volt, and thanked me for the diligence I had used." She begged the Scottish envoy to convey her most heartfelt congratulations to Mary, renewed her pledge to become the child's godmother, and, if possible, to be present at the baptism. For the very reason that Elizabeth grudged Mary her good fortune, she wished—always the play-actress eager to convince the audience of her own greatness—to appear before the world as a magnanimous patroness.

Everything seemed to have been admirably settled, and the omens pointed to peace and friendship. On the one hand, it would be impossible for Elizabeth to contest this male heir's twofold claim to the English succession; and, on the other hand, the certainty that her little son would in due time become King of England would bridle Mary Stuart's impatience for the English crown. Once more the clouds which had from the first hovered over Mary Stuart's destiny seem to have been happily dispelled; but, as had happened again and again, when life was prepared to give her peace and happiness, her own inmost nature drove her to fashion unrest for herself. A destiny does not acquire meaning and form from the chance happenings of the outer world; "character is destiny"; it is invariably the innate and primal laws of being that shape a life to high issues or destroy it.

CHAPTER TEN

A Terrible Entanglement

(JULY TO CHRISTMAS 1566)

IN THE tragedy of Mary Stuart the birth of her son signified the close of the first act. Only with the opening of the second act did the situation assume a thoroughly dramatic character, aquake with internal dissensions and uncertainties. New characters appeared on the stage; the play was performed in a changed theatre; the tragedy became personal instead of political. Hitherto Mary had had to contend, somewhat ineffectively, against the rebels in her own country and against her enemies across the border; but now new powers had accrued to her, which made her mightier than all the Scottish lords put together. Simultaneously, however, her own senses rose in revolt, so that the woman in her warred against the queen. For the first time the fervour of her blood gained precedence over the will-to-power. With the levity of passion, the awakened woman destroyed what the monarch had sedulously preserved. In an ecstasy of love scarcely paralleled in history, forgetting every other claim, she flung herself recklessly into an abyss, dragging down with her honour, law, morals, crown, and country—displaying characteristics which no one had suspected in her, whether in the diligent and worthy princess or as the woman who (Queen-Dowager of France as well as Queen of Scotland and the Isles) seemed to be indifferently awaiting the course of events. During the year that ensued Mary increased the dramatic intensity of her life a thousandfold, and in this one year she shipwrecked her existence.

At the opening of the second act, Darnley appeared once more on the scene, likewise modified, and in tragical lineaments. He was alone, uncompanioned, for no one could have confidence in the man who had so shamelessly betrayed his confederates. The ambitious youth was embittered and full of impotent wrath. Having done the utmost a man can do for a woman, he expected, in return, on Mary's part, gratitude, self-sacrifice, and perhaps even love. Instead, his wife, who no longer needed him, showed him nothing but repulsion. She was inexorable. The alarmed conspirators, wishing to take vengeance on Darnley, had, on the sly, confided to Mary the bond he had signed with them before Rizzio's murder. This proof of her husband's complicity did not disclose to Mary anything she had not already guessed, but it confirmed her in her disdain for Darnley's treachery and cowardice, so that she found it hard to forgive herself because her fancy had been ensnared by a man who was as worthless as he was handsome. Her detestation of him was, in part, a detestation of her own mistake. Darnley had become as loathsome to her as some horrid and venomous creature which one cannot bear to touch and, least of all, admit to the familiarities of conjugal intimacy. She could not endure breathing the same air as her husband; his proximity was as oppressive to her as a nightmare. But one thought monopolized her by day and by night: how to get rid of him, how to free herself from a position which had become intolerable.

This notion of freeing herself from Darnley was not, to begin with, overshadowed by the wish-dream of a deed of violence. Mary Stuart's trouble was not peculiar to herself. Like thousands of other women, after a brief period of marriage she felt profoundly disappointed in her husband; so gravely disappointed that the man was now a stranger to her, with the result that the thought of his embraces and even of less intimate association with him had become insufferable. In such instances divorce seems the obvious and logical way out of the difficulty, and Mary discussed the possibility with Moray and Lethington. They pointed out to her that a divorce so soon after the birth of her child would be likely to lead to widespread gossip about her relations with Rizzio, so that ill-natured tongues innumerable would proclaim her child a bastard. It would, they declared, damage James's title to the throne if his name were spotted by scandal, and therefore the queen, at all costs to herself, must refrain from trying to divorce her husband.

Well, there was another possibility. While continuing to refuse herself to Darnley as a wife in the full sense of the term, Mary might keep up appearances. The pair could live together in the eyes of the world as king and queen, while leaving one another free as far as their private lives were concerned. Evidence that Mary considered this way out is furnished by the report of a conversation with Darnley in which she suggested his taking a mistress—if possible the Countess of Moray, wife of Darnley's chief enemy. Although the proposal was made jestingly, it was seriously intended by Mary to show her husband that she would not be mortified by his seeking sexual gratification elsewhere. Unfortunately for her scheme, however, Darnley was in thrall, and wished for no other woman in the world than his proud and strong wife. He was crazy to possess her once more, perpetually demanding the restoration of his conjugal rights; and the more ardently he wooed her, the more scornfully and decisively did she repel his advances. Her coldness, her aversion, served only to increase his ardour. Again and again he returned to the charge, giving her ever fresh reason to deplore the haste with which in the eyes of law and religion she had conceded a husband's privileges to this graceless young man, whom she now abhorred, and to whom she was irrevocably bound.

In this cruel situation Mary Stuart did what human beings are so apt to do in such circumstances. She evaded decision, refrained from open combat, and took refuge in flight. Almost all her biographers have declared it incomprehensible that she did not take a longer rest after giving birth to her child, but in four weeks forsook both castle and baby in order to take boat to Alloa, one of the estates of the Earl of Mar. In reality this flight is perfectly explicable. By the time her little James was four weeks old, an end had come to the period during which, without some special pretext, she could refuse to give herself to her unloved husband. Darnley would, without any breach of ordinary conventions, become more and more importunate. Day after day, night after night, he would clamour to possess her, and she could not endure to accept as a lover the husband whom she had ceased to love. What could be more natural, then, than that she should run away from him, to place between herself and him a distance which would free her mind while freeing her body? Through the ensuing weeks and months, during the whole of the summer and far on into autumn, she saved herself by renewed flight, wandering from castle to castle, from hunting-lodge to hunting-lodge. If in these circumstances she did her best to amuse herself, if in Alloa and elsewhere Mary Stuart, who was not yet twenty-four years of age, thoroughly enjoyed herself whenever she could, reviving the masked balls and other entertainments of Chastelard's and Rizzio's days, if, unteachable as ever, she killed time merrily—this only shows with what rash nonchalance she could thrust the memory of unhappy experiences away from her. Once Darnley made a timid attempt to assert his position. He rode over to Alloa, but was brusquely received, and was not invited to stay the night. Mary had done with him. Her feeling for him had burned up and died down again like a straw fire. He had been no more than one of those blunders which one wants to forget as soon as possible; that was what Henry Darnley had become for Mary who in the folly of her love had made him lord of Scotland and lord of her own body.

Darnley no longer counted for her. Even in Moray, her half-brother, although she had been outwardly reconciled to him, her confidence had not been fully restored; and never again would she wholly trust Lethington. Yet she needed someone in whom she could put her trust. Alike as queen and as woman, throughout her life Mary Stuart was consciously and unconsciously in search of the steadfast antipode to her own restless and inconstant nature.

Since Rizzio's death, Bothwell had become the only man on whom she could rely. Strong though he was, life had ruthlessly driven him hither and thither. In youth, during the rebellion of the Scottish lords, he was exiled because he refused to make common cause with them. Though he was a Protestant, he was loyal to Mary of Guise, defending her against the Lords of the Congregation, and continuing to resist them when the cause of the Catholic Stuarts seemed lost. In the end, however, he had had to flee the country. In France he was appointed commanding officer of the Scottish lifeguards, and while he held this honourable position at court, some of his asperities were smoothed off without any diminution in the elemental energy of his nature. Bothwell was too much the warrior to be content with a sinecure. As soon as James Stuart, his deadly enemy, turned against the queen, he sailed across the sea to battle for the daughter of the House of Stuart. Whenever, thereafter, Mary needed a stout helper against her intriguing subjects, Bothwell was ready to man the breach. On the night of

Rizzio's murder, he jumped out of a first-story window in order to fetch help; his boldness and circumspection rendered the queen's flight possible; his military renown was so alarming to the conspirators that they hastened to capitulate. No one in Scotland had hitherto done Mary such excellent service as this sturdy soldier, who was now about thirty years of age.

Bothwell produces the impression of a figure hewn out of black marble. Like Colleoni, the great condottiere, his Italian prototype of a century before, he looked coolly and challengingly athwart the times in which he lived, a man through and through, with all the harshness and brutality of overpowering virility. His family name of Hepburn had for centuries been honoured in Scotland, but one might rather have thought him of Viking or Norman stock, sprung from those untamable sea-reivers. Though a man of fair education, who could speak excellent French and had a taste for collecting books, he was full of the swashbuckling spirit of a born rebel against peaceful civic order, retaining the adventurousness of all outlaws, of such men as Byron's Corsair. Tall, broad-shouldered, of exceptional bodily strength, equally skilled with the broadsword and the rapier, and able to steer a ship through a storm at sea, his confidence in his own powers gave him great moral (or rather unmoral) valour. He was afraid of nothing, and the law of the stronger was the only law by which he would abide—the law that would enable him to seize ruthlessly and to defend what he had grasped. But this predatoriness of his had nothing in common with the petty brawls and calculations of the other Scottish lords, whom he, ever heedless, despised, because they always assembled in large numbers for their raids and carried these out under cover of darkness. He would league himself with no man, taking his course arrogantly and challengingly in defiance of laws and customs, striking down with the mailed fist any who got in his way. Unconcernedly he did whatever he liked, permissible or unpermissible, in broad daylight. Yet for all his violence, for all his disregard of established standards (such as there were, in those days), and though he was so completely amoral, Bothwell had the merit of straightforwardness. Amid his peers, whose characters were so untrustworthy and whose actions were so ambiguous, he stands out like a beast of prey, fierce and yet royal, a panther or a lion amid slinking wolves and hyenas. Not a moral, not a humane figure, but at least a man, such as man was in the prime.

For this reason, other men hated and feared him, but his frank brutality gave him extraordinary power over women. We hardly know whether this ravager of women was handsome. Such portraits of him as have come down to us are unsatisfactory. But from these, and from such descriptions as we have of him, we cannot but think of him as he might have been painted by Franz Hals, and of that Dutch artist's "Laughing Cavalier"—a young and bold warrior, with his hat jauntily cocked over one eye, and ready to stare everyone out of countenance. Some describe James Hepburn, Earl of Bothwell, as ill-favoured. But a man need not be handsome in order to win the favour of women. The aura of virility that radiates from these forcible personalities, their arrogant savagery, their ruthless violence, their atmosphere of war and victory, radiate sensual seduction. Women are apt to fall passionately in love with a man whom they simultaneously fear and admire, one who arouses in them a sense of horror and peril which exerts a mysterious lure. When such a being is not merely ultra-masculine, a bull-like and savage male animal, but is also, as was Bothwell, courtly and cultured, shrewd and adroit, he becomes irresistible. Wherever he went, this adventurer, seemingly without effort, made conquests among the fair sex. At the French court his amours were notorious; in Mary Stuart's own circle he enjoyed the favour of one of her ladies-in-waiting; in Denmark, for his sake, a woman left her husband and her property. Yet, these triumphs notwithstanding, Bothwell was far from being a typical seducer, a Don Juan, a woman-hunter, for he did not seriously hunt women. Since he was a man of fighting temperament, his victories in this field came too easily and with too little risk. Bothwell took possession of women as his Viking ancestors had done; they were but casual booty, which came his way in the intervals between carousing and gaming, between riding and fighting; and he accepted the conquests willingly enough as earnest of his powers in the manliest of all manly sports. He took women, but he did not give himself to them. He took them because forcible seizure was the most natural expression of his will-to-power.

At first Mary Stuart paid no heed to the man in Bothwell, who was for her but one among her more trusty vassals. Just as little did Bothwell see in the queen a young and desirable woman. With his usual bluntness and unrestraint he had openly commented on her appearance in an unseemly manner, saying: "She and Elizabeth rolled together would not suffice to make one proper woman." They showed no erotic leaning towards one another. At one time, indeed, the queen had been inclined to forbid Bothwell's return to Scotland, having heard that he had spread impudent rumours about her while in France; but as soon as she had had experience of his valour and skill as a soldier, she was glad to rely on him. One mark of favour followed another. He was appointed Lieutenant of the Border and, as previously said, was confirmed in his hereditary position as Lord Admiral of Scotland. He also became commander-in-chief of the forces in the event of war or rebellion. The escheated lands of the outlawed rebels were transferred to him; and, as a special mark of friendliness, the queen herself chose a wife for him, Lady Jane Gordon, sister of Mary's faithful counsellor, the Earl of Huntly. There could not be a better proof of the fact that at this juncture there was no love-affair between Bothwell and Queen Mary.

A man of so commanding a nature as Bothwell is given power or wrests it to himself. Soon Bothwell had become the queen's chief adviser, the real ruler of the Scottish realm. The English ambassador reported with annoyance: "His influence with the Queen excels that of all others." This time Mary had made a sound choice. At length she had discovered a viceroy or chief minister who was too proud to accept bribes from Elizabeth or to traffic with the other Scottish lords to secure trifling advantages. Having this doughty soldier as her loyal servant, she could maintain the upper hand in her own country. Ere long the nobles realized how much the queen's authority had been strengthened through Bothwell's military dictatorship. They complained: "His arrogance is so great that he is hated more than David ever was." They would have been glad to clear him out of the way. But Bothwell was not a Rizzio to allow himself to be butchered unresistingly, nor a Darnley who could simply be thrust aside. Familiar with the amiable little ways of the Scottish lords, he was always attended by a strong body-guard, and at a nod from him the borderers would have risen to support him. Little did he care whether court intriguers loved him or hated him. Enough that they should fear him and that, so long as his sword was ready to his hand, the unruly rabble of his peers would not dare to lay a hand on the queen. At Mary's express desire, his bitterest enemy, Moray, had been reconciled to him; therewith the ring of power had been closed, the weights duly balanced. Mary Stuart, now that her position was safeguarded by Bothwell, was contented with a purely representative position; Moray continued to preside over the conduct of home affairs, while Lethington had diplomatic matters in charge. For the first time since Mary had been queen, order and peace were re-established in Scotland. One man worthy of the name had worked this miracle.

The more power became concentrated in Bothwell's hard hands, the less remained to wield for him to whom authority rightly accrued, the king. By degrees this little shrank to a mere name, to nothing at all. No more than a year had passed, but how distant seemed the days of the young queen's passion for Darnley, when he had been acclaimed king and, in glittering harness, had ridden forth to do battle against the rebels. Now, after the birth of his son, when he had done his duty by his wife and the kingdom, the unhappy man found himself thrust into the background and despised. He might speak, but no one listened; he might go whithersoever he pleased, but unaccompanied. He was not summoned to the council nor invited to festivities, and he grew desperately lonely. In all directions he sensed scorn and hatred. A stranger, a foe, he stood among foes in his own country, in his own house.

This complete eclipse of Darnley, this sudden change from hot to cold, may have been explicable on the ground of the spiritual change that had occurred in his wife; but her open manifestation of contempt for him was a political move, and a political folly. Reason should have taught Mary to leave this vain and ambitious young man at least a semblance of power and prestige, and not to expose him as cruelly as she did to the ruthless disdain of the Scottish lords. Such mortifications may make even a weakling strong and hard. Darnley, who had hitherto been a mere fool, grew by degrees malicious and dangerous. He could no longer restrain his wrath. When, attended by armed guards (he had learned caution since Rizzio's murder), he rode forth on prolonged hunting expeditions, his guests would hear him utter open threats against Moray and many other Scottish lords. On his own initiative he wrote diplomatic dispatches to foreign potentates, describing his wife as "unsteadfast in the faith," and offering himself to Philip II as the true defender of Catholicism. He considered that, as the great-grandson of Henry VII, he was entitled to his share of royal power; and, however soft and yielding his youthful spirit, from time to time a determination to assert his honour flickered in the depths. In truth we are not entitled to term this unhappy man dishonourable, but only to speak of him as a weakling; and it seems probable that Darnley was led into despicable paths by perverted ambition, by an irritable self-assertive impulse. At length, the bow having been stretched too tightly, he formed a desperate resolve. At the end of September he rode from Holyrood to Glasgow, having openly proclaimed his intention to leave Scotland for foreign parts. He would no longer fritter away his time in the northern realm. He had been refused the powers which rightly belonged to him as king. So be it; he cared nothing for the empty title. He was given no task worth performing in the Scottish kingdom, so he would go elsewhere. At his command a ship was made ready on the Clyde, and preparations were pushed forward for departure.

What did Darnley mean by this singular threat? Had some warning already reached his ears? Had he been given a hint that a plot against him was in the wind; and had he decided, feeling incapable of defending himself against his enemies, to flee to some region where he would be beyond the reach of poison or dirk? Was he tortured by suspicion or hunted by dread? Or was he merely showing off, making a diplomatic gesture of defiance, in order to alarm Mary Stuart? Between these various possibilities it is impossible to decide, all the more seeing that mixed feelings are usually at work in every resolve, so that each of the hypotheses may be partially true. For here, when we have to penetrate the shadowy depths of the heart, historical lights grow dim. Only with caution, groping one's way, guided by suppositions, can one venture farther into the labyrinth.

This much is certain, that Mary was greatly alarmed by the tidings of Darnley's intended departure. A deadly blow would be inflicted on her reputation if the father of her child were to quit the kingdom before the formal celebration of little James's baptism. It would be particularly dangerous now, so soon after the Rizzio scandal. The stupid young fellow might work her infinite mischief by giving his tongue free rein at the court of Catherine de' Medici or at that of Elizabeth Tudor. What a triumph it would be for her two rivals, how it would hold her up to the mockery of the world, if the husband she had so passionately loved were thus to divorce himself from her bed and board! Hastily she summoned her council of State; and, to get ahead of Darnley, she penned a diplomatic dispatch to Catherine de' Medici declaring herself innocent of any wrongdoing against the fugitive. "Il veult estre tout et commander partout, à la fin il se mest en ung chemin pour estre rien."

But the alarm was premature, for Darnley did not set sail. He could find strength for a bold gesture, but not for a bold deed. On September 29, 1566, the very day on which the lords of the council sent their warning missive to Paris, Darnley turned up in Edinburgh, at ten o'clock in the evening, in front of the palace of Holyrood. Yet he refused to enter the building so long as any of the lords of the council remained there, another instance of childish and scarcely explicable behaviour. Did he dread sharing the fate of Rizzio? Was it only from caution that he refused to enter the palace so long as he knew his enemies to be there? Or did the humiliated man wish to be publicly begged by Mary to come home again? Had he perhaps only paid this visit in order to discover what effect his threat of flight from Scotland had produced? Here we are faced by a mystery, as almost always where Darnley's behaviour and fate are concerned.

Mary speedily made up her mind. She had learned the use of a special technique in her dealings with her husband when he wanted to play the lord and master or the rebel. She knew that, just as on the night after Rizzio's murder, she must quickly undermine his willpower before, in his youthful stubbornness, he could work mischief. Away, then, with moral considerations, with prudery or other niceties of feeling! Once more she played the yielding wife. To mould him to her will, she did not shun extreme measures. Dismissing the lords of the council, she went out to Darnley, who was defiantly waiting outside the door, and led him, not only into the palace, but presumably, into Circe's Island, into her own bedroom. And lo! the charm worked, as it had done before, and would always work with this youth who was a slave to his passion for her. Next morning he had been tamed, and was once more in leading-strings.

But, just as on the night after Rizzio's murder, the man thus befooled had to pay the price for his folly. Darnley, again believing himself lord and master, unexpectedly encountered in the reception-room the French ambassador and the lords of the council. Mary, like her "dear sister" Elizabeth in the matter of the Moray comedy, had provided timely witnesses. In their presence she loudly and urgently inquired of Darnley, "for God's sake," to tell her why he wanted to leave Scotland, and whether anything in her conduct had given occasion for such a step. This was an unpleasant surprise for Darnley, who had a moment before believed himself lover and beloved, and now had to appear as an accused person before the lords of the council and the French ambassador, du Croc. He stood there moodily, this tall young fellow, with his pale, beardless boyish countenance. Had he been a true man, had he had any grit in him, now would have been the moment to show it. Masterfully he should have stated his grievances, presenting himself before his subjects and his wife, not as accused, but as accuser and king. But one who has a "heart of wax" does not venture to resist. Like a criminal caught in the act, like a schoolboy who is being scolded and is afraid of bursting into tears, Darnley stood in the great hall, biting his lips, and maintaining an impenetrable silence. He gave no answer. He made no accusation, but neither did he excuse himself. Now the lords of the council, who found this silence of his embarrassing, addressed him courteously, asking him how he could forsake "so beautiful a queen and so noble a realm." In vain! Darnley would not answer. This defiant and menacing silence grew more and more oppressive to the assembly. Obviously the unfortunate wight was finding it hard to restrain himself, and it would have been a terrible scene for Mary Stuart if he had found energy to persist in his accusatory silence. But now Darnley grew weak. When du Croc and the lords plied him persistently "avec beaucoup de propos," he at length reluctantly acknowledged that nothing in his wife's conduct had given him occasion for the intended journey. This admission, which put Darnley in the wrong, was all that Mary wished. Her reputation had been established before the French ambassador. She could smile once more and, with a final wave of her hand, show herself thoroughly satisfied with Darnley's declaration ("qu'elle se contentait").

But Darnley was by no means satisfied. His gorge rose because he had again been outwitted by this Delilah, because he had been lured from the bulwarks of his silence. Immeasurable must have been the torment of the man thus befooled when, with a magnanimous gesture, the great actress "forgave" her husband the king before the foreign envoys, whereas he probably had ground for playing the accuser. Too late did he recover his poise. Abruptly he broke off the conversation. Without a courtly farewell to the lords of the council, without embracing his wife, stiff as a herald who had issued a declaration of war, he quitted the room. His only words as he departed were: "Madam, you are not likely to see me again for a long time." But the lords and Mary Stuart smiled and drew a deep breath of relief when the "proud fool" who had come full of brazen impudence now went away with hanging head. His threats no longer alarmed anybody. Let him stay away as long as he liked, and the farther away the better, both for him and for others.

Nevertheless, the man whom no one seemed to want was needed after all. He was urgently summoned home. After a long postponement the formal baptism of the young prince had been fixed for December 17, 1566, at Stirling Castle. Imposing preparations had been made. Elizabeth, who was to be godmother, would not indeed be present. Throughout life she carefully avoided meeting Mary Stuart. The English queen, however, overcoming her notorious avarice, had sent a costly gift by the Earl of Bedford, a massive silver font, richly gilt. The French, Spanish, and Savoyard ambassadors were also on hand; nor would any member of the Scottish nobility who was of note absent himself from the ceremonial. On so representative an occasion, it would have been most unseemly to exclude Henry Darnley, who, however unimportant personally, was the father of the child and the nominal king of the country. But Darnley, who knew that this was the last occasion on which he would be needed, was not so readily to be snared. He had had his fill of public life, had been informed that the English ambassador was instructed to refuse him the title of "Your Majesty," while the French ambassador, on whom he called, sent down an amazingly presumptuous message announcing his intention of walking out of one door of the room when Darnley entered the other. At length the worm turned, although even now, when his vanity had been pricked, he could manage nothing better than a childishly malicious gesture. Still, the gesture was effective. Darnley came to Stirling Castle but kept in retirement there. He made his demonstration by confining himself to his apartments, neither participating at the baptism of his son nor attending dances and masques. Instead of Darnley, Bothwell, the new favourite, splendidly attired, received the guests. From time to time murmurs of impatience were heard among them, and Mary had to outdo herself in friendliness and cheerfulness lest the skeleton in the household should become too obvious, lest the lord and master, the father and the husband, in his barred chamber on the upper story, should succeed in completely spoiling the festal mood of his wife and her friends. Once more he had shown—by keeping out of the way—that he was still on hand, thus reminding people effectively of his existence.

But the rod was already in pickle to punish him for his boylike mutiny. A few days later, at Christmas Eve, it struck. The unexpected happened. Mary Stuart, who had been so unconciliatory, decided, upon Moray's and Bothwell's advice, to pardon the murderers of Rizzio. Therewith Darnley's worst enemies, the conspirators whom he had betrayed, were recalled to Scotland. Darnley, however stupid he might be, could not fail to recognize that this put him in mortal danger. If the clique of Moray, Lethington, Bothwell, and Morton should be re-formed, the hunt would be up, so far as he was concerned—a hunt of which he would be the quarry. There must be some hidden significance when his wife came to terms with the assassins, and a price which he by no means wanted to pay.

Like a beast with bloodhounds on its trail, Darnley fled from Stirling Castle to join his father in Glasgow. Not ten months had yet elapsed since Rizzio's death and burial, yet his murderers were again fraternizing, and something sinister was imminent. The dead do not like to sleep alone; they always demand companions in the tomb, and always they send fear and horror as heralds.

In truth something dark and heavy and ominous seemed to have been brooding over Holyrood for the last few weeks, something as chill and depressing as a north-east wind. That evening of the baptism at Stirling, when hundreds of candles were lighted to show the strangers the splendours of the Scottish court, and to welcome the friends who had come from afar, Mary Stuart, who for brief spaces of time could master her will, had summoned all her energies. Her eyes flashed with simulated happiness; she charmed the guests by her merriment and cordiality; but hardly had the lights been extinguished when her feigned cheerfulness came to an end. Now, at Holyrood, it was cruelly quiet, and yet more cruelly quiet in the depths of her soul. The queen was seized by an inscrutable melancholy foreign to her temperament. Her face was shadowed, and she seemed profoundly disturbed. She no longer danced, no longer called for music. Moreover, since her ride to Jedburgh, at the end of which she had been lifted from her horse half-dead with fatigue, she had never fully recovered. She complained of pains in the side, stayed day after day in bed, and shunned all scenes of merriment. She would not stay long at Holyrood, but moved on week after week, for brief sojourns at one castle after another, driven by a terrible unrest. Some disturbing element was at work in her, and she seemed to be listening with tense curiosity to the working of that which was painfully burrowing within her. Something new, something hostile, had gained ascendancy over her usually sunny temperament. Once the French ambassador found her lying on her bed, sobbing bitterly. The experienced old man was not deceived when, ashamed at being detected in tears, she began to talk of the pain in her left side which had made her weep. He recognized at once that her troubles were spiritual and not bodily, the troubles, not of a queen, but of an unhappy woman. "The Queen is not well," reported du Croc to Paris, "but I think the real cause of her illness is a sorrow which she cannot forget. Again and again she says: 'Oh that I could die!'"

Moray, Lethington, and the Scottish lords in general did not fail to see that their sovereign was in a gloomy mood. Still, being better trained in the art of war than in the science of psychology, they could see no cause for her trouble but the obvious one of her connubial disappointment. "She finds it intolerable," wrote Lethington, "that he should be her husband, and that there is no way in which she could be rid of him." Du Croc, however, old and wise, had spoken truth when he referred to "a sorrow which she cannot forget." An inward and invisible wound of the spirit was torturing her. The sorrow she could not forget was sorrow that she had forgotten herself and her honour. Sorrow that she had disobeyed law and custom, that a passion had suddenly seized her like a beast of prey, and was now gnawing at her entrails, an immeasurable, unquenchable passion, beginning as a crime and from which she could be freed only by further and yet further crimes. Now, in her alarm, filled with shame and self-torment, she was striving to hide this terrible secret from herself and the world, though she could not fail to know that to hide it was impossible. Already she was subject to a stronger will than her conscious will; she no longer belonged to herself, but only to her passion.

CHAPTER ELEVEN

The Tragedy of a Passion

(1566–1567)

MARY STUART'S passion for Bothwell was one of the most notable in history. Those devouring loves of classical antiquity that have become proverbial hardly excel it in frantic intensity. It shot skyward like a sheet of flame into ecstasy; its ardours spewed themselves forth into crime. When mental states are thus intensified, it is foolish to scrutinize for logic and rationality the actions of those in whom they rage, since it is of the essence of uncontrollable impulses to be irrational. Passions, like illnesses, can neither be accused nor excused; they can only be described with ever-renewed astonishment not untinged with horror in face of the elemental forces which disclose themselves from time to time in nature and not infrequently in human beings, violent discharges of energy which are not amenable to the measuring-rod of customary human laws. Their expression does not belong to the realm of the conscious, but to the subconscious impulses of man, and is quite outside the circle of his personal responsibility. It is just as senseless to sit in judgment upon an individual who happens momentarily to be a prey to an overwhelming passion as it would be to call a thunderstorm to account or wish to hold an assize upon the eruption of a volcano. So Mary Stuart, a product of her epoch both in the mental and the moral sphere, must not be condemned out of hand, seeing that her actions were temporarily governed by something irrespective of her normal and hitherto moderate and sedate outlook on life. With eyes closed and ears stopped, drawn as it were by a magnet, she moved along her path towards disaster and crime. No advice could influence her, no call could awaken her. Not until the fires had burned themselves out would she come to her senses, consumed and distraught.

In one who has passed through such a furnace, life itself has been incinerated.

So massive a feeling cannot take hold of a person twice in the same lifetime. Just as an accumulated store of gunpowder goes up in one huge explosion, so in such an overwhelming passion are the reserves of emotion completely expended. Mary Stuart's voluptuousness glowed at white heat for no more than half a year. Nevertheless, during this brief space her heart knew such an ecstasy that all subsequent feelings appeared to her as wraiths in a mist. Certain writers, such as Rimbaud, and certain musicians, such as Mascagni, spend themselves in a single work, and when this work is finished they lie exhausted and impotent for ever more: thus is it, too, with certain women who give their all in one access of passion, instead of spreading their love, as do more moderate natures, economically over decade after decade. Such women's love and passion is a concentrated extract, their ardours are compressed into one convulsive episode, they drink the cup to the dregs, and for them there exists no salvation and no way back. Mary Stuart was a supreme example of this kind of love, of love that is spendthrift because it despises contumely and death, of love that is truly heroic, that allows passion to have its fullest range and to exhaust the emotions even should this lead to self-destruction.

At a first glance one may well be puzzled to account for so speedy a transformation of her affection for Darnley into her elemental passion for Bothwell. Yet such a development was both logical and natural; for, like every other art, love needs to be learned, tested, and practised. Never, or rarely—as with the arts—is the first essay in love a perfect success; and Shakespeare, the profoundest psychologist of all time, knew this well, showing that calf-love is merely a tentative and initial stage to the real passion which may flame up on a day to come. One of the most admirable touches in his immortal tragedy of love is that he did not, as any lesser artist or expert judge of the human soul might have done, allow Romeo's infatuation for Juliet to begin without a prelude, but that he made it arise as a sequel to an earlier amour for some Rosalind or the other. A fugitive and stray feeling is swept away by genuine passion; there is a prentice introduction, half unwitting, to the conscious artistry of the artist in love.

Shakespeare shows in this splendid instance that there can be no full knowledge without foreboding, no wholehearted pleasure without a preliminary sojourn in the ante-rooms of pleasure, and that, if feeling is to soar into the infinite, it must first have been kindled in a narrow and finite realm. Only because Romeo is already in a state of inward tension, because his strong and passionate spirit craves for fuller experience of passion, does his will-to-love, having directed itself haphazard and blindly towards Rosalind, the first-comer, then, becoming sighted, and fully aware of the difference, direct itself anew and swiftly towards a supreme object, exchanging Rosalind for Juliet. "When half-gods go, the gods arrive."

In like manner Mary Stuart, awakening from the long twilight of her youth, was carried away by a blind affection for Darnley, precisely because he was comely and young and made his entry into her orbit at a propitious hour. But the lad's dull breath was too weak to fan her inward glow. He could not lift her into the paradise of ecstasy, where the glow would have burned itself out. It continued, therefore, like a smoored fire, to excite her senses and nevertheless disappoint them—a distressing condition in which the fires struck inward because their outward expression had been stifled. As soon, however, as he came who had the power to relieve her from this torment, he who gave air and fuel to this stifled glow, the repressed flames rushed up to heaven and down to hell. Just as Romeo's feeling for Rosalind vanished without a trace when his genuine passion for Juliet was aroused, so did Mary Stuart completely forget her sensual inclination for Darnley in the unresting and voluptuous feeling for Bothwell.

We possess two sources of information relating to the story of Mary's love for Bothwell. In the first place there are the State papers and other contemporary official documents, and there are the chronicles and the annals of the time. As second source, we have a number of letters and poems ascribed to her. The recorded facts and the self-revelation of the letters and verses dovetail into one another with the utmost precision. But the genuineness of the letters and poems is denied by those champions of Mary Stuart who, in the name of their own moral codes, believe that they must defend her against a passion against which she herself was quite defenceless. There is, of course, some ground for doubt as to the authenticity of letters and sonnets which have come down to us only in transcribed, translated, and perhaps mutilated texts. The holograph versions, which would have been irrefutable evidence, were destroyed—we know when and by whom. For James, her son, had but shortly succeeded to power when, as a measure of protection for his mother's honour as a woman, he consigned the original papers to the flames. Ever since then an embittered fight has been raging as to the authenticity of these "Casket Letters," a party strife wherein religious motives and national served as foundation for charge and countercharge in the assize upon Mary Stuart. For one who is above party it is all the more essential that he should go warily in his judgments. In any case his conclusions can never be anything more than personal ones, since the original letters have long since been destroyed and, in the last resort therefore, he has to depend upon his individual deductions.

Nevertheless, if a true portrait of Mary is to be drawn, if her real character is to be depicted, an author is bound to decide one way or the other; he must make up his mind to accept these letters and poems as authentic or to declare them spurious. He cannot be allowed merely to shrug his shoulders and mutter: "Maybe they're genuine—and, then again, maybe they're not." For these writings, if authentic, are a pivot whereon the whole subsequent psychical development of the woman turned. If we cast the die in favour of their genuineness, then it behoves us to prove and make perfectly clear the reasons for such an assumption.

As will be subsequently related in fuller detail, the letters and sonnets in question were found in a silver casket after Bothwell's flight from Carberry Hill. It goes without saying that such missives as Mary actually wrote to her lover must have been incautious and compromising. She had always been venturesome, not to say foolhardy, and had never learned to hide her feelings when she spoke or wrote. Next, the huge delight of her adversaries at the discovery of the originals shows that these must have contained revelations injurious or shameful to the queen.

However, those who describe the Casket Letters as forgeries do not go so far as to deny that some such genuine letters may have existed. Their contention is that, during the brief interval between the discovery of the casket and the official examination of the letters, some of the Scottish lords had substituted malicious falsifications for the originals, so that the documents laid before parliament were by no manner of means those discovered in the casket. Who was responsible for this accusation? Nobody in particular. The Scottish lords of council in Edinburgh, immediately the booty had been handed over to Morton, assembled on the selfsame day and solemnly swore to the authenticity of the documents as soon as the casket was opened. Parliament, too, at a later date (and among the members were personal friends of the queen), examined the script carefully and uttered no word of doubt. Subsequently, at the York Conference, they were again overhauled; and for a fourth time, at Hampton Court, they underwent close scrutiny. Each time they were compared with Mary's writing, and each time they were declared authentic and coming from Mary's own hand. More convincing still is it that Elizabeth had the texts printed and circulated among the courts of Europe. Now, although we have many reasons to distrust the actions of the Queen of England, we can hardly credit the assumption that she would compromise her high position by going to the length of forgery, since at any moment discovery was possible. Elizabeth was an able politician, and as such too careful to let herself be caught in a petty snare. The only person who, for repute's sake, should have protested vehemently if the letters and sonnets were forgeries, namely Mary Stuart herself, was content to utter a feeble and quite unconvincing protest. Furthermore, she tried by underground means to hinder their production at the Conference of York. One cannot but ask "why?" if, indeed, the documents were forgeries, seeing that this would have greatly strengthened her position. An additional reason for believing that Mary suspected that her enemies had got hold of the originals is that she commanded her representatives to repudiate wholesale her authorship of everything alleged to be written by her hand, and this before any inquiry had been held. Of course this is not of very great evidential value, for, in political matters, Mary was never a stickler where truth was concerned. Moreover she held that her "parole de prince" was of far greater worth than any amount of proof against her. Even when Buchanan published the letters in his *Detection,* and they were eagerly read at all the courts, Mary raised no cry of protest; she did not then declare them to be "false and feigned, forged and invented" to her "dishonour and slander." She was content to call her sometime Latin master a "defamatory atheist." When writing to the Pope or to the King of France and her other relatives, she never mentioned a word about forgery of her letters and love-verses. Nor was any suggestion of forgery made by the French court, to which transcripts of the letters were sent immediately after their disclosure. Among her contemporaries none cast the shadow of a doubt upon their authenticity, or raised a voice to confute so spiteful an accusation, or mooted the suggestion that fraudulent papers had been slipped into a batch of original ones. It was not for a century or so after James had rid the world of his mother's love-letters and poems that the hypothesis as to their falsification was first propounded, and this in a well-meant endeavour to describe a spirited and impulsive woman as an innocent creature incapable of doing wrong or committing a crime if such a course seemed to her necessary. These kindly souls wish us to believe that Mary was the hapless victim of a base conspiracy.

Unquestionably, the attitude of Mary's contemporaries seems to prove the authenticity of both letters and love-ballads; and in my opinion, when considered from the stylistic and psychological standpoint, the evidence is no less forcible. Take the verses alone. Who was there in the Scotland of that day capable of producing a whole cycle of poems in the French tongue and at such short notice? Did any living person in sixteenth-century Scotland possess such a genius for poetry as not only to reproduce the literary style of the queen but to show so intimate an acquaintance with her hidden thoughts and feelings? No doubt there have been many remarkable forgeries of historical documents and important letters, and in the realm of literature we are acquainted with a number of apocryphal poems and other imaginative compositions; but whether we think here of Macpherson's *Ossian* or of the Königinhof Manuscript, and the like, we are concerned with skilful reproductions of the style of long-past epochs. There is, however, no record of any attempt to palm off a whole sonnet-cycle upon a living author. How absurd to suppose that rough Scottish lairds, barons, and earls, to whom poesy was the most alien thing on earth, would be able, animated by the desire of compromising their queen, to produce eleven sonnets in French. Again, I ask, who was this nameless genius, this magician, who possessed the gift for composing in a foreign tongue a sequence of love-verses so precisely in the style of the queen that the work could be attributed to her pen without raising a doubt in the minds of any of her relatives, her friends, or her contemporaries? Not one of her champions has so far answered this question. Not even Ronsard, not even du Bellay, could have done as much. How ridiculous, then, to ascribe such a talent to the Mortons, the Argylls, the Hamiltons, or the Gordons, who could wield the sword well enough, but did not know French sufficiently to carry on a dinner-table talk.

No unprejudiced person can doubt the genuineness of the poems; and since the style of these sonnets is in perfect harmony with that of the letters, we have to admit that the latter are authentic and were written by Mary herself. Maybe in the course of the translation into Latin and into Scots certain details were doctored, or tampered with, and it is obvious that a few interpolations were made. A final consideration, a psychological one, has to be adduced in favour of the letters being Mary's. If a suppositious "gang of criminals" inspired by hatred and malice had set to work forging letters, would not the forgers have produced documents showing beyond question that the alleged author was a contemptible creature, a lascivious and spiteful wanton? They would have been wasting their pains if, in their desire to injure Mary, they had produced as forgeries the extant Casket Letters, which exculpate her rather than incriminate her, exhibiting as they do Mary's horror at her foreknowledge of and complicity in the intended crime against young Darnley. For what these documents show forth is not the voluptuousness of passion but its bitter distress. The letters are like the muffled cries of one who is being burned alive.

Although, as already said, the letters are in Mary's style, they are rough-hewn. They manifest a wild and confused flow of thought and feeling, were evidently written in haste and disorder by a hand that (one feels) was tremulous with excitement. All these things are fully accordant with what we know from other sources regarding the queen's overstrained mental condition during the days from which they date, and they correspond to the writer's actions at the same period. None but the most skilful of psychologists could have imagined so perfect a spiritual background for the known facts. Moray, Lethington, and Buchanan, who by turns and haphazard, have been mentioned as the forger by professional champions of Mary's honour, were neither Shakespeares nor Balzacs nor Dostoievskys, but little souls, able to finesse and to cheat when trickery would serve their turn, but utterly incompetent, putting pen to paper, to produce word-pictures so admirably representing Mary Stuart for all time. First let the genius who forged these letters be produced! We, who know that Mary in times of stress always poured her heart out in verse, can have no doubt that she composed both letters and poems. This granted, we can have no better testimony than her own as to her state of mind at this juncture.

The verses reveal the beginning of her unfortunate passion. Three or four lines disclose that Mary's love for Bothwell did not arise by a slow process of crystallization, but seized an unsuspecting woman as its prey. The immediate occasion was, apparently, a crude act of bodily possession, an onslaught by Bothwell that was half or wholly rape. In her sonnet the darkness is dispelled by a lightning-flash:

Pour luy aussi, ie gete mainte larme.
Premier quand il se fit de ce corps possesseur,
Du quel alors il n'auoyt pas le cœur.

[Full many a tear have I wept because of him.
The first was shed when he took possession of my body,
Whose heart did not then belong to him.]

Instantly we are made to feel the situation. For weeks Mary had been thrown into close companionship with Bothwell. As chief adviser, and as commander of her armed forces, he had accompanied her from castle to castle. Since she had so recently chosen a beautiful and high-born lady as his wife, and had graced the wedding with her royal presence, it never occurred to her to think of him as a suitor; she was a queen, he, a vassal; her position was inviolable. She could, therefore, travel about her realm with him unconcerned. But some of Mary's most charming qualities, her lack of caution and her sense of security, had always been a danger to her. One can picture the scene. Presumably she had allowed him some trifling liberties, showing towards him that coquetry which twice already had led to disaster, in the cases of Chastelard and of Rizzio. He was alone with her for hours; she talked with him more confidentially than was customary; jested and sported with him. But Bothwell was no Chastelard, no romantic lute-player and languishing troubadour; Bothwell was not a Rizzio, an upstart with a flattering tongue; Bothwell was a man with hot senses and hard muscles, a creature of impulse and instinct, who would not shrink from any audacity. Such a man does not lightly allow himself to be led on and stimulated. Abruptly, he must have seized her, this woman who had long been in a vacillating and irritable state of mind, whose passionate nature had been aroused by her foolish fondness for Darnley—aroused but not assuaged. "Il se fit de ce corps possesseur"; he took her by storm or violated her. Who, at such moments, can distinguish between the two? They are moments of intoxication when a woman's longing to give herself and desire to defend herself interlace. On Bothwell's side the act of possession was probably just as little premeditated as it had been on Mary's. The embrace was not the fulfilment of a tender inclination which had been growing in ardour over a lengthy period of time, but an impulsive act of lust devoid of spiritual tone, a purely physical capture.

The effect on Mary Stuart was overwhelming. Something wholly new invaded her life like a thunder-clap. In taking possession of her body, Bothwell had also raped her soul. Both of her husbands, the fifteen-year-old boy Francis II and the beardless Darnley, had lacked virility; they had been weaklings. In her experience of sexual relations Mary had hitherto bestowed herself magnanimously, to confer pleasure on her partner, remaining mistress and queen even in this intimate sphere; she had never played the passive role, had never been possessed by force. In this encounter with Bothwell, which left her amazed senses tingling with surprise, she came for the first time into close contact with the primitive male, one who trampled upon her femininity, her modesty, her pride, her sense of security; and, therewith, he caused a voluptuous uprush from a universe within herself hitherto unsuspected.

Before she realized the danger and before she even thought of warding it off, she had already been conquered. This taking of her body by storm gave vent to a geyser of feeling—of feeling which, in the first moment of alarm, may have been dominated by wrath, by fierce hatred of the ruffian who had thus brutally ravaged her womanly pride. But it is one of the profoundest mysteries of our composite souls, as we find in external nature, that extremes meet, and especially in the realm of feeling. The skin cannot distinguish between intense heat and intense cold; frost can burn like fire. A woman may pass in one moment from hatred into love, from mortified pride to uttermost humility; she may desire and affirm with all the wealth of her body that which, a moment before, she has repudiated and regarded with loathing.

The upshot in the present case was that, henceforward, a woman who had been tolerably reflective was consumed by an inner fire. What had hitherto been the pillars sustaining her life (honour, dignity, repute, pride, self-confidence, and reason) collapsed. Having once plunged into deep waters, she wished for nothing better than to sink in them. A new and strange voluptuousness seized upon her. Avid and intoxicated, Mary wished to enjoy so novel a sensation at the cost of self-destruction. Humbly she kissed the hand of the man who had annihilated her womanly pride and had taught her the ecstasy of self-surrender.

This passion was something immeasurably vaster than her fondness for Darnley. With Darnley she had played at self-surrender; now it had become deadly earnest. With Darnley she had merely wanted to share the crown, her sovereign authority, her life. To Bothwell she wished to give, not this, that, or the other, but all that she had on earth, impoverishing herself to enrich him, lustfully debasing herself from her high estate in order to uplift him to the skies. With an unwonted thrill, Mary flung aside restraints, that she might seize and hold him who had become for her the only man in the world. She knew that her friends would forsake her, that people in general would revile her and look upon her with contempt. But these realities gave her another pride in place of that which had been shattered, and she enthusiastically proclaimed the fact:

Pour luy depuis iay mesprise l'honneur
Ce qui nous peut seul prouoir de bonheur.
Pour luy iay hasarde grandeur et conscience.
Pour luy tous mes parents i'ay quiste, et amys,
Et tous aultres respects sont apart mis. . . .
Pour luy tous mes amys i'estime moins que rien. . . .
Ie veux pour luy au monde renoncer:
Ie veux mourire pour luy faire auancer. . . .
Pour luy ie veux rechercher la grandeure,
Et faire tant qu'en vray connoistra,
Que ie n'ay bien, heur, ni contentement,
Qu'a l'obeyr et servir loyammant.
Pour luy i'attendz toute bonne fortune.
Pour luy ie veux guarder santé et vie. . . .

[For him since then I have despised honour,
Which alone can provide us with happiness.
For him I have risked dignity and conscience,
For him I have forsaken all my relatives and friends,
And all other considerations have been put aside. . . .
For his sake I have come to regard my friends as less than nothing. . . .
For his sake I would fain renounce the world,
I would gladly die that he might rise. . . .
For him alone I wish to be great,
And I shall so behave that he will recognize
That I have neither wellbeing nor luck nor contentment
Than in obeying and serving him loyally.
I hope for him nothing but good fortune.
For his sake I wish to retain health and life. . . .]

Unduly tensed feelings affect the mind profoundly. Storms of passion liberate unfamiliar and unique energies in women such as Mary, who had hitherto been reserved and indifferent. During these weeks her mental and bodily life seemed multiplied tenfold, and she showed capabilities she had never shown before nor was ever to show again. She spent eighteen hours in the saddle, and then sat up nearly all night writing letters. Though as poetess she had hitherto composed no more than brief epigrams and casual fragments of verse, under the stimulus of fresh inspiration she penned the sonnet cycle in which her pleasures and her pains were manifested with wonderful command of language. Ordinarily incautious, at this time she concealed her sentiments most effectively, with the result that for months none suspected her intimacy with Bothwell. His lightest touch made her senses reel, yet before the eyes of the world she addressed him as calmly as any other subordinate; she preserved a cheerful mien while her nerves were twitching and her mind was filled with despair. A daimonic super-ego took possession of her, lending her a strength which far transcended her natural powers.

But these achievements had to be paid for by a terrible collapse. When this ensued, day after day she remained in bed, utterly exhausted; or else she wandered for hours from room to room in a state of partial stupefaction, sobbing and groaning, exclaiming "je voudrais être morte," clamouring for a knife with which to stab herself. Thus her vitality would wane as strangely as it came to her rescue again.

Nothing can show more plainly than does the famous Jedburgh episode how much her body had been exhausted by the frenzy of passion. On October 7, 1566, in an affray with a border brigand, Bothwell was dangerously wounded. The news reached Mary on her way to the town, where she was about to hold an assize. Though her first impulse was to ride forthwith to Hermitage, twenty-five miles away, she restrained the impulse lest such behaviour should arouse remark. There can be no doubt, however, that she was profoundly distressed by the tidings, for du Croc, the French ambassador (who was the most dispassionate observer in her entourage, and who could not as yet have had an inkling of her liaison with Bothwell), reported to Paris: "Ce ne luy eust esté peu de perte de le perdre." Lethington, too, noticed how absent-minded she was; but, being equally ignorant of the true state of affairs, he opined that her "thought and displeasure had their root in the King."

Not until a week had elapsed and the assize was over did the queen ride over to Hermitage Castle accompanied by Moray and others of her lords. She spent two hours by the wounded man's bedside, and rode back to Jedburgh the same afternoon. On dismounting, she fell into a faint which lasted two hours. Thereafter she was feverish and delirious. Then her body suddenly stiffened; she neither saw nor felt anything. Her courtiers and the doctor stood round, contemplating her with alarm. Messengers were sent in all directions to fetch the king and the bishop—the latter to administer extreme unction. For a week Mary hovered between life and death, since seemingly her secret wish to die had sapped her vital forces. What shows, however, that the collapse was mental rather than physical, that it was, indeed, a characteristic hysterical attack, is the fact that as soon as Bothwell, now regaining health and strength, was brought to Jedburgh in a horse-litter, the queen took a turn for the better and, a fortnight after her suite had supposed her to be dying, she was well enough to be in the saddle once more. Danger had threatened her from within, and from within it had been overcome.

Though restored in body, for the next few weeks the queen was much distraught in mind. Comparative strangers noticed that she had become "a different person." Something in her aspect and her manner underwent modification; her usual levity and self-confidence vanished. Her demeanour was that of one sorely afflicted. She shut herself up in her room, and through the closed door her ladies could hear her sobbing. But though it was her custom to be frank and outspoken, on this occasion she confided in no one. Her lips remained closed, and none guessed the secret which burdened her mind by day and by night

A terrible feature of Mary's infatuation for Bothwell, that which made it at once splendid and gruesome, was that from the first the queen must have known her love to be sinful, and disastrous to the plans she had most at heart. Her awakening from the first embrace must have been like that of Tristan and Iseult from the effects of the love-potion, when they recalled that they were not living by themselves in the infinite realm of love, but were bound to this world by numerous ties and duties. So Mary probably realized her situation. She who had given herself to Bothwell was another man's wife; and Bothwell, another woman's husband. This was a twofold adultery into which the turmoil of the senses had led her. How long was it—two weeks, or three, or four—since she herself, Mary Queen of Scotland and the Isles, had signed and issued an edict declaring adultery and every form of illicit lust to be capital offences? From the outset her insane passion was, therefore, branded as a crime. Having committed a crime, she could save herself from punishment only by further criminal offences. If ever she and Bothwell were to be wedded, she would have forcibly to rid herself of her husband, and Bothwell to divorce his wife. This love-plant could bear none but poisoned fruit. In so desperate a plight, Mary's courage rallied though she realized that she would never again enjoy peace of mind and knew that henceforward she was past saving. As always, her intrepid nature came to her aid, were it no more than an endeavour to try vain hazards and to challenge fate. She refused to draw back like a coward; she would not draw back; she would, with head erect, march forward to the abyss. Though she should lose all, there would be joy in her torment, since she would lose all for her lover's sake.

Entre ses mains et en son plein pouuoir,
Ie metz mon filz, mon honneur, et ma vie,
Mon pais, mes subjects, mon âme assubiectiè
Est toute à luy, et n'ay autre vouloir
Pour mon obiect que sens le disseuoir
Suiure ie veux malgré toute l'enuie
Qu'issir en peult. . . .

[Into his hands and into his full power
I put my son, my honour, and my life,
My country, and my subjects; my subjugated heart
Is his alone; and I have no other wish
In life than, without deceiving him,
To follow him, despite all the troubles
That may result. . . .]

"Despite all the troubles"! Though it be a thousand times a crime she means to follow the path which leads nowhere. Having given herself wholly, body, soul, and destiny, to the man she loved so abjectly, the only thing that remains to be dreaded is that she may lose him.

The most obnoxious feature of her situation, the utmost extremity of her torment, remains to be told. Mad folly notwithstanding, Mary

Stuart was too shrewd not to recognize that she had once more given herself in vain, that the man towards whom her whole being turned did not really love her. Bothwell had possessed her, as he had possessed many another wench, sensually, swiftly, and brutally. He was as ready to leave her in the lurch as he had been ready to leave other women when the hot fit was over. For him, the rape of Mary Stuart had been no more than a passing adventure. In her despairing verses she discloses her knowledge that the man who had worshipped her body for a fleeting moment did not love her mind.

Vous m'estimes legier je le voy,
Et si n'avez en moy nul asseurance,
Et soubçonnes mon cœur sans apparance,
Vous deffiant à trop grande tort de moy.
Vous ignores l'amour que ie vous porte;
Vous soubçonnez qu'autre amour me transporte,
Vous estimes mes parolles du vent,
Vous depeignes de cire mon las cœur
Vous me penses femme sans iugement;
Et tout cela augmente mon ardeur.

[I see that you esteem me inconstant,
And have no faith in me,
And suspect my heart without just cause,
Suspecting me to my own detriment.
You do not realize the love I bear you;
You suspect that another love is carrying me away,
My words you look upon as light as wind,
You picture my tired heart as though of wax,
You think me a woman lacking in judgment,
And all this does but intensify my love.]

Instead of turning away proudly from her unappreciative lover, instead of exercising a modicum of self-control, Mary, carried away as she was by passion, flung herself on her knees before the indifferent Bothwell, in the hope of retaining him. Painful was the way in which her previous arrogance was now replaced by self-abasement. She implored, she supplicated, she extolled her own merits, offering herself to her lover, to the man who would not love her, after the manner of a salesman making the most of his goods. So completely had she lost all sense of personal dignity that she, who had once been queenly and self-reliant, retailed to him like a chaffering market-woman the sacrifices she had made for him, and went on to emphasize her submissiveness.

Car c'est le seul desir de vostre chere amye,
De vous seruir et loyaument aymer,
Et tous malheurs moins que riens estimer,
Et vostre volunté de la mien suiure.
Vous conoistres avecques obeissance
De mon loyal deuoir n'omettant la science
A quoy i'estudiray pour tousiours vous complaire
Sans aymer rien que vous, soubs la suiection
De qui ie veux sens nulle fiction
Viure et mourir. . . .

[For it is your beloved's sole desire,
To serve you and love you faithfully,
And to count all misfortunes as less than nothing,
And to place your will before mine own.
You will know how obediently
Never forgetting my duty
I shall study to please you always
Loving none but you, under whose guidance
I wish, without any reserves
To live and die. . . .]

With consternation we recognize the disappearance of the self-assertive impulse in a young woman who has hitherto been afraid of no sovereign ruler in the world and of no earthly peril, and who now debases herself by exhibiting a most shameful and spiteful jealousy. Bothwell must have given Mary cause to believe that he was more attached to the wife whom she had provided for him than he was to herself, and that he had no inclination to desert his wife for the queen. Now, therefore (is it not horrible that a great love can make a woman so paltry?), she proceeded to disparage Lady Bothwell in the most ignoble and malicious way. She tried to stimulate his erotic masculine vanity by telling him that his wife did not show enough ardour when in his embraces. The gossip must have been passed on to her by some intimate of the Bothwell household.

"Quant vous l'aymez, elle usoit de froideur," she writes, implying that Lady Bothwell surrendered herself hesitatingly, frigidly, instead of with the warmth of true passion. In contemptible self-praise, she tells him how much she, the adulteress, is sacrificing for Bothwell, whereas his wife reaps advantages and pleasure from his greatness. Let him stay then with herself alone, not allowing himself to be humbugged by the letters and tears and conjurations of that "false" woman.

Et maintenant elle commence à voire
Qu'elle estoit bien de mauuais iugement
De n'estimer l'amour d'vn tel amant
Et vouldroit bien mon amy desseuoir,
Par les escripts tout fardes de scauoir. . . .
Et toutesfois ses parolles fardez,
Ses pleurs, ses plaints remplis de fictions,
Et ses hautes cris et lamentations
Ont tant guagné que par vous sont guardes
Ses lettres escriptes ausquells vous donnez foy
Et si l'aymes et croyez plus que moy.

[Now she begins to see
That she has made a great mistake
In not valuing the love of such a lover
And would gladly deceive you, my beloved,
By writing letters stuffed with knowledge. . . .
Nevertheless, her inflated words,
Her tears, her fictitious plaints,
Her loud cries and lamentations,
Have so won you over that you have kept
Her letters, in which you believe,
And thus you love her and trust her more than me.]

More and more despairing do her cries become. She is the only woman worthy of his love; he must not forsake her for an unworthy wife. He must put away this creature and unite his lot with that of his queen and lover who is ready to walk beside him whatsoever may befall, through life and into the very jaws of death. Mary implores Bothwell to ask what proof he will of her everlasting devotion, for she is prepared to sacrifice all—house, home, possessions, crown, honour, and child. Let him take everything from her, so long as he keeps her who has wholly given herself to him, body, soul, and destiny.

For the first time a lambent ray was shed upon the background of this tragical landscape; the scene was flooded with light by Mary's frenzied avowals. Bothwell had possessed her in a casual way as he had possessed so many others, and so far as he was concerned, that would have sufficed. Queen Mary, however, a thrall to him both with her soul and her senses, all fire and ecstasy, wanted to bind him to her for ever. Now, for this ambitious man, happy in his recent marriage, a mere liaison had no charm. At most, Bothwell might have thought it advantageous to remain, for a while, on terms of intimacy with the woman in whose gift were the supreme honours and dignities of Scotland, to have Mary as concubine without disturbing his relations towards his legal wife. This did not suffice the queen, who was of a regal disposition; nor the woman, who cared not to share a lover, but wanted him for herself alone. Yet how could she bind him to her side, this wild and unbridled adventurer? Her promises of fidelity, her asseverations of humility, could not be particularly alluring to Bothwell. They were more likely to bore him, for he must have heard them too often from other feminine lips. Only one prize was calculated to attract so greedy and ambitious a man: the highest, which so many had coveted—the crown. However disinclined Bothwell may have been to go on playing the part of lover to a woman whom he did not love, he could not but find it a seductive thought that this woman was a queen, and that by her will he might become king of Scotland.

At the first glance such a notion must have seemed preposterous. Mary Stuart's lawful spouse, Henry Darnley, was alive, and bore the title of king. There was no room for another bearing that title. Yet this preposterous thought was the only link that could keep Mary and Bothwell together, the former yearning for love and the latter for power. He was a strong man, craving for freedom and independence; she was completely under his spell; nothing could permanently bind him to her but the crown. In her infatuation, forgetting honour, prestige, dignity, and law, she was ready to pay the price.

Even though she could bestow the crown on Bothwell only through committing a crime, she would not shrink from crime.

Just as Macbeth could fulfil the witches' demoniacal prophecy, could become king, only by the slaughter of a whole royal kinship, so Bothwell's path to the throne must lead him over Darnley's corpse. Blood must be spilled before his blood and Mary's could mingle.

Moral scruples never troubled Bothwell. We cannot doubt that so bold a man as he must have been ready enough to slay a king in order to wear a crown. Even if the written promise, said to have been found among the papers in the casket, the letter in which Mary avers in so many words that she will marry Bothwell in defiance of objections that might be raised by her relatives and others, were ultimately proved to be a forgery, yet the earl was so sure of his ground that he needed no signed and sealed document to force the queen to carry out any plan that might mature in his mind. Often had she complained to him, as to all and sundry, that the thought of her irreparable union with Darnley oppressed and mortified her; over and over again, in her love-verses (and we may well surmise in private interviews too), she assured Bothwell that her one and only desire was to bind herself to him for ever; why, then, should he hesitate to risk the most foolhardy deeds when he knew himself to be backed up by such plain-spoken assurances?

He knew, likewise (though nothing was openly said in the matter), that he could count upon the support of the Scottish lords, since they were unanimous in their hatred for their tiresome and vicious young master who had not kept faith with them but had shamelessly betrayed them in the Rizzio and in other affairs. Nothing would please them better than that by some means the king could be got out of the country. Bothwell was present, too, at Craigmiller Castle during the famous conference, attended by the queen, when all conceivable ways of freeing Mary and Scotland from Darnley were discussed. The highest dignitaries of the realm, Moray, Lethington, Argyll, Huntly, and Bothwell, were agreed in trying to strike a bargain with their sovereign lady. If she would recall Morton, Lindsay, and Ruthven, who had been banished on account of their complicity in Rizzio's murder, they, for their part, would "find the means that Your Majesty shall be quit of him." At the time they merely spoke of getting "quit of him" by legal measures, such as a divorce. Mary herself made the riddance conditional on its not bringing any slur upon her son. Lethington hinted that she could leave ways and means to her faithful servants, and that they should so act as to bring no "prejudice to your son." Moray, too, who as Protestant was even less scrupulous in such questions, is reported as saying that he would "look through his fingers and will behold our doings, saying nothing of the same." The proposals, however, made Mary uneasy, so that she insisted: "I will that ye do nothing through which any spot may be laid upon my honour or conscience." Behind these dark sayings there lurked a sinister meaning, which Bothwell was the last man in the world to misconstrue. This point comes out perfectly clear: Mary Stuart, Moray, Lethington, and Bothwell, the star performers of the tragedy, were determined to rid themselves of Darnley. One problem alone remained to be solved: how was the deed to be executed? Was it to be done by gentle means or by force?

Bothwell, since he was the boldest and the most impatient member of the Scottish aristocracy, preferred force. He could not and would not wait, since he was not, like the others, moved merely by the wish to sweep the troublesome youngster out of the path, but by the determination to succeed to crown and realm. Though the others might be satisfied to wish, while watching the progress of events, he had to act resolutely. There is reason to suppose that, on the quiet, at this juncture he was already on the look-out for confederates among the Scottish lords. Once more, however, the lights of history burned low, since the preparations for a crime are naturally made in dark places. We shall never know how many of the lords were implicated in this matter, whether as confederates or acquiescent onlookers. It seems possible that Moray knew of the scheme, but refrained from active participation. Lethington, on the other hand, appears to have behaved less cautiously. The most trustworthy information is derived from Morton's dying confession. He had just returned from outlawry full of hatred for Darnley, the traitor. Knowing this, Bothwell bluntly proposed that they should co-operate in the murder of Darnley. Morton's experience after the assassination of Rizzio, when his associates left him in the lurch, made him cautious. He insisted upon safeguards. Was the queen privy to the affair? Bothwell, eager for Morton's aid, did not hesitate to answer in the affirmative. But Morton knew that verbal assurances were apt to be repudiated when a plot such as this had achieved its goal, so he refused to move in the matter without the queen's written approval. He demanded one of those famous bonds, wherewith he could exonerate himself in case of need. Bothwell promised that a bond should be forthcoming. Manifestly, however, the pledge was futile, for the queen would be able to marry him after the murder only if she remained in the background and could affect surprise when the deed was done.

Once more, then, Bothwell was thrust back on his own resources, and proved equal to the occasion. Still, the way in which Morton, Moray, and Lethington had received his approaches showed him that they were nowise opposed to the scheme, and that he might consider himself to have a free hand. If not by their signatures to a document, they had at least declared their assent by a silence full of meaning and by a friendly aloofness. Now that Mary and Bothwell and the Scottish lords were of one mind, Darnley's fate was sealed.

Everything was prepared. Bothwell made arrangements with a few hardy caitiffs, agreeing with them as to the place and method of the murder. One thing was lacking—the victim. Darnley, however much of a nincompoop, must have had an inkling of what awaited him. For several weeks he refused to go to Holyrood so long as the Scottish lords were there. He did not feel safe at Stirling Castle, now that Rizzio's assassins, those men with whom he had broken troth, had been readmitted to Scotland by Mary's act of clemency. Refusing invitations and firmly resisting lures, he stayed in Glasgow. His father, the Earl of Lennox, was there with other trusty friends and allies. Here he had a stronghold. On the Clyde was a vessel, and in case of need he could embark and make his escape by sea. Then, as if at the most dangerous hour fate wanted to protect him, during the early days of January 1567 he fell ill of smallpox, this providing him with a welcome pretext for staying weeks longer in safe harbourage at Glasgow.

The king's illness interfered with the plans made by Bothwell. He was waiting impatiently in Edinburgh. For some unknown reason the earl was now in a hurry. Perhaps he was eager for the crown; perhaps he thought there were too many initiates, so that the scheme would soon be blown upon; anyhow he wished to bring matters speedily to a head. Yet how could Darnley, already suspicious and now ill in bed, be attracted to the place of slaughter? An open summons would warn him. Neither Moray nor Lethington nor anyone else at court was in the young monarch's good graces, or likely to be able to persuade him to return. One person in the world had power over the poor weakling, one to whom he was devoted, and who had twice succeeded, ere this, in making him subservient to her will. Mary, if she feigned affection for the man who wanted nothing but her love, might perhaps lull his suspicions to sleep. None other could achieve this colossal deception. Since she herself was no longer mistress of her will, but blindly obeyed the orders of him to whom she had given her heart, Bothwell had merely to issue his commands, and the incredible happened, or that happened which our modern feelings make incredible. On January 22, Mary Stuart, who for weeks had avoided any contact with her husband, rode to Glasgow, ostensibly to visit the young fellow, but really to entice him back to Edinburgh, where death awaited him.

CHAPTER TWELVE

The Path to Murder

(JANUARY 22 TO FEBRUARY 9, 1567)

THE CURTAIN now rises on the most sinister act in the tragedy of Mary Stuart—the most sinister and the most obscure. Yet there is no conflict of testimony as to the journey she made to Glasgow to visit her ailing husband when the conspiracy to murder him was in full swing. It is one of the most incontestable actions of her life. Here, as so often, arises the question whether Mary Queen of Scots was really an Atrides figure, was, like Clytemnestra, able with well-feigned wifely care to make ready the bath for her husband on his return from Troy, while Ægisthus, her paramour, with whom she had planned the murder of Agamemnon, was waiting in the shadow with the sharpened axe. Was she a second Lady Macbeth, who with gentle and flattering words led King Duncan to the bedroom in which Macbeth was to slay him? Was she one of those fiendish criminals whom the unruly passion of love will often produce out of women who have been devoted wives? Or was she a mere tool in the hands of the brutal bully Bothwell, unconsciously (in a trance, as it were) obeying an irresistible command; a puppet, unaware of the preparations that were being made for the dreadful deed? Modern sentiment rises in revolt against the theory that she was a deliberate criminal, that a woman who had previously shown herself animated with humane sentiments could have been party to the butchering of her husband. Repeated attempts have been made, and will still be made, to put another, a kindlier interpretation upon her journey to Glasgow. Again and again one tries to regard as untrustworthy the utterances and documents which incriminate her. One scrutinizes the Casket Letters, the verses, the sworn testimony, in the honest hope of convincing oneself that the exculpations devised by Mary's defenders are satisfactory. In vain! With the best will in the world to believe them, we find that these special pleadings have no convincing force. The more closely we scrutinize the exonerations, the more futile do they seem when confronted with the iron chain of fact.

How can anyone imagine that loving care impelled Mary to seek out her husband on his sick-bed that she might withdraw him from a safe refuge in order to have him better tended at home? For months the wedded couple had lived apart. Darnley had been "in a manner exiled from her presence" . . . though "with all humilitie he requiryth hir favour, to be admitted to hir bed as hir husband." She bluntly refused to allow him his conjugal rights, and there is ample evidence that such conversations as she had of late had with Darnley were disfigured by hatred and contentions. The Spanish, the English, and the French ambassadors write at great length in their reports about the estrangement as insuperable, inalterable, a thing which must be taken as a matter of course. The Scottish lords had publicly advocated a divorce and yet more forcible means of solving the difficulty. So indifferent had the pair become to one another that, when Darnley received tidings that Mary lay dangerously ill in Jedburgh, and that the last sacrament had been administered, he made no immediate move to visit her. Not even with a microscope can the observer find any intact filaments of love in this marriage at the stage the rupture had now reached. Tenderness was over and done with. Preposterous, therefore, is the assumption that loving care instigated Mary's journey to Glasgow.

Still, we have to consider the last argument of those who wish to defend the queen through thick and thin. Perhaps her journey was designed to put an end to the breach between herself and her husband? Perhaps she visited him in order to become reconciled to him? Unfortunately even this last straw breaks in the hands of her uncompromising defenders; or, rather, it is broken by a document in her own writing. Only one day before she set out for Glasgow, in a missive to Archbishop Beaton, she unreflectingly (for Mary Stuart never dreamed that her letters would continue to testify against her long after she was dead) gave vent to the most acrimonious utterances concerning Darnley. "And for the King our husband, God knows always our past towards him, and his behaviour and thankfulness to us is likewise well known to God and the world. Always we perceive him occupied and busy enough to have inquisition of our doings which, God willing, shall aye be such as none shall have occasion to be offended with them, or to report of us in any ways but honourably, howsoever he, his father, and their abettors, seek, which we know was no good will to make us have ado, if their power were equivalent to their mind: but God moderates their forces well enough, and takes the means of execution from them; for, as we believe, they shall find none, or very few, approvers of their counsels or devices imagined to our displeasure." Is that the voice of reconciliation? Are those the sentiments of a loving wife who, full of distress, is hastening to her sick husband's bedside? But here is another incriminating circumstance. Mary undertook the journey, not simply to visit Darnley and come home again, but with the fixed intent of having him conveyed forthwith to Edinburgh. Surely this was excess of zeal? Was it not contrary to the rules of medical art and the prescriptions of reason to take a man not yet convalescent from smallpox out of his bed in mid-winter, and to convey him on a two-day journey in a litter? In her "loving care" for him she intended to carry him off in this way, as is shown by her having brought a litter along with her, that Darnley might have no cause for objection to the removal, and could be transported as soon as possible to Edinburgh, where the conspiracy to get rid of him was in active progress.

Still, lest we should unjustly accuse a fellow-mortal of murder, let us ask whether there can be found any justification for her defenders' contention that she was not privy to the conspiracy. Unfortunately there is extant a letter sent by Archibald Douglas which effectually disposes of this hypothesis. Unless she had forcibly closed her eyes to what was going on, she could not fail to be aware of it. She knew that the pardoned lords were deadly enemies of Darnley and that they had sworn vengeance against him. They had shown her the bond in which Darnley pledged himself to join them in Rizzio's murder. Furthermore, Lethington told her that means would be found, without tarnishing her honour, to free her from the "proud fool and bloody tiranne." The aforesaid letter shows that Archibald Douglas, the chief agent of the conspirators, sought Mary out on her journey to secure her plain assent to the plot for Darnley's assassination. Even if we may suppose that she refused such assent, and declined to be a party to the affair, what are we to think of a wife who keeps silent when she has been informed that her husband's murder is being planned? Why did she not warn Darnley? Why, above all, though she must now have been convinced that his enemies intended to slay him, did she bring him back into the region where his murder would be comparatively easy? In such circumstances silence is something more than mere complicity; it is the tendering of secret aid, for one who is informed of a conspiracy and does not try to prevent its being carried out is at least guilty of failure to intervene.

No unprejudiced investigator can fail to recognize Mary's complicity in her husband's murder. However, if this complicity was a crime, it was a "crime passionnel"—one of those terrible actions for which not the individual but his passion is responsible, at a time when passion has full sway.

One who wishes to plead extenuating circumstances can only do so on the ground of "diminished responsibility" through passion, and not on the ground that she knew nothing of the matter. She was not acting boldly, joyfully, in full awareness, and under the promptings of her own will, but at the instigation of an alien will. I do not think it can be justly said that Mary went to Glasgow in a spirit of cold calculation in order to bring Darnley back into the danger zone; for, in the decisive hour (as the Casket Letters prove), she was filled with repulsion and horror at the thought of the role which was imposed on her. Doubtless she had beforehand talked over with Bothwell the plan of removing Darnley to Edinburgh, but one of her letters shows with remarkable clearness how, as soon as she was a day's journey away from her controller, and thus partially freed from the hypnotic influence he exercised upon her, the slumbering conscience of this magna peccatrix began to stir. We must draw a clear distinction between her, as one of those who are driven into crime by mysterious forces, and those who are criminals through and through; for at the moment when Mary began the actual carrying out of the plan, when she found herself face to face with the victim whom she was to lead to the slaughter, she was no longer inspired by hatred or by vengeful sentiments, and her innate humanity struggled desperately against the inhumanity of her commission. At the moment of the crime, and even when she was engaged in transferring Darnley to the place of assassination, the true womanliness of her nature surged up. But this revulsion of feeling came too late. In the Kirk o' Field affair, Mary was not only the huntress cunningly seeking her prey; she herself was also the quarry. Behind her she could hear the crack of the huntsman's whip. She trembled at the thought of the bullying wrath of her lover Bothwell should she fail to lead the victim to the sacrifice; and she trembled, likewise, lest, through weakness, she should forfeit the earl's love. Only on the ground that Mary was suffering from a paralysis of the will, and did not at the bottom of her soul will her own deed, only when we recognize that she was inwardly in revolt against the actions that were forced upon her, can we at least sympathetically understand a deed which, from the outlook of abstract justice, was unpardonable.

We can understand the gruesome story of those hours only in the light of the famous letter which she wrote to Bothwell from the ailing Darnley's bedside; nothing but this missive gives the repulsive deed a reconciling glimmer of humanity. The letter, as it were, removes a wall to give us a glimpse into the dreadful hours in Glasgow. It is long past midnight. Mary Stuart is seated at the writing-table in a strange room. A fire flickers on the hearth, throwing shadows on the lofty walls. This fire does not warm either the lonely room or the woman's freezing soul. Again and again a shudder runs down her back. She is tired, would gladly sleep, but cannot do so owing to the way her mind is worked up. She has lived through too much during these last weeks, during these last hours. Her nerves are still tingling with excitement. Horrified at the thought of the deed about to be committed, but blindly obedient to the behests of the man who has mastered her will, as Bothwell's slave she has undertaken this evil journey in order to remove her husband from safety to certain death.

She has not found her task easy, so far. At the door of the house she was stopped by a messenger from Lennox, Darnley's father. The old man had had his suspicions aroused. Why should his son's wife, who had sedulously avoided her husband for months, and had obviously come to hate him, hasten in this way to his bedside now that he had fallen sick? Old men are ready to forebode evil; and perhaps Lennox called to mind that, whenever Mary Stuart, since Rizzio's murder, had shown any kindliness towards her husband, it had been in pursuit of personal advantage. However, she managed to satisfy the emissary and was admitted to Darnley's bedroom. Like Lennox, the young man was mistrustful, remembering how often she had played tricks on him. The first thing he wanted to know was why she had brought a litter along. In face of such questions, it needed all her presence of mind lest, by a stammer, by a blush, or by pallor, she should betray herself. Still, dread of Bothwell quickened her powers in the art of deception. With fondling hands, with consoling words, she at length put Darnley's suspicions to sleep. Thus she undermined his will, made him her pliant tool. Already on the first afternoon, half the work had been done.

Now she was alone with him in the small hours. The candles flickered in ghostly fashion, and so silent was the room that she was afraid her thoughts would become audible, and the sighs of her uneasy conscience. She could not sleep; she could not rest; she felt an irresistible longing to confide to someone the troubles that burdened her spirit, to pour out in words the anguish of her soul. But Bothwell, the only man on earth to whom she could speak about these things, was far away. So secret were they, that she was afraid to admit them even to herself. Still, as a relief, she began to commit her thoughts to paper, in a letter to her lover, a long, rambling letter. She would not finish it that night, nor yet the next day, nor yet the night following; for it was really a dialogue with herself. In the act of committing a crime, the criminal was wrestling with her conscience. It was the expression of intense fatigue, of the uttermost confusion. Words of folly and words of profound significance, laments and idle chatter and despairing complaints, succeed one another pell-mell. We have a vision of black thoughts fluttering through the darkness like bats. Hatred flames up between the lines; compassion overcomes it for a moment; but the dominant note is one of ardent love for him who has mastered her will and whose hand has thrust her into this abyss. Her letter-paper has come to an end, so she goes on writing on the back of the pages of a memorial—on, on, on, for she feels that horror will choke her unless she continues to pour out words to the man now linked to her in the bonds of crime as well as in the bonds of love.

But while the pen between her trembling fingers seemed to move of its own volition over the paper, she noticed that she lacked power to say what she wanted to say, to bridle, to arrange her thoughts. What she inscribed on these sheets seemed to her to well up from unknown depths of her mind, so that she excused herself for incoherence, and begged Bothwell to read the letter twice over. This is what makes the epistle of three thousand words so unique a human document, that it is not written alertly and clearly, but confusedly and stumblingly. It is not Mary's conscious mind that is speaking, so much as an inner self, the voice of trance and fatigue and fever—the subconsciousness with which it is so hard to get into touch, the realm of feeling that knows no shame. Overtones and undertones, clear ideas and such as would never be expressed by one with full awareness, are mingled in this document written by one who had temporarily lost the power of self-concentration. She repeats herself, contradicts herself, gives vent to a flow of jumbled thoughts in the extremity of her passion. Very few documents have been preserved that reveal so admirably as this the hyperexcitability of one who is in the course of committing a crime. No Buchanan and no Lethington, no one with an ordinary though shrewd intelligence, could, for all his culture and ability, have imagined with such magical faithfulness the hallucinated monologue of a profoundly troubled heart; could have imagined the desperate situation of the woman who, while the deed is in full progress, finds no other escape from pricks of conscience than in writing to her lover; who writes in search of forgetfulness, of self-exculpation; who takes refuge in writing to dull, in the quiet of the night, the sound of the monitory beating of her own heart. Once more we cannot but think of Lady Macbeth, wandering by night through the dark corridors of Dunsinane Castle, assailed by dreadful memories, and, in the monologue of a sleep-walker, recounting the incidents of her crime. None but a Shakespeare or a Dostoievsky could have imagined such a scene; none but they, or their master, Reality.

[The French original having been destroyed, the quotations from the second letter to Bothwell that follow are taken from the English translation at the Record Office; *State Papers relating to Mary Queen of Scots,* vol. II, number 65.]

"I am weary, and am a sleepe, and yet I cannot forbeare scribbling so long as ther is any paper. . . . Excuse it, yf I write yll; you must gesse the one halfe; but I am glad to write unto you when other folkes be a sleepe, seeing that I cannot doo as they doo, according to my desyre, that is betwene your armes my dear lyfe." With overwhelming impressiveness she describes how delighted Darnley has been by her unexpected coming. One can fancy oneself looking at the poor youth, his face flushed with fever, and still disfigured by the eruption. He has been alone, languishing for a sight of his fair young wife. Now, of a sudden, he finds her sitting by his bedside. "He said that he did dreme, and that he was so glad to see me that he thought he shuld dye." Again and again, indeed, the old suspicions flame up in him. Her coming seems incredible, but he has been too sore at heart, and is now too glad to see her, to dwell on the possibility of further deception, often though she has deceived him. It is sweet for a man who is weak and ill to believe in loving assurances, so easy to persuade a vain man that he is loved. Ere long Darnley was once more her slave, just as he had become during the night after Rizzio's murder, and he begged her forgiveness for everything he might have done to displease her. "I avowe that I have done amisse . . . and so have many other of your subjects don, and you have well pardonid them. I am young. You will saye that you have also pardoned me many tymes and that I returne to my fault. May not a man of my age, for want of counsell, fayle twise or thrise and mysse of promes and at the last repent and rebuke him selfe by his experience? Yf I may obtayn this pardon I protest I will neuer make faulte agayne. And I ask nothing but that we may be at bed and table togiether as husband and wife; and if you will not I will never rise from this bed. . . . God knoweth that I am punished to have made my God of you and had no other mynd but of you."

Once more we look through this letter into the shadowy room that is so distant both in time and space. We picture Mary Stuart sitting by the sick man's bed and listening to this outburst of love and humility. Now she ought to rejoice, for her scheme has been successful; she has once more made the simple-minded lad soft and yielding. But she is too much ashamed of her deceit to rejoice. At the climax of her success she is overcome with loathing as she contemplates her own deed. Gloomily, with averted eyes, with disordered senses, she sits beside her husband, so that even Darnley is at length struck by something obscure, something incomprehensible, in this beloved woman. The poor dupe tries to console the deceiver! He wants to help her, to cheer her up, to make her happy. He implores her to stay the night in his room, dreaming, poor fool, once more of love and tenderness. It is heartbreaking to a reader of this letter to note how the weakling again clung trustfully to his wife, again felt sure of her. He could not turn away his eyes from her, or cease from enjoying the delight of renewed confidential association from which he had so long been debarred. He begged her to cut up his meat for him. In his folly, he blurted out secret after secret, revealing the names of those whom he had been employing to spy upon her. Not knowing of her passion for Bothwell, he told her of his own fierce hatred of Bothwell and Lethington.

Naturally enough, the more he gave himself away, the harder he made it for his wife to betray him, unsuspecting and helpless. Despite herself, she was touched by the credulity of her victim. She found it difficult to go on playing this despicable comedy. "You have never heard him speake better nor more humbly; and if I had not proofe of his hart to be as waxe and if myne were not as a dyamant, no stroke but coming from your hands could make me but to have pitie of him." We see that she no longer hated Darnley, that she had forgotten all the ill the poor deceitful creature had done her. At the bottom of her soul she would gladly have spared him. She shifted the burden of vengeance on to Bothwell's shoulders. "You are the cause thereof. For, my own revenge, I wold not doo it." It is Bothwell's command, which she must obey in defiance of her conscience. For love's sake, and for no other reason, she must do this horrible thing, must turn the childlike trust of her husband to account. She burst out angrily: "You make me dissemble so much that I am afrayde thereof with horrour, and you make me almost to play the part of a traitor. Remember that if it weare not for obeyeng I had rather be dead. My heart bleedith for yt."

But a thrall cannot defy orders. He can but groan when the lash drives him forward. Once more she insists that what she does is done by Bothwell's will and not her own: "Alas! and I never deceived anybody; but I remitt myself wholly to your will. And send me word what I shall doo, and whatsoever happen to me, I will obey you. Think also yf you will not fynd som invention more secret by phisick, for he is to take physick at Cragmillar and the bathes also."

We see that she would at any rate be glad to secure an easier death for her unhappy husband, and to avoid the gross act of violence that had been planned. Had she not become so completely subordinate to Bothwell, had there still remained in her a spark of moral independence, she would, even at this late hour, one feels, have saved Darnley. But she will not venture on disobedience, being afraid that this will cost her Bothwell, whose wishes she has pledged herself to carry out; and also afraid (this is a brilliant flash of psychological insight, which no forger could have imagined) that Bothwell would, in the end, despise her for having shown compassion. "I shall never be willing to beguile one that puttith his trust in me. Nevertheless you may doo all, and doo not estyme me the lesse therefor, for you are the cause thereof." She flings herself, figuratively, on her knees before him in a last despairing appeal that he will reward by his love the torment that she is now suffering for his sake.

"Now if to please you, my deere lyfe, I spare neither honor, conscience, nor hazard, nor greatnes, take it in good part, and not according to the interpretation of your false brother-in-law, to whom I pray you, give no credit against the most faythfull lover that ever you had or shall have. See not also her" [the Countess of Bothwell] "whose faynid teares you ought not more to regarde than the true travails which I endure to deserve her place, for obteyning of which, against my own nature, I doo betray those that could lett me. God forgive me, and give you, my only frend, the good luck and prosperitie that your humble and faythfull lover doth wisshe vnto you, who hopeth shortly to be an other thing vnto you, for the reward of my paynes."

One who listens to the unhappy woman's tortured heart speaking out of this letter will not term her a murderess, although throughout these days and nights she was serving the cause of murder. We feel, as we read, that her reluctance is really stronger than her will. We feel that her honest spirit has been besmirched by these deceptions; perhaps during many of these hours she was much nearer suicide than murder. But herein lies the disaster of such subjection as hers. One who has surrendered his will to another's keeping can no longer choose his own path; he can only serve and obey. She therefore stumbled onward, bondmaid of her passion, unwitting and yet at the same time cruelly aware, towards the abyss of her deed.

On the second day Mary Stuart made the prescribed arrangements; the more subtle, the more dangerous part of the scheme had been carried through. She had allayed the suspicions in Darnley's mind, so that the ailing, stupid youth was now "the merriest that ever you saw." Though still feeble, still disfigured by the marks of the recent smallpox, he ventured on little endearments. He tried to kiss her, to put his arms round her, and she found it hard to conceal her disgust and impatience. Obedient to Mary's wishes, as obedient as she was to Bothwell's commands, this thrall of a thrall declared himself ready to return with her to Edinburgh. Trustfully he allowed himself to be carried out of his safe retreat and installed in the litter, his face wrapped in a linen cloth to hide its disfigurement. Now the victim was on the way to the slaughter-house, and Mary had fulfilled her cruel task. The rough and bloody deed was to be Bothwell's affair, and that harsh borderer would find it a thousand times easier than Mary Stuart had found the preceding acts of deception.

The litter advanced slowly, accompanied by a guard of riders, along the wintry road. The royal pair, seemingly reconciled after months of severance and dissension, were returning to Edinburgh. Edinburgh? Yes, but where in Edinburgh? To Holyrood Palace, one might suppose, the royal residence, a comfortable abode. No, Bothwell, the all-powerful, had made other arrangements. The king should not return to his own home at Holyrood, for there might still be danger of his spreading the infection. Why not, then, send him to Stirling, or to Edinburgh Castle, an impregnable fortress, or house him as guest in some other princely dwelling, or perhaps in the episcopal palace? No, and yet again no! Strangely enough there was chosen for his residence a modest and isolated building that no one would have dreamed of; not a princely habitation at all, but a house "in a solitar place at the outmost part of ye town, separat from all companie—ane maist rewynous hous quhair no man had dwelt seven yearis of befoir"—a house hard to watch and to protect. One cannot but ask who had chosen for the king this suspiciously remote house in Kirk o' Field, to which the approach was by an alley bearing the ominous name of Thieves' Row. Bothwell had chosen it, Bothwell, who was now "all in all." Again and again one comes across the same red thread in the labyrinth. Again and again, in letters, documents, and utterances, the trace of blood leads us back to this sinister figure.

A small habitation, unworthy of a king, it lay among untilled fields, the nearest adjoining residence being that of one of Bothwell's henchmen. It contained no more than an ante-room and four rooms. On the ground floor a bedroom was made ready for the queen, who now expressed a strong desire to care tenderly for the husband she had of late neglected. One of the rooms on the upper story was set in order for the king, and the other of the two first-floor rooms was allotted to his three servingmen. Certainly the place was richly furnished for the occasion, carpets and tapestries being brought from Holyrood, and one of the fine beds which Mary of Guise had imported from France. Another of these beds was supplied for the queen's bedroom.

Now Mary could not do enough to display her affection for Darnley. Though she slept only two nights in the Kirk o' Field house, she came over frequently to companion him, attended by her train—and we must not forget that for months before this she had sedulously avoided him. The nights she slept in the room under Darnley's were probably the fifth and seventh of February. Everyone in Edinburgh was to know that the king and the queen were once more a loving couple, the reconciliation being thus advertised to the world. This change of mood must have produced a strange impression upon the Scottish lords who, only a few days before, had discussed with the queen the removal of Darnley by all possible means. Now had come this over-emphasized affection! The ablest of the nobles, Moray, was quick to draw his conclusions. He did not doubt for a moment that, in the sequestered house, evil was to befall the King of Scotland, and diplomatically he made his preparations.

Perhaps there was only one person in Scotland who honestly believed in Mary's change of heart—Darnley himself, the unhappy husband. His vanity was tickled by the attention she paid him; he was proud to find that the Scottish lords, who for so long had treated him with contempt, now visited him in his sick-bed making low obeisances and showing concern in their faces. In a letter to his father, dated February 7, he assured Lennox how rapidly his health was improving under "the loving care of my love the Queen, who doth use herself like a natural and loving wife." Within a few days the last traces of the dreaded and usually disfiguring disease had disappeared. His doctors had assured him of this, and that he would be able to remove to his palace. The horses had been ordered for next Monday. Another day, and he would be back in Holyrood, to share bed and board with his wife and, once more, to be king in his own country and lord of his wife's heart.

But before this Monday, February 10, came Sunday, February 9, 1567, and that evening high festival was to be held in Holyrood. Two of Queen Mary's most faithful servants were to be married; there were to be a banquet and a dance, at which the queen had promised to appear with her ladies. But this manifest affair was not to be the main event of the day. There was something else in the wind, as time would show. On Sunday morning, the Earl of Moray took leave of his sister for several days, ostensibly to visit his wife, who was lying ill at one of his castles. This departure was a bad sign. Whenever Moray suddenly withdrew from the political scene, he had good reason for the step. Always his disappearance foreshadowed a rising or some other misfortune; and always on his return he was able to produce an alibi, to show that he had had nothing to do with the affair, although he would not fail to reap any advantages that were derivable from it. Not a year had elapsed since, on the morning after the murder of Rizzio, he had ridden into Edinburgh as innocently as he was now riding away from it the morning before a still more horrible crime was to be perpetrated, leaving to others the deed and the danger, while intending to garner the honour and the profit.

Something else happened which might have given reason for thought. We learn that Mary had already issued orders for the removal of her costly bed with its fur covering from her bedroom in Kirk o' Field back to Holyrood. This seemed natural enough, since she proposed to sleep in Holyrood that night, and not in Kirk o' Field; the next day there would be an end to the separation. Yes, that is a natural way of accounting for the order; but subsequent events were to throw an ominous light upon the removal of the costly bed on this particular day. At the time, however, neither in the afternoon nor in the evening of Sunday were there signs that anything was amiss, and the queen's behavior was as ordinary as possible. During the day, accompanied by her friends, she visited her husband, now almost recovered. In the evening she sat with Bothwell, Huntly, and Argyll among the wedding company and made merry with them. Still, once again, after night had fallen, though it was cold and wintry, she visited the forsaken house in Kirk o' Field to see Darnley. What a touching demonstration! She bade farewell to the festal party at Holyrood, merely that she might sit a little longer with her husband and converse with him. She stayed at Kirk o' Field until eleven. Let the reader carefully note the hour. Then she returned to Holyrood on horseback, well attended, the little procession being made conspicuous by the torches that were carried to light it on its way. The doors of the palace were opened wide, for Edinburgh was to see that the queen had returned from her loving visit to her husband, was to hear the skirl of the bagpipes to which the wedding company was dancing. Conversing in the most friendly way with all and sundry, the queen moved among the company. Not till after midnight did she retire to her sleeping-apartment.

At two o'clock in the morning there came a thunderous crash, a frightful explosion "as if five-and-twenty cannon had been fired simultaneously." Immediately thereafter, suspicious-looking figures were seen rushing away from the house where the king lodged. A wave of terror swept through the awakened city. The gates were opened, and messengers hastened to Holyrood to report the terrible news that the lonely house in Kirk o' Field had been blown up, together with the king and his servants. Bothwell, who had been present at the wedding festivities (wishing, like Moray, to have an alibi) while his henchmen were preparing for the deed, was awakened from his sleep, or at any rate was roused from the bed where he was pretending to sleep. Hastily donning his clothes, accompanied by armed men, he made his way to the scene of the crime. The corpse of Darnley and that of the servant who slept in his room were found in the garden, clad only in their shirts. The house had been completely destroyed by an explosion of gunpowder. Bothwell contented himself with ascertaining these details, making as if he was greatly surprised at what had happened. Since he knew the real undercurrent of the affair better than anyone else, he did not try to elucidate the truth. He merely commanded that the corpses should be laid out on a bier, and after half an hour returned to the palace. There he told the queen, likewise, as it seemed, just aroused from sleep, the bare fact that her husband the king, Henry of Scotland, had been murdered by unknown malefactors in an incomprehensible way.

CHAPTER THIRTEEN

Quos Deus Perdere Vult...

(FEBRUARY TO APRIL 1567)

PASSION CAN work wonders. It can awaken superhuman energy. By its irresistible pressure it can evoke titanic forces from a previously tranquil soul, and can drive a hitherto well-regulated and law-abiding person to crime. The nature of passion is, however, such that, after intense ebullitions and wild outbreaks, a phase of exhaustion ensues. That is what distinguishes one who becomes a criminal through passion from a born, or a habitual criminal. The casual and passionate criminal is, as a rule, only equal to the occasion as regards the commission of the crime, but proves unable to deal with its consequences. Acting under stress of impulse, with his mind concentrated on the deed that is to be done, his energies are tensed upon this one and only aim. Thereafter, as soon as the deed is done, his impetus fails, his resolution subsides, at the very time when a cool and calculating criminal devotes himself to a purposive struggle against the representatives of law and morality. The energies of the habitual criminal are held in store for dealing with what will come after the crime.

Mary Stuart (and we think the better of her for this) was unfitted to cope with the situation into which her thraldom to Bothwell had brought her. Though she was a criminal, she had only become one through irresponsible passion, under the promptings of another will than her own. She had lacked the strength to forbid her husband's murder, and after it she was in a state of collapse. Two possibilities were open to her. She might break off all relations with Bothwell, who had done more than, at the bottom of her soul, she had desired. Or, on the other hand, she might help to conceal the crime, feigning sorrow in order to avert suspicion from him and from herself. Instead, Mary did the stupidest thing anyone in so suspicious a situation could possibly do. She did nothing. She betrayed herself through dull inaction. Like a mechanical toy, having been wound up by the influence of a stronger nature than her own, she had, as if in a trance, automatically done whatever Bothwell wanted. She had gone to Glasgow, beguiled Darnley, brought him back with her to Kirk o' Field. Now the clockwork mechanism had run down, and she made no further move. At the very time when skilful play-acting was needed to convince the world of her own and her lover's innocence, she dropped the mask. As if petrified, she displayed a horrible rigidity and nonchalance which could not fail to concentrate suspicion upon her.

Such spiritual numbness, such passivity and indifference, at the very time when active misrepresentation, vigorous defensive, and extreme presence of mind are essential, are by no means uncommon. Inertia of this sort is a reaction from excess of tension, the outcome of a revenge taken by nature on those who have unreasonably overtaxed their forces. On the evening after Waterloo, Napoleon's daimonic energy of will was in abeyance. He was mute and passive, could give no instructions to anyone, although in that hour of catastrophe it was essential for him to take active measures to avert the crowning disaster. Strength seemed to have run out of him as wine runs out of a barrel when the spigot has been removed. In like manner, Oscar Wilde collapsed in the hours before his arrest. Friends had warned him; there was still time for him to escape; he had funds, could have taken train to Dover and crossed the Channel. But, frozen stiff, he sat in his room waiting and waiting—as if for a miracle or for annihilation. Only by such analogies, which could be multiplied a thousandfold by students of history and biography, can we explain Mary Stuart's foolish passivity, which concentrated suspicion upon her during the weeks following her husband's murder. Before the murder, no one had suspected her intimacy with Bothwell, and her visit to Darnley at Glasgow might easily have been supposed to be the outcome of a desire for reconciliation. After the crime, however, the widow became the centre of interest. It was incumbent upon her to make her innocence plain by brilliant misrepresentation. Yet the unhappy woman would appear to have been seized with loathing at the thought of such hypocrisy. Instead of doing her best to avert natural suspicion, she made herself seem more culpable than she actually was by manifesting the most callous indifference to her husband's death. Like a woman who has determined to drown herself, she closed her eyes while flinging herself into the water, that she might see nothing more, feel nothing more, hoping only for the oblivion of non-existence. Criminology can hardly find a more signal example of the person who has become a criminal through passion, and in whom, after the crime, complete paralysis ensues. Quos deus perdere vult . . . Whom the gods would destroy, they first make mad.

What would an innocent, an honest, a loving woman, be she queen or commoner, do when, at dead of night, tidings are brought that her husband has been murdered by unknown miscreants? Would she not rage and storm? Would she not scream for the immediate arrest of the guilty? If a queen, she would instantly cast into prison those upon whom a glimmer of suspicion rested. She would appeal to her subjects to help her; she would ask neighbouring sovereigns to seize any that attempted to cross her frontiers. As in France, when her boy-husband Francis II had died, she would have gone into seclusion, showing no inclination for social amusements until weeks, months, or years had elapsed; and, above all, never resting until every participant in the crime had been brought to justice.

Such would have been the behaviour, in these circumstances, of an affectionate widow, innocent of her husband's murder. Logically, therefore, such also should have been the behaviour of a guilty widow. From calculation she would have played the innocent, for what can safeguard a criminal better than to act as if he had neither part nor lot in the crime? Instead, after Darnley's murder, Mary Stuart displayed a callousness that could not fail to arouse dark suspicions in the minds even of her well-wishers. She showed neither the gloomy wrath she had shown after the assassination of Rizzio, nor yet the seemly melancholy prescribed for her by French court etiquette after the premature death of Francis II. She had penned a touching elegy on Francis, but she did not consecrate her poetic talent to enshrining the memory of Darnley. Instead, during the first hours after the crime, she calmly signed lengthy and confused dispatches to the courts of Europe—an account of the murder so worded as to avert suspicion from herself. In this remarkable tale the facts were so distorted as to imply that the crime had not been primarily directed against the king but against herself. According to the official version of the story, the conspirators had intended the nocturnal explosion at Kirk o' Field to destroy both the wedded pair, and nothing but the chance that she had left the house in order to participate in the wedding festival at Holyrood had saved the queen from perishing with the king. Her hand did not tremble as she signed the following statement: "The matter is horrible and strange, as we believe the like was never heard in any country. . . . By whom it was done, or in what manner, appears not yet. We doubt not but, according to the diligence which our Council has begun already to use, the certainty of all shall be known shortly and the same discovered, which we wot God will never suffer to lie hid; we hope to punish the same with such rigour as shall serve as an example . . . for all ages to come."

This distortion of the facts was, of course, too great to mislead public opinion. For, in reality, as all Edinburgh knew, the queen had left Kirk o' Field at 11 P.M., attended by a great train and numerous torch-bearers, while Darnley remained in the lonely house. Everyone in the capital was aware that she was not spending the night with her husband, and therefore the murderers, hiding in the darkness, could not possibly have had any designs upon her life when, three hours later, they blew up the house. Besides, the explosion was nothing more than a smoke-screen, intended to hide the real fact that Darnley was strangled or smothered (probably before the explosion). Thus the stupidity of the official account served only to intensify the conviction of Mary's complicity.

Strangely enough, little hubbub was raised about the matter in Scotland, and the indifference of her subjects, as well as Mary's own, served during these days to intensify the animus of the foreign world. For this much is true in the above-mentioned report, that the affair was horrible and strange, so that the like had never been recorded in the blood-stained annals of history. The King of Scotland had been murdered in his own capital; his house had been blown up. What happened? Did the town quiver with excitement and indignation? Did the Scottish lords hurry from their castles to Edinburgh in order to defend the queen, who was also declared to have been endangered by the plot? Did priests denounce the crime from their pulpits? Did the law-courts do their utmost to discover and condemn the criminals? Were the gates of the city closed? Were hundreds of suspects arrested and racked? Was the border guarded? Were the ports watched? Was the corpse of the slain king carried through the streets, attended by a mournful procession of the nobles of the land? Was a catafalque erected in one of the public squares, surrounded by guards and torch-bearers, so that the deceased king could lie in state? Was parliament summoned, to be informed about the crime, and to take the necessary steps to avenge it? Did the Scottish lords, the defenders of the throne, solemnly swear to punish the assassins?

Nothing of the kind happened. Nothing happened. An incomprehensible silence followed the thunder-clap. The queen secluded herself in her apartment instead of making a public utterance. The Scottish lords were silent. Neither Moray nor Lethington raised a finger, not one of those who had bowed the knee before their king. They neither blamed the deed nor extolled it. With dour quietude they waited upon events. It was plain that open discussion of the king's murder would be inconvenient, since nearly all of them had been accessories before the fact. The burghers, in their turn, stayed quietly at home, not venturing to do more than mutter their suspicions. They knew it was inexpedient for such as they to meddle in the affairs of the great.

To begin with, therefore, what happened was precisely what the assassins had hoped. No one seemed to look upon the murder as anything more than a petty and undesirable incident. Perhaps there has been no other occasion in European history when a court, a nobility, the population of a capital, has made so little stir about the killing of a king. Even the most obvious and simple measures for the elucidation of the crime were conspicuously neglected. There was no official or legal inquiry at the site of the murder. No report was called for. No proclamation was issued. Everything, as if designedly, was left shrouded in darkness. No post-mortem examination was made by such experts as then existed. Even today we do not know whether Darnley was strangled, smothered, stabbed, or poisoned before the house was blown up in order to hide the traces of the crime. This much only is certain, that his corpse, with a blackened face, was found at some distance from the house. By Bothwell's orders, the body was interred with unseemly haste, lest too many people should have a chance of examining

it. Let the earth quickly cover the remains of Henry Darnley. Let the dark affair be speedily shuffled out of sight, before it stank to heaven.
The world became convinced, therefore, that persons of high standing must have been responsible for the murder. Such was the reason why Henry Darnley, King of Scotland, had not been vouchsafed a burial worthy of a king. Not with pomp and circumstance was the coffin borne through the streets of the city, followed by a mournful widow, by earls and other persons of rank and station. No royal salutes were fired nor were the bells tolled in the church towers. Secretly, and by night, the entombment in the chapel took place. Dishonourably and hastily was the body of Henry Darnley, King of Scotland, lowered into the grave, as if he himself had been a murderer, instead of the victim of hate and greed. Read one Mass over him, and that will suffice! His tormented soul will no longer disturb the peace of Scotland! . . . Quos deus perdere vult . . .

Mary Stuart, Bothwell, and the other Scottish lords hoped that, with the nailing-on of the coffin-lid, the whole matter would be hushed up. Lest, however, inquisitive folk should make trouble, lest Queen Elizabeth should complain that nothing had been done to throw light upon the crime, it was decided to show a semblance of activity. To obviate a serious inquiry, Bothwell commanded a spurious one. A bogus search was to be made for the "unknown assassins." True, the whole city knew their names. Too many confederates had been needed to surround the house, to buy large quantities of gunpowder, and to store it in sacks at the site of the explosion for them to pass unobserved. The sentries at the gates knew only too well who had made their way back into Edinburgh that night after the explosion. Since, however, the queen's council was now practically reduced to Bothwell and Lethington, the prime actor and the chief confederate, who needed only to look in the mirror to see the guilty parties, the council sedulously maintained the pretence that the crime had been the work of "unknown miscreants," and issued a proclamation offering a reward of two thousand pounds Scots to anyone who would put the authorities upon the track of the guilty. Two thousand pounds Scots, equivalent to £165 English, was a respectable sum in those days, and a fortune for any poor citizen of Edinburgh, but everyone knew that if he should blab he would be more likely to have a dirk between his ribs than the two thousand pounds in his pouch. Bothwell established a military dictatorship. His retainers, the borderers, masterfully patrolled the streets, armed to the teeth, a plain menace to whosoever might think of trying to earn the reward by indiscreet revelations.

When attempts are made to repress truth by force, it seeks an outlet by cunning. What could not be said in the open and by day could be posted on the walls during the night. The morning after the issue of the proclamation, placards were pasted up in the market-place and even on the gates of the royal palace at Holyrood. These placards denounced as the murderers Bothwell, his accomplice Sir James Balfour, together with the queen's servants Bastien and Joseph Rizzio. Other names were mentioned in other lists. Two names, however, were found in them all, Bothwell and Balfour, Balfour and Bothwell.

Had she not been, as it were, under a spell, had not her reason been completely overmastered by passion, had not her will been in thrall, there is one thing which Mary Stuart would certainly have now decided upon, when the popular voice was speaking so plainly; she would have broken off all connexion with Bothwell. Had even a gleam of reasonableness persisted in her darkened mind, she would have had nothing more to do with him. At any rate she would have avoided converse with him until, by some clever scheming, she had secured "official" proof of his innocence. Meanwhile, under one pretext or another, she would have dismissed him from the court. The one thing which she should have avoided was allowing this man, whom current talk declared to have been the murderer of her husband the King of Scotland, to continue to hold sway in the late king's house. Above all, since public opinion unanimously regarded him as the chief of the assassins, she should have avoided making him chief of the inquiry which ostensibly aimed at the discovery of the "unknown miscreants."

But this was not the limit of her folly. On the illicit proclamations, besides Bothwell and Balfour, her two servants Bastien and Joseph Rizzio had been denounced as confederates. What, then, should Mary have instantly done? Common sense demanded that she should hand over this pair of understrappers to the court for trial. Instead of doing so, committing a blunder which was tantamount to self-incrimination, she privately dismissed the two men from her service. They were furnished with passports and hastily smuggled across the border. It was the very opposite of what she should have done to safeguard her own honour. Even crazier was her conduct in another respect. Prudence demanded that she should mourn more conspicuously for her assassinated spouse than she had mourned for Francis II. Instead, after a bare week in retreat, she left Holyrood to visit Lord Seton in his castle. She could not even bring herself to make the requisite gesture of court mourning, and as if to flaunt her folly in the face of the world, she received as visitor at Seton House—whom? James Bothwell, the man whose portrait was being hawked in the streets of Edinburgh with the legend: "This is the king's murderer."

But Scotland is not the world. Although the conscience-stricken lords and the intimidated burgesses held their peace, making as if, with the king's interment, all interest in his murder had come to an end—at the courts of London, Paris, and Madrid the dreadful deed was by no means regarded with the same equanimity. For Scotland, Darnley had been nothing more than a tiresome foreigner, of whom the world could be rid in the usual way as soon as he became too much of a nuisance. For the courts of Europe, Darnley was a crowned and anointed king, scion of an illustrious family, a man of the highest rank; his cause was theirs. It need hardly be said that no one believed the official report for a moment. From the first, throughout Europe, it was universally held that Bothwell had been the murderer-in-chief and that Mary had been his confidante. Even the Pope and the papal legate denounced the unhappy woman in the strongest terms. But what chiefly disturbed the minds of foreign princes was not so much the murder itself. The sixteenth century was not greatly troubled about moral questions, or likely to be squeamish about a bagatelle such as a political assassination. It was but a couple of generations since Machiavelli had published *The Prince,* and ever since (as indeed before!) murder for "reasons of State" had been regarded as a trifling matter, or at most a venial sin. There was scarcely a royal house in Europe without some such skeleton in its cupboard. Henry VIII had made no bones about the execution of wives he wanted to get rid of. Philip II would not have liked to be pressed with questions about the murder of his son Don Carlos. The Borgias (Pope Alexander III and his son Cesare) have an evil reputation as poisoners. Still, there is a distinction to be drawn. The aforesaid princes did their dark deeds by proxy, and liked to keep their own hands "clean." What her fellow-sovereigns expected from Mary Stuart was a strenuous and personable attempt at self-exculpation, and what they took amiss was her ostentatious indifference. Coldly at first, and then with rising indignation, they watched their imprudent sister, who did nothing to avert suspicion, who refrained from having a few commoners hanged and quartered, who went on amusing herself by playing pall-mall and had as her chosen companion the man who was unquestionably the chief instigator of the murder. With honest anger Mary's trusty ambassador in Paris reported that her impassivity was making a very bad impression. "You yourself have become the object of calumny here, being regarded as having planned and commanded this crime." With a frankness which will for ever redound to the credit of this churchman, he told the queen that, unless she atoned for the murder in the most explicit and uncompromising manner, it would be better for her to have lost her life and her all.

Here were plain words from a friend. Had there been a spark of reason left in her mind, had she still possessed any will of her own, this exhortation would have stirred her. Queen Elizabeth's letters of condolence convey an even plainer message. For, by a remarkable coincidence, no one in the world was better fitted to understand Mary Stuart in this terrible crisis than the woman who, throughout life, was her harshest adversary. Elizabeth, contemplating Mary's crime, seemed to be watching herself in a mirror; for Mary was in the same situation, exposed to universal and probably justified suspicion, as Elizabeth herself had been in the days of her most ardent passion for Robert Dudley. Just as in Mary's case an unwanted husband, so in Elizabeth's case an inconvenient wife, had to be swept out of the path to clear the way to a fresh marriage. With or without Elizabeth's knowledge (the mystery of that matter will never be solved), murder had been committed when, one morning, Amy Robsart, Robert Dudley's wife, had been slain by "unknown miscreants." As, now, all glances were suspiciously directed at Mary Stuart, so, then, they had been directed at Elizabeth Tudor. Why, Mary Stuart herself, at that time still Queen of France, had made mock of the cousin who, wishing to marry her Master of the Horse, had connived at his making an end of his own wife. With the same confidence as now the world regarded Bothwell as the murderer, so then it had regarded Dudley as a murderer and the Queen of England as his confederate. Thus the memory of her own former troubles made Elizabeth the best, the most trusty adviser, of her sister in misfortune. With much shrewdness and force of character, Elizabeth had saved her honour by promptly commanding an inquiry—fruitless, of course, but nevertheless an inquiry. In the end she had stilled gossip and scandal by renouncing her dearest wish, that of marrying the gravely compromised Leicester. This renunciation made the world believe that the Queen of England could have had no part in the murder. Elizabeth wanted a like renunciation on the part of the Queen of Scotland.

Elizabeth's letter under date February 24, 1567, is further remarkable in its sincerity as a missive from one human being to another. It really has the human touch. "Madam," she writes, in genuine concern, "my ears have been so much shocked, by my distress, and my heart appalled, at hearing the horrible report of the abominable murder of your husband, my slaughtered cousin, that I have scarcely as yet spirit to write about it: but although nature constrains me to lament his death, so near to me in blood as he was, I must tell you boldly that I am far more concerned for you than I am for him. Oh, Madam! I should neither perform the office of a faithful nor that of an affectionate friend, if I studied rather to please your ears than to preserve your honour: therefore I will not conceal from you that people, for the most part, say 'that you will look through your fingers at this deed, instead of revenging it,' and that you have not cared to touch those who have done you this pleasure, as if the deed had not been without the murderers having had that assurance. I implore you to believe me that I myself would not for all the gold in the world cherish such a thought in my heart. I would never allow so evil a guest to harbour in my heart by having so bad an opinion of any sovereign, and still less of one to whom I wish as much good as my heart can conceive or as you yourself could desire. Therefore I exhort you, counsel you, and implore you to take this affair so much to heart that you will not be afraid to wreak vengeance even on him who stands nearest to you, should he be guilty; and that no consideration whatever will withhold you from giving the world a proof that you are as noble a ruler as you are a righteous woman."

Elizabeth, apt to be so double-faced, probably never wrote a more sincere or kindly epistle than this. To Queen Mary, despite her numbed senses, it must have come like a pistol-shot, and at length awakened her to realities. Here was another accusing finger directed against Bothwell. Again she was assured that any consideration for him would be taken as evidence of complicity in her husband's murder. But, let me reiterate, Mary Stuart's condition during these weeks was one of complete enslavement. She was so "shamefully enamoured," wrote one of Elizabeth's spies in his report to London, "that she had been heard to say she would go with him to the world's end in a white petticoat, leaving all rather than forsake him." Appeals were uttered to deaf ears; reason could make no headway against the stir in her blood. Because she had forgotten herself, she believed that the world would forget her and her crime.

For a while, throughout the month of March 1567, Mary might well believe that her passivity was having the right effect. Scotland was silent, the legal authorities were blind and deaf, and Bothwell (strangely enough!) with the best will in the world, was unable to lay his hands upon the "unknown miscreants"—although the name of the murderer-in-chief was being whispered in every house. All knew who was the guilty man, but all were afraid to claim the promised reward and utter the dreaded name out loud. At length a voice was raised in denunciation. The murdered king's father, the Earl of Lennox, was in high repute among the Scottish nobles, and the authorities had to pay heed to him when he complained that weeks had elapsed without bringing the murderers of his son to justice. Mary Stuart, since the leader of the assassins was her paramour, and since Lethington, who had been a confederate, guided her with his counsels, gave an evasive answer, saying that she would do her best and would bring the affair before parliament. But Lennox knew that these words meant nothing, and reiterated his demands. It was essential, he said, to arrest forthwith those whose names had been anonymously placarded in Edinburgh.

So specific a demand was not easy to elude. Again, however, Mary shuffled. She would be glad to do what Lennox asked, but so many names had been placarded, most of them of persons who, obviously, had nothing to do with the murder. Let her father-in-law himself declare the names of those whom he regarded as guilty. She hoped, doubtless, that fear of Bothwell, the dictator, would prevent Lennox from mentioning the latter's name. Meanwhile, however, Lennox took steps to secure his own safety and to strengthen his position. He got into touch with Elizabeth, and placed himself under her protection. Meticulously, therefore, he named the persons against whom he demanded an investigation. First came Bothwell, then Balfour, then David Chalmers, and some of Mary Stuart's and Bothwell's serving-men, who had long since been spirited across the border lest their tongues should be loosened by the rack. Now, to her consternation, Mary began to realize that the comedy of "looking through her fingers" had come to an end. Lennox's persistence, she felt, must be backed up by the energy and authority of Queen Elizabeth. By this time, too, Catherine de' Medici had plainly intimated that she regarded Mary Stuart as "dishonoured," and that Scotland need expect no friendship from France so long as the murder had not been properly investigated in the law-courts. There was a swift change of scene, replacing the contention that inquiry was "futile" by another comedy, that of a public legal inquiry. Mary was compelled to agree that Bothwell (small folk would be dealt with later) should defend himself before a court of his peers. On March 28, 1567, a summons was sent to the Earl of Lennox, commanding him to appear in Edinburgh on April 12 and formulate his charges against Bothwell.

Bothwell was by no means the man to present himself in a penitent's robe and humbly bow before his judges. If he was ready for a trial by his peers, it was only because he was determined that there should be a "cleansing"—not a sentence, but an acquittal. He made his preparations with his customary energy. First of all he induced the queen to put him in command of all the fortresses in Scotland, thus gaining control of the available weapons and ammunition throughout the country. He knew that might was right, so he summoned his borderers to Edinburgh and equipped them as if for battle. Shamelessly, with the audacity and lawlessness characteristic of the man, he established a reign of terror in Edinburgh. He publicly announced that, if he could discover by whom the "treasonable painted tickets" were designed and posted, he would wash his hands in their blood—this threat being intended as a warning to Lennox. He swaggered about with his hand on his sword-hilt, while his followers had their dirks ready, openly declaring that they had no mind to allow the lord of their clan to be arrested as a criminal. Let Lennox dare to come and accuse him! Let the judges try to condemn the dictator of Scotland!

Such preparations were too unambiguous to leave a doubt in Lennox's mind as to what awaited him. He might go to Edinburgh to accuse Bothwell, but there was little chance that Bothwell would allow him to leave the city alive. Once more he turned to his patroness Elizabeth, who thereupon sent an urgent letter to Mary warning her for the last time that any open breach of the peace would expose her to suspicion of complicity.

"Madam," wrote the English queen to the Scottish, "I should not be so unfeeling as to trouble you with this letter were it not that we are commanded to love the afflicted and that the cry of the unfortunate impels me. I learn, Madam, that you have issued a proclamation to the effect that the judicial proceedings against those suspected of participation in the murder of your late husband and my deceased cousin will take place on the twelfth of the present month. It is of extreme importance that matters should not be obscured, as they very well might be, by secrecy or cunning. The father and the friends of the deceased have humbly begged me to ask you to postpone the inquiry, because they have noticed that these scoundrelly persons are trying to achieve by force what they cannot achieve by law. In my love for you, therefore, I cannot act otherwise than I now do, since you are the person most concerned, and I wish to tranquillize those who are innocent of so unspeakable a crime. Were you yourself not guiltless, this would be reason enough to rob you of your dignity as a princess and to expose you to the contempt of the multitude. Rather than such a thing should happen to you, I should wish for you an honourable tomb instead of a dishonourable life."

This new appeal to Mary's conscience could not fail to arouse her benumbed senses. We cannot be certain, however, that the exhortation reached the Queen of Scotland in time. Bothwell was on guard, fearing neither death nor the devil, and least of all the English queen. The special messenger to whom the letter had been entrusted for delivery was detained at the gates of the palace by Bothwell's underlings. He was told that the queen was asleep and could not receive him.

The special messenger, bearing a missive from on· queen to another, wandered disconsolately about the streets. At length he obtained audience of Bothwell, who impudently opened the letter directed to Mary Stuart, read it, and thrust it into his pocket. We do not know whether he ever showed it to Mary, nor is the matter of importance. She was his bondslave, who dared to do nothing opposed to his will. It is even recorded that she was foolish enough to wave her hand to him from the window when, surrounded by his riders, he set forth to the Tolbooth. Thus she wished success to the notorious murderer on his way to participate in the comedy of justice.

Even if Mary Stuart never received Elizabeth's last warning, she was none the less warned. Three days before, her half-brother Moray took leave of her. He was, he told her, seized with a desire to travel through France to Italy, for he wanted "to see Venice and Milan." Mary had had ample experience to show her that the sudden disappearance of Moray from the political theatre foreboded stormy weather, and that his determination to be absent from the comedy of justice was intended to signify disapproval. On this occasion, indeed, Moray was plain-spoken enough, and did not conceal the true reason for his journey. He told everyone who cared to listen to him that he had tried to arrest Sir James Balfour as one of the chief participants in the murder, and that Bothwell, wishing to protect a confederate, had prevented his doing so. A week later, in London, he candidly informed the Spanish ambassador de Silva that he felt it would be dishonourable to stay any longer in the Scottish kingdom while so strange and terrible a crime remained unpunished. We may assume, then, that James spoke candidly to his sister before taking leave. We know for a fact that Mary was in tears when he quitted her apartment. But she could not restrain him from going. Her energy had departed since she had become Bothwell's slave. She could only let things take the course prescribed by a stronger will than hers. The queen in her was subjugated, and she was nothing but an amorous woman.

On April 12, the comedy of justice, which began challengingly, ended in like manner. Bothwell rode to the Tolbooth, sword strapped to his side, dagger in his belt, surrounded by a train of armed followers, in the spirit of a warrior setting forth to storm a fortress. The number of the clansmen has perhaps been exaggerated, but according to current reports it was four thousand. Lennox, on the strength of an ancient edict, had been forbidden to bring more than six men with him if he entered the city. Lennox felt in no mind to face "justice" thus backed by overwhelming force. He knew that Elizabeth's letter asking for a postponement of the proceedings had been sent to Mary, and that moral force was on his side. He was content, therefore, to send one of his feudatories to the Tolbooth, to read a written protest. The chief accuser being absent, the judges, some of whom had been intimidated, and others bribed by lands or money or titles, found it convenient to avoid exhaustive inquiry. They were freed from a burden. After deliberating among themselves upon a matter which had been decided beforehand, they unanimously exonerated Bothwell from "any art and part of the said slauchter of the King" on the ground that "no accusation had been brought against him." This exculpation might have seemed insufficient to a man of honour, but Bothwell held it as a triumph. Harness clinking, he rode through the city, brandishing his drawn sword, and publicly challenging to a duel anyone who might venture to declare him guilty or in part guilty of the late king's murder.

The burgesses, however, murmured among themselves that the law had been brought into contempt. Mary's friends looked askance, with "sore hearts." "It was pitiful," writes Melville, her most loyal friend, "to watch this excellent princess hastening to destruction without anyone calling her attention to the danger she was running." But Mary refused to listen and would accept no warning. A morbid delight in preposterous hazards drove her farther and farther. Circumspection became impossible to her; she would not ask and would not hearken; but could only rush to her doom, the slave of her feelings. The day after Bothwell flaunted his freedom in the streets of Edinburgh, she inflicted a humiliation on the whole country by conferring upon this notorious criminal the highest honour Scotland could offer. At the opening of parliament Bothwell bore the insignia of the nation, the crown and the sceptre. Who could doubt that this man who now carried the crown in his hands would tomorrow be wearing it? Bothwell, indeed, was not a man to hide his light under a bushel, and his boldness was one of his least unamiable characteristics. Impudently, energetically, and frankly, he demanded his reward. Without shame, "for his great and manifold gud service" he asked for the gift of the strongest castle in the country, Dunbar. Then, since the Scottish lords complied with his will, he determined to force from them their consent to his marriage with Mary Stuart. On the evening when the sittings of parliament closed, as dictator he invited the whole company of them to supper in Ainslie's Taverne. The wine flowed freely, and when most of those present were already half-seas-over (we recall the famous scene in *Wallenstein*), he laid before the lords a bond which not only made them pledge themselves to defend him against every calumniator but also to approve him, "noble puissant lord," as a worthy husband for the queen. The bond ran as follows: "That James Earl of Bothwell, Lord of Hailes, Crichton, and Liddesdale, Great Admiral of Scotland, and Lieutenant of all the Marches, being calumniated by malicious report and divers placards, privily affixed on the Kirk of Edinburgh and other places, by evil-willers and privy enemies, as art and part in the heinous murder of the King, late husband to the Queen's Majesty, and also by special letters sent to her Highness by the Earl of Lennox accused of the said crime, had submitted to an assize, and been found innocent of the same by certain noblemen his peers, and other barons of good reputation; the undersigned united to defend and bear him harmless against his privy or public calumniators bypast or to come." The signatories to this instrument, including eight earls, among whom were the Earls of Morton, Huntly, and Argyll (Justice-General), Glencairn, Cassilis, and Rothes, together with eleven barons, peers of parliament, united to declare that they considered Bothwell a proper person to recommend the widowed queen to accept as husband, pledging themselves "on their honour and fidelity . . . to further, advance, and set forward such marriage betwixt her Highness and the said noble lord." In pursuit thereof they would "spend and bestow" their "lives and goods, against all that live or die," as they might "answer to God" upon their own "fidelities and conscience."

Only one of the company, the Earl of Eglinton, misliking the bond, slipped away from the tavern before it was signed. The others obediently subscribed their names, for Bothwell's stalwarts surrounded the house—though many of the signatories were perhaps determined, when occasion offered, to break their pledged word. They knew that what is written in ink can be washed out with blood. Anyhow, no one entered a protest against signing. After this formality the company went on carousing gaily, and the merriest among them may well have been Bothwell, for now he had gained his ends. A few weeks later, and the Queen of Scotland and the Isles would wed the murderer of her husband as heedlessly as did Hamlet's mother wed Claudius. Quos deus perdere vult . . .

CHAPTER FOURTEEN

A Blind Alley

(APRIL TO JUNE 1567)

AS THE Bothwell tragedy advances towards its climax, we are again and again reminded of Shakespeare. The resemblance of the situation to that of *Hamlet* is obvious on the face of it. In both cases we have a king who has been murdered by his wife's lover; in both cases the widowed queen shows unseemly haste in marrying her husband's murderer; alike in the tragedy of real life and in the tragedy conceived by the playwright, we note the enduring consequences of a murder whose concealment and repudiation demand more effort than was requisite for the performance of the crime. Even stronger, even more striking, are the analogies between many scenes of Shakespeare's Scottish tragedy and those of the historical tragedy in sixteenth-century Scotland. Whether wittingly or unwittingly, *Macbeth* was created in the atmosphere of the Mary Stuart drama; the happenings staged by Shakespeare's imagination in Dunsinane Castle had previously been staged in fact at Holyrood Palace. In both cases, after the murder had taken place, there was the same isolation, the same oppressive spiritual gloom, the same ghastly festivals in which none dared to take pleasure and from which one after another slipped away because the ravens of black disaster were already circling round the house. Often we find it hard to distinguish whether it is Mary Stuart we are watching as she wanders by night through the apartments, sleepless, confused, tormented by pangs of conscience, or whether it is Lady Macbeth wailing: "All the perfumes of Arabia will not sweeten this little hand." Is it Bothwell, or is it Macbeth, who becomes harsher and more resolute after he has committed his crime; who more and more boldly challenges the enmity of Scotland—though he knows well enough that his courage is futile, and that ghosts are stronger than a living man? In both cases alike, a woman's passion is the motive power, but the man is appointed to do the deed; as extraordinarily similar are the atmospheres, the oppression that lours over the tormented spirits, husband and wife chained together by the crime, each dragging the other down into the same dark abyss. Never in history or in literature have the psychology of assassination and the mysterious power exerted after death by a victim upon a murderer been more magnificently depicted than in these two Scottish tragedies, one in the realm of fable and the other in that of real life.

Are such remarkable similarities the product of chance? Have we not good ground for assuming that, in *Macbeth,* Shakespeare was dramatizing and sublimating the tragedy of Mary Stuart? The dramatist was three years old when the tragedy of Bothwell and Mary Stuart was played; he was a man of forty when he wrote *Macbeth.* The impressions of childhood exert an ineffaceable influence upon a poet's mind, genius transmuting stimuli that have acted in childhood into imperishable realities. We cannot doubt that Shakespeare had been informed about the happenings in the palace at Holyrood. In his youth at Stratford he must have heard many details and legends about the Scottish queen who had thrown away her kingdom and her crown in pursuit of a frenzied passion, and who, in punishment, had been prisoned in one English castle after another. In 1587 Shakespeare had already been in London for a year, a play-actor, and probably trying his prentice hand as playwright, when the bells in the London churches pealed to announce that at length the head of Elizabeth Tudor's chief adversary had been cut off, and that Henry Darnley had dragged his unfaithful wife down to join him in the tomb. When, in Holinshed's *Chronicles of England, Scotland, and Ireland,* the dramatist came to read the story of the Thane of Cawdor who slew Duncan and usurped the crown of Scotland, may we not suppose that he interwove his memories of the tragical fate of Mary Queen of Scotland and the Isles into the substance of his drama? We cannot, indeed, either affirm or deny that Shakespeare, in writing his tragedy, was influenced by his knowledge of the life and death of Mary Stuart. This much, however, is certain, that only those who have studied and understood the psychology of Lady Macbeth after the murder of Duncan will be able fully to understand the moods and the actions of Mary Stuart during those dark days at Holyrood—to understand the torments of a woman strong of soul, who was yet not strong enough to face up to the darkest of her deeds.

The most amazing part of the resemblance between the two tragedies, that conceived by the playwright and that recorded by historians and biographers, is the resemblance in the changes which took place in Mary Stuart and in Lady Macbeth after the crime had been committed. Before the murder Lady Macbeth had been a loving, warm-hearted, energetic woman, strong of will and fired by ambition. Her supreme desire was to help the man she loved and lift him to greatness, and she might have penned many of the lines from Mary Stuart's sonnet: "Pour luy ie veux recercher la grandeure. . . ."

Ambition supplies her with abundant energy until the deed. Lady Macbeth is crafty, shrewd, and resolute while the crime is still only willed, proposed, and planned, while the hot, red blood has not yet flowed over her hands and over her soul. With cajoling words like those used by Mary to lure Darnley to Kirk o' Field, she lures Duncan into the bedchamber where the dagger is awaiting him. But immediately after the crime she becomes a different woman, losing both strength and courage. Conscience burns within her like a furnace. Delirious, with rigid gaze, she wanders through the rooms of the castle, a horror to her friends and a terror to herself. Her brain is overwhelmed by one desire, the longing to forget, the morbid yearning for surcease from thought, the craving for death. So was it, likewise, with Mary Stuart after Darnley's murder. She had been completely transformed, not only in mind, but in aspect as well, so that Drury, one of Elizabeth's spies, reported to his royal mistress that never, without a severe illness, had a woman changed in outward appearance in so brief a time and so remarkably as had the queen.

There was nothing now about her to recall the cheerful, talkative, self-confident woman she had been only a few weeks before. She was silent, and shunned company. Perhaps, like Macbeth and Lady Macbeth, she continued to hope that the world would be silent if she herself were silent, and that the black waves would recede. But when questioning voices became urgent; when, at night, from the streets of Edinburgh, the names of the murderers were shouted up at her windows; when Lennox, her slain husband's father, and Elizabeth, her enemy, and Seton, her friend, made common cause with the rest of the world in insisting that the criminals must be called to account, she lost her head. She knew that she must do something to hide the crime, to exculpate herself. But she lacked the will for defence, and could not find words that would be convincing though deceptive. As if in a trance, she listened to the voices from London, from Paris, from Madrid, and from Rome, exhorting her and warning her; but none of them could awaken her from her stupor. She listened to them only as one buried alive might listen to the footsteps of those who passed by his grave—defenceless, impotent, and despairing.

She knew that it was incumbent upon her to play the sorrowful widow, to shed the tears that might make people believe her innocent. But her throat was dry as well as her eyes; she could not speak and could not dissemble. Things went on in this way for week after week, until at length she could bear no more. As a hunted beast turns at bay, as Macbeth, seeking safety, added new murders to the murder which was already clamouring for vengeance, so Mary Stuart at length threw off her intolerable inertia. No longer did she care what the world thought of her, and whether her actions were wise or foolish. Movement had become essential to her, speedier and speedier movement, to outrun the warning and the threatening voices. On! On! Anything, now, but stillness and reflection, for self-communings forced her to recognize that no skill could save her. One of the mysteries of the human mind is that, for a brief time, speed can overcome anxiety. Just as a coachman who feels and hears the bridge breaking down beneath his carriage flogs his horses into the gallop which can alone rescue him from the danger, so Mary Stuart spurred the black charger of her destiny onward in her despair, hoping to outrun her thoughts, to escape from her own criticism. Neither to think nor to know nor to hear nor to see any more; only on and on into frenzy! Better a terrible end than terror without end. Just as a falling stone drops with a steadily accelerating velocity as it plunges deeper into the abyss, so do people act more hastily and more foolishly when they can see no issue from their troubles.

Mary Stuart's actions during the weeks after the murder cannot be explained on reasonable grounds, but only as the outcome of unconquerable anxiety. One would have thought that even in her frenzy she might have told herself that she was flinging her honour to the winds and exposing herself to universal condemnation. That all Scotland, all Europe, would regard her marriage to the murderer of her husband within a few weeks of the crime as an outrage. If she had spent a year, or better two years, in retirement, since memories are short, the world might have forgotten. Then, by adroit diplomatic manœuvres, various reasons might have been found for her choice of Bothwell as husband. But Mary was flying towards destruction when, without a decent interval of mourning, she was in such haste to set her murdered husband's crown on the murderer's head. Yet this was the crazy course she took.

Only one explanation of such behaviour is possible in the case of a woman who, in general, was shrewd and tolerably circumspect. Mary Stuart was under duress. Manifestly she could not wait, because waiting would disclose a shameful secret. To anyone with insight into such matters it must have been obvious that the only explanation of the way in which Mary rushed into marriage with Bothwell was that the unhappy woman knew herself to be with child. She knew herself to be with child, not with a posthumous son of King Henry, but with the fruit of an adulterous passion. A queen of Scotland must not give birth to an illegitimate child, least of all under conditions likely to proclaim from the house-tops her complicity in her husband's murder. For in that case it would inevitably be disclosed how voluptuously she had passed with her lover what should have been the days of her mourning for her husband, and even a poor reckoner could have counted up the months to decide whether Mary had become Bothwell's mistress shortly before or shortly after the murder of Darnley. Either supposition would have been equally disgraceful. Nothing but a prompt legitimization through marriage could save her child's honour, and perhaps to some extent her own. If she were already Bothwell's wife when the child came into the world, pre-conjugal relations with him might seem excusable. In any case the infant would bear Bothwell's name, and Bothwell would know how to defend its rights. Not a month, not a week, must be lost. It was a horrible choice by which she was faced, but no doubt it seemed less shameful to her to marry in haste the murderer of her husband than to bring a fatherless child into the world. Only on such a supposition does the apparent unnaturalness of Mary's behaviour during these weeks become comprehensible. Other interpretations serve merely to obscure the picture. At all times women suffering from this particular dread have been driven by it to foolish and criminal deeds. Mary, the queen, was but one among millions of her sex rendered distraught by an unwelcome maternity. No other theory can explain the insensate, the tragical haste of her marriage to Bothwell.

She was in a dreadful situation, and no demon could have imagined a crueller one. On the one hand, knowing herself to be with child, she was in a desperate hurry; but this hurry proclaimed her complicity in Darnley's murder. As Queen of Scotland, as widow, as a woman of the highest rank and station, watched closely by Edinburgh, by Scotland, by the whole European world, Mary must have known that so notorious a man as Bothwell, universally regarded as the murderer of Darnley, was the last whom she ought to marry; but, as a helpless woman, she knew him to be her only saviour. She ought not to marry him, and yet was compelled to marry him. That the real cause for haste might not be disclosed, some other reason for a speedy wedding must be invented. A pretext must be found which would outweigh the legal and moral objections to the proposed union.

But how can a queen be constrained to marry a man of lower degree? The code of honour of those days recognized only one possibility in such a case. If a woman had been forcibly robbed of her honour, it was the violator's duty to re-establish her honour. Only if, as a wife, she had been raped, could Mary Stuart find the glimmer of an excuse for marrying Bothwell. Only in that case could the illusion be diffused among the populace that she had not married Bothwell from free will, but under compulsion of the inevitable.

So fantastic a plan for escape could appeal only to a woman in a blind alley. Nothing but madness could engender such madness. Mary, who in general was courageous and resolute at decisive moments, shrank back when Bothwell proposed this tragical path to her. "I wish I were dead, for I see that all will turn out ill," she wrote in her distress. But whatever moralists may think about Bothwell, he always remained a splendidly bold desperado. Little did he care that before the eyes of Europe he had to parade himself as a shameless robber, the ravisher of a queen, a villain who heeded neither law nor morals. Though the gates of hell should yawn in his path, he was not the man to hesitate when there was a crown to win. He was not appalled by any danger, resembling in this Mozart's Don Giovanni who jeeringly invited the statue of the murdered Commander to the death-feast. Beside him shuddered his Leporello, his brother-in-law Huntly, who, for a few sinecures, had just consented to his sister's divorce from Bothwell. Huntly, being less stalwart, soon took fright, hastened to the queen, and tried to dissuade her from the proposed venture. Bothwell, who was ready to defy a world in arms, was not troubled by the defection of this confederate. Nor did it affright him that the plan for the abduction of Mary had probably been blown upon. (In actual fact, one of Elizabeth's spies reported the scheme to London in a dispatch sent the day before it was carried into effect.) Nor did it matter to the earl whether the abduction would be regarded as genuine or spurious, so long as it brought him to his goal, the kingship. His only law was his own will, though death and the devil stood in the way; and he had power enough over Mary to drag her whithersoever he pleased.

Once more we learn from the Casket Letters that Mary was inwardly rebellious to the harsh will of her new lord and master. She had an inkling that this fresh deception would not impose upon the world. Still, as before, she obeyed him to whom she had surrendered her will. As submissively as when she helped to lure Darnley to Edinburgh, so, though with a heavy heart, she lent herself to the proposed "abduction"; and, scene after scene, the comedy of this collusive rape was carried out, strictly according to plan.

On April 21, 1567, only nine days after the extorted acquittal of Bothwell, two days after, at the famous supper-party in Ainslie's Taverne, Bothwell had compelled most of the Scottish lords to consent to the proposed marriage; exactly nine years and two days since Mary's betrothal, or "handfasting," to the Dauphin of France in the great hall of the Louvre—the queen, who had hitherto shown little maternal affection, was seized with an urgent desire to visit her little son at Stirling. The Earl of Mar, guardian of Prince James, gave her a suspicious welcome, for all sorts of rumours had come to his ears. Mary was not allowed to see her baby boy alone, since the Scottish lords were afraid of her kidnapping James and handing him over to Bothwell. It had become plain that she no longer possessed any will of her own, and would, without demur, carry out the most criminal instructions of her tyrant. If there had been any idea of such a kidnapping, it was frustrated by Mar's caution.

After seeing her son, Mary rode back towards Edinburgh, attended by only a few riders, among whom were Huntly and Lethington, undoubtedly parties to the plot for her "abduction." When the queen and her train reached Almond Bridge, between Linlithgow and Edinburgh, six miles from the capital, she found Bothwell, with eight hundred cavalrymen, blocking her way. This overwhelmingly superior force "attacked" the queen's troops. Of course there was no fighting, for Mary Stuart, "wishing to avoid bloodshed," forbade her attendants to resist. It was enough for Bothwell to seize the bridle of her palfrey for the queen to "surrender," and allow herself to be led off to the desired captivity at Dunbar. An over-zealous captain, who wished to set out for reinforcements and try to "rescue" the "prisoner," was given a broad hint that Mary was a consenting party to the capture. Huntly and Lethington were dismissed unhurt. No one was to be injured in this "affray." The only thing necessary was that Mary herself should remain in the "custody" of her beloved ravisher. For more than a week ensuing she shared his bed at Dunbar, while simultaneously in Edinburgh, with great haste (and with wheels greased by corruption), Bothwell's divorce from his wife was carried through the ecclesiastical courts, both Protestant and Catholic. As far as the former were concerned, the shabby plea was put in that Bothwell had had adulterous relations with a servingmaid. The Catholic court made the belated discovery that his marriage with Lady Jane Gordon was null and void because the pair were related in the fourth degree. At length this dark business was over. Then the world could be informed that Bothwell had carried off the unsuspecting Mary with the strong hand, and had raped her at Dunbar. Nothing but marriage to the man who had possessed her against her will could restore the honour of the Queen of Scotland.

This "abduction" was too obviously accordant with the wishes of those concerned for anyone to believe that the Queen of Scotland had really been "carried off by force and raped." Even the Spanish ambassador, who was well affected towards Mary, reported to Madrid that the whole affair had been play-acting. Strangely enough, however, it was those who were best in a position to see through the pretence that now behaved as if the alleged abduction and rape had been genuine. The Scottish lords, who had meanwhile already signed a bond for the removal of Bothwell, made a grotesque pretence of taking the comedy of the abduction seriously. With a touching display of fidelity they protested themselves enraged because the queen of their country had been seized and detained against her will, to the dishonour of Scotland. With unwonted unanimity they declared themselves ready, as loyal subjects, to rescue the helpless lamb from the clutches of the wicked wolf Bothwell. Bothwell had at length given them a long-desired excuse for, under the mask of patriotism, attacking the military dictator. They hastily got together to "rescue" Mary from his clutches, and thus prevent the marriage which, only a week earlier, they had agreed to promote.

Nothing could have been more distressing to Mary than this sudden determination of her "loyal" nobles to protect her against her "ravisher." They were plucking from her hands the cards she had so carefully and deceitfully arranged. Since she had no wish to be "liberated" from Bothwell, but desired to be bound to him for ever, she now found it necessary to make short work of the lying statement that Bothwell had carried her off by force. Whereas yesterday she had wanted to blacken him, today it was incumbent on her to whitewash him, and thus to destroy the whole effect of the farce she had been playing. To prevent any serious charge being brought against Bothwell, she became the most zealous defender of the ravisher. His behaviour had, indeed, "been rather strange at first; but since then he had given her no grounds for complaint." As no one had assisted her to resist the abduction, she had been "compelled to modify her first disinclination and to give serious attention to his proposal." More and more deplorable grew the situation of this unhappy woman, entangled in the thorny thicket of her passion. The last veils were stripped from her, leaving her naked to the scorn of the world.

It was with consternation that Mary's friends watched her return to Edinburgh in the beginning of May. Bothwell was leading her horse by the bridle; and to show that she came with him of her own free will, his spearmen were ostentatiously unarmed. Vainly did those who honestly wished well to Mary Stuart and to Scotland warn the queen of the error of her present courses. Du Croc, the French ambassador, told her that if she married Bothwell, this would put an end to the friendship with France. One of her most trusty adherents, Lord Herries, threw himself at her feet, imploring her to think better of what she was doing; while Sir James Melville, as ever a loyal and sagacious adviser, had to flee from the wrath of Bothwell when, at the last moment, he tried to hinder this unhappy marriage. All her adherents were heavy-hearted because this splendid woman was in thrall to a dastardly adventurer; and they foresaw that the mad haste with which she was wedding the murderer of her husband would lose her both her crown and her honour. Good days had dawned for her opponents. The gloomy prophecy of John Knox was being disastrously fulfilled. John Craig, who had succeeded Knox as minister at St. Giles's, refused at first to have the banns published in the kirk. He openly stigmatized the marriage as "odious and slanderous before the world." Not until Bothwell threatened him with the gallows did he lend himself to promoting the marriage.

Mary, however, had to bow her neck lower and lower beneath the yoke. For now, when everyone knew how urgently the queen needed this marriage, she was shamelessly blackmailed by those whose help and approval were requisite. Huntly demanded and secured the return of all the estates that had been escheated to the crown, this being his payment for consenting to his sister's divorce from Bothwell. The Catholic bishop received manifold offices and dignities; but the highest price was demanded by the Protestant minister, who insisted upon the queen's public humiliation. Since the urgency of her need was well known, she was compelled to declare that she, a Catholic princess, on the maternal side a descendant of the Guises, would have her marriage celebrated in accordance with the Reformed, that is to say heretical, rites. By acceding to this demand, Mary Stuart flung away the last card which might have enabled her to secure the support of Catholic Europe and to retain the favour of the Pope, the sympathies of

Spain and France. Henceforward united Catholicism would be against her. Terribly true had become the words of the sonnet:

Pour luy depuis iay mesprise l'honneur
Ce qui nous peut seul prouoir de bonheur.
Pour luy iay hasarde grandeur et conscience.
Pour luy tous mes parents i'ay quisté et amys.

[For him since then I have despised honour,
Which alone can provide us with happiness.
For him I have risked dignity and conscience.
For him I have forsaken all my relatives and friends.]

Nothing now could save her, since she had forsaken herself. The gods will not accept such foolish sacrifices as hers.

It will be hard to find in the pages of history a more painful description of a wedding than that of Mary's third marriage on May 15, 1567; the picture is one of the utter debasement of an unhappy queen. Her first marriage, to the dauphin, afterwards Francis II of France, had been a resplendent occasion. Tens of thousands had acclaimed the young bride who was Queen of Scotland and was to be Queen of France. From far and wide the nobility of France, the envoys of all lands, had assembled to watch the dauphiness's progress to Notre Dame, attended by the royal family and the flower of French chivalry. The second marriage had been a quieter affair. No longer at high noon, but between five and six o'clock in the morning, the priest had wedded her to the great-grandson of Henry VII. Still, the Scottish nobles had been on hand, and the foreign ambassadors likewise, while the good people of Edinburgh kept high festival throughout the day. But this third marriage, that to Bothwell—who at the last moment had been created Duke of Orkney—was perpetrated as secretly as a crime. In the small hours (four o'clock), when the city was still asleep, a few persons assembled, almost furtively, in the old chapel of Holyrood. It was not three months since Darnley's murder, so his widow was married in her "dule-weed." The chapel was almost empty. Numerous guests had been invited, but few of them wished to grace the occasion by their presence, or to see the Queen of Scotland accept a wedding-ring from the hand of him who had slain Darnley. Almost all the Scottish lords had stayed away, with or without excuse. Moray and Lennox had left the country; Lethington and Huntly, who were half in the plot, absented themselves; and the only man to whom, as a devout Catholic, Mary had hitherto been able to disclose her most secret thoughts, even her father-confessor, had taken leave of her for ever. Her spiritual director had sadly acknowledged that he regarded her henceforward as lost. No one in whom there persisted a spark of honour wished to witness the marriage of Darnley's murderer to Darnley's widow, or the alleged consecration of this crime by religious rites. Fruitlessly had Mary implored the French ambassador to be present so as to give the wedding a semblance of respectability. Du Croc, her good friend, steadfastly refused to attend. His presence would have signified the assent of France. "Had I gone, one might have believed that my King had had a hand in these affairs." Besides, he did not wish to recognize Bothwell as the queen's consort. The marriage service was read by Adam Bothwell, Bishop of Orkney, assisted by the Reverend John Craig. No Mass was said, no organ sounded, short work was made of the ceremony. No arrangements were made for a dance or a banquet that evening. Nor, as when Mary had wedded Darnley, was money scattered among a rejoicing crowd, with cries of "Largesse, largesse!" The capital was as cold, as empty, and as chill as a new-made grave; and the few witnesses of this strange wedding were as mournful and silent as mutes at a funeral. There was no procession through the streets. The wedded pair hastened from the doleful chapel to lock themselves up in the privacy of their own apartments.

For, at the very moment when, after blindly straining forward to her goal, Mary had achieved her purpose, she underwent a spiritual collapse. She had fulfilled her wish of making Bothwell her own. Up to the hour of the wedding she had persisted in the illusion that a union with him, the formal sanctification of their love, would rid her of her anxieties. But now, when she no longer had a purpose to fulfil, no object on which to fix her gaze, her eyes were opened, and she stared round her—into vacancy. Discord between the pair seems to have begun directly after the wedding. As invariably happens when two persons have dragged one another down towards destruction, each was inclined to blame the other for what had gone awry. On the afternoon of the wedding-day, du Croc, who visited Mary at her request, found her in despair. Night had not yet fallen, but a chill spectre had arisen to separate Mary from Bothwell. "Repentance has already begun," reported the French ambassador to Paris. "When I went to see Her Majesty on Thursday afternoon, I noticed something strange in the manner of her and her husband, which she sought to excuse; saying that if she was sad, it was because she wished to be so, and she never wished to rejoice again. All that she wished for was death. Yesterday, while she and her husband were together, shut up in their cabinet, she cried out aloud for a knife with which to kill herself. Those who were in the outer chamber heard her. They fear that unless God comes to her aid she will, in her despair, do herself a mischief." Soon there were other trustworthy reports of dissension between the newly wedded pair. Bothwell, indeed, was said to regard the divorce from his pretty young wife, Lady Jane Gordon, as invalid, and spent nights with her instead of with Mary. "From the day of the wedding," reports du Croc once more, "there was no end to the fears and the plaints of Mary Stuart." Now that the blinded woman had forced the hand of fate, she knew that all was lost, and that death would be better than the life of torment she had brought upon herself.

This ghastly honeymoon endured for three weeks and was a time of agony throughout. Whatever the pair tried to do in the hope of holding together and of saving themselves proved futile. When in the public eye, Bothwell, indeed, made a parade of respect and affection for the queen, feigning love and humility; but his words and gestures counted for nothing in view of his dreadful record. The populace was gloomy, and looked askance at the pair of criminals. Vainly did the dictator, since the nobles held aloof, woo the favour of the commonalty, playing the liberal, the kindly, the pious ruler. He attended the services of the Reformed Church, only to find that the Protestant clergy were as hostile to him as the Catholic. He wrote humbly worded letters to Elizabeth, which she left unanswered. He wrote to Paris, but his epistles were ignored. Mary summoned the Scottish lords, but they held aloof in Stirling. She demanded the custody of her child, but the Earl of Mar refused to surrender little James to her care. A horrible silence surrounded the queen and Bothwell. To give the semblance of security and cheerfulness, Bothwell hastily improvised a masque and a regatta. This water-pageant was held at Leith, and Mary graced it with her presence, to watch her consort ride at the ring and review the troops. Wanly she smiled at her spouse. The common folk, always ready for a show, assembled in great numbers, but did not rejoice. The country seemed paralysed with fear, which was likely, in a moment, to blaze up into wrath.

Bothwell was not the man to be carried away by sentiment. An experienced seaman, he could read the signs of a coming storm. With inveterate resolution he prepared to meet all hazards. He knew that his enemies aimed at his life, and that matters would soon be decided by an appeal to arms. Hastily, therefore, he sharked up what riders and foot-soldiers he could, in order to be prepared to resist attacks. Mary sacrificed everything left to her in order to aid him in paying his mercenaries; she sold her jewels, borrowed such moneys as she could, and at length (though this was a grievous affront to the English queen) decided that the silver-gilt font Elizabeth had sent her for little James's christening should be committed to the melting-pot in the hope of prolonging the agony of her own rule. In threatening silence, however, the Scottish lords gathered together, enveloping the palace like a thunderstorm which might at any moment shoot forth its lightnings against the royal pair. Bothwell was too familiar with the cunning of his erstwhile associates to trust the semblance of tranquillity. He knew well enough that they were planning to strike him out of the darkness, and he would not await their onslaught in unfortified Holyrood. On June 5, barely three weeks after the wedding, he and Mary rode from Edinburgh to the stronghold of Borthwick, a few miles south of the capital in the direction of the border, where his principal strength lay. There, Mary, as a last hope, issued a summons for June 12, addressed to her "subjects, noblemen, knights, esquires, gentlemen, and yeomen," who were to assemble under arms, provided with a week's supply of food. Obviously Bothwell designed, by a sudden attack, to strike down his enemies before they had gathered their own forces.

But this flight from Holyrood gave the Scottish lords courage. Hastily they moved upon Edinburgh, occupying the capital without resistance. Sir James Balfour, who had been Bothwell's chief assistant in the murder, was ready and willing to betray his confederate, so that a couple of thousand riders were able to gallop off to Borthwick to seize Bothwell before he could get his troops together and equip them for battle. Bothwell, however, would not allow himself to be taken like a wild beast in a snare. He jumped out of a window before the main body of his enemies under Morton and Hume arrived on the scene, and spurred away, leaving Mary behind. The Scottish lords did not, at this juncture, venture to use arms against their queen, being content with the attempt to persuade her to detach herself from Bothwell. She, however, was still in thrall to her ravisher. During the night, hastily dressing herself as a boy, she mounted her horse and, soon joined by her husband, rode with him to Dunbar, leaving all else in order to live or die with Bothwell.

One little sign ought to have convinced the queen that her cause was lost. For on the day of her flight from Edinburgh to Borthwick Castle there suddenly disappeared, "without leave-taking," her last adviser, Maitland of Lethington, the only man who, during these weeks when she had been distraught by passion, had continued to show some degree of loyalty. Lethington had followed his mistress a long way on the gloomy descent to ruin, and perhaps—Bothwell apart—no one had done more than he to weave the net of murder around Darnley. But now he felt that the wind had changed and was blowing in full force against the queen. A typical diplomatist, one of those who always trim their sails to the breeze of power, he would no longer help in a cause he knew to be lost. While the ride to Borthwick was in progress, he quietly turned his horse and rode back to join the other side. The last rat had deserted the sinking ship.

Mary was unteachable; she could be neither intimidated nor warned. In this astonishing woman danger served only to intensify the courage that gave her greatest follies a romantic glamour. Reaching Dunbar on horseback, in male attire, she found there no royal robes, no harness, no equipment. What matter? This was not the time for courtly state, now that war had been declared. From a woman of the people she borrowed a feminine outfit—"a red petticoat, with sleeves tied with points, a partlet, a black velvet hat and a muffler." Little did she care if her appearance was unqueenly, so long as she could ride beside the man who was all that remained to her on earth, and for whom she had sacrificed everything. Bothwell quickly mustered what forces he could. The "subjects, noblemen, knights, esquires, gentlemen, and yeomen" had failed to assemble. Scotland was no longer loyal to its queen. With two hundred mercenary harquebusiers as shock-troops and a rabble of poorly armed peasants and borderers (not more than about twelve hundred men in all) on June 14 the queen and Bothwell rashly abandoned Dunbar and set forth to attack Edinburgh. The insignificant army was driven onward by the sturdy will of the earl, who hoped to take the Scottish lords by surprise. He knew that foolhardiness can sometimes save a situation in defiance of reasonable calculation.

At Carberry Hill, six miles from Edinburgh, on Sunday, June 15, the two rabbles (they are not worthy the name of armies) came face to face. The queen's troops, now swelled by reinforcements to three thousand five hundred, outnumbered those of her enemies. But few of the lords of the realm, few of the nobility and gentry, were fighting under the royal banner of the Scottish lion. Except for the beforementioned harquebusiers (mercenaries) the queen's main supporters were Bothwell's moss-troopers, whose lust for battle was almost wholly in abeyance. Less than half a league away, on the other side of the stream, were the forces of her adversaries, well mounted gentlefolk, adequately armed, and trained for combat. The standard under which they were prepared to fight was a strange one for those who had been accomplices in the late king's murder. It was of white silk, and upon it was painted the dead body of Darnley, with the infant James praying before it, in the words: "Judge and avenge my caus, O Lord!" Thus the very men who had participated in the slaying of Darnley now wished to represent themselves as Darnley's avengers, and to proclaim themselves as having taken up arms only against his murderer, not in rebellion against the queen.

The two banners fluttered bravely in the wind. But there was no bravery in the hearts of those who formed either body of combatants. Neither side would advance to the attack across the burn. Both parties stood watching one another warily. Bothwell's borderers had no mind to let themselves be slaughtered for a cause beyond their understanding. The Scottish lords, on their side, had certain scruples which rendered them unwilling to use spears and swords against their rightful queen. To bring a monarch to his death by a cleverly devised hole-and-corner conspiracy, thereafter to hang a few poor devils of the lower orders and solemnly proclaim their own innocence—little matters of that sort did not occasion them any pricks of conscience. But in open day to assail a sovereign ruler conflicted with the feudalist notions which still swayed their minds.

Du Croc, the French ambassador, present on the battlefield as a neutral observer, did not fail to notice that neither side was eager for the fray, and therefore hastened to offer his services as mediator. Under a flag of truce, with an escort of fifty horse, the Frenchman crossed the brook to parley with Bothwell and the queen.

It was a strange audience. Mary, who had been accustomed to receive the French ambassador beneath a royal canopy, and robed in court attire, was sitting on the stones, clad as aforesaid, with a short kilt which barely covered her knees. But she was no less dignified, no less proud, than if she had been in full panoply of State. She could not master her wrath. As if she were still queen of the situation as she was still virtually queen of the country, she demanded that the Scottish lords should immediately make their submission. The lords, she said, had formally acquitted Bothwell, but now they were accusing him of the murder. They had asked her to marry Bothwell, and now dared to make a crime of her having done so. No doubt, in these respects, Mary's indignation was justified; but the hour of right had passed, and the hour of might had come. While Mary was parleying with du Croc, Bothwell rode up. The ambassador saluted him, but did not shake hands. Now Bothwell had his word to say. He spoke clearly, and without reservations. Not a shade of fear troubled his audacious countenance. Du Croc himself had, unwillingly, to admit the unshaken courage of the desperado. "I must acknowledge," wrote the ambassador in his report to the King of France, under date June 17, 1567, "that I saw in him a great warrior, who spoke with self-confidence, and was well able to lead his followers boldly and skilfully. I could not but admire him, because he was well aware that his enemies were resolute, and that he could not count upon the fidelity of a bare half of his own forces. Nevertheless he was undismayed." Bothwell proposed that the issue should be decided by single combat between himself and anyone of equal rank whom his enemies chose to appoint. His cause was just, and God would be on his side. Banteringly he told the Frenchman to watch the proposed duel from a neighbouring hillock. That would be good sport. The queen, however, would hear nothing of the proposal. "No, no," she interposed, "I will not suffer that; I will fight out the quarrel by his side." She still hoped that her enemies would submit to her authority. A born romanticist, she was now, as ever, lacking in the sense of reality. Du Croc speedily realized that his mission was fruitless. The fine old fellow would gladly have helped the queen if he could, and the tears came to his eyes, but so long as she stood by Bothwell there was no hope for her. Farewell, then. He bowed courteously, turned his horse, and rode slowly back to the Scottish lords.

The parley was finished. It was time for the battle to begin. But the rank and file had better sense than their leaders. They saw that the great men had been conversing amicably. Why should poor wretches shoot one another or cut one another down on such a fine afternoon? Bothwell's soldiers idled about, and when Queen Mary, as a last hope, ordered them to attack, they refused to advance. They had been loafing on the hillside for six or seven hours, and now the little force began to crumble away. As soon as the lords perceived this, they dispatched two hundred cavalrymen to cut off Bothwell's and the queen's retreat. Mary saw the danger, and, being still a woman in love, she thought, not of her own danger, but of Bothwell's. She knew that none of her subjects would lay a hand on herself, but that his enemies would not spare him, for Bothwell left alive might betray things which these belated avengers of Darnley would not like to have made public. For the first time in her life, therefore, she mastered her pride. She sent a messenger under a flag of truce to Kirkcaldy of Grange, asking him to come alone for a parley.

Reverence for the sacred command of a monarch had a magic effect. Kirkcaldy of Grange halted his riders. He went alone to Mary Stuart, and, before saying a word, he knelt to pay homage. Then he stated his conditions. The queen must leave Bothwell and return with the Scottish lords to Edinburgh. Bothwell could ride whithersoever he pleased. No one would pursue him.

Bothwell (a wonderful scene, and a wonderful man!) stood looking on without a word. He said nothing to Kirkcaldy nor yet anything to the queen to influence her decision. One cannot but feel he was ready to ride alone against the two hundred who were waiting at the foot of the hill, prepared, at a wave of Kirkcaldy's hand, to charge the hostile lines. Only when he heard that the queen had agreed to Kirkcaldy's proposal did Bothwell step to her and embrace her—for the last time, though neither of them knew this. Thereupon he mounted his horse and galloped off, followed only by a couple of servants. The dream was over, and the time of awakening had come.

The awakening came, dreadful, inexorable. The Scottish lords promised to conduct Mary back to Edinburgh with all due honour, and it is probable that such had been their intention. But hardly did she, seated on her jennet and wearing lowly attire, begin to ride through the ranks of the common soldiers, when, fired with scorn, they venomously reviled her. So long as the iron hand of Bothwell had protected the queen, the hatred of the populace had been kept in restraint. Now, when she was no longer thus safeguarded, contempt broke forth. A queen that had capitulated was no longer a queen to these rebel soldiers. They thronged round her more and more closely, inquisitively at first, then challengingly, with shouts of "Burn the whore! Burn the murderess!" Kirkcaldy laid about him with the flat of his sword, but in vain. More and more of the rebels closed around her, and held aloft, full in her sight, the banner demanding God's vengeance upon Darnley's murderer. This unroyal progress, this running of the gauntlet from Carberry Hill to Edinburgh lasted from six in the evening until ten. The populace thronged from the villages and from all the houses of the city to enjoy the spectacle of a captured queen. Again and again the press became so great that the ranks of the soldiers were broken. Never did Mary Stuart suffer a more profound humiliation than on this day.

But this proud woman might be humiliated; she would not bend. As a wound does not burn fiercely until it is cleansed, so Mary did not really feel her defeat until she was faced by this poison of scorn. Her hot blood, the blood of the Stuarts, the blood of the Guises, boiled. Instead of behaving prudently, she railed at the lords, holding them responsible for her contumelious treatment by the people. Like an angry lioness she roared at her enemies; she would hang them, would have them crucified; and suddenly she seized the Earl of Lindsay's hand, saying: "I swear, by this hand which is now in yours, that I will have your head." As always, in times of danger, her excess of courage led her into folly. Although the Scottish lords now had her safe in their hands, she openly used the most abusive language against them, expressing the utmost contempt for their misbehaviour, instead of maintaining a prudent silence or trying to win her subjects over by cajolery.

Probably her rage made the lords harsher than they had at first intended to be. At any rate, now that they felt she would never forgive them, they did their utmost to make the unruly woman feel her defencelessness. Instead of installing their queen in the palace of Holyrood, which lay without the city walls, they compelled her to ride past Kirk o' Field into Edinburgh, where the streets were filled with the rabble. There, through High Street, she was led to the provost's house, as if to the pillory. The door was locked upon her. Not one of her noblewomen or servantmaids was admitted. A night of despair followed. For days she had not changed her clothes. Since the morning she had not had a morsel of food. Terrible had been her sufferings from sunrise to sunset—a period in which she had lost her kingdom and her lover. Outside in the street there assembled, as before a wild beast's cage, a foul-tongued mob, to shout words of the coarsest opprobrium. Not until now, when the lords believed that her spirit was broken, did they try to negotiate with her. They did not ask much. Their only demand was that she should break away from Bothwell for ever. But the defiant woman could fight more boldly for a lost cause than for a hopeful one. Contemptuously she rejected their proposal, and one of her adversaries admitted later: "Never have I seen a more valiant woman than was the Queen on this occasion."

Since the Scottish lords could not by any threat induce Mary to forsake Bothwell, the cunningest among them tried to gain the same end by craft. Maitland of Lethington, her old and at one time her faithful adviser, used finer means. His appeal was to her jealousy, for he told her (perhaps it was true, perhaps false; who knows since the words were uttered by a diplomatist?) that Bothwell had been unfaithful to her, that during the few weeks of their marriage he had resumed intimate relationships with his divorced wife, had told Lady Jane Gordon that he regarded her as his lawful spouse and the queen as no more than a concubine. But Mary knew that she was surrounded by cheats, none of whose words were to be trusted. The information served only to drive her into a frenzy, with the result that Edinburgh saw the degrading sight of the Queen of Scotland behind barred windows with her dress torn, her breasts exposed, her hair hanging down, raging like a maniac, sobbing and shrieking, while she declared to the populace, touched in spite of frenzied hate, that it was their duty to free her, since she was being kept in duress by her own subjects.

The situation had become impossible. The Scottish lords would have been glad to yield a step or two. They felt, however, that they had now gone too far to retreat. It had become impossible for them to dream of reinstalling Mary Stuart in Holyrood as queen. Yet they could not leave her in the provost's house, surrounded by a raging mob, without incurring formidable responsibilities and arousing the anger of Elizabeth and all other foreign princes. The only man among them who had both courage and authority, Moray, was across the border. In his default, the other lords did not venture to come to a decision. The best they could do was to remove the queen to some safer retreat, and for this purpose they selected Lochleven Castle. That stronghold was on an island in the lake of the same name. It belonged to Margaret Douglas, Moray's mother, who would naturally not be too well disposed towards the daughter of Mary of Guise, for whom her lover James V had forsaken her.

The ominous word "imprisonment" was carefully avoided in the lords' proclamation. The queen was only "secluded" that "the person of Her Majesty might be kept from any communication with the aforesaid Earl Bothwell, and that she might not get into touch with those who wished to safeguard him from the just punishment of his crime." The measure they adopted was a half-measure, a provisional measure, dictated by fear, and prompted by an uneasy conscience. The rising against Queen Mary did not yet venture to declare itself a rebellion. All the blame was still laid upon the fugitive Bothwell. The secret determination to dethrone Mary was hidden away under cowardly though courteous words. To humbug the populace, which was still clamouring for judgment and execution of the "whore," on the evening of June 17 Mary Stuart was conveyed to Holyrood under a guard of three hundred men. But as soon as the citizens had gone to bed, a little procession was formed to conduct the monarch to Lochleven. This gloomy ride lasted until dawn. In the twilight of dawn, when the waters of the lake were beginning to show themselves more clearly, she approached the solitary, inaccessible fortress where she was to stay, who knew how long? She was rowed thither, and the gates clashed to behind her. The passionate and gloomy ballad of Darnley and Bothwell was finished. Now began the melancholy envoy, the chronicle of perpetual imprisonment.

CHAPTER FIFTEEN

Deposition

(SUMMER 1567)

FROM THIS day, June 17, 1567, when the Scottish lords prisoned their queen in Lochleven Castle, Mary did not cease, until the day of her death, to be a focus of European unrest. She incorporated a new-fangled problem, a revolutionary problem of far-reaching import. What was to be done with a monarch who was in sharp conflict with the people, and had proved unworthy to wear a crown? In this instance there can be no doubt that the sovereign lady had been to blame. By yielding to passion, Mary had brought about an impossible, an intolerable situation. Against the will of the nobility, the commonalty, and the clergy, she had chosen for husband a man wedded to another woman, and a man universally regarded as the murderer of her late husband, the King of Scotland. She had disregarded law and defied morality. She still stubbornly refused to admit that her foolish marriage was invalid. Even her best friends were agreed that she could not continue to rule Scotland with this assassin by her side.

What means were there of compelling the queen to abandon Bothwell or, as an alternative, to abdicate in favour of her son? There were none. In those days subjects had no constitutional rights against a monarch. Public opinion counted for nothing where a king or a queen was concerned. The people were not entitled to blame his or her actions; jurisdiction came to an end before the steps of a throne. The king was not, as today, the chief citizen of the State over which he ruled, but was himself the State, or stood above the State. Once he had been crowned and anointed, he could neither lay down his office nor make it over to another. No one could rob the anointed of the Lord of his dignity, so that, from the absolutist outlook, it was easier to deprive a ruler of his life than of his crown. He could be murdered, but could not be deposed, for to use force against him signified an infraction of the hierarchical ordering of the cosmos. With her criminal marriage Mary had put the world in this dilemma. Her fate would decide, not an isolated conflict, but a philosophical principle.

That was why the Scottish lords, although the ceremonies were respected, were in so feverish a hurry to find a satisfactory solution. Looking back across the centuries, we can see that they felt uneasy at their own revolutionary deed, at having imprisoned their sovereign; and the fact is that they were prepared to make things easy for Mary's reinstatement. It would be enough for her to admit her error by acknowledging her marriage with Bothwell to have been illegal. Then, though weakened doubtless in her hold on popular affection and in her authority, she could still have effected an honourable return to Holyrood, and could have chosen a worthier husband. But Mary remained unyielding. Regarding herself as infallible, she could not recognize that the rapid succession of scandals—that of Chastelard, of Rizzio, of Darnley, and of Bothwell—had led people to regard her as incorrigibly light-minded. She would not make the slightest concession. In the face of Scotland, in the face of the world, she defended Bothwell the assassin, maintaining that she could not separate herself from him, for, if she did so, his child, which she bore in her womb, would be a bastard. She continued to live in cloudland. A confirmed romanticist, she could not face realities; and, with a stubbornness which you may call foolish or splendid as you please, defied those who had marshalled their forces against her in a way that would lead her to a violent death. Nor her alone, for her grandson, Charles I, would in due time pay with his life for his claim to be an absolute ruler.

Still, at the outset she could count upon a certain amount of aid. So conspicuous a struggle between a sovereign ruler and her people could not leave the other crowned heads of Europe indifferent. Elizabeth, above all, was strongly on the side of the cousin she had so often opposed. This change of front on the part of the Queen of England, her ardent espousal of the cause of her rival, is usually regarded as one more sign of Elizabeth's inconstancy. No doubt the Tudor monarch was fickle, was a weathercock in petticoats, but in this instance her behaviour was consistent. If she now stood shoulder to shoulder with the Queen of Scotland and the Isles, this does not mean that she was siding with Mary Stuart the woman, the woman whose recent behaviour had naturally aroused so much suspicion. Elizabeth was a queen supporting another queen, supporting the principle that sovereign rights are inviolable, and therefore fighting for her own cause as well as Mary's. She did not feel sure enough of the loyalty of her nobles to look on inert while rebellious subjects took up arms against the queen of a neighbouring kingdom and flung her into prison. In defiance of Cecil, whose inclination was to extend assistance to the Protestant Scottish lords, Elizabeth was determined to force these rebels to return to their allegiance, thus defending herself while defending her cousin. For once, her words had the ring of truth when she said she was profoundly moved by what had happened. She hastened to promise her sisterly support to the prisoned queen, while at the same time blaming Mary's conduct as a woman. She drew a sharp distinction between her private views and the position she adopted as a crowned head.

Probably in July 1567, Elizabeth wrote to Mary as follows: "Madam, it hath been always held for a special principle in friendship that prosperity provideth, but adversity proveth friends; whereof at this time finding occasion to verify the same with our action, we have thought meet, both for our professions and your comfort, in these few words to testify our friendship, not only by admonishing you of the worst, but also to comfort you for the best. . . . Madam, to be plain with you, our grief hath not been small, that in this your marriage so slender consideration hath been had, that as we perceive manifestly, no good friend you have in the whole world can like thereof: and if we should otherwise write or say we should abuse you, for how could a worse choice be made for you, than in great haste to marry such a subject, who besides other notorious lacks, public fame hath charged with the murder of your late husband, besides the touching of yourself also in some part, though we trust in that behalf falsely? And with what peril have you married him that hath another wife alive, whereby neither by God's law nor man's yourself can be his lawful wife, nor any children betwixt you legitimate! Thus you see plainly what we think of the marriage, whereof we are heartly sorry that we can conceive no better, what colourable reason soever we have heard of your servant to induce us thereto. We wish, upon the death of your husband, the first care had been to have searched out and punished the murderers; which having been done effectually—as easily it might have been in a matter so notorious—there might have been many more things tolerated better in your marriage than that now can be suffered to be spoken of. And surely we cannot but for friendship to yourself, besides the natural instinct that we have of blood to your late husband, profess ourselves earnestly bent to do anything in our power to procure the due punishment of that murder against any subject that you have, how dear soever you hold him."

These are plain words, and cutting as a knife. They show that Elizabeth, who had doubtless been kept well informed by her spies and Moray about all that happened at Kirk o' Field, was convinced of Mary's complicity in the murder of Darnley. With very little periphrasis, she pointed to Bothwell as the actual murderer, and did not try to wrap up the unpalatable assurance in courtly or diplomatic words. The above-quoted letter shows, beyond question, that Elizabeth Tudor was prepared to support Mary Stuart the queen, and not her cousin Mary the woman, because in supporting the queen she was fighting for her own hand. In this remarkable letter Elizabeth continues: "Now for your comfort in such adversity as we have heard you should be in—whereof we cannot tell what to think to be true—we assure you, that whatsoever we can imagine meet to be for your honour and safety that shall lie in our power, we will perform the same; that it shall well appear you have a good neighbour, a dear sister, a faithful friend; and so shall you undoubtedly always find us and prove us to be indeed towards you; for which purpose we are determined to send with all speed one of our trusty servants, not only to understand your state but also, thereupon, so to deal with your nobility and people, as they shall find you not to lack our friendship and power for the preservation of your honour and greatness."

Elizabeth kept her word. She charged her special messenger to enter the strongest possible protest against the measures the rebels were taking against Mary, and to let the Scottish lords know that in the event of their using any violence towards her cousin she was determined to declare war. She fiercely reproved them for their presumptuousness in proposing to hold judgment upon an anointed queen. There was nothing in Holy Writ to justify subjects in deposing their heaven-given ruler. In no Christian monarchy was there any law authorizing subjects to touch the person of their prince, to prison him, or hale him before a court of assize. Elizabeth had been as much outraged as had been the Scottish lords by the murder of her cousin, the late king, and as much outraged as they by the queen's marriage to Bothwell. But she could neither tolerate nor condone their subsequent behaviour towards their queen. By God's ordinance they were her subjects and she was their ruler, and they therefore had no right to call her to account, since it was opposed to nature to make the head subordinate to the feet.

For the first time, however, Elizabeth encountered open resistance on the part of the Scottish lords, although most of them had been for years in her pay. Since the murder of Rizzio, they had known well enough what they might expect should Mary regain power. Neither their threats nor their cajoleries had induced her to forsake Bothwell; and they still had a lively memory of the invectives and menaces of vengeance which she had shrieked at them during the ride from Carberry Hill to Edinburgh. They had not got rid, first of Rizzio, then of Darnley, and then of Bothwell, in order to become once more the powerless subjects of so incalculable a woman. It would suit them enormously better to have as monarch Mary Stuart's little son James, for a child could not order them about, and during the long period of his minority they would remain undisputed rulers of the country.

Nevertheless, the Scottish lords would not have found courage to defy Elizabeth had not chance put into their hands an unexpected and deadly weapon against Mary. Six days after the affair at Carberry Hill, an act of despicable treachery to Bothwell on the part of his confederate Sir James Balfour gave them what they wanted. Balfour, rendered uneasy by the change in the political weather, saw a chance of saving his skin by fresh rascality. He informed the Scottish lords that Bothwell, now a fugitive, had sent a valet, George Dalgleish, to Edinburgh, in search of a casket containing important documents, which Dalgleish was to smuggle out of the capital. The valet was promptly arrested, was put to the torture, and revealed the hiding-place of the documents. Under a bed was thereupon found a silver casket which had been given to Mary by her first husband Francis, and which subsequently, with all her other treasures, she had made over to her lover Bothwell. In this coffer or casket, protected by cunningly devised locks, Bothwell had been accustomed to keep his private documents, Mary's promise to marry him, her letters to him, and presumably certain papers which were compromising to the Scottish lords. One may suppose that he had thought it would be too dangerous to take this casket with him upon the flight to Borthwick. He had hidden it away in Edinburgh before leaving, intending to have it brought to him in due course by a trustworthy servant. His bond with the Scottish lords, the queen's promise to marry him, and her private letters might serve him, some day, for blackmailing purposes or for self-exculpation. With the documents in his possession he could, on the one hand, bring pressure to bear on the queen should she prove fickle and, on the other hand, guard himself against the Scottish lords should they wish to accuse him of the murder of Darnley. His first thought when he found himself in temporary security after his flight from Carberry Hill was to get these important pieces of evidence once more into his own keeping. It was an almost incredible piece of luck for the Scottish lords to be able to seize them, since they were then in a position to destroy whatever might compromise themselves, while ruthlessly using against the queen whatever was to her detriment.

For one night the Earl of Morton had charge of this precious find. Next day the other lords were summoned (it is important for the reader to note that among them were Catholics and friends of Mary Stuart), and in their presence the locked coffer was broken open. It contained the famous Casket Letters as well as the sonnets written or alleged to be written by Mary. Without troubling here to reopen the question whether the translations which have come down to us faithfully represent the original text, as far as the letters are concerned, or whether the sonnets were genuine—this much is certain, that the documents found or alleged to have been found in the casket had a disastrous influence upon the fate of Queen Mary. Thenceforward the Scottish lords became far bolder, more self-assured. In their jubilation they hastened to spread the news far and wide. The very same day, before there could have been time to copy the documents, and still less to falsify them, they sent a message to Moray in France giving him an oral summary of the most incriminating. They made the French ambassador acquainted with their discovery; they arrested and examined all of Bothwell's servants they could lay hands upon, and took minutes of their evidence. Their general line of conduct after the opening of the casket would be incomprehensible had not its contents provided damnatory confirmation of Mary Stuart's complicity. At one stroke the queen's situation had grown far worse.

For the discovery of the letters at this critical juncture could not but enormously strengthen the position of the rebels. It gave them, at last, the moral ground they needed to support them in their rebellion. Hitherto they had been content to talk of Bothwell as guilty of the late king's murder, but had carefully avoided pressing him too hard lest the refugee should proclaim them to the world as confederates. The only grievance they had been able to allege against the queen, so far, had been that she had married her husband's murderer. Now, however, thanks to the opportune "discovery" of the letters and sonnets, they were able to convince the most unsuspicious that Queen Mary had been privy to the crime. Her (to say the least of it) extremely indiscreet written avowals gave the practised and cynical blackmailers the very lever they wanted for putting pressure upon the queen and breaking her obduracy. Now they could compel her "of her own free will" to make over the crown to her son; or, if she refused, could publicly accuse her of adultery and of being accessory to her husband's murder.

I should have written "arrange for her to be accused" rather than "accuse." The Scottish lords knew that Elizabeth would never allow them to claim jurisdiction over the queen. They therefore remained prudently in the background, pulling strings to secure that a formal trial should be instigated by a third party. The requisite inflaming of public opinion against Mary Stuart was gladly undertaken by a man who hated her, John Knox. After the murder of Rizzio, this agitator and fanatic had thought it wise to quit the country. Now, when his gloomiest prophecies concerning the "bloody Jezebel" and the disasters her misconduct would bring about had been fulfilled in every particular and even outdone, he returned to Edinburgh clad in the prophet's mantle. From his pulpit came demand after demand that the sinful papist woman should be put upon trial; in the uncompromising vernacular of the Old Testament, the priest clamoured for an assize upon the adulterous queen. Nor was Knox's a solitary voice. Sunday after Sunday the sermons of the preachers of the reformed religion became more acrimonious. No more in the case of a queen than in that of the lowliest woman in the land were adultery and murder to be overlooked. They went so far as to demand the execution of Mary Stuart, and their perpetual incitation did not fail of its effect. Hatred soon spread from the kirk into the street. Excited at the thought of seeing a woman of such exalted position led as a sinner to the scaffold, the mob, which hitherto in Scotland had sung small, now began to insist upon the public trial of the queen. "The women were most furious and impudent against her, yet the men were bad enough." Every poor woman in Scotland knew that the pillory and the scaffold would have been her lot had she been proved guilty of adultery. Was this one woman, because she was called a queen, to lecher and to murder unpunished, and to escape the fire? More and more savage became the cries: "Burn the whore!" The English ambassador, honestly alarmed, reported to London his fear lest the tragedy which had begun with the murder of David the Italian and with the slaying of the queen's husband would end with the execution of the queen.

The Scottish lords had all that they wanted. They could bring up their heavy artillery, to batter down Mary Stuart's resistance to a "voluntary" abdication. The document had been already drawn up to fulfil John Knox's insistence upon a direct accusation of the queen, for "a breach of the law" and for "incontinence with Bothwell and others." If she still refused to abdicate, the letters found in the casket, the letters which proved her to have been privy to the murder, could be read in open court, disclosing her shame. Therewith the rebels would have justified themselves before the world. They did not think that Elizabeth or any other monarch would in that case intervene on behalf of a woman whose own letters showed her to be a murderess and an adulteress.

Armed with this threat of a public trial, Sir Robert Melville and

Lord Lindsay arrived at Lochleven Castle on July 25, 1567. They brought with them three parchments for the queen to sign if she wished to avoid being put on her trial. In the first of them Mary was to declare that she was weary of queenship and was content to lay aside the burden of the crown, a burden which she had neither power nor inclination to sustain any longer. The second parchment announced her consent to the coronation of her son; the third, her approval of Moray's appointment as regent.

Melville was the chief spokesman. He, of all the rebellious nobles, was most sympathetic to her. Twice he had intervened to avert open conflict, and to urge her to repudiate Bothwell. But on both occasions she had refused, knowing that if she gave way to his demands the child she carried in her womb, Bothwell's child, would be born a bastard. Now, however, after the discovery of the Casket Letters, her position had become much more difficult. At first she passionately refused to sign the parchments. She burst into tears, declaring that she would rather forfeit her life than her crown. Ruthlessly, and in the crudest colours, Melville explained what awaited her if she persisted in her refusal: a public reading of the letters, the interrogation of Bothwell's servants, her own examination and condemnation. With horror Mary began to realize the result of her heedlessness, and how she had involved herself in shame and disgrace. By degrees her stubborn resistance was overcome by her fears. After prolonged hesitation and fierce outbursts of indignation and despair, she gave way in the end and signed the three documents.

An agreement had been come to. But, as usual with the Scottish "bonds," neither party to the contract had any intention of being bound by it. The Scottish lords would, nonetheless, read Mary Stuart's letters in parliament and would trumpet to the world that she had been privy to Darnley's murder, hoping thereby to make her return to the throne impossible. Mary herself did not for a moment regard herself as discrowned merely because she had affixed her signature to the pieces of parchment. To her, the divine right of a queen was as much a part of herself as the warm blood that coursed through her veins, oaths to the contrary notwithstanding. Considerations of her word of honour counted for nothing with her as compared with the only thing which gave the world reality to her.

A few days later the little king was crowned. The populace had to put up with a less impressive spectacle than an auto-da-fé in the public square. At the coronation the Earl of Atholl carried the crown, Morton the sceptre, the Earl of Glencairn the sword, and the Earl of Mar bore in his arms the little boy who was henceforward to be known as James VI of Scotland. Since John Knox preached the coronation sermon, the world was given to understand that the new-made king had for ever put away from him the errors and snares of papistical doctrines. There was great jubilation among the crowd outside the gates; the church bells pealed; bonfires were lighted throughout the country. For the moment, and only for the moment, joy and peace were restored to Scotland.

Now, when the burden and heat of the day had been borne by others, Moray, the man of finesse, returned home in triumph. Once more his perfidious policy of absenting himself when danger was in the wind had been justified by results. He kept in the background during the murder of Rizzio, and again during the murder of Darnley; he took no active part in the rebellion against his sister; his loyalty was unsmirched and no blood bespecked his hands. Time had been working on his side. Since he knew how to wait and to hold aloof, there accrued to him without effort and without taint of dishonour what he had been artfully scheming for. Unanimously the Scottish lords offered him the regency.

Moray, able to command others because he knew how to command himself, did not show himself unduly eager. He was too clever to accept this position of dignity and power as a gracious gift, since those who offered it to him were men whom he intended to rule. He also wished to present himself in the light of a loving and devoted brother, who had no thought of claiming the authority of which his sister had been forcibly bereft. It was a psychological master-stroke on his part so to arrange matters that the regency should be forced on him, through the insistence of both parties, the rebel lords and the dethroned queen.

The stagecraft of his visit to Lochleven was admirable. The unhappy woman, as soon as she caught sight of him, flung herself sobbing into her half-brother's arms. Now at length, she hoped, she would find consolation, support, and friendship; and, more than all, she expected to receive the boon of the good counsel of which she had so long been deprived. Moray, however, instead of responding cordially, assumed a harsh reserve. Leading her to her room, he told her plainly what he thought of her folly and misconduct, without saying a word to arouse in her any hope of considerate treatment. Much perturbed by James's bitterness and coldness, the queen wept once more, but tried to excuse herself and explain or extenuate her behaviour. Moray listened to her in silence, with a gloomy countenance, his main object being to intimidate her.

Then Moray left his sister to her own devices for the night; a night of alarms, poisoned by the anxiety he had aroused in her, which he wished to burn deeper and deeper. She, poor woman, was with child; she had had no tidings of what was going on in the outer world, for no one was allowed to visit her; she could not tell whether a shameful trial and a horrible death might not be awaiting her. She did not sleep a wink, and next morning was utterly broken. When they met again, Moray thought fit to utter a few words of consolation. He hinted that if she made no attempt to escape or to get into communication with the foreign powers, and especially if she would no longer seek reunion with Bothwell, it was possible, just possible, that he and her other well-wishers would try to save her honour before the world. This glimmer of hope sufficed to bring comfort to the despairing woman. She embraced her brother, and implored him to assume the regency. Then only would she feel that her son was safe, the kingdom well governed, and she herself freed from danger. She begged him again and again to become regent, and Moray went on allowing her to beg him, before witnesses, for a long time, until at length he magnanimously agreed to accept from her hands the position he had already determined to hold. Having gained his end, now that his sister no less than the Scottish lords wanted him to be regent, he departed well satisfied, leaving Mary likewise consoled, since she knew that the power would be held in her brother's strong hand, and she hoped that the famous letters would not be made public.

But no one has pity for the powerless. As soon as Moray was installed as Lord Regent, he naturally determined to do that which would make the restoration of his sister for ever impossible. He was resolved to render her queenship morally impossible. There was no further word of her liberation from prison, and all preparations were made to keep her there for the rest of her life. Although he had promised both Elizabeth and Mary to safeguard the latter's honour, on December 15, 1567, he had the compromising documents found in the silver casket, the letters and sonnets, read aloud in the Scottish parliament, examined by those assembled, and unanimously declared to be in the dethroned queen's handwriting. Four bishops, fourteen abbots, twelve earls, and somewhere near fifty of the lesser lights of the nobility and gentry (among whom were not a few that were friendly to the queen) swore to the genuineness of the letters and the sonnets.

On this occasion not a single voice, not even that of any of those friendly to the queen (and this fact is of great evidential value), expressed the slightest doubt as to the authenticity of the documents. Thus the meeting of the Scottish parliament became a tribunal. Invisibly the queen was present at an assize held by her subjects. After the reading and examination of the letters, the illegal actions of the Scottish lords during late months, their rebellion, their taking prisoner of the queen, and so on were formally approved; and it was expressly declared that Mary had deserved her fate, since she had had "art and part" in the murder of her lawful husband. This was said to be "proven by the letters written with her own hand before and after the deed to James Bothwell, who had been mainly instrumental in the murder, and also by her shameful marriage to Bothwell immediately after the murder." In order that the world at large should be informed as to Mary's guilt, and should learn that the worthy Scottish lords had risen in rebellion only under the stimulus of moral indignation, copies of the letters were sent to the foreign courts, that thereby Queen Mary might be publicly stigmatized as an adulteress. Moray, the Lord Regent, and the Scottish lords in general, hoped that, with this red brand on her forehead, Mary would never again venture to claim the crown of Scotland.

But Mary was too strongly fortified by her sense of divine right to be shaken by public humiliation. No brand, she felt, could mark a forehead which had worn a crown and been duly anointed. No judgment and no command would ever make her bow her head. The more violent the attempt to cast her down from her high estate, the more resolutely would she resist. A will such as hers cannot long be prisoned. It breaks through the strongest walls, snaps the bars of any cage. If you put such a woman as Mary Stuart in chains, she will strain against her bonds so forcibl that stronghold and hearts will quake.

CHAPTER SIXTEEN

Farewell to Freedom

(SUMMER 1567 TO SUMMER 1568)

NO IMAGINATIVE writer but Shakespeare could have adequately encompassed the Bothwell tragedy as a drama or a work of fiction; but a British writer of less weight has, with considerable success, described the romantic and touching postlude at Lochleven Castle—Walter Scott. Yet anyone who has read *The Abbot* in childhood will continue, throughout life, to regard this historical "fiction" as more vivid and even more truthful than what is called historical "truth," for, when a gifted imaginative writer sets to work, the beautiful legend he constructs will often gain the victory over reality. We have all had our early emotions touched by these scenes, which have made a deep impress on our affective life and have permanently influenced our sympathies, for the elements of romance were ready to the writer's practised hand: there were the grim jailers who kept watch over the unhappy queen; the calumniators who blotted her scutcheon; she herself, young, kindly, and beautiful, able to transform her enemies' cruelty into clemency, to inflame the hearts of the men with whom she came into contact until they were filled with a spirit of chivalry and self-sacrifice. The setting, too, was no less romantic than the motif—the gloomy stronghold on an island in a lovely lake. From the dormer-window Mary could catch glimpses of her beautiful Scottish realm with its forests and mountains, its perpetual charm. In the far distance she could discern the chill waters of the North Sea. The poetic energies in the hearts of the Scottish people have been, so to say, embodied in this romantic episode of Mary at Lochleven; and when once such a legend has been created, it comes to form a lasting element in the blood of a nation. For each successive generation it is re-creative, arousing fresh faith. Like an imperishable tree, it throws forth new blossoms year after year, possessed of a higher truth beside which the arid truths of documents wither. What has once been thus created by the immortal power of imaginative genius maintains itself in virtue of its beauty. Those who, in a later, maturer, and more sceptical epoch, try to elicit the facts that underlie so impressive a legend find that these facts are repellently bald—like a prose paraphrase of a magnificent poem.

The supreme danger of legend, however, is that those who give it currency tend to ignore that which is genuinely tragical in favour of that which is merely sentimental. Thus the balladesque tale of Mary Stuart's imprisonment at Lochleven makes no mention of the innermost, the most human of her distresses. Sir Walter Scott stubbornly omits to relate that Queen Mary was with child by the murderer of her previous husband, and thus leaves out of account the full horror of her position during those months of humiliation. For if the babe she bore in her womb were (as was likely enough in the circumstances) to come prematurely into the world, the pitiless calendar of nature would disclose for all to read when she had first given herself to Bothwell. There is little or no doubt that she had done so before the formal wedding—maybe at a time when surrender to his embraces signified adultery; maybe during the period of mourning for Darnley, at Seton, or in the time of her strange wanderings from castle to castle; maybe (and probably) while Darnley was still alive. No one can fully understand Mary's distressful state of mind at Lochleven who fails to recall that the birth of Bothwell's child would betray to a censorious world the date at which her fatal passion for the earl had begun.

What actually occurred in this respect remains a mystery from which the veil has never been lifted. We do not know how many months Mary had been with child when she was imprisoned at Lochleven; we do not know when she was freed from the burden of this undesired pregnancy; we do not know whether the child came into the world alive or was still-born; if the pregnancy was brought to a premature conclusion, we do not know at what stage. Obscurity and suppositions envelop the whole affair; the witnesses are contradictory; and only this much is certain, that Mary had good reason for keeping the birth secret. It is suspicious enough that in none of her letters does she say a word about the birth of Bothwell's child. According to the reports of Claud Nau, Sieur de Fontenay, who was her private secretary at this time, she gave birth at Lochleven to twins, prematurely; and, since she had her apothecary with her in the castle, we may guess that the prematurity was assisted. According to another account, which equally lacks confirmation, the fruit of her union with Bothwell was not twins born too early to be viable, but a living daughter, who was secretly shipped to France, to be brought up there in a nunnery, ignorant of her royal descent. The key that might have unlocked these mysteries has been sunk for ever in the waters of Lochleven.

The fact that Queen Mary's guardians helped her to cover up the mystery of the birth of Bothwell's child at Lochleven Castle shows that they were not the hard-hearted jailers of the legend. Lady Douglas of Lochleven, to whose care the queen had been committed, had, more than thirty years before, been mistress of King James V, to whom she had borne six children, the eldest being now the Regent Moray. After King James's death she married Earl Douglas of Lochleven, and by him had seven children. A woman who had thirteen times experienced the pangs of labour and who had suffered the spiritual distress of bearing her first children out of wedlock was well able to understand and sympathize with Mary Stuart's pitiable plight. The stories of her harshness towards the royal prisoner may be regarded as fabulous, and we cannot doubt that Mary, though a prisoner, was treated as an exalted guest. The dethroned queen had a suite of rooms, her own cook, her own apothecary, four or five ladies-in-waiting or female domestics; she had the free run of the castle and the island; and she seems even to have been allowed the pleasures of the chase. If we strip the story of her life at Lochleven of sentimental trammels, we shall come to the conclusion that her treatment at the castle was extremely considerate. For, though the sentimentalists would fain have us overlook the fact, Mary had (to say the least of it) been somewhat remiss in her conduct, having married the murderer of her husband three months after the crime. As regards the question of her complicity in the murder, were she to be re-tried by a modern court of justice, the best plea that could be put in for her would be "extenuating circumstances" on the ground of her spiritual thraldom to Bothwell. If this woman whose behaviour had been a scandal to Europe and who had thrown the country over which she ruled into renewed disorder was kept in seclusion for a while, this was to her own advantage as well as to that of Scotland. During these months of retreat, she was given a chance of calming her over-stimulated nerves, of regaining command of her will, which had been paralysed by her infatuation for Bothwell. In a word, imprisonment at Lochleven saved her for a time from the dangers to which she would otherwise have been exposed by her own foolhardiness, unrest, and impatience; safeguarded her from the opportunity for committing numerous follies.

In any case Mary's detention at Lochleven must be regarded as mild punishment for what she had done amiss, when compared with what befell her accomplice and lover. Notwithstanding the solemn pledges that had been given, Bothwell became a hunted outlaw; a price of a thousand crowns had been set on his head; and his best friends in Scotland would have betrayed and sold him for that sum. The earl, however, was not so easy to get hold of. Having vainly attempted to rally the borderers, he fled to the Orkneys, hoping thence to levy war against the Scottish lords. Regent Moray, however, dispatched four warships against him, and Bothwell escaped capture only by taking to sea in a nutshell of a boat. This little vessel was intended merely for coasting traffic among the islands, but in it, through stormy weather, the earl made his way to Norway, arriving with torn sails, and being taken on board a Danish warship. Bothwell hoped to remain unrecognized, and borrowed a suit of ordinary clothing from some of his shipmates. He thought he would fare better if regarded as a pirate than if he were known to be the outlawed consort of the Queen of Scotland and the Isles. He was recognized, however, carried hither and thither, and at length set at liberty in Denmark. But even there, when fortune seemed to favour him, this adventurer wrecked his chances by seducing a Danish girl under promise of marriage. She brought a suit against him.

Meanwhile, the authorities in Copenhagen had learned of what crimes Bothwell was accused in Scotland, so that the axe seemed ready for his neck. Diplomatic couriers hastened hither and thither. Moray demanded his extradition, and Queen Elizabeth was yet more urgent in the matter, wanting him as witness for the crown against Mary Stuart. The latter's French relatives, however, were secretly working upon the King of Denmark, in order to prevent the surrender of one whose testimony might have proved so defamatory to the Queen of Scots. He was kept in rigorous confinement, and in prison he was safer than he would have been at large. Day after day, however, the man whose boldness was notorious in a hundred fights and forays had to dread lest he should be sent back to Scotland in chains, to perish under fearful tortures as a regicide. He was continually moved from one prison to another, kept behind strong bars like a dangerous beast, and he knew well that nothing but death would free him. Intolerably lonely and inactive, this vigorous man, who had been the terror of his enemies and the darling of the fair sex, now week after week, month after month, year after year, had to endure the living death of perpetual imprisonment. Could there be conceived a more horrible torture for one whose natural element was activity and freedom, one who loved the chase, who had ridden often to battle surrounded by his faithful retainers, who had enjoyed the favour of women wherever he went and had taken delight also in the things of the spirit? Now this paralysing inactivity in one prison-cell after another! We learn from credible reports that he became frenzied in his solitude, dashing himself against the bars and the walls, to die insane in 1578, at the age of forty-two, after ten years of purgatory. Of the many who suffered death and martyrdom for Mary Stuart, Bothwell, the man whom she had most ardently loved, atoned longer and more horribly than any other.

Did Mary Stuart continue to think of Bothwell? Was she still in thrall to him, in spite of time and distance? Or was her glowing bondage gradually dissolved? The latter is true, for, as we shall learn, she entertained various schemes for other marriages and, to pave the way for these, begged the Pope to annul the "forced" wedding to Bothwell. She also sent a messenger to Denmark, and induced the earl to sign a document agreeing to the dissolution of their marriage. It is plain that, as soon as she had risen from childbed, she was able once more to exercise the old lure and become again a centre of disturbance. She drew a young man into her charmed circle, and involved his fate with hers.

The biographer of Mary Queen of Scotland and the Isles finds reason again and again to complain that the portraits of her which have come down to us were limned by mediocre artists, so that they give us no insight into her true nature. They show nothing more than a charming, tranquil, kindly, gentle face, making no disclosure of the sensual charm this extraordinary woman must have exerted. Wherever she went she won friends, even from among her foes. As bride and as widow, on every throne and in every prison, she radiated an aura which aroused sympathy and made the environing atmosphere warm with friendliness. Very soon after her arrival at Lochleven, she awakened so much interest in the young Earl of Ruthven (son of the man who had been among the leaders in the murder of Rizzio) that the Scottish lords thought it expedient to remove him from his position as jailer. Thereupon she exercised her witchery upon another stripling, George Douglas, youngest son of Lady Douglas of Lochleven, and therefore Moray's half-brother, though not Mary's blood relation. Within a few weeks George was ready to do anything for her and became the chief assistant in her flight.

Was he merely this? Was not George Douglas something more during her months of imprisonment at Lochleven? Did his liking for her remain purely chivalrous and platonic? Ignorabimus. Anyhow, Mary turned the young fellow's fondness to practical account, using her customary arts of deception and cunning. A queen can always exert another lure in addition to personal charm, for the man who wins her hand may win to power. We guess, though we do not know, that Mary made Lady Douglas of Lochleven more pliable by talking of the possibility of a marriage to George. At any rate, it was not long before the supervision over the imprisoned queen's movements was slackened, and Mary forthwith concentrated her thoughts and activities upon plans for escape.

The first attempt, on March 25, 1568, miscarried, although it had been carefully thought out. Every week a washerwoman with some other girls came across to the island in a boat. Douglas had a talk with this laundress, who agreed to exchange clothes with the queen. Safeguarded against recognition by the laundress's coarse clothing and by a thick muffler, Mary walked boldly past the sentries at the castle gates. She was already being rowed across the lake, towards the shore where George Douglas was to await her with horses, when it occurred to one of the oarsmen to dally with the slender, muffled woman who was clad as a laundress. Wanting to see whether her face was as pretty as her figure, he tried to draw aside the muffler, which Mary obstinately held with her slender and delicate white hands. These hands, being well cared for, were obviously out of keeping with her dress. The boatmen became alarmed, and although the queen angrily commanded them to continue on their course, they put about and took her back to prison.

The attempt at escape was promptly reported to Edinburgh, and thenceforward the prisoner was kept under closer supervision. George Douglas was forbidden to re-enter the castle. From the neighbourhood, however, he managed to communicate with the queen, and conveyed tidings from her to her supporters. For by now, after a year of Moray's regency, although Mary had been exposed to public opprobrium as a murderess, fresh supporters came to her aid. Some of the Scottish lords, especially the Huntlys and the Setons, being no friends to the regent, were faithful to her cause. Strangely enough, however, Mary found her most trusty adherents to be the Hamiltons, who had hitherto proved her fiercest adversaries. Of course there had been an old feud between the Hamiltons and the Stuarts. The Hamiltons came next in power to the Stuarts among the great families, and had long hoped to secure the crown for a member of their clan; now there had suddenly dawned the possibility of gaining their ambition by marrying off one of their number to Queen Mary. Since politics have no concern with morality, this fine scheme immediately led them to espouse the cause of the woman for whose execution as murderess they had been clamouring a few months before. We need hardly suppose that Mary seriously intended to marry one of the Hamiltons. Had she forgotten Bothwell so soon? More likely she only toyed with the proposal in order to escape from Lochleven. George Douglas, to whom (in the desperation of a prisoner) she had also promised her hand in marriage, went on with the preparations for her escape. By May 2, 1568, everything was ready; and, as always when courage would serve her turn better than prudence, Mary was equal to the occasion.

The flight from Lochleven was as romantically effected as was proper to the romantic life of this queen. Mary Stuart or George Douglas had enlisted the services of a lad of sixteen, Willie Douglas, who served as page in the castle, which he had entered as a foundling in infancy. Willie was a bright youth, who played his role well. Under the strict regime that now prevailed at Lochleven it was decreed that, when the family supped in the great hall and the guards also came in to supper, the gates should be locked and the keys should be laid on the table close to the hand of the castellan, Sir William Douglas, Laird of Lochleven, who would keep them under his pillow during the night. On the evening in question, the sharp-witted youngster, while serving at table, dropped a napkin over the keys, and then, when the company had been richly supplied with wine and was carrying on a cheerful conversation, he made off with the keys enveloped in the napkin. Thereafter everything was carried out as had been pre-arranged. Mary Stuart put on the dress of one of her tirewomen; the boy ran downstairs, unlocked the doors, and when the disguised queen had made her exit, he locked them again from the outside. On the way to the Kinross shore, he dropped the bunch of keys into the lake and, to increase the difficulty of pursuit, he towed all the castle boats behind him as he rowed Mary to the shore, where George Douglas and Lord Seton were awaiting her with fifty riders. Now the little force, with the liberated queen in their midst, galloped off through the darkness to Lord Seton's castle of West Niddry, where they halted for the night. With freedom, her courage returned.

Such is the balladesque story of the escape of Mary Stuart from Lochleven Castle, an escape in which she was aided by the devotion of two Douglases: George, who was in love with her, and little Willie, who was likewise devoted to her. The reader who wishes to study the details as seen by a romantic writer may turn to the pages of Sir Walter Scott's *The Abbot*. Sober historians do not accept this legend at its face value. They incline to believe that the lady of Lochleven and her son Sir William, the castellan, may have been less innocent than they appeared, and that the pretty tale of the method of escape was merely devised to excuse Mary's guardians for deliberate negligence. But why should we dispel this last romantic glow in the life of Mary Queen of Scotland and the Isles? Already clouds were gathering on the horizon; her most adventurous days were over, and for the last time in her life did this young woman inspire and feel the emotion of genuine love.

Having been escorted by Lord Seton from West Niddry to Hamilton Castle, which was to be the headquarters of her faction, by the end of a week Mary Stuart found herself leader of an army of six thousand men. It seemed, for a time, as if all might go well with her, and as if the stars in their courses were fighting for her. Not merely had the Huntlys, the Setons, and the Hamiltons rallied to her cause, but, in addition, large numbers of the Scottish nobility and gentry; eight earls, nine bishops, and more than a hundred lairds. This was strange, and yet not so strange as it might seem at first sight, for in Scotland no one ever became an effective ruler without arousing rebellion against him among the nobility. The Lord Regent's strictness had had the customary result. The blue blood of Scotland would rather serve under a tender queen, were she a hundred times a murderess, than under the severe and stubborn Moray. The foreign world was hastening to congratulate the liberated queen on the reestablishment of her rights. Beaumont, the French ambassador, sought her out to pay his respects to her as lawful ruler of Scotland. Elizabeth sent a special messenger to congratulate her cousin upon the joyful news of the escape. During the year of imprisonment her position would seem to have been greatly strengthened.

But, as if under stress of a premonition, Mary, generally courageous and eager for the fray, now shunned having recourse to arms. She would prefer a reconciliation with her half-brother, would be content with a semblance of monarchical power. If he would vouchsafe her that much, she would confirm him in the regency. As events were soon to show, the strength with which she had been animated while subject to the iron will of Bothwell had been dissipated by her subsequent hardships. All that she now craved for was liberty, peace, and rest—these things and the semblance of majesty. But Moray was not inclined to make terms with her, and to rule by his half-sister's grace. His ambition and Mary's were children of the same father, and there were not wanting those who would strengthen Moray in his determination to resist. At the very time when Elizabeth was sending congratulations to Mary, Cecil was vigorously urging the Lord Regent to make an end of Mary Stuart and of the Catholic party in Scotland once and for ever. Moray did not delay. He knew that, so long as his sister was at large, there could be no peace in the realm. He wanted to deal roundly with the rebel lords and to make an example of them. With his usual energy he hastily assembled an army, less numerous than Mary's, but better led and better disciplined. Without waiting for reinforcements, he marched from Glasgow. At the village of Langside, now a suburb of that great city, the issue between Stuart and Stuart, between queen and regent, between brother and sister, was fought out on May 13, 1568.

The battle of Langside was brief but decisive. There was not, as there had been at Carberry Hill, prolonged parleying, with hesitation on either side. Mary's riders boldly attacked the enemy forthwith. Moray, however, had chosen his position with care; the hostile cavalry was mowed down by a fierce fire before it could storm the hill, and Mary's lines were broken by a savage counter-thrust. In three-quarters of an hour all was over. The queen's last army fled precipitately, abandoning its artillery, and leaving three hundred dead on the field.

Mary was watching the fight from a neighbouring eminence. As soon as she saw that the day was lost, she mounted and galloped away, attended by a few riders. Seized with panic, she had no thought of further resistance. She rode many, many miles without pause, as we learn from her letter to her uncle, the Cardinal of Lorraine. "I have suffered injuries, calumnies, captivity, hunger, cold, heat, flying—without knowing whither—fourscore and twelve miles across the country, without once pausing to alight, and then lay on the hard ground, having only sour milk to drink, and oatmeal to eat, without bread, passing three nights with the owls." Today in Scotland Mary's weaknesses and follies have in great measure been forgotten by her people; they find excuses for her mad passion, and they remember her chiefly by the sad story of these last days of freedom and flight. Either they think of her as the prisoner at Lochleven Castle, or else as a weary woman galloping on and on through the darkness, braving all hazards rather than that of surrender to her foes. Thrice before had she made night-rides after this fashion: the first time with Darnley when she escaped from Holyrood; the second time in male attire from Borthwick Castle, being joined by Bothwell soon after she left, for their escape to Dunbar; the third time with George Douglas, from Lochleven to West Niddry Castle. Thrice before in this manner had she saved her freedom and her crown. On the present occasion she saved only her life.

Three days after the rout at Langside, Mary reached Dundrennan Abbey, near the town of Kirkcudbright on the Solway Firth. Here was the limit of her realm; thus far she fled like a hunted beast. For her, who had yesterday been a queen, there was no safe spot left anywhere in Scotland, no stronghold there to which she could return. In Edinburgh was the pitiless John Knox; there she would have to face the scorn of the mob, the hatred of the clergy, and maybe the pillory and the stake. Her last army had been defeated, her last hope had vanished. Now she must choose. Behind her lay the kingdom she had lost; in front of her, the sea, with its trackless roads leading in every direction. She might return to France; she might cross the firth to England; she might make her way to Spain. She had been educated in France, had friends and relatives there, many who were fond of her, poets who had sung her praises, noblemen who had been her companions; once before this land had received her hospitably, had given her a splendid coronation. But for the very reason that she had been queen there, decked out with the glories of this world, the greatest lady in the land, she was unwilling to return thither as a beggar, as a petitioner, with torn clothing and tarnished honour. She could not endure to think of the sneering countenance of Catherine de' Medici, of seeking alms, or of taking refuge in a convent. Nor was there anything more agreeable in the idea of entrusting herself to the tender mercies of Philip of Spain. Never would that bigot forgive her for having married Bothwell in accordance with the rites of the Protestant Church, and with the blessing of a heretical priest. Thus only one possibility remained open to her, not a choice but a necessity. She must take refuge in England. During the most hopeless days of her imprisonment, had not Elizabeth written to her encouragingly: "You can at any time count on the Queen of England as a true friend"? Had not her cousin solemnly promised to have her reinstated as queen? Had not Elizabeth sent her a ring as a token, which Mary need only produce to be sure of sisterly aid?

Too hastily, as always when she made important decisions, Mary now took one of the most momentous decisions of her life. Without any preliminary demand for safeguards, she wrote from Dundrennan Abbey to Elizabeth: "You are not ignorant, my dearest sister, of the great part of my misfortunes; but those which induce me to write at present have happened too recently yet to have reached your ear. I must therefore acquaint you as briefly as I can that some of my subjects whom I most confided in, and had raised to the highest pitch of honour, have taken up arms against me, and treated me with the utmost indignity. By unexpected means, the Almighty Disposer of all things delivered me from the cruel imprisonment I underwent; but I have since lost a battle, in which most of those who preserved their loyal integrity fell before my eyes. I am now forced out of my kingdom, and driven to such straits that, next to God, I have no hope but in your goodness. I beseech you, therefore, my dearest sister, that I may be conducted to your presence, that I may acquaint you with all my affairs. In the meantime, I beseech God to grant you all heavenly benedictions, and to me patience and consolation, which last I hope and pray to obtain by your means. To remind you of the reasons I have to depend on England, I send back to its Queen this token of her promised friendship and assistance. Your affectionate sister, M.R."

The die had been cast. On May 16, 1568, Mary embarked in a fishing-smack, crossed the Solway Firth, and landed at the little port of Workington in Cumberland. When Mary reached this turning-point in her fate, she was not yet twenty-five years of age, and yet her life was finished. She had enjoyed all possible earthly splendours, climbed to all possible earthly altitudes, and plumbed life's abysses. Within a brief space of time, amid fearful mental tension, she had experienced extraordinary contrasts, had buried two husbands, lost two kingdoms, undergone harsh imprisonment, and, by the pathway of crime, had with renewed pride remounted the steps of the throne. These weeks, these years, had been weeks and years of flame, whose reflex shines down to us through the ages. Now the fires were burning low and the best of her had been consumed. What remained was but dross and ashes, poor vestiges of these magnificent ardours. As a mere shadow of her former self, Mary Stuart went forward into the twilight of her destiny.

CHAPTER SEVENTEEN

Weaving a Net

(MAY 16 TO JUNE 28, 1568)

THERE CAN be no doubt that Elizabeth Tudor was genuinely perturbed to learn of Mary Stuart's arrival in England. This uninvited guest was extremely embarrassing. For the past year a sense of monarchical solidarity had led Elizabeth to support Mary as far as lay within her power against the rebellious Scottish lords. Polite diplomatic assurances were easy, so the Queen of England frequently declared herself to be full of sympathy and love for her Scottish "sister." Such assurances were extravagantly worded. Not once, however, did Elizabeth invite Mary to come to England; on the contrary, she persisted in her long-standing policy of doing all in her power to avoid a personal encounter with her cousin. Now the tiresome woman had unexpectedly landed on English soil, was in the country over which she had recently and arrogantly proclaimed her right of sovereignty. She came uninvited, and her first words after her arrival were a reminder of pledges of friendship which Elizabeth had meant to be taken no more than metaphorically. In the letter dispatched from Workington on May 17, to follow up the letter from Dundrennan, Mary did not trouble to inquire whether Elizabeth would receive her as a guest, but assumed that such a reception was her unquestioned right. "I entreat you to send for me as soon as possible, for I am in a pitiable condition, not only for a queen, but for a gentlewoman, having nothing in the world but the clothes in which I escaped, travelling across country the first day, and not having since ever ventured to proceed except in the night, as I hope to declare before you, if it pleases you to have pity, as I trust you will, upon my extreme misfortune."

Pity was, indeed, Elizabeth's first impulse. It must have been gratifying to her pride that Mary, whom she would gladly have dethroned, had lost the Scottish crown without Elizabeth herself having stirred a finger in the matter. What a spectacle for the world, could Elizabeth raise from her knees and clasp in a sisterly embrace the woman who had once been so proud a rival; if Elizabeth could pose as protectress and benefactor. She honestly desired, therefore, to invite the fugitive to stay with her. "I have learned," reported the French ambassador, "that in the Privy Council, the Queen ardently espoused the cause of the Queen of Scotland, giving everyone present to understand that it was her intention to receive Mary with the honour appropriate to the latter's former dignity and greatness, and not to her present fallen fortunes." Elizabeth was endowed with a strong sense of historical responsibility; and had she acted on her first impulse to abide by her written assurances, she would have saved Mary Stuart's life and her own honour.

Elizabeth, however, did not stand alone. Her main prop was Cecil, the man with cold, steel-blue eyes, who dispassionately moved piece after piece upon the political chessboard. Knowing herself to be a creature of impulse, sensitive to every change in atmospheric pressure, the English queen had been shrewd enough to select as chief adviser this sober-minded and prosaic calculator, whose puritanism made him detest the passionate, unbridled Mary, a man who, as a strict Protestant, hated her as Catholic, and who—as his private papers prove—was absolutely convinced of her complicity in the murder of Darnley. He hastened to check Elizabeth's move to help her cousin. As a statesman, he was prompt to realize that any support given by the English government to the claims of the dethroned Queen of Scotland ("the daughter of debate, who discord fell doth sow") would involve far-reaching complications. To receive Mary in London with royal honours would imply a recognition of her right to be restored to the Scottish throne, and would pledge England to support her with arms and money against Moray and the Scottish lords. Cecil, who favoured the rebellion in Scotland, was not in the least inclined for such a reversal of policy. He regarded Mary as the arch-enemy of Protestantism and as the most conspicuous peril to England. He found it possible to persuade Elizabeth how dangerous it would be to show friendliness to Mary. Elizabeth was all the more disposed to listen to Cecil's counsel by the news that some of her own leading nobles had paid honour to the fugitive Mary. The mightiest of the Catholic peers, the Duke of Northumberland, invited her to his castle; the Duke of Norfolk, premier peer of England, though a Protestant, visited her. Everyone who came into contact with the fugitive seems to have been captivated. Elizabeth, suspicious by nature, and preposterously vain, soon abandoned any thought of inviting to her court a princess who might outshine her, and might become a rallying-centre for the malcontents of her realm.

Within a few days, therefore, Elizabeth got the better of her humane inclinations and decided against soliciting Mary's presence at the English court, while determined to keep the fugitive on English soil. Elizabeth, however, would not have been Elizabeth had she acted unequivocally. She showed her usual ambiguity—a quality which always confuses people's minds and disturbs the world. Now began the period in which Elizabeth Tudor undeniably sinned against Mary Stuart. Fortune gave her the victory she had dreamed of for years. Her rival, regarded as the exemplar of chivalric virtues, had been publicly disgraced by her own misconduct; she who had wished to usurp the crown of England had forfeited that of Scotland; she who had arrogantly proclaimed her rights was now a petitioner for Elizabeth's aid. Two possibilities were open to Elizabeth. She might heap coals of fire on Mary's head by generously granting the right of asylum. On the other hand, she might, for political reasons, refuse Mary safe harbourage on English soil. Either course would have been justified. A plea for aid may be granted or denied. Both by divine law and by human, however, it must be accounted base to refuse the petitioned help and yet detain a hapless fugitive. No excuse can be found for Elizabeth's rejection of Mary's plea for aid, and for then, under false pledges and by the secret use of force, detaining Mary on English ground. It was this perfidious conduct on Elizabeth's part, weaving a net round the abased and conquered queen of Scotland, which drove Mary farther and farther along the road of despair and crime.

Elizabeth's behaviour at this juncture was a more grievous offence, and blots the English queen's character more darkly, than the subsequent sending of Mary to the scaffold. There was not a shadow of pretext for detention. When Napoleon, after taking refuge on the *Bellerophon,* claimed British hospitality, Britain was entitled to reject his demand as farcical. For, at that juncture, France and Britain were at war; Napoleon was commander of the enemy forces, and had for nigh upon two decades been hounding the war-dogs at Britain's throat. But when Mary landed at Workington, England and Scotland were not at war. Elizabeth Tudor and Mary Stuart had for years been affectionately addressing one another as friends, cousins, and sisters; and when, a day or two before, from Dundrennan, Mary dispatched the ring, the "token of promised friendship and assistance," she bore in mind Elizabeth's words that no other person on earth would give her so cordial a hearing. She could rely, moreover, on the knowledge that Elizabeth had granted the right of asylum to Moray and Morton, to the murderers of Rizzio and the murderers of Darnley, their crimes notwithstanding. Only, when Mary came to England, it was not now with a claim to England's throne, but with the modest request to be allowed to live at peace in England; or, failing this, to be given free passage to France.

It need hardly be said that Elizabeth was well aware of a complete lack of excuse for taking Mary prisoner. So was Cecil, for there is a memorandum in his own handwriting, *Pro Regina Scotorum,* in which we read: "She must be helped, seeing that she came of her own free will into England, relying upon our Queen." Thus both Elizabeth and her Lord High Treasurer knew perfectly well, at the bottom of their hearts, that in weaving a net round Mary they were acting unjustly. But what would a statesman be worth if he could not, in ticklish circumstances, fabricate pretexts and procedures, make something out of nothing or nothing out of something? If there was no solid ground for arresting the fugitive, one must be discovered; since Mary had done no wrong to Elizabeth, an offence must be faked up. Caution was needed, since the whole European world was on the watch. The net must be carefully and inconspicuously woven, and then drawn tighter and tighter round the defenceless victim, before she realized what was afoot. Matters must be so arranged that, if she thereupon endeavoured—too late—to escape, her ill-judged movements would only ensnare her more hopelessly.

The weaving of the net began with an exchange of civilities. Two of Elizabeth's chief advisers, Lord Scrope, the warden of the Western

Marshes, and Sir Francis Knollys, the vice-chamberlain, were sent post-haste to Carlisle, whither Mary had now removed. Their mission was manifold and obscure. They were to convey to Mary assurances of their queen's distinguished consideration, to deplore the fugitive's misfortunes—and to allay the Scottish queen's fears, lest she should prematurely appeal to the foreign courts for help. The most important part of their mission was secret. They were to keep watch over the woman who was at this time already a prisoner, were to bar the doors against inadvisable visitors, and were to intercept letters. To sustain them in the use of force, should force be needed, fifty halberdiers were ordered to Carlisle. Scrope and Knollys were also commissioned to report whatever Mary Stuart said. For what Cecil and his royal mistress most eagerly awaited was some incautious utterance of Mary's which might serve as an excuse for openly proclaiming the imprisonment which, in default of it, virtually existed.

The two emissaries discharged their mission to the best of their ability, and it is to their report that we owe some of the most vivid of the extant characterizations of Mary. Again and again we find that she inspired respect and admiration in the most unlikely quarter. Sir Francis Knollys wrote to Cecil: "Surely she is a rare woman, for as no flattery can abuse her, so no plain speech seems to offend her, if she think the speaker an honest man." Reporting to Queen Elizabeth, Lord Scrope and Sir Francis wrote: "We found her in her answers to have an eloquent tongue and a discreet head, and it seemeth by her doings she hath stout courage and a liberal heart adjoined thereunto." But, they went on to say, she was extremely proud, that victory was what she had most at heart, and that, in comparison with this, wealth and everything else in the world were of little importance to her. Such a description was hardly calculated to placate the jealous and suspicious Elizabeth, whose heart could only thereby be hardened against her rival.

Mary Stuart, likewise, had quick apprehensions. She speedily realized that the condolences and courtesies of these envoys were empty words, and that their friendly conversation was intended to mask some hidden purpose. Only by degrees, and sugared with compliments, did they administer the bitter medicine they had brought—the news that

Elizabeth would not receive the fugitive until she had purged herself of the murder charge. This formula had been excogitated in London to mask the blunt determination that Mary should be kept prisoner, and to provide a moral justification for her imprisonment. It may be that Mary took these perfidious assurances at their face value, and failed to see the net that was closing round her; or it may be that she thought it expedient to assume ignorance. Anyhow she declared that she would have no difficulty in exculpating herself, but that of course she would only do so before someone of equal rank with herself, namely before the Queen of England. The sooner the better. She would like to go to Elizabeth at once and confidently fling herself into her sister's arms. She urgently desired to make her way to London forthwith, in order to refute the calumnies that were levelled against her honour. She gladly offered to accept Elizabeth as arbiter—no one else in the world.

The implications were sufficient for Elizabeth. By admitting that her guilt was open to discussion, Mary provided Elizabeth with a pretext for involving the refugee in a tedious trial. Of course the proceedings must not be begun hastily, in such a way as to induce Mary to alarm the world prematurely. Her senses must be lulled by honeyed assurances, so that she might unresistingly uncover her throat to the knife. Elizabeth wrote in moving terms, concealing the fact that the Privy Council had already decided upon Mary's imprisonment, and wrapping up in honeyed phrases the refusal to receive the Scottish queen at the English court. "Madam," wrote Elizabeth, "I learn by your letter and by my Lord Herries your desire to justify yourself in my presence of the things charged against you. Oh, Madam, there is no creature living more desirous to hear it than I, or who will more readily lend her ears to such answer as shall acquit your honour. But, whatever my regard for you, I can never be careless of my own reputation. I am held suspect for rather wishing to defend you herein, than opening my eyes to see the things these people condemn you in." After this skilfully phrased repudiation, there comes a yet more refined allurement. Elizabeth went on (the wording should be carefully noted): "And I promise on the word of a prince, that no persuasion of your subjects or advice of others shall ever induce me to move you to anything dangerous to you or your honour." The letter grows more eloquent and more urgent: "If you find it strange not to see me, you must put yourself in my place, and then you will understand it would be difficult for me to receive you before your justification. But once honourably acquitted of this crime, I swear to you before God, that among all worldly pleasures that will hold the first rank."

These are gentle, consolatory, cordial words. But they are the wrappings of a hard kernel. Henry Middlemore, the envoy who brought the epistle, was further commissioned to make it clear to Mary that what was in prospect for her was not an opportunity for a personal justification to Elizabeth, but a judicial or quasi-judicial investigation into what had happened in Scotland, although the true nature of the proceedings was, for the time being, to be decorously veiled by styling them a "conference."

At the words "trial," "investigation," "judicial inquiry," Mary Stuart's anger found vent: "I have none other judge than God!" she exclaimed. "Marry, I know mine own estate and degree, although, according to the good trust I have reposed in the Queen, my good sister, I have offered to make her the judge of my cause. But how can that be, when she will not suffer me to come at her?" Threateningly she declared (a true word!) that Elizabeth would gain no advantage by holding her fast in England. Then she took up her pen: "Prithee, Madam, abandon the thought that I came hither in order to save my life. Neither the world nor Scotland has repudiated me. I came hither to win back my honour, and to find support that would enable me to chastise those that have falsely accused me; but not in order to answer them as if they were my equals. For among all princes I chose you as my next of kin and my 'perfaite amye,' that before you I might accuse my accusers, because I believed you would regard it as an honour to yourself to be called upon to help in re-establishing the honour of a queen unjustly accused." She had not fled from a prison in Scotland in order to be confined "quasi en un autre" on English soil. In conclusion she demanded, what it was always futile to demand from Elizabeth, namely plain speaking and unambiguous behaviour; either to be helped, or else to be set at liberty. She would "de bonne voglia" justify herself before Elizabeth, but would not do so in the form of a trial by the mightiest of her subjects, unless these were brought before her with bound hands; being fully aware of her position as a ruler by divine right, she would not meet any subject on equal terms; she would rather die.

Mary Stuart's attitude was legally incontestable. The Queen of England could exercise no jurisdiction over the Queen of Scotland; Elizabeth had no right to institute an inquiry concerning a murder which had taken place in another kingdom; she possessed no right to intervene in a conflict between a foreign princess and the latter's subjects. Of course Elizabeth was aware of this, and therefore redoubled her cajoleries in order to lure Mary Stuart out of an impregnable position on to the slippery ground of a quasi-judicial inquiry. It was not, she said, as a judge, but as a friend and sister that she desired these dark matters to be cleared up; the exculpation was an indispensable preliminary to the gratification of her dearest wish to see Mary face to face and to enjoy the knowledge that Mary had been restored to her queenship. In order to gain the end she had in view, Elizabeth gave one important pledge after another, implying that never for a moment did she doubt the Scottish queen's innocence, that the proposed conferences had nothing whatever to do with Mary Stuart, but were simply directed against Moray and the other rebels. One lie followed hard upon the heels of another. She gave a binding pledge (we shall see later how it was kept) that nothing should be disclosed at the inquiry which could tarnish Mary Stuart's honour. As a further deception, Elizabeth explained to those who were to hold the conferences that, whatever the result of the inquiry, Mary Stuart's royal position would be unaffected.

While Elizabeth was being thus prodigal of friendly assurances and undertakings, Cecil was quietly pursuing a different path. To make Moray consent to the investigation, the regent was assured that there was not the remotest thought of his sister's reinstatement. (We see that double tongues and double faces are not the invention of latter-day statesmen!) Mary was not deceived by the manœuvres of her "dear sister and cousin." She strenuously defended herself, writing letter after letter, sweet and bitter by turns. In London, however, the net was drawn closer all the time. By degrees measures were taken to intensify spiritual pressure upon the captive, to show her that, if she persisted in her refusal, force would be used. Such amenities as she had been allowed were withdrawn. She was no longer permitted to receive visitors from Scotland. If she left Carlisle Castle to take the air, she was accompanied (that is to say watched and guarded) by a hundred riders. Carlisle was too near the coast, from which rescue by boat was possible. Thus, in the middle of July, despite her protests, she was removed to Bolton Castle in the North Riding of Yorkshire—her new prison being described as a "very strong, very fayre, and very stately house."

Even now the iron hand was velvet-gloved. The Queen of Scotland was assured that the removal was only due to Elizabeth's kindness and consideration, that correspondence between the pair might be accelerated. Mary would have more liberty at Bolton, and would be better protected from the risk of attack on the part of her enemies. What was possible to Mary beyond empty protest? She could not effectively resist. Return to Scotland was impossible; she could not make her way to France; and her position grew more sordid day by day. She lived upon the bread of charity, and the very clothing she wore was borrowed from Elizabeth. Utterly alone, cut off from communication with her friends, surrounded by her adversary's subjects, she gradually became more pliable.

At length, as Cecil had hoped and planned, she made the great mistake for which he and Elizabeth had been so impatiently waiting. In a moment of fatigue and weakness she acquiesced in the scheme of an inquiry. This was the greatest blunder of her life. Her position had so far been invincible; as long as she insisted that Elizabeth had no jurisdiction, had no right to deprive her of her freedom—that, as the queen's and as England's guest, no one could compel her to submit to alien jurisdiction—nothing could be undertaken against her. Mary's courage, however, great though it was, came only in flashes, and she lacked the stamina essential to a sovereign ruler. Having once consented, it was vain for her to impose conditions. She felt that the ground had been cut from under her feet. "There is nothing," she wrote on June 28, "which I would not undertake upon your word, for I have never doubted your honour and your royal good faith."

But one who has surrendered unconditionally cannot, thereafter, attempt to make terms. The conqueror insists upon his rights, while the conquered have no rights whatever. Vae victis!

CHAPTER EIGHTEEN

The Net Closes Round Her

(JULY 1568 TO JANUARY 1569)

AS SOON as Mary Stuart foolishly consented to an investigation by an "unbiased conference," the English government devoted itself to ensuring that there should be the bias it wanted. Whereas the Scottish lords would be allowed to appear before the tribunal, equipped with all their proofs, Mary was to be represented only by two confidential agents. Solely from a distance and through intermediaries could she levy her counter-accusation against the rebel lords, who, for their part, could speak freely with their own voices, and could form cabals among themselves. By this perfidious arrangement the captured queen was at one stroke reduced from the offensive to the defensive. The fine pledges which were previously given her might now be ignored. Elizabeth, who had declared it incompatible with her honour to receive Mary Stuart until the proceedings were over, did not hesitate to admit the rebel Moray to her presence. This little matter did not trouble her "honour." No doubt the determination to force Mary into the dock was still carefully veiled, for appearances must be kept up before the eyes of the foreign world. The Scottish lords, it was said, would have to "justify" their rebellion. But this justification, which Elizabeth sanctimoniously demanded, meant nothing more than that they would have to state the reasons why they had taken up arms against their queen. That implied a request to them to disclose "the whole truth" about Darnley's murder, giving them a weapon of which the point was to be directed against Mary Stuart. If the Scottish lords would be strenuous enough in their accusations, legal reasons could be excogitated in London for continuing to keep the Scottish queen in prison, and a specious excuse would be provided for what was really an unwarrantable detention.

Conceived as a huge piece of humbug, this conference (which cannot be called a judicial procedure without libelling justice) unexpectedly degenerated into a comedy of a very different character from that which Cecil and Elizabeth had designed. For hardly had the parties to the affair been brought together round a table that they might accuse one another, when it appeared they had very little desire to produce documents and state facts, and both sides knew perfectly well why. As a unique feature of this trial, accusers and accused had been confederates in the same crime. The murder of Darnley was a thorny matter for them all. Both would prefer to maintain silence about it since both had had "art and part" therein. If Morton, Lethington, and Murray should produce the Casket documents and maintain, on the strength of these, that Mary Stuart was a confederate in the murder or at least an accessory before the fact, the honourable lords would, no doubt, have been right in their deductions. Mary Stuart would also have been right in showing that those who accused her had likewise been accessories before the fact, and had at least approved the murder by their silence. If the accusers put the letters in as evidence, Mary, who had learned from Bothwell the names of the signatories to the bond for murder, and perhaps had the document in her possession, could tear the mask from the faces of the posthumous royalists. Nothing was more natural, therefore, than the lukewarmness of both parties to the action; nothing could be plainer than their common interest in settling the matter out of court, and allowing poor Henry Darnley to rest quietly in his tomb. "Requiescat in pace!" was the pious prayer of everyone concerned.

The result was a great surprise to Queen Elizabeth. When the Conference of York had been duly opened, Moray was content to put in a plaint against Bothwell, who happened to be hundreds of miles away, and not in a position to denounce his confederates. The regent carefully refrained from making any accusation against Mary Stuart, and seemed to have forgotten that, a year before, she had been openly accused of the murder in the Scottish parliament. These chivalrous knights did not enter the lists with the impetuosity Cecil had hoped for. They did not fling the incriminating letters on to the table. Furthermore, it was a remarkable (and not the least remarkable) feature of this ingenious comedy that the English commissioners, likewise, showed themselves little inclined to ask questions. The Duke of Northumberland, being a Roman Catholic, was perhaps better disposed towards Mary Stuart than towards Elizabeth, his own queen. The Duke of Norfolk, for reasons which will presently be revealed, was also in favour of compromise. The grounds for an understanding were not difficult to find. Mary's royal title and her liberty were to be restored, while Moray was to retain the power which was all he cared about. Though Elizabeth wished for a thunderstorm which would annihilate her adversary—morally at least—the weather proved balmy.

Instead of openly hurling facts and documents at one another, the commissioners carried on conversations in a friendly spirit behind closed doors. Their mood grew more and more genial. After a few days, instead of holding a strict assize, accusers and accused, commissioners and judges, were collaborating to bring about a decent burial of the conference which Elizabeth had intended to be an imposing State-trial of Mary Stuart.

The heaven-born intermediary between the two parties was the Scottish secretary of State, Maitland of Lethington. In the obscure business of Darnley's murder he had played one of the most sinister parts; and, since he was an admirable diplomatist, of course a double one. When, at Craigmillar, the Scottish lords had proposed to Mary that she should rid herself of Darnley by divorce or in some other way, Maitland had been their spokesman, and had conveyed the sinister assurance that Moray would "look through his fingers." Lethington had also furthered Mary's marriage to Bothwell, had "chanced" to be on hand at the "abduction" of Queen Mary, and had deserted her for the Scottish lords only twenty-four hours before the end. If the queen and the Scottish lords were to shoot at one another in deadly earnest, he was likely to find himself between two fires, so that he was eager, by fair means or foul, to bring about a compromise.

His first step was an attempt to intimidate Mary Stuart by telling her that if she proved unyielding the Scottish lords would make a ruthless use of the evidence against her, although it should put her to open shame. To convince her what deadly weapons her enemies possessed, he had the Casket documents privately copied by his wife (who had been Mary Fleming), and then sent the copies to Mary Stuart.

It need hardly be said that, in disclosing this evidence to Mary, Maitland was betraying his comrades, and was infringing the accepted rules of legal procedure. But his fellow-peers capped his perfidy by (under the table, so to say) handing the Casket Letters to the Duke of Norfolk and the other English commissioners. This was to load the dice against Mary, since it could not fail to prejudice against her those who were to act as her judges but who had thus been "nobbled." Norfolk, in particular, was dumbfounded by the reek which emerged from this open Pandora's box. Since right and justice were far from being the chief concern of those who presided over the conference, the English commissioners hastened to report to Elizabeth: "The said letters and ballades do discover such inordinate love betweene her and Bothwell, her loothsomness and abhorringe of her husband that was murdered, in such sorte as everie good and godlie man can not but detest and abhorre the same."

This report, so disastrous to Mary Stuart, was extremely welcome to Elizabeth Tudor. She knew now what incriminating material could be produced at the conference, and she determined not to rest until Moray had been forced to produce it. The more Mary showed herself inclined for compromise, the more did Elizabeth insist upon a disclosure of all the facts. It seemed as if the Duke of Norfolk's "detestation and abhorrence," now that he had had a private glimpse of the contents of the famous casket, would prove fatal to Mary.

But gamesters and politicians must never give up the game as lost so long as they still hold a card in their hand. At this juncture Lethington made a sharp curve. He called on Norfolk and had a long private conversation with the premier peer of England. Immediately afterwards Norfolk himself made a sharp curve. Saul had been converted into Paul. The man who had seemed prejudiced against the Queen of Scots as one of her judges became her most zealous assistant and partisan. Instead of guiding the conference towards a public inquiry such as Elizabeth wanted, he began to work in the interests of the Scottish queen. Nay more, he urged Mary against renouncing the Scottish crown and against abandoning her claim to the English succession; he stiffened her back and steeled her hand. At the same time he strongly advised Moray against producing the letters in open court, and Moray suddenly changed front after his private conversation with Norfolk. The regent became mild and conciliatory, fully agreeing with Norfolk that Bothwell must be held solely responsible for Darnley's murder and that Mary Stuart should be exonerated. A gentle thaw had begun. Within a few days spring weather came, and friendship smiled over this remarkable house.

What had induced Norfolk to swing round in this way, so that he disregarded the instructions of his own sovereign, and from being an adversary of Mary Stuart became one of the Scottish queen's closest friends? We can hardly suppose that Lethington had bribed him with money. Norfolk was the wealthiest nobleman in England; his family was of hardly less importance than that of the Tudors; neither Lethington nor all Scotland could have furnished enough money to influence him. Nevertheless, Lethington had bribed him, though not with dross. He had offered the young widower the only bribe which could appeal to so powerful a man, namely more power. Why should not the Duke of Norfolk marry Queen Mary and thus secure the right of succession to the English crown? There is magic in the thought of wearing a kingly diadem which can make a coward brave, an indifferent man ambitious, and a philosopher a fool. That was why Norfolk, who a few days before had been strongly advising Mary voluntarily to renounce her royal rights, now urged her to cling to them. It was only because of her right of succession to the English throne that Norfolk wished to wed Mary Stuart, for by this marriage he would rank with the Tudors.

To modern sentiment it cannot but seem extraordinary that a man who had just been denouncing Mary to Elizabeth as a murderess and an adulteress, who had been so righteously indignant about the Scottish queen's unsavoury love-affairs, should almost in the same breath decide upon making this woman his wife. Naturally enough, therefore, the whole-hearted defenders of Mary Stuart declare that, in the aforesaid private conversation, Lethington must have convinced Norfolk of Mary's innocence, and of the fact that the Casket Letters were forgeries. There is, however, no documentary evidence in support of such a hypothesis; and some weeks later Norfolk, in conversation with Elizabeth, was still describing Mary Stuart as a murderess. Nothing can lead the historian more hopelessly astray than to apply to a long-past century the moral standards of a later date. The value of a human life is not an absolute value, but one which varies from time to time and from place to place. We ourselves are much laxer in our judgment of political assassinations than were our grandfathers in the nineteenth century, though we may not have reverted without qualification to the sixteenth-century outlook that such matters are trifles. In the days of Mary Stuart and Elizabeth Tudor conscientious scruples were rare; morality was based, not upon Holy Writ, but upon Machiavelli's *The Prince.* One who aspired to a throne would wade through slaughter to reach it, undeterred by sentimental considerations. The scene in *King Richard III* in which Anne Neville consents to give her hand in marriage to the slayer of her husband ("Was ever woman in this humour wooed? Was ever woman in this humour won?") was penned by a contemporary of the fourth Duke of Norfolk. It seemed nowise incredible to the playgoers who witnessed its performance. To become king a man would poison his father or his brother, would involve thousands of innocent persons in a war, would sweep people ruthlessly out of his path. In the Europe of those days it would hardly be possible to find a ruling house in which such crimes were not committed. When a crown was at stake, a boy of fourteen would marry a woman of fifty, or a girl would wed a man old enough to be her grandfather. No one bothered, in such cases, about virtue or good looks or dignity or morals. The aspirant to a throne married without a qualm someone who was feeble-minded, crook-backed, or paralysed; a syphilitic, a cripple, or a criminal. Why, then, should it be supposed that the ambitious Norfolk would have been troubled by moral scruples when this young, beautiful, and hot-blooded queen declared herself ready to become his wife? Norfolk was not concerned with what Mary Stuart had done or might have done to others, but with what she would or could do for him. A man with more imagination than intelligence, he already fancied himself at Westminster in Elizabeth's place. Betwixt night and morning there had been a change of scene. Lethington's clever hand had drawn aside the net which was being woven round Mary Stuart, and he who was to have been a severe judge had been transformed into a wooer and a helper.

Elizabeth, however, had excellent tale-bearers, and her senses were kept alert by her suspicions. "Les princes ont des oreilles grandes qui oyent loin et près," she once said triumphantly to the French ambassador. A hundred trivial signs convinced her that in York potions were being brewed which would disagree with her. She sent for Norfolk and told him archly how a little bird had informed her that "he would a-wooing go." Norfolk was no hero. His father had been attainted by Henry VIII, and only that monarch's death had saved the third duke of Norfolk from execution. Like Peter with his "I know not the man," Norfolk, who had so recently become Mary Stuart's suitor, repudiated the implication. Those who affirmed that he desired to wed an adulteress and murderess were calumniators. "Madam," said he, "that woman shall never be my wife who has been your competitor, and whose husband cannot sleep in security on his pillow."

But Elizabeth knew what she knew, and afterwards was able to say proudly: "Ils m'ont cru si sotte, que je n'en sentirais rien." When, in one of her tantrums, she seized an eavesdropper at her court to give him a violent shaking, she soon shook all his secrets out of his sleeve. She took prompt and energetic measures. On November 25, 1568, the proceedings were transferred from York to the Painted Chamber at Westminster. Here, a few paces from her own palace, and immediately under her watching eyes, Lethington could not play his double game so easily as he had played it at York, two hundred miles away, and with fewer spies around him. Furthermore, Queen Elizabeth, now that she knew some of her commissioners to be untrustworthy, supplemented them by persons on whom she could absolutely rely, above all, appointing her favourite Leicester. As soon as her hands were on the reins, the inquiry proceeded at a smart trot along the prescribed road. Moray, her sometime pensioner, was bluntly told "to defend himself," this implying that he must not shrink from the "extremity of odious accusations," but must produce his proofs of Mary's adultery with Bothwell and must lay the Casket Letters on the table. Forgotten now was Elizabeth's solemn pledge that nothing should be brought up "against the honour" of Mary Stuart. Still, the Scottish lords remained uneasy. They shilly-shallied, hesitated to produce the letters, and restricted themselves to general charges. Since Elizabeth would have shown her bias too plainly by a blunt command that they should produce the letters, she had recourse to hypocrisy. Professing herself to be convinced of Mary's innocence, she said that her one desire was to save her "good sister's" honour, and that, to this end, it was essential for her to have evidence which would refute the "calumny." She wanted the letters and the love-poems to Bothwell to be exposed upon the conference table. It was necessary to her scheme that Mary Stuart should be hopelessly compromised.

Under this pressure the Scottish lords at length gave way. A little comedy of resistance was played, indeed, for Moray did not himself actually put the letters on the table, but merely showed them in his hand, and then allowed them to be "snatched" from his secretary. Elizabeth had triumphed. The documents were in open court. They were read aloud forthwith; and, next day, were read aloud once more before the full assembly. The Scottish lords had long since sworn that the documents were genuine, but this previous oath did not suffice Elizabeth. As if foreseeing that in centuries to come the authenticity of the letters and sonnets would be disputed by the defenders of Mary Stuart's honour, she insisted that their handwriting must be closely compared with that of the letters she had herself received from Mary. This comparison must be effected in full view of the conference. While it was taking place, Mary's commissioners walked out of the room (is not this additional and strong evidence of the genuineness of the letters?), declaring, truly enough, that Elizabeth had broken her pledge to produce nothing which would be derogatory to the honour of Mary.

But what did law and right count for in these proceedings, where the person chiefly implicated was not allowed to participate, although her enemy, Lennox, could act as her accuser? Hardly had Mary's commissioners withdrawn, when the other commissioners unanimously agreed that Elizabeth could not receive Mary Stuart until the Scottish queen had been purged from the charges against her. Elizabeth thus reached her goal. At length she had been given the desired pretext for repelling the advances of the fugitive. Henceforward it would not be difficult to find an excuse for continuing to keep the Queen of Scots "in honourable custody"—a euphemism for imprisonment. One of those devoted to Elizabeth's cause, Archbishop Parker, could jubilantly exclaim: "Now our good Queen has the wolf by the ears!"

With this "temporary conclusion," the necessary preliminaries had been achieved for the slaughter of Mary's reputation. Now the axe of judgment might be wielded. She could be declared a murderess, could be handed over to Scotland, where John Knox would have no mercy on her. At this juncture, however, Elizabeth held her hand, and the blow did not fall. Always when a final resolve was needed, whether for good or for evil, this enigmatic woman lacked courage. Was she stirred by one of those generous and humane impulses which were common enough in her? Was she ashamed at having broken her royal word to safeguard Mary Stuart's honour? Was she moved by diplomatic considerations? Or are we to suppose, as was usually the case in her unfathomable temperament, that she was prompted by mixed motives? Anyhow, Elizabeth refrained from using the opportunity of ridding herself of her adversary once and for all. Instead of having a speedy and severe sentence passed, she postponed the final decision in order to negotiate with Mary. Substantially, what Elizabeth wanted was to be freed from the troubles caused her by this defiant, ambitious, unyielding, self-reliant, and courageous woman—to humiliate Mary, to draw her teeth and cut her claws. Elizabeth proposed, therefore, that, before a final judgment was passed, Mary should be given an opportunity for protesting against the documents; and, under the rose, the Queen of Scotland was informed that if she consented to abdicate she would be acquitted, could remain free in England, and be supplied with a pension. At the same time, since she must hear the crack of the whip as well as be tempted by a lump of sugar, Mary was told there was considerable chance of a public condemnation, and Knollys, the confidential agent of the English court, reported that he had frightened her as much as he could. Elizabeth loved to combine or alternate caresses with punishment.

But Mary Stuart was not to be either intimidated or decoyed. As soon as danger became imminent, she rallied her forces. She refused to examine the documents. Recognizing too late that she had been inveigled into a trap, she reiterated her old contention that it was not possible for her to put herself upon the same footing with her subjects.

Her royal word that the accusation and the documents were false must count for more than any proof or contention. She refused to purchase by abdication an acquittal from a court whose jurisdiction she did not recognize. Resolutely she declared that she would not hear another word about the possibility of renouncing her crown. "I will die rather than agree; and the last words of my life shall be those of a Queen of Scotland."

The attempt at intimidation had miscarried; Elizabeth's half-heartedness was faced by Mary's stalwart determination. Again the English queen hesitated, and did not venture upon open condemnation. As so often happened, Elizabeth shrank from the final goal of her own will. When the definitive sentence came, it was not annihilating, as had been designed, but perfidious like the whole affair. On January 10, 1569, the Westminster Conference announced that nothing had been adduced against Moray and his faction which "might impair their honour or allegiance." These words explicitly condoned the rebellion of the Scottish lords. As to Mary, the decision of the conference was ambiguous. The commissioners announced that nothing had "bene sufficiently proven or shown by the Scottish lords against the queen their sovereign, whereby the Queen of England should conceive or take any evil opinion of her good sister for anything yet seen." Superficially considered, this might be regarded as an exculpation. The proofs of Mary's guilt were insufficient. But the last clause had a sting in its tail. It implied that various things had been adduced of a highly suspicious and injurious nature, but not enough to convince so good a queen as Elizabeth. The sting was more than Cecil needed for his purposes. Henceforward a heavy cloud of suspicion would rest over Mary Stuart, and a "sufficient" ground had been discovered for keeping the defenceless woman in prison. For the moment Elizabeth had conquered.

But she had gained a Pyrrhic victory. So long as she kept Mary Stuart prisoner, there were two queens in the realm of England; and while both lived the land would never know quiet. Injustice always leads to disorder; that which is done too craftily is done badly. By robbing Mary Stuart of her freedom, Elizabeth Tudor robbed herself of her own. By treating Mary as an enemy, she gave Mary the right to be one; Elizabeth's breaking her word gave Mary the right to break her word; every lie on the English queen's part justified another lie on the part of the Queen of Scotland. Year after year Elizabeth would have to pay for not having followed her first and most natural instincts. Too late would she realize that magnanimity would have been a better policy. If, after the brief ceremonial of a cool reception, Elizabeth had left Mary free to go whithersoever she pleased, Mary's life thenceforward would have been like a stream whose waters run to waste in the sands of the desert. To whom could the woman thus contemptuously dismissed have turned for refuge? Neither judge nor poet would have intervened any longer on her behalf. Tainted by the breath of scandal, humiliated by Elizabeth's generosity, she would have wandered aimlessly from court to court. Moray would have made it impossible for her to return to Scotland; neither in France nor in Spain would she have been received, an unwelcome guest, with any great show of respect. Her temperament being what it was, she would probably have become involved in new love-affairs, unless she had followed Bothwell to Denmark. Her name would have counted for little in history; or, at most, she would have been mentioned derogatorily as a queen who had married the murderer of her husband. It was Elizabeth's injustice which saved Mary from this obscure and pitiable fate. By trying to debase Mary, Elizabeth lifted her on to a higher plane, and equipped her with the halo of martyrdom. As the shamefully deceived, as the unjustly imprisoned, as a romantically touching figure, as the innocent victim of a cruel use of force, she has been justified by history as against her unjust cousin. Nothing has done so much to make Mary Stuart a centre of undying legend, and nothing has done so much to detract from Elizabeth's moral greatness, as the English queen's failure to be generous in this decisive hour.

CHAPTER NINETEEN

Years Spent in the Shadows

(1569-1584)

NOTHING eludes description more effectually than a vacuum, nothing can be more difficult to picture than monotony. Mary Stuart's imprisonment was such a prolonged non-existence, such an empty, starless night. With the decision of the Westminster Conference, the rhythm of her life had been definitively interrupted. Year followed year, as at sea wave follows wave, sometimes more eventful, sometimes more tranquil; never again would she be stirred to the depths in her solitude, whether by unqualified happiness or by unqualified torment. A destiny which had been so moving and so passionate became uneventful, and therefore doubly unsatisfying. Thus in a sort of piaffing trot passed her twenty-eighth, twenty-ninth, thirtieth year. A new decade of her life opened, vacant and chill as the last had been at the close. Followed the thirty-first, the thirty-second, the thirty-third, the thirty-fourth, the thirty-fifth, the thirty-sixth, the thirty-seventh, the thirty-eighth, the thirty-ninth year. Merely to write the numbers is fatiguing. But to understand her cruel fate we have to dwell upon them, to understand the interminable duration of her spiritual agony; for each of these years had hundreds of days; each day had too many hours, and not one of these hours was irradiated by joy. Then came the fortieth year, and she was no longer a young woman, nor yet a strong one, but ageing, weary, and out of health. Slowly there dragged themselves out the forty-first, the forty-second, and the forty-third year, until at length death had compassion on her when her fellow-mortals had none, and relieved her weary spirit from imprisonment.

There were many changes for her during these years, but only in minor and indifferent matters. Sometimes she was well, sometimes ill; sometimes she was hopeful, and a hundred times she was disappointed;

sometimes she was more harshly and at other times more clemently treated; occasionally Elizabeth would write her angry letters, to be followed by others that were kindly worded: but in general there was nothing but dull uniformity, a garland of colourless hours which slipped vacantly through her fingers. Outwardly her prison-hours changed from time to time. Now she would be detained in Bolton Castle, now at Chatsworth or Sheffield or Tutbury or Wakefield or Fotheringay. But only the names were different. They all had the same walls of impenetrable stone, and were really the same prison since they all deprived her of freedom. The monotonous procession of the days, the weeks, and the months was marked by the circling of the sun, the moon, and the stars. Night followed day and day followed night summing up the months and the years. Kingdoms passed and were renewed; kings rose and fell; women grew up, bore children, and withered; beyond the coasts and the mountains the world continued in process of unceasing change. Only this one life was perpetually in the shadows, cut off from its roots, no longer bearing either blossom or fruit. Slowly, slowly, as if poisoned by impotent yearning, Mary Stuart watched the withering of her youth, the ticking-out of her life.

Paradoxically enough, the most cruel feature of this endless imprisonment was that, to outward seeming, it was never cruel. A self-reliant person can react against crude violence, can reply to humiliation by bitterness; always the mental stature can be increased by fierce resistance. Nothing but vacancy makes us absolutely impotent. Always the walls of a padded cell, against which the fists of the prisoner cannot even hurt themselves, are more unendurable than the hardest lock-up. No flogging, no abusive language, arouses so hopeless a frame of mind as the violation of freedom under the mask of obsequiousness and with devoted assurances of respect; no kind of scorn is more dreadful than that which assumes the form of politeness. This feigned consideration, not shown to the suffering human being, but to her rank, was the treatment to which Mary Stuart was unceasingly subjected. Always a respectful entourage of guardians, a masked watch, "honourable custody" by those who, hat in hand and with profound obeisances, followed hard upon her heels. Throughout these years never for a minute was Mary Stuart's queenship forgotten. She was granted all kinds of valueless conveniences and petty freedoms, while the most important thing in life was withheld—true liberty.

Elizabeth, sedulous to maintain her prestige as a humane sovereign, was clever enough to avoid treating her adversary vengefully. She would take great care of her "good sister"! When Mary was out of health, anxious inquiries came from London; Elizabeth would offer the services of her own physician, would express a wish that the prisoner's food should be prepared by her own domestic staff. No evil tongues should whisper that she was trying to rid herself of an inconvenient rival by poison. No one should complain that she was keeping an anointed queen in a prison cell. All that had happened was that she had urgently begged her Scottish sister to live in some of her fine English country mansions or castles as a permanent guest! Certainly it would have been much more convenient and safer for Elizabeth to keep the unyielding woman in the Tower of London, a much less costly plan than the one she adopted. But, having a wider experience of the world than her ministers of State, who again and again recommended her to take this precaution, Elizabeth persisted in avoiding the odium she would have incurred by sending Mary to the Tower. Her cousin should be treated as a queen, while entangled in a noose of reverence and fettered with golden chains.

Penurious though she was, Elizabeth was able, in this instance, to overcome her avarice, with a grudging heart providing for the maintenance of her uninvited guest no less than fifty-two pounds a week throughout these nineteen years. Since, in addition, Mary received a pension of £1200 a year from France, she was well supplied with funds. She could live like a sovereign ruler at whichever castle or manor was her residence for the time. She was allowed to install a royal canopy in her reception-room, keeping queenly state, though a prisoner. She had a silver table-service; her rooms were lit with costly wax candles in silver sconces; the floors were covered with Turkey carpets —a rare luxury at that time. So abundantly were her apartments furnished, that dozens of wagons drawn by four-horse teams were needed when she was removed from one mansion to another. For her personal service she had a number of ladies-in-waiting, tire-women, and chambermaids. In the best days there were fifty of them to make up her personal staff. A miniature court with major-domos, priests, physicians, secretaries, paymasters, chamberlains, keepers-of-the-wardrobe, tailors, dressmakers, and cooks—whose numbers the frugal Queen of England desperately endeavoured to cut down, while Mary Stuart with no less tenacity defended herself against any invasion of her privileges.

But that no cruelly romantic imprisonment was designed for the queen who had fallen from power was shown at the outset by the choice of George Talbot, sixth Earl of Shrewsbury, a great nobleman and true gentleman, as her guardian in chief. Down to June 1569, when Elizabeth appointed him to this post, he might reckon himself a fortunate man. He had great possessions in the northern and midland counties, nine castles of his own, so that he had lived quietly on his estates as a minor prince in the by-paths of history, remote from offices and dignities. Untroubled by political ambition, this serious-minded man had been well satisfied with life. His beard was grizzled, and he must have thought that nothing was likely to disturb his rest until Elizabeth unexpectedly forced upon him the distasteful task of keeping watch and ward over her ambitious rival, who had been embittered by ill treatment.

His predecessor, Sir Francis Knollys, drew a breath of relief on being informed that Shrewsbury was to supersede him in the perilous charge, and declared: "As sure as there is a God in heaven, I would rather endure any punishment than continue this occupation." For it was an unthankful task, this "honourable custody," whose rights and limits were extremely vague, so that it was one which required immense tact. Mary was at one and the same time a queen and not a queen; in name she was a guest, but in fact she was a prisoner. Thus, as a gentleman, Shrewsbury had to play the part of a polite host, but as a jailer in Elizabeth's confidence he had to restrict his "guest's" liberties in various disagreeable ways. He was the controller of her doings, and yet could present himself before her only when making obeisance; he must be strict, but under the mask of subserviency; he must entertain her, and yet perpetually watch her. As if the situation were not already enough complicated, it was further involved by the fact that Lady Shrewsbury had been the notorious Bess of Hardwick. She had buried three husbands. Talbot was her fourth, and she reduced him to despair by her unceasing gossip. She was a weathercock, too, intriguing, now against Elizabeth, now in her behalf, sometimes favourable and sometimes antagonistic to Mary Stuart. Poor Shrewsbury had a difficult time of it among these three women, being the loyal subject of one, married to the second, and bound to the third by invisible bonds. For fifteen years he was not really the prisoned queen's guardian but her fellow-prisoner; and in his person once more was fulfilled the mysterious curse which made her bring misfortune to all whom she encountered upon her tragical path.

What did Mary Stuart do during these vacant and unmeaning years? She seemed to spend her time quietly and comfortably enough. Outwardly regarded, her daily round did not differ from that of other women of rank who lived year after year in a manor-house or a castle. When she felt well enough, she would go out riding—hawking or hunting—surrounded by the inevitable "guard of honour"; or she would play pall-mall or some other outdoor game in order to keep herself, as far as possible, in good bodily condition. There was no lack of company. Visitors would come from neighbouring country mansions to pay their reverence to the interesting prisoner; for it must never be forgotten that, however powerless she might be at the moment, she was still the next heir to the English throne, and if anything untoward should happen to Elizabeth, Mary might reign in her stead. That was why far-seeing persons, Shrewsbury not excepted, thought it expedient to remain on good terms with her. Even Elizabeth's favourite and intimate friends, Sir Christopher Hatton and the Earl of Leicester, wishing to keep a foot in both camps, would, behind their patroness's back, send letters and greetings to her rival. Who could tell whether it might not be necessary, ere long, to bend the knee before her, and to ask for some sinecure. In various ways, therefore, although kept in the wilds, Mary Stuart was continually in receipt of information as to what went on at the English court and in the wider world of Europe. Lady Shrewsbury told her a great deal about Elizabeth which this other Bess would have done better to keep to herself. Then, by various underground channels, news was continually flowing in from Rome. It must not be supposed that Mary Stuart's exile was that of a prisoner in a dungeon. She was not completely forsaken. On the long winter evenings music could help to pass the time agreeably.

Not now, of course, as in the days of Chastelard, did young poets sing madrigals to her. Banished for ever were the masques of Holyrood; and this impatient heart had no room left any longer for love and passion. The inclination for such adventures was ebbing with her youth. Of her more enthusiastic adherents there only remained with her Willie Douglas, who had helped her to escape from Lochleven; and among all the men who formed her little court (no more Bothwells or Rizzios, alas!) she prized above the rest the physician. For she was often ill, suffering from rheumatism, and from an inexplicable pain in the side. Often her legs were so greatly swelled that she could scarcely move, could get relief only in hot springs; while from the lack of exercise the body which had been so slender gradually became flaccid and obese. Seldom now was her will tensed as of old. Gone for ever were the long day's gallops through the Scottish countryside, when she was journeying merrily from castle to castle.

The longer her seclusion lasted, the more did she take pleasure in domestic occupations. For hours she would sit, dressed in black like a nun, at her broidery-frame, stitching with her lovely white hands those remarkable gold embroideries many of which have come down to us. At other times she would read her favourite books. There is no trustworthy record of her having had any love-affairs during the nineteen years of her imprisonment—beyond the fugitive scheme for a marriage with the Duke of Norfolk. Since her tenderness could no longer flow out towards a Bothwell, or any other lover, it was directed more gently and with less exuberance to those creatures who never deceive us, domestic pets. Mary imported from France the gentlest and cleverest of all hounds, spaniels; she had an aviary and a dovecot; she personally cared for the flowers in the garden, and saw to it that the women of her suite should not suffer from want of anything; the ordinary cares of a housewife occupied her mind, now that she no longer felt the stirrings of passion. A casual observer, a passing guest who failed to look into the depths, might suppose that the ambition which had once shaken the world had died down in her, that all earthly desires had subsided. Frequently, in her flowing widow's weeds, the ageing woman went to hear Mass said; she kneeled devoutly on the prie-dieu in her chapel; sometimes, though rarely now, she still wrote verses in her prayer-book or upon a loose sheet of paper. No longer did she pen ardent sonnets, but poems breathing piety or resignation, in which she repudiated longing for any other kingdom than the kingdom of heaven, hoped to become reconciled with God and man and with her own fate!

This, for instance:

Que suis ie helas et quoy sert ma vie
Ien suis fors qun corps priue de cœur
Un ombre vayn un object de malheur
Qui na plus rien que de mourir en uie....

[What am I, alas, and of what use my life?
I am naught but a body without a heart,
A vain shadow, a creature of misfortune,
Whose only future is one of living death.]

Always she produced the impression of having abandoned thoughts of worldly power, of being one who quietly awaits the coming of that last grim visitor who can alone bring peace on earth.

Yet this was but semblance. In reality her pride was undiminished, and she had but one thought—that of recovering freedom and sovereignty. Not for a moment did she seriously desire to become reconciled with her lot. Work at the broidery-frame, reading, conversation, and reverie served only to conceal her real work, which was conspiracy. From the first to the last day of her imprisonment Mary was perpetually plotting, and wherever she went, her habitation was a centre of intrigue. Work went on in her apartments feverishly by day and by night. Behind closed doors Mary, with the aid of her two secretaries, composed holograph diplomatic letters to the French and Spanish ambassadors, to the papal legate, to her adherents in Scotland and in the Netherlands. At the same time she sent imploring or tranquillizing, humble or proud letters to Elizabeth, who had long ceased to answer them. In a hundred different disguises her messengers made their way to and from Paris and Madrid. Secret signs were agreed upon; ciphers were elaborated, and changed month by month; an overseas correspondence with the enemies of Elizabeth went on day after day. All the members of the little court—

as Cecil knew perfectly well, and therefore was continually trying to have its numbers reduced—worked as a general staff aiming to promote her escape. Her fifty servants paid visit after visit to the neighbouring villages, to gather news, for the local population was bribed under cover of alms-giving, and was part of the gossamer organization which kept Mary in touch with Madrid and Rome. Letters were smuggled in and out with the washing, in books, in hollow sticks, beneath the lids of ornamental boxes, or in other ingenious hiding-places. New tricks were continually being devised to elude Shrewsbury's vigilance. For instance, the lining of a shoe would be opened up, to hide between the layers a message written in invisible ink; or wigs were worn in which rolls of paper could be concealed. In the books which Mary Stuart received from Paris or from London, letters were underlined in accordance with a code, and important messages could thus be transmitted. The most compromising documents would be stitched beneath the inner sole of his shoe by the confessor. Mary Stuart, who in youth had learned how to elaborate and to decipher cryptograms, directed the whole diplomatic service; and this exciting amusement of frustrating Elizabeth's precautions kept her intelligence alert, replacing outdoor sports and other amusements. She flung herself with her usual heedlessness and ardour into this conspiratorial activity, with the result that often enough, when messages and pledges had come by some new route from Paris, from Rome, or from Madrid, she could succeed in convincing herself that she was once more in possession of real power, could regard herself as a centre of European interest. The thought that Elizabeth knew her to be dangerous and yet could not bend her will, that despite the vigilance of those who kept watch over her she could conduct a campaign from her prison and modify the destinies of the world, was, perhaps, the only pleasure which diverted and refreshed her mind during those long and vacant years.

Marvellous, indeed, was her energy, the vigour she continued to show though in chains; but it was tragical, likewise, through its futility. For Mary never had any luck in her undertakings. The conspiracies she was continually instigating were foredoomed to failure. The game was too unequal. The individual is always weak in face of an effective organization. Mary Stuart was alone, whereas Elizabeth was the head of a great State, was in command of ministers, police, soldiers, and spies; and besides, one can fight better from a government office than from a prison. Cecil had ample resources at his disposal; he could spend freely and, watching with a thousand eyes, could easily checkmate the attempts of this lonely and inexperienced woman. At that time the population of England was about three million. A large number, no doubt; but the authorities kept close watch on suspects; every foreigner who landed on the English coast was under strict observation; there were spies in the taverns, in the prisons, upon the ships that crossed the Channel. When these means failed to elicit the desired information, there was no hesitation in employing a stronger instrument—the rack.

The superiority of collective force over individual force was soon manifest. One after another of Mary's self-sacrificing friends was, in the course of her years of imprisonment, dragged into the vaults of the Tower and tortured into avowing the schemes and the names of his confederates. One plot after another was crushed by this brutal method. Even when, now and again, Mary Stuart was able, by way of the embassies, to smuggle her correspondence abroad, it took weeks before her letters could reach Rome or Madrid; and many weeks more before her correspondents in the foreign capitals made up their minds to answer these dangerous dispatches; and many weeks more before the answer could get back to her. How supine, then, was the help which was offered; how intolerably lukewarm did it seem to the impatient woman who was always waiting for armies and armadas to be sent to set her free. The prisoner, the solitary, thinking day and night of his own sad fate, is always inclined to believe that those who live in the free and active world must be thinking as much about him as he thinks about himself. Of course, it is not so.

Vainly, therefore, did Mary Stuart continue to represent her liberation as the most important step towards the Counter-Reformation, as the first and most noteworthy thing the Catholic Church could do to safeguard its position. Those to whom she addressed these instigations were calculators and procrastinators, and were not agreed among themselves. The armada was not equipped; its main promoter, Philip II of Spain, prayed much, but ventured little. He was not inclined, on behalf of the imprisoned Scottish queen, to declare a war whose outcome no one could foresee. Now and again he or the Pope would send money, to help her to bribe conspirators. But the plots were poor things, badly planned, and promptly ferreted out by Walsingham's spies! Only a few mutilated corpses on Tower Hill served, from time to time, to remind the populace that, at some castle in the north, there lived a royal prisoner who obstinately persisted in her claim to be the rightful queen of England; to show the multitude that there were still fools and heroes ready to throw away their lives on behalf of this woman's alleged rights.

It was plain to all intelligent persons that Mary's incessant plotting would in the end drag her down to destruction; that she was leading a forlorn hope when, from her prison, she declared war against one of the mightiest monarchs of that day. As early as 1572, after the failure of the Ridolfi conspiracy, her brother-in-law Charles IX angrily declared: "The poor foolish woman will not desist until she loses her head. She will certainly bring about her own execution. If she does so, it will be her own fault, for I can do nothing to hinder her." These were harsh words from a man whose own heroism sufficed only to make him, during the Massacre of St. Bartholomew, fire upon unarmed fugitives from a safe window in the Louvre.

From the outlook of chill reason, Mary behaved foolishly in preferring the hopeless part of conspiracy to making a convenient but cowardly capitulation. It is probable that a timely renunciation of her royal pretensions would have unlocked the doors of her prison-house, and if so, during all these years, she had the key in her own hands. She need merely humble herself, solemnly abandon her claim alike to the Scottish and to the English throne, and England would have set her at liberty. England would have been glad to do so. Several times Elizabeth—not from magnanimity but from fear, because the accusing presence of this dangerous prisoner was a nightmare to her—endeavoured to build a golden bridge for Mary; again and again she was ready to negotiate with her "dear sister," and offer an easy compromise. But Mary would rather remain a crowned prisoner than be a queen without a throne; and Knollys had rightly judged her when, during the first days of her imprisonment, he said of her that she had courage to hold out so long as there was left no more than a span of hope. She was keen-witted enough to understand that, if set free as a queen who had abdicated, she could enjoy nothing more than a pitiful freedom; that all that could then await her would be a shameful existence in some out-of-the-way corner; and that it was her present abasement which would give her a great position in history. Stronger than the bars of her prison-house were the barriers imposed by her formal declaration that she would never abdicate, and that the last words she uttered on earth would be those of a Queen of Scotland.

Very narrow are the limits between folly and foolhardiness, for the most heroic actions can always be regarded as foolish. In concrete affairs Sancho Panza is shrewder than Don Quixote, and from the standpoint of a "reasonable" man Thersites is more reasonable than Achilles; but Hamlet's words, "Rightly to be great is not to stir without great argument, but greatly to find quarrel in a straw when honour's at the stake," will remain the acid test of a heroic nature. Beyond question Mary Stuart's resistance was almost hopeless against such overwhelming superiority of force; yet we should do wrong to call it absurd because it was in the end unsuccessful. Throughout these years, and more effectively as year followed year, this seemingly powerless and lonely woman, by her defiance, incorporated an immense power; and, for the very reason that she shook her chains, again and again she made England quake and Elizabeth's heart tremble. We regard historical happenings in a false perspective when we look upon them only from the convenient standpoint of posterity, which sees effects as well as causes. When the hurly-burly's done, when the battle's lost or won, it is easy to stigmatize him who has been vanquished as a fool because he ventured a dangerous combat.

For nigh on twenty years the decision of the struggle between these two women hung in the balance. Many of the conspiracies instigated to restore Mary Stuart to the throne of Scotland or to establish her on that of England might, with better luck and more adroitness, have proved fatal to Elizabeth. Twice or thrice, the Tudor queen escaped only by a hair's breadth. First of all the Duke of Northumberland rebelled at the head of the Catholic nobles. The whole of the north was in an uproar, and Elizabeth found it hard work to remain mistress of the situation. Then, yet more dangerous, came the Duke of

Norfolk's intrigue. The flower of the English nobility, and among them some of Elizabeth's closest friends, such as the Earl of Leicester, supported his scheme for marrying the Scottish queen, who, lest he should be a laggard in love (what would she not do to promote her triumph?), wrote him the most affectionate letters. Through the intermediation of Ridolfi, the Florentine, Spanish and French troops were ready to land on English soil. Had not Norfolk (as shown by his before-mentioned repudiation of his marital scheme) been a weakling and a coward, had not chance, wind, and storm, the sea and betrayal, wrought against the enterprise, the page would have been turned, roles exchanged. Mary Stuart would have gone to live at Westminster while Elizabeth Tudor would have languished in the Tower or have been in her coffin.

The execution of Norfolk, the fate of Northumberland and of all the others who, during these years, had laid down their lives for Mary's sake, did not deter her last suitor. Another wooer appeared upon the scene, Don John of Austria, illegitimate son of Charles V and half-brother of Philip II, the victor of Lepanto, exemplar of chivalry, the first warrior of Christendom. Excluded from the Spanish succession by his bastardy, he had attempted to found a kingdom for himself in Tunis. Then there offered a chance of mounting the Scottish throne by a marriage to the imprisoned queen. His army was being equipped in the Netherlands, and a plan had been made for the deliverance of Mary when Don John was struck down by the fate that awaited all her helpers. He died prematurely. . . .

It was luck that failed, rather than cunning. If we look clearly into the matter of this prolonged struggle between Elizabeth and Mary, luck always favoured the former, whereas disaster invariably dogged the latter's courses. Force against force, personality against personality, the women were fairly matched. Not so their respective stars. Once luck had definitely turned against Mary, once she had been dethroned and imprisoned, all her attempts miscarried. The fleets sent against England were scattered by storms; her messengers lost their way; her suitors died or were slain; her friends lacked vigour in the decisive hour; and whoever tried to help her was working for his own destruction.

Profoundly moving, therefore, was what Norfolk said upon the scaffold: "Nothing that was begun by her or for her has ever turned out well." Evil had pursued her from the time when Bothwell had become her lover. It was equally fatal to love her or to be loved by her. Whoever wished her well did her harm; whoever served her invited death to tap him on the shoulder. As the loadstone mountain in the Arabian tale attracted ships to their wreck because of the iron they had on board, so did she tend to involve all who came near her in her own unhappy fate. That is why her name has become invested with the sinister magic of death. The more hopeless her cause, the more fiercely did she fight. Her long and melancholy imprisonment, instead of breaking her pride, stiffened her to renewed defiance. Of her own free will, though aware that what she did was futile, she challenged the final award of destiny.

CHAPTER TWENTY

War to the Knife

(1584-1585)

THE years sped by. Days, weeks, months, passed like tenuous clouds over the skies of Mary's solitude, and were barely noticed in the monotonous course of her life. Nevertheless, time was laying its mark upon her and her contemporaries, and was transforming the world about her. She had reached her fifth decade, an ominous period in a woman's vital span; and still Mary Stuart remained a captive, still was she deprived of her freedom. Gently, age began to touch her; the hair at her temples was turning grey; her body began to thicken, her general appearance slowly assumed a more matronly aspect, and a quiet melancholy took possession of her soul, a sadness which she sublimated into religious fervour. Deep in her heart, the woman within must have come to realize that the days of love were gone for ever. What could not be fulfilled now must remain unfulfilled to all eternity. Evening had drawn in, and the dark nighttime was at hand. It was long since a wooer had sued for her; perhaps no man would again present himself as a possible lover. In a brief space, maybe, life would be irreclaimably closed. Was there any sense in waiting, and again waiting, for a miracle to happen, for the miracle of liberation, for the miracle of aid coming to her from an indifferent world? During recent years a feeling had been growing stronger with every passing day, that this long-suffering woman was weary of the struggle, and that slowly she was making up her mind to renounce all and accept a compromise. Ever more frequently did she ask herself whether it was not mad and useless to allow herself to wilt away like a flower in the shade, unloved, unremembered; whether she would not be better advised to buy her freedom, and of her own free will to renounce the crown. Mary Stuart, for all her courage, was finding that captivity pressed too heavily upon her tired spirit; life had become so empty that her craving for power was slowly changing into a mystical longing for death. This explains her mood on the morning of her execution, when she wrote the heart-rending lines:

O Domine Deus! speravi in te.
O care mi Jesu! nunc libera me.
In dura catena, in misera poena, desidero te;
Languendo, gemendo et genu flectendo,
Adoro, imploro, ut liberes me.

[O Lord my God, I have hoped in Thee.
O dear Lord Jesu, set me free.
Though hard the chains that fasten me,
And sore my lot, yet I long for Thee;
I languish, and groaning bend my knee,
Adoring, imploring: set me free.]

Since none came to deliver her, Mary turned more and more to her Redeemer. Far better to commit her soul into His hands than to continue to live so empty an existence, to continue waiting and uncertain, expectant and full of hope, only at last to be frustrated once more. Let an end be made—whether good or bad, whether through victory or complete relinquishment of her claim, she no longer cared. And since Mary Stuart herself desired this end with every energy of her nature, accomplishment could not fail to ensue.

The longer the struggle continued, the more tenacious had the two antagonists become. Mary Stuart and Elizabeth Tudor confronted one another defiantly. In the political arena the English queen secured one success after another. She had composed her differences with France; Spain dared not declare war; her hand lay heavy upon malcontents at home and abroad. But one enemy remained to deal satisfactorily with: a woman within her own borders, a woman conquered and yet unconquerable. Only when this last foe had been set aside could Elizabeth look upon herself as a genuine victress. For Mary Stuart, too, Elizabeth Tudor remained the only survivor upon whom to concentrate the full fury of her hatred.

In a fit of despairing moodiness she made a last appeal to the humane feelings of her sister in destiny, writing an epistle whose plaintiveness is most affecting. "I cannot, Madam, suffer it any longer; and, dying, I must discover the authors of my death. The vilest criminals in your gaols and born under your authority are admitted to be tried for their own justification, and their accusers and the accusation against them are made known to them. Why should not the same privilege be accorded to me, a sovereign queen, your nearest relative and your legitimate heir? I think that this last quality has been hitherto the principal cause of exciting my enemies against me, and of all their calumnies for creating division between us two, in order to advance their own unjust pretensions. But, alas! they have now little reason and still less need to torment me longer on this account; for I protest to you on mine honour that I now look for no other kingdom than that of my God, whom I see preparing me for the best end of all my sorrows and adversities." Then she added a final plea: "I entreat you, for the honour and grievous passion of our Saviour and Redeemer, Jesu Christ; once more I beseech you to permit me to withdraw from this kingdom to some place of rest, there to seek solace for my poor body, so worn and wearied with unceasing grief, and, with liberty of my conscience, to prepare my soul for God who daily summons me. . . . Give me this contentment before I die that, seeing all things set at rest between us, my soul, delivered from my body, may not be constrained to pour out its complaints before God for the wrong you have suffered to be done me here below. . . ."

Elizabeth turned a deaf ear to this moving appeal, and no compassionate word dropped from her lips. But Mary Stuart, too, henceforward kept silent and clenched her fists. Hatred now possessed her, a cold and fierce and enduring hatred, all the more ardent because it was concentrated upon one individual, the last of her enemies to remain alive, since the others had either died a natural death or had been put away by their foes and adversaries. It was as if a demon of death emanated from the person of Mary Stuart, a demon that assailed as indiscriminately those she loved as it assailed those she hated, slaying or maiming her supporters and her antagonists alike. The accusers at the York Commission of Inquiry, Moray, Morton, and Lethington, died violent deaths; those who at York sat in judgment upon her, Northumberland and Norfolk, lost their heads on the block; those who conspired against Darnley and those who did the same by Bothwell, the traitors of Kirk o' Field, of Carberry Hill, and of Langside, betrayed themselves, as in the case of Lindsay and Kirkcaldy; those she abhorred, the whole band of wild, ruthless, and dangerous men who loved life so greedily, the lords and earls of Scotland, slew one another, thus settling age-long disputes with the point of a dirk. The arena had been wellnigh emptied of combatants. One alone remained for Mary to wrestle with and to hate: Elizabeth Tudor. Thus the combat had degenerated into a duel. One would have to remain victorious; the other needs must be vanquished. The hour for trafficking and compromise had gone by; now it was a struggle for life or for death.

Mary Stuart rallied her remaining energies for this ultimate struggle. Her last hope had to be taken from her. She would have to submit to a final and profound affront. This had ever been the case with Mary: her superb courage, her unlimited resoluteness, were never greater than when all was lost or seemed to be lost. Her true heroism shone forth whenever there was nothing more to expect.

Mary's last hope, now, was that she might come to an understanding with her son. For during the tedious and uneventful years that had crumbled away behind her, and during which her fresh and youthful visage had been changed into a sere and pallid countenance, a child had grown to boyhood, the son of her womb, with her own blood coursing in his veins. She had left her infant behind at Stirling Castle when she rode forth to Edinburgh, where Bothwell's troopers surrounded and abducted her. Never since then had she set eyes on James. Ten years passed, fifteen years went by; now the baby she had clasped in her arms was a stripling of seventeen, James VI, King of Scotland. Soon he would be a full-grown man. Qualities of both his parents were mingled in his disposition. He possessed a queer makeup; his body was plump and stocky; his speech was heavy, his tongue unwieldy; his spirit lay under a pall of anxiety and shyness. A superficial glance conveyed the impression that the boy was abnormal. He withdrew from social intercourse, was alarmed at the sight of naked steel, trembled before dogs. His ways were uncouth, his manners far from polished. The delicate and ingrained charm of his mother was completely lacking. Nor was he musical; indeed he loved neither music nor the dance; he could not participate in gay and pleasant conversation. But he acquired foreign languages with ease, had an excellent memory, and a certain shrewdness and resoluteness manifested themselves where his personal advantage was concerned. Unhappily, many of the father's unworthier traits had been transferred to the son; for James was infirm of purpose, had no true sense of honour, and was never to be depended upon. Elizabeth once asked irritably what one could expect from this double-tongued fellow. James, like Darnley, was twisted hither and thither by almost anybody he came in contact with. Generous impulses remained totally alien to his nature; cold and calculating ambition governed his decisions; and his unwavering coolness towards his mother can be understood only when we consider it without any reference to accepted ideas of filial piety and sentiment.

The lad had been mainly educated and taught Latin by one of Mary's bitterest enemies, George Buchanan, the author of the defamatory pamphlet *Detection;* and all his life James had been brought up to believe that his mother had encompassed his father's death, and that from her places of captivity across the border she contested his right to reign though he was crowned King of Scotland. From the outset it had been dinned into his ears that he must look upon his mother as a stranger and as an obstacle in the way to his own achievement of power. Even if a tender and childlike longing to meet the woman who had given him birth still lingered in James's heart, he could never have attained his object, for the English and Scottish wardens of both prisoners kept too keen a watch on their movements —indeed, just as Mary was Elizabeth's prisoner so was James the prisoner of the Scottish lords and of various regents during his minority. Nevertheless, from time to time a letter would pass over the border. Mary Stuart sent occasional presents to her boy, playthings, too, and once she got him a little monkey. Most of these communications and gifts were returned to the sender, because Mary would not bend her pride to addressing the child as king. So long as she persisted in calling James VI "Prince of Scotland," and refused him his regal title, the lords maintained that her letters were an insult to their sovereign. Not even a formal relationship between mother and son was possible if she and he respectively continued to stand upon their royal prerogatives and looked upon the possession of power as of more importance than the ties of blood; if she persisted in maintaining that she alone was queen and sovereign lady of Scotland, while he considered that he alone was king and sovereign lord of the same realm.

Mary and James could perhaps begin to draw together if she curtailed her pretension of alone being the reigning sovereign of Scotland. Despair and weariness might exercise more power over her proud and impatient spirit than any other means of persuasion. Of course, even if she yielded on a point or two, she had no intention of wholly renouncing her privilege to bear the title of queen. She intended to live and die with the crown upon her consecrated head. But she was now prepared, at the price of regaining freedom, at least to share the royal sovereignty with her son. For the first time her thoughts turned to compromise. Let James rule the land and call himself king; but let her retain her title of queen, so that her renunciation might at least be gilded with a little honour. Could not some formula be found? Negotiations at first promised well. But James VI, perpetually at the mercy of his threatening nobles, carried on the parleyings in a spirit of cold calculation. Without scruple, he bargained simultaneously with everyone, playing off Mary against Elizabeth and Elizabeth against Mary, using one religion as a lever against the other. He was content to sell his favour to the highest bidder, since for him the struggle did not concern his honour. What he hoped to win out of the barter was the recognition of himself as the sole and unlimited monarch of Scotland, and at the same time to secure his own succession to the English throne. He was not satisfied with being the accredited heir of one only of these two women, but must bear that relation to both. Quite prepared to remain Protestant if by doing so he added to his advantages, he was, nevertheless, equally amenable to the idea of entering the Catholic Church if the old faith offered him a handsomer price; the seventeen-year-old monarch was not even dismayed by the notion of marrying Elizabeth, if these nuptials were likely to make him King of England the sooner. Yet Elizabeth Tudor was by this time a jaded and worn-out piece of womanhood, nine years older than Mary Stuart, and the fiercest and most embittered enemy of James's mother. For Darnley's son these contemptible quibbles were no more than matters of deliberate calculation. For Mary, on the other hand, the undying child of illusion, shut away as she was from the world and its events, the parleyings to and fro acted like a bellows upon the glowing brazier of her final hopes, so that she truly believed she might come to an understanding with her son and yet retain her title of queen.

But Elizabeth was fully awake to the peril that such a reconciliation entailed for herself. Any outcome of the sort must be hindered. She quickly took a hand in the game. Sharp-eyed and cynical as she was, it would prove no difficult affair to decoy the unscrupulous careerist: she need but trade upon his weakness. Knowing the uncouth youngster to be madly in love with the chase, Elizabeth sent him gifts of the finest horses and hounds she could lay hands on. His counsellors were handsomely bribed; and he himself—who like all the Scottish nobles and gentry was perennially short of money—was offered a yearly pension of five thousand pounds. Finally the promise of the English succession was dangled before his eyes. Money, as always, decided the issue. While Mary, ignorant of these counter-intrigues, was making diplomatic contacts with the Pope and with Spain in an endeavour to bring Scotland into the Roman Catholic fold, James VI was signing a treaty with Elizabeth wherein were incorporated the clauses which might accrue to his benefit, but where no mention was made of Mary Stuart's liberation. No thought was given to the captive, for she had become a creature of no consequence to James her son since she had no advantages to offer. As if Mary had ceased to live, he came to a workable arrangement with Elizabeth, his mother's cruellest foe. The woman to whom he owed his existence might disappear for all he cared, or must at least not enter the circle of his life. No sooner was the bond between himself and Elizabeth signed, no sooner had he got the promised pension in hand and become the master of some fine hunting dogs and horses, than, at a moment's notice, he broke off negotiations with Mary Stuart. Why should he bother about behaving courteously to a woman who had lost all power? He anounced that he was under the necessity "of declining to associate her with himself in the sovereignty of Scotland"; nor could he "treat with her otherwise than as Queen-Mother." Thus a son heartlessly abandoned his royal mother to life-long captivity. Realm, crown, power, freedom, had been snatched out of her grasp by her rival. The childless enemy thus completed her vengeance, for she had brought about the defection of Mary Stuart's son.

Elizabeth's triumph on this occasion shattered Mary's last hopes. Once again she realized that her enemy had sold and betrayed her. Having lost her husband, her brother, and her subjects, she now lost her child; henceforward she was to stand alone. Her disappointment was only equalled by her disgust. She need consider nobody's feelings for the future! Just as well, perhaps! Since her own child denied her, she would deny him. Since he had nearly bartered away her rights to the crown of Scotland, she would pay the youngster back in his own coin. She accused him of having forgotten the "duty and obligation" he owed her, and threatened to bestow her malediction "and invoke that of heaven on my ungrateful son"; further, she affirmed that, unless James became a convert to the Church of Rome, she would debar him from his rights to the crowns of England and of Scotland. She would rather, "if he perseveres in the heresy of Calvin," transfer these rights to a foreign prince—to the King of Spain, for instance, should that monarch consent to fight for her freedom and to humiliate the assassin of her best hopes, Queen Elizabeth of England. No longer was her son or her country of importance to her. All she needed now was freedom, liberty to live her own life, once more to be victor in the arena. Even the boldest venture seemed natural to her. One who has lost everything has nothing left to risk.

Year after year anger and embitterment had accumulated within this tortured and humiliated woman; year after year she had hoped and negotiated and compromised and conspired. Her cup was now full, and even overfull. A flame of hatred streamed upward against the torturer, the usurper, the wardress of her imprisonment. No longer was it as one queen against another or as one woman against another that Mary Stuart hurled herself tooth and nail against Elizabeth Tudor. A petty incident brought things to a head. The Countess of Shrewsbury, a confirmed scandal-monger and peculiarly malicious slanderer, declared that Mary Stuart had entered into amorous relationships with the earl, her husband and Mary's jailer. Such gossip was not meant to be taken seriously, but Elizabeth, who had always been at pains to show up the moral lapses of her rival, quickly seized the opportunity in order to acquaint the continental courts of her cousin's fresh misdemeanour. It was, then, not enough that she should have power taken from her, that she should be deprived of her freedom, that the affection of her son should be alienated from her; now her fair name must be besmirched, and she, who lived like a nun, who dispensed with any form of pleasure or of love, was to be held up before the eyes of the world as an adulteress. Wounded pride made her wrath blaze high. She demanded immediate reparation, and Lady Shrewsbury "upon her knees" denied that there were any grounds for the infamous reports spread abroad against the Queen of Scots. But Mary knew well who was responsible for the speedy extension of the rumours initiated by her jailer's wife; she guessed the secret and malignant joy of her perennial foe at having so luscious a morsel of calumny to serve up to the courts of Europe; and she determined to counter the blow that had been dealt her in the dark by a blow dealt in the open. Impatience had long possessed her soul to exhibit this so-called virgin queen in true colours. She who set herself up as a model of virtue and righteousness would hear the truth at last as between one woman and the other.

Mary, therefore, wrote a letter (to outward seeming a friendly one, but, in truth, one of the spiciest documents in the English archives) to Elizabeth, narrating in the frankest language the gossip anent the English queen's private life and morals that was being disseminated by the Countess of Shrewsbury. The ostensible motive was, as I have said, a friendly one; but Mary's real object was to show her "dear sister" how slight were the latter's claims to pose as an exemplar of good morals or as an authority upon ethical standards. Every word in this epistle seems like a fresh blow, whose punch was backed up by despair and hate. All the fearful things one woman can say to another are herein stated; Elizabeth's faults of character are flung vindictively in her face; the most hidden secrets of her womanhood are ruthlessly unveiled. "Bess of Hardwick" had indulged her tongue beyond the limits of the excusable, had declared Elizabeth to be so vain and to hold so exalted an opinion of her own loveliness as to make her hearers believe she must be the Queen of Heaven. Never was she satiated with flattery, continually forcing her ladies into the most absurd exaggerations; her uncontrolled vulgarity was displayed in the way she would, when vexed, mishandle these same gentlewomen and the tiring-maids in her suite. She had actually broken the finger of one and had slashed another with a knife on the hand because of some lack of dexterity in the serving of a meal.

These items, however, were nothing when compared to other revelations, such as that Elizabeth had a running sore on the leg (a hint that she might have inherited syphilis from her father); that she had lost her youth prematurely, but nevertheless continued to lust after men. That "infinies foys," countless numbers of times, she had gone to bed with Leicester; nor had he been her only paramour; that she sought her pleasure anywhere and everywhere; that she never wanted to lose her freedom to make love and to have her desires satisfied by ever fresh lovers. At night she had been known to slip out of her own bedchamber, wearing nothing more than a nightgown with, maybe, a shawl flung about her for warmth's sake, and creep into the room of some man of her choice; these illicit delights had to be paid for dearly. Mary heaped name upon name, detail upon detail. But the deadliest bolt of all, Elizabeth's bitterest wound to her pride as a woman, about which Ben Jonson blabbed freely in the taverns he frequented, was not spared the English sovereign: "She says, moreover, that indubitably you are not like other women, and it is folly to advance the notion of your marriage with the duc d'Anjou, seeing that such a conjugal union could never be consummated." There Elizabeth had it plain and flat; her secret was known to all; everyone knew that because of her physical imperfection she could only gratify her lust but never her natural sexual appetite, that she could only play at love but was debarred entirely from wedlock and motherhood. One woman alone had the courage to tell the mightiest of queens this ultimate and terrible truth; one captive woman alone, after twenty years of pent-up hatred, of stifled anger, of imprisoned energies, rallied her forces to deal this ghastly assault upon the heart of her tormentor.

After such an explosion, reconciliation was impossible. The woman who had composed the letter, and the woman who was intended to read it, could no longer breathe the same air or live in the same country. "Hasta al cuchillo," as the Spaniards say, war to the knife, war to the death—such was the only issue. After more than two decades of double dealing, of obstinate spying and irreconcilable enmity, Mary Stuart and Elizabeth Tudor had brought their historic combat into the light of day. The Counter-Reformation had used every conceivable diplomatic art, but neither side had as yet had recourse to arms. What was to be proudly (and afterwards derisively) styled the "Invincible Armada" was being slowly and laboriously built in Spain. But, despite the inflow of wealth from America, the court of that unhappy land was always short alike of money and of resolution. Philip the Pious resembled John Knox in looking upon the removal of an adversary who adhered to another creed as an act well pleasing to Almighty God. Would it not be cheaper and easier to hire a few bravos who would forthwith rid the world of Elizabeth, the protectress of heresy? The age of Machiavelli and his pupils was not troubled by moral considerations when power was at stake. Here the stakes were colossal: faith against faith, south against north, the admiralty of the world.

When politics are heated white-hot in the furnace of passion, moral and legal scruples are thrown to the winds; no one bothers about honour or decency, and even assassination is glorified. Through the excommunication of Elizabeth in 1570 and of William the Silent in 1580, the two chief enemies of Catholicism had been outlawed by the Roman Church; and after the Pope had expressly approved the Massacre of St. Bartholomew, every Catholic was assured that he would be doing a praiseworthy deed if he succeeded in assassinating either of these hereditary foes of the true faith. A vigorous thrust with a dagger, a skilfully aimed pistol bullet, might free Mary Stuart from captivity and place her on the throne at Westminster, with the result that England and the world would be regained for Rome. The Jesuits were busily and secretly going to and fro across the Channel. The Spanish government did not hesitate to avow that the murder of Elizabeth was one of its chief political aims. Mendoza, Spanish ambassador in London, referred frequently in his dispatches to "killing the queen" as a laudable enterprise. The Duke of Alva, governor of the Netherlands, approved the scheme. Philip II, lord of two continents, drafted with his own hand a plan which he hoped that "God would favour."

Matters were to be decided, not by diplomatic arts, nor by open warfare, but by the assassin's knife. There was not much to choose between England and Spain as to methods. In Madrid, the killing of Elizabeth was decided on in a secret conclave, and was endorsed by the king. In London, Cecil and Walsingham and Leicester were agreed upon making short work of Mary Stuart. There were to be no more hesitations and no more expedients. The account had long been overdue, and its settlement would be marked by a line drawn in blood. The only question was, which would act more promptly, the Reformation or the Counter-Reformation, London or Madrid? Would Mary Stuart sweep Elizabeth Tudor out of her path, or would Elizabeth make an end of Mary?

CHAPTER TWENTY-ONE

"The Matter Must Come to an End"

(SEPTEMBER 1585 TO AUGUST 1586)

"THE MATTER must come to an end." Such was the incisive formula in which one of Elizabeth's ministers of State impatiently summarized the sentiment that prevailed throughout England. Nothing is harder for an individual or a nation to bear than long-continued uncertainty. The assassination of the other great protagonist of the Reformation, William the Silent, who was killed by a Roman Catholic fanatic in June 1584, showed England plainly enough that the poniard had already been sharpened for the heart of Queen Elizabeth. It was a known fact that one conspiracy followed close upon another. The general feeling, therefore, was that the moment had come to make an end of the prisoned Scottish queen who laid claim to the throne of England as well, and who was the centre of innumerable conspiracies. The evil must be cut at the roots. In September 1584, the Protestant section of the English nobility and gentry drew up a Bond of Association pledging all good citizens to slay without scruple any conspirator who plotted against the queen. Furthermore, "pretenders to the throne in whose favour these men conspired" were "to be deprived of all rights as claimants to the succession," and were to be held personally responsible for such plots. Next the Bond of Association was confirmed by a statute (27 Elizabeth, 1585) entitled *An Act for the Security of the Queen's Royal Person, and the Continuance of the Realm of Peace.* Everyone who participated in an attack upon the queen or who merely sanctioned it became liable to the death penalty. It was further decided that everyone accused of entering into a conspiracy against the queen should be tried by a jury of twenty-four persons appointed by the crown.

This gave Mary Stuart plain notice of two facts: first of all, that her royal rank would no longer protect her from a public trial; secondly, that even a successful attempt on Elizabeth's life would bring her no advantage, but would cost her her own head. This was like the last flourish of trumpets which demands a surrender of an obstinate fortress before the final assault. If there were any further hesitation, no quarter would be given. Ambiguities between Elizabeth Tudor and Mary Stuart were over and done with. There was to be no more shilly-shallying.

There were other signs that the days of a courteous interchange of letters and of amiable hypocrisies were over, that the last round in the long struggle had opened, that there was to be no more consideration shown, that war to the knife had been declared. The English court decided, in view of the unceasing conspiracies against Elizabeth, that Mary Stuart should be more strictly guarded in future. Shrewsbury, being too much of a gentleman to be a good jailer, was "released" from his office. In very truth Shrewsbury thanked Elizabeth on his knees for having restored him to freedom after fifteen years of a jailership that had made him a prisoner as well as Mary. He was replaced in his guardianship by Sir Amyas Paulet, a fanatical Protestant. Now Mary Stuart could, without exaggeration, speak of having been reduced to "servitude," for her friendly guardian had been replaced by an inexorable jailer.

Amyas Paulet, a hard-bitten Puritan, one of the excessively "just" who model their behaviour upon the Old Testament worthies but who cannot be pleasing to a good God, made no secret of his determination that thenceforward Mary Stuart's life was to be as uncomfortable as possible. The task of making himself disagreeable, of robbing her of the small favours Shrewsbury had granted her, was a delight to Paulet. He wrote to Elizabeth saying that he expected no mercy should Mary escape from his custody, since such an escape would be possible only through gross negligence on his part. With the cold and clear systematism of one who regards himself as a slave to "duty," he contemplated the guardianship of Mary Stuart and the making it impossible for her to do any harm as a task assigned to him by God. He had no other ambition than to be an exemplary jailer. He was a new Cato, whom no temptation could lead astray; and no inner promptings of tenderness would ever induce him to modify his harshness. The ailing and weary woman was not, in his eyes, a princess who deserved compassion for her misfortunes, but merely his queen's arch-enemy, who must be treated as Antichrist personified. As for her illness, he wrote cynically: "The indisposition of this Queen's body, and the great infirmity of her legs, which is so desperate as herself doth not hope of any recovery, is no small advantage to her keeper, who shall not need to stand in great fear of her running away, if he can foresee that she be not taken from him by force." He fulfilled his task with a malicious delight in his own efficiency, entering his observations of the captive night after night in a manuscript book. Even though history has made us acquainted with more cruel, violent, and unjust jailers than Paulet, there is scarce a record of any who was as well able as he to take pleasure in his detestable duties.

His first step was to cut the hidden threads by means of which Mary Stuart had still been able to communicate with the outer world. Her prison-house was surrounded by sentries, whose cordon was kept intact by day and by night. The domestic staff, which had hitherto passed freely in and out, and had been able to transmit oral and written messages, had their leave stopped. No member of Mary's court could go abroad without a special permit, and must then be accompanied by a soldier. Mary was forbidden to continue the bestowal of alms upon the poor of the neighbourhood, Paulet perspicaciously recognizing that this pious practice made the recipients ready to smuggle information. The regulations were tightened day by day. Parcels of laundry, of books—whatever passed in or out—were scrutinized as closely as baggage is at a modern custom-house, and in this way the possibility of secret correspondence was cut off. Nau and Curle, Mary's secretaries, sat twiddling their thumbs, for their occupation was gone. They had no letters either to write or to decipher. Neither from London nor from Scotland nor from Rome nor from Madrid did news trickle through bringing hope to Mary in her loneliness. Soon Paulet deprived her of her last enjoyment. Her sixteen horses ate their heads off in Sheffield since she was forbidden the chase or even a ride to breathe the fresh air. Terribly narrowed were the bounds of her existence under Sir Amyas Paulet's "guardianship," so that she was at length indisputably prisoned, and felt as if she were already in her coffin.

It might have been more creditable to Elizabeth had she chosen a less strict jailer for her sister the queen. Still, as far as seeing to Elizabeth's immunity from the risk of assassination was concerned, one cannot but recognize that no more trusty watch-dog could have been chosen than this cold-blooded Calvinist. Paulet admirably discharged the duty of isolating Mary Stuart from the world. Within a few months she began to feel as if she were kept under a bell-glass. Not a word, not a letter, from outside reached her. Elizabeth had every reason to be satisfied with the new jailer, and expressed her most heartfelt thanks to Paulet for all he was doing. "If you knew, my dear Amyas, how much indebted I feel to you for your unparalleled care, how thankfully I recognize the flawlessness of your arrangements, how I approve your wise orders and safe measures in the performance of a task so dangerous and difficult, it would lighten your cares and rejoice your heart."

Strangely enough, however, Elizabeth's ministers of State, Cecil and Walsingham, were, to begin with, by no means pleased with the "precise fellow," Sir Amyas Paulet, for his pains. The complete severance of Mary Stuart from her secret correspondence with foreign parts ran counter to their wishes. It did not suit them at all that the Scottish queen should be deprived of every chance for carrying on conspiracies, or that Paulet, by establishing a cordon round her, was guarding her against the consequences of her own incaution. What Cecil and Walsingham wanted was, not an innocent Mary Stuart, but a guilty one; they wanted her, whom they regarded as the perpetual cause of unrest and plotting in England, to continue her plots until she could be caught in her own net. Their main desire was that "the matter should come to an end"; they looked forward to the trial, condemnation, and execution of Mary Stuart.

In their view, the only way of safeguarding Elizabeth was to make an end of her adversary; and since Sir Amyas Paulet, by the rigorous methods he adopted, had rendered it impossible for Mary to initiate any further plots, a plot must be instigated by provocative agents, and the prisoner induced to take part in it. What Cecil and Walsingham required was a conspiracy against Elizabeth, and plain proof that Mary Stuart was involved in it.

As a matter of fact, a plot to kill Elizabeth was ready to their hands. The plot was, so to say, a permanent one. Philip of Spain had established on the continent an anti-English conspiratorial centre; in Paris resided Morgan, Mary Stuart's confidential agent, supplied with funds from Spain, his business being to carry on unceasing machinations against England and Elizabeth. Here more and more young enthusiasts were enlisted. Through the intermediation of the Spanish and French ambassadors, links were maintained between the malcontent Catholic nobility in England and the chancelleries of the Counter-Reformation. But an important point had escaped Morgan's notice, namely that Walsingham, one of the ablest and most unscrupulous directors of provocative agents that ever existed, had planted upon Morgan some of his own spies under the guise of devout Catholics, so that the very messengers whom Morgan placed most confidence in were really in Walsingham's pay. What was planned on behalf of Mary Stuart was betrayed to England, time after time, before any steps had been taken to put the scheme into execution. Now, at the close of the year 1585, when the scaffold was still dripping with the blood of those who were executed for the part they had played in the latest conspiracy, the English authorities became aware that fresh action was about to be taken for the assassination of Elizabeth. Walsingham had a full and accurate list of the names of the Catholic nobles in England who had assured Morgan of their willingness to support any move to put Mary Stuart upon the throne. Walsingham need merely give a sign, and a liberal use of the rack would enable him to fill the gaps in his knowledge.

Walsingham's technique, however, was more subtle, more far-sighted, and more perfidious. Of course, if he wished, he could nip the conspiracy in the bud. It would not suit his purposes, however, merely to send a few noblemen to the block or to have some of the lesser conspirators hanged, drawn, and quartered. What would be the use of cutting off five or six heads of the hydra of this unceasing conspiracy if, next morning, two new heads would have taken the place of each? "Carthage must be destroyed" was Cecil's and Walsingham's motto; they were determined to make an end of Mary Stuart; and for this purpose no minor conspiracy would suffice. They would need to prove the existence of widespread activities in favour of the imprisoned Queen of Scots. Instead, therefore, of stifling Babington's plot in the germ, Walsingham secretly encouraged it; manuring it with good wishes, supplying it with funds, furthering it by assumed indifference. Thanks to his skill as director of provocative agents, what had at first been no more than an amateurish conspiracy of a few country gentlefolk against Elizabeth, developed into the famous Walsingham plot for ridding the world of Mary Stuart.

There must be three stages in the affair if Mary Stuart was to be slain in due form of law. First of all, the conspirators must be induced to commit themselves to a scheme for Elizabeth's assassination. Secondly, it was necessary that they should acquaint Mary Stuart of their intention. Thirdly (and this was the most difficult requisite), Mary herself must be persuaded to approve the plan, by a document in her own handwriting. Her complicity and her guilt must be proved up to the hilt, for Elizabeth would be dishonoured if Mary were put to death in default of the desired proof. Rather than that, manufacture evidence of Mary's guilt! Rather than that, cunningly press into her hand a dagger with which she could slay herself.

The work of the English official conspirators against Mary Stuart began by a mitigation of the rigorousness of her imprisonment. Walsingham, it would seem, did not find much difficulty in persuading Sir Amyas Paulet, the pious Puritan, that, instead of maintaining so strict a cordon round Mary as to make it impossible for her to initiate or participate in any conspiracies, it would be better to entangle the royal prisoner in a plot. Anyhow, Paulet modified his treatment of Mary in accordance with the scheme of the English general staff. One day this man, who had hitherto been so inexorable a jailer, came to see Mary and told her, in the most friendly terms, that it had been decided to remove her from Tutbury to Chartley. Mary, little guessing the machinations of her enemies, could not conceal her delight. Tutbury was a gloomy stronghold, more like a prison than a castle; Chartley, on the other hand, was a pleasant place enough, with the added advantage that in the neighbourhood lived Catholic families friendly to her, and from whom she might expect aid. At Chartley she would be able to go out riding once more if her health allowed it; and, there, perhaps, she would have a chance of getting news from her relatives and friends across the seas, a chance (with courage and skill) of regaining what she would prize most of all—her liberty.

Behold, one morning, Mary Stuart was astonished. She could scarcely believe her eyes. As if by magic, Sir Amyas Paulet's encirclement had been broken through. A cipher dispatch came to hand, the first she had received for months. How clever of her friends to have at length found means for outwitting her inexorable jailer! What an unexpected delight! She was no longer cut off from the world, but would again be kept informed of the plans that were being made to set her free. Nevertheless, some instinct warned her to be cautious, and in her reply to Morgan she advised him: "Keep yourself from meddling with anything that might redound to your hurt, or increase the suspicion already conceived against you in these parts, being sure that you are able to clear yourself of all dealings for my service hithertill." But this mood of suspicion did not last long. It was dispelled when she learned by what clever artifices her friends (really they were her intended assassins) would keep up communications with her. Every week a barrel of beer was sent from Burton for the queen's servants, and her friends persuaded the drayman to let them replace the bung of the barrel with a corked tube in which letters could be concealed. Thenceforward communications were carried on with the regularity of a postal service. Week after week "the honest man," as the drayman was styled in the correspondence, brought his barrel of beer to the castle; once it was safely in the cellar, Mary's butler removed the corked tube which carried the incoming letter, while last week's empty barrel, in like manner, conveyed an outgoing letter. The honest man, it need hardly be said, was well paid for his services.

But what Mary Stuart did not know was that the drayman was paid over again by the English authorities, and that Sir Amyas Paulet knew all that was going on. It was not Mary Stuart's friends who had excogitated this method of communication, but Gifford, one of Walsingham's spies, who had presented himself to Morgan and to the French ambassador as Mary's confidential agent. Thus Mary's secret correspondence could be fully supervised by her political enemies. Every letter to or from Mary was, on its way, inspected by Gifford (whom Morgan regarded as his most trustworthy henchman), was deciphered by Thomas Phelippes, who was also in Walsingham's employ and was clever at ciphers. When the missive had been decoded, a copy was promptly sent to London. This work was done with so much dispatch that the correspondence between Mary Stuart and the French embassy went on briskly without the parties at either end suspecting that it had been tampered with.

Mary Stuart congratulated herself. At length she had outwitted Sir Amyas Paulet, the stiff Puritan, who examined the laundry on its way to and from the wash, had shoe-soles inspected, kept her under close observation as if she were a criminal. She smiled as she thought what a rage her jailer would be in if he knew that, despite all his sentries, despite locks and bars, she was week after week exchanging letters with Paris, Madrid, and Rome; that her agents were working busily on her behalf; that armies and navies were making ready in support of her cause; that daggers were being sharpened to pierce the hearts of her enemies. Sometimes, maybe, she showed her delight too plainly, thus giving herself away beneath Sir Amyas Paulet's watchful eyes, now that she was stimulated by the cordial of renewed hope. Paulet, on his side, was much better justified in smiling coldly to himself when, week after week, he saw the fresh supply of beer being brought by the "honest man" (the only name by which this worthy is known), when he noted the haste with which Queen Mary's butler went down to the cellar to secure the precious letter. Paulet knew that what his prisoner was about to read had long since been deciphered by the English agent, and that copies were on their way to Walsingham and Cecil. These ministers of State would learn from the decoded letters that Mary Stuart had offered the crown of Scotland and the right of succession to the crown of England to Philip of Spain if he would help her to escape. Such a letter, they knew, might be useful in appeasing James VI if he should take it into his head that his mother was being too harshly treated. They read that Mary Stuart, in her holograph dispatches to Paris, was urging the invasion of England by Spanish troops. This would be useful, too, when the Scottish queen was brought to trial. Unfortunately for their scheme, however, they could not for a long time discover anything in the letters to show that Mary Stuart sanctioned a plan for the assassination of Elizabeth

Tudor. The prisoner had not made herself as guilty as Queen Elizabeth's advisers wished; she had not yet done enough for them to set their murder-machine in motion by demanding a public trial of the prisoner; they wanted definite proof of Mary Stuart's "consent" to the killing of Elizabeth Tudor. To secure this last turn of the screw, Walsingham now devoted his best energies. Therewith began one of the most incredible though documentarily attested acts of perfidy known to history—the "frame-up" by which Walsingham made Mary Stuart privy to a plot of his own manufacture, the so-called Babington conspiracy, which was in reality a Walsingham conspiracy.

Walsingham's plan was masterly, and was, in a sense, justified by results. What made it so repulsive that, after the lapse of centuries, one's gorge rises when one contemplates the details, was that Walsingham, to further it, appealed to one of the finest of human qualities, the touching faith of youthful romanticists. Anthony Babington, whom the authorities in London chose as their unwitting tool, merits our sympathy and admiration, for he threw away his life under stress of a noble impulse. A young country gentleman, married and well-to-do, scion of an ancient Northumberland family that later settled in Derbyshire, he lived for the most part on his estate, which was close to Chartley. The reader will readily understand why Walsingham selected Chartley as Mary Stuart's latest residence. Walsingham had long since known that Babington, a devout Catholic, greatly attached to Mary Stuart, was instrumental in furthering her secret correspondence with foreign parts. It is one of the privileges of youth to be profoundly moved by sympathy for the victims of a tragical destiny. Such an unsuspicious idealist, a "pure fool," would suit Walsingham's purposes far better than a hired spy, for the prisoned queen would be only too eager to put her trust in young Babington. She knew that he was not moved by pursuit of gain, or by personal fondness for her, but by chivalric sentiment, which in him was accentuated almost beyond the verge of sanity. It is most probably a posthumous and romantic invention, the assertion that Babington had been page to Mary Stuart for a time when she was under Shrewsbury's custody, and had then fallen to her charms. Presumably he never met her, and served her only from delight in service, from Catholic fervour, from adventurous enthusiasm, all these combining to make him devote himself to the woman whom he regarded as the rightful Queen of England. Heedless, unwary, and loquacious, as emotional young people are prone to be, he recruited adherents from among his friends, inducing various individuals of his own creed and station to join him. A strange circle of conspirators was formed, including a fanatical priest named Ballard, a desperado aptly called "Savage," and various young gentlemen with more money than brains, who had read Plutarch's *Lives* and entertained cloudy dreams of heroism. Soon, however, their ranks were swelled by clearer-headed and more resolute persons than Babington and his intimates; above all by a certain Gifford, whom Elizabeth was subsequently to reward for his services with a pension of one hundred pounds per annum. The hotheads among them decided that it would not be enough to set the prisoned queen at liberty. Impetuously they determined upon a far more dangerous deed: upon the assassination of Elizabeth, the "usurper."

The latest adherents to the plot, and the most ardent among the conspirators, were, it need hardly be said, Walsingham's spies, insinuated among the young idealists as provocative agents; for Walsingham designed, not only to keep himself fully informed as to what was going on, but also, and above all, to jog the elbow of Babington the enthusiast. For Babington, as the documents clearly show, had, with his friends, originally designed nothing more than, from his country-house as base, to effect Mary Stuart's rescue from prison. The thought of murder was foreign to his nature.

But a mere scheme for the carrying-off of Mary Stuart would not suffice Walsingham, would not enable him to send the troublesome prisoner to the block. He needed a full-dress conspiracy for assassination. His agents, therefore, kept up their work of incitation until Babington and the latter's friends finally agreed to take action along the line desired by Walsingham. On May 12, 1586, the Spanish ambassador, who was throughout in touch with the conspirators, was able to report to King Philip the agreeable tidings that four Catholic gentlemen who were granted the entry to Elizabeth's court had solemnly sworn to make an end of the queen with poison or dagger. The provocative agents had done their work satisfactorily; at length Walsingham's murder-conspiracy was well on the way.

But this only fulfilled the first part of Walsingham's plans. The snare was fastened at one end. The other end needed to be firmly attached. The plot for the murder of Queen Elizabeth had been successfully instigated. Now came the harder part of the business, the securing of the unsuspicious prisoner's "consent" to the "removal" of her rival. Once more Walsingham whistled up his gang of spies. He sent some of his emissaries to Paris, the headquarters of the Catholic conspiracy, with instructions to complain to Morgan, agent of Philip II and of Mary Stuart, that Babington & Co. were lukewarm in the cause. They could not make up their minds to the assassination, but hesitated and procrastinated. It was urgently necessary to stimulate their fervour, and nothing could do this so effectually as a word from Mary Stuart. Were Babington once convinced that the queen he honoured and admired approved the murder, he would be prepared to take action. It was essential, therefore, so the spies assured Morgan, for him to induce Queen Mary to write something that would enhance Babington's zeal.

Morgan hesitated. One may guess that his suspicions were aroused, that he had glimpsed Walsingham's game. However, the English minister's agents persisted in assuring him that nothing more was needed than a few formal lines. At length Morgan gave way; but, to guard against any lack of caution, he sent to Mary a draft of the letter he wanted her to write to Babington. The queen, who had full confidence in Morgan, copied this missive word for word.

At length the connexion Walsingham desired between Mary Stuart and the conspiracy had been brought about. Morgan's caution, however, stood him and the queen in good stead, for Mary's first letter to the conspirators, though cordial enough, was noncommittal. What Walsingham needed was the queen's plain "consent" to the proposed attempt upon Elizabeth's life. Acting on his instructions, therefore, his agents set to work once more upon the other end of the snare. Gifford made it plain to the unhappy Babington that, now Mary had shown her confidence in him, he must respond by giving the captive queen a full account of his plan. A thing so dangerous as an attempt upon Elizabeth's life must not be undertaken without the express approval of Mary Stuart; and, thanks to the weekly visits of the "honest man," there was a safe way of conveying all necessary information to Queen Mary and of getting her royal instructions in return. Babington, the "pure fool," with more courage than wit, walked into the trap. He sent a long missive addressed to his "très chère souveraine," disclosing every detail of the plot. Why should not the unhappy queen be consoled in her captivity by knowing what was afoot? Why should she not be informed that the hour of her liberation was at hand? As unsuspiciously as if his words were to be conveyed to Queen Mary by heavenly messengers, absolutely unaware that whatever he wrote would be read by Walsingham's emissaries before it would be read by Mary, the poor wretch blabbed the whole plan of campaign. "Myself with ten gentlemen and a hundred of followers will undertake the delivery of your royal person from the hands of your enemies. For the dispatch of the usurper, from the obedience of whom we are by the excommunication of her made free, there be six noble gentlemen, all my private friends, who for the zeal they bear to the Catholic cause and Your Majesty's service will undertake that tragical execution." Ardent resolution, and a clear understanding of the risk that was being run, are made plain by this foolish though candid letter, which cannot but touch the hearts of those who read it after the lapse of centuries. Surely it would touch Queen Mary's heart too? She was not likely to be so cautious or sober-minded as, from cowardice, to refuse answer and encouragement to those who were chivalrously ready to devote themselves to her service.

It was upon Mary Stuart's ardour and heedlessness, the qualities she had so often shown, that Walsingham was counting. If Mary approved Babington's scheme for "the dispatch of the usurper," Walsingham would have gained his end. Mary would have relieved him from the unpleasant need for compassing the secret murder. She would have walked into the open trap.

The disastrous letter was sent. Phelippes, as usual, deciphered it and sent a copy to Walsingham. The unaltered original, scrupulously resealed, was dispatched to the unsuspecting recipient by way of the beer-barrel. On July 10, 1586, it was in Mary Stuart's hands, when two notables in London, Cecil and Walsingham, the prime movers in this perfidious plot, were eagerly waiting to know how she would reply to it. The moment of greatest tension had come. The fish was nibbling at the bait. Would the tempting morsel be swallowed hook and all, or would it be left uneaten? Well, we must look at the affair for a moment from Cecil's and Walsingham's point of view, for some will admire though others will condemn their political methods. However abominable the means Cecil used for the destruction of Mary Stuart, we must remember that this statesman was throughout working for an ideal. He believed that by ridding the world of the hereditary enemy of Protestantism he was merely acting in accordance with an inexorable necessity. As for Walsingham, whose business it was to frustrate plots against his sovereign, we could hardly expect him to be more scrupulous than his adversaries, to renounce espionage, and to countenance nothing which persons with more exalted standards would regard as immoral.

What about Elizabeth? Throughout life she gave ample evidence of concern for her reputation before the tribunal of posterity. Are we to suppose that on this occasion she knew how, behind the scenes, a murderous machine was being constructed, more sinister and dangerous than any of the accepted means of public execution? Were these repulsive practices undertaken by her chief advisers with her knowledge and consent? Mary Stuart's biographer is forced to inquire what part the Queen of England played in this sinister plot against her adversary.

The answer is that Elizabeth played a double role. We have plain evidence that she knew about Walsingham's machinations; that from first to last she tolerated, approved, and perhaps actively furthered the provocative agency of Cecil and Walsingham. History can never acquit her from the charge of looking on and perhaps assisting while the prisoner under her care was being lured to destruction. Still I must reiterate that Elizabeth would not have been Elizabeth if she had acted unambiguously. Capable of any falsehood, any misrepresentation, any form of deception, this extraordinary woman was, nevertheless, not without a conscience, and was never wholly immoral or ungenerous. In decisive moments, her finer impulses were always stirred. Even now she felt uneasy at the prospect of deriving advantage from such base practices. For suddenly, when her ministrants were getting ready to garnish the sacrifice, she made a strange movement in favour of the victim. She sent for the French ambassador, who had been instrumental in conveying Mary Stuart's correspondence from and to Chartley, without a notion that those whom he employed as messengers were creatures of Walsingham. "Sir," she said to him roundly, "you are in frequent communication with the Queen of Scotland. I would give you to know that I am aware of all that goes on in my kingdom. I have myself been a prisoner, in the days when my sister Mary ruled this land as queen, and am therefore familiar with the strange expedients used by prisoners to corrupt servants and effect secret communications." With these words Elizabeth appeased her conscience. She had conveyed a clear warning to the French ambassador, and therewith to Mary Stuart. She had said as much as she could without betraying her servants. If Mary did not desist from the enterprise, Elizabeth could wash her innocent hands and say proudly: "At any rate I gave full warning at the last moment."

But Mary Stuart would not have been Mary Stuart had she allowed herself to be frightened from her intended courses by a warning, if she had learned to act cautiously and thoughtfully. Still, to begin with she was content with a brief and noncommittal acknowledgment of Babington's letter—so brief that her enemies were disappointed, but Phelippes reported to Walsingham: "We attain her very heart at the next." She hesitated awhile, and Nau, her secretary, urgently advised her against involving herself in so dangerous an affair by putting pen to paper. But the plan was too exciting, the conspiracy too promising, for Mary Stuart to control her dangerous longing for intrigue. "Elle s'est laissée aller à l'accepter," remarked Nau with manifest concern. For three days she was closeted in her room with her two secretaries, Nau and Curle, writing a detailed answer to the various proposals. On July 17, a few days after getting Babington's missive, she dispatched her rejoinder by the usual route in the beer-barrel.

Phelippes was loitering in the neighbourhood of Chartley that he might decipher this momentous letter forthwith. As chance would have it, one of these days when Mary Stuart was out driving, she caught sight of the rascal, and was struck by his pock-marked countenance. He beamed at her genially, for he knew that the fruit of his labours was about to be garnered. The hopeful Mary fancied he must be one of the emissaries of her friends, come to the neighbourhood in order to prepare the way for her liberation. But Phelippes had a much more urgent and perilous task in hand. As soon as he had taken her missive from its cache, he set to work busily deciphering it. It began with generalities.

Mary Stuart expressed her thanks to Babington, and made three separate proposals for the coup de main which was to get her safe away from Chartley. Of course these matters were not without interest to the spy, but they were not of decisive importance. Then, however, Phelippes's heart almost stopped beating from delight, for he came to a passage that conveyed what Walsingham so greatly desired, Mary Stuart's "consent" to the murder of Elizabeth Tudor. To Babington's remark that "to dispatch the usurper" there were "six noble gentlemen, all my private friends," prepared to "undertake that tragical execution," Mary replied unambiguously: "The affairs being thus prepared and forces in readiness both without and within the realm, then it shall be time to set the six gentlemen to work, taking order that, upon the accomplishment of their design, I may be suddenly transported out of this place, and that all of your forces in the same time be on the field to meet me in tarrying for the arrival of the foreign aid, which then must be hastened with all diligence."

What more was needed? Thus Mary Stuart disclosed "her very heart," by approving the plan for the murder of Elizabeth. At length Walsingham's plot had reached fruition. Commissioners and creatures, masters and servants, could congratulate one another, could clasp one another's befouled and soon to be blood-stained hands. "Now you have documents enough," wrote Phelippes triumphantly to Walsingham. Sir Amyas Paulet, likewise, knowing that the execution of Queen Mary would soon free him from his jailership, was filled with pious exultation. "God has blessed my exertions," he wrote, "and I rejoice that He has thus rewarded my faithful services."

Now, when the bird of paradise was caught in the net, Walsingham need no longer hesitate. His plan had proved successful; his unsavoury machinations had been carried to a safe conclusion; but so sure was he of his position that he could not refrain from the gloomy pleasure of playing with his victim for a few days more. If he duly sent the deciphered and copied letter of Mary Stuart to Babington, there would be no harm in giving Babington a chance to answer, and perhaps thereby procuring additional items for the indictment. Something, however, must have made Babington aware that his mysteries were being probed. His courage failed, for the nerves of the most valiant man may give way under stress of an invisible and incomprehensible danger. He ran hither and thither like a hunted rat. Mounting a horse, he rode forth into the country. Then, as aimlessly, he returned to London and (a Dostoievsky touch!) visited Walsingham, the intriguer who was playing with his fate. His obvious intention was to discover, if possible, whether he was suspect. Walsingham, tranquil as ever, disclosed nothing, and let Babington take leave unmolested. Perhaps the fool would give additional proof by some act of stupidity. Babington, however, felt that the atmosphere was threatening. He scribbled a note to a friend, using heroic words in the attempt to keep up his courage. "The fiery furnace is made ready in which our faith will be tested." At the same time he sent a last word to Mary Stuart, telling her to trust and hope.

By now Walsingham had all the proofs he needed, and he struck hard. One of the conspirators was arrested, and this showed Babington that the game was lost. In an outburst of despair he proposed to Savage that they should hasten to the palace and make an end of Elizabeth. But it was too late. Walsingham's catchpoles were already on their trail, and only for a moment could the pair evade capture. Whither could they flee? The roads were blocked, the ports were watched, they were short of money and provisions. For ten days they hid in St. John's Wood, then a few miles from London, though now not far from the heart of the huge city—ten days of horror. But hunger was pitiless, and at length drove them to a friend's house, where they received food and where the last sacraments were administered to them. Then they were arrested and led back in chains through the streets of London. The only mercy these two bold young men could expect in the vaults of the Tower was that of the rack, while the bells of the London churches were pealing in triumph. The populace was lighting bonfires and inaugurating processions to celebrate the rescue of Elizabeth, the revealing and foiling of the conspiracy, and the imminent destruction of Mary Stuart.

Meanwhile at Chartley the prisoner had enjoyed a few hours of unfamiliar happiness. Her nerves were tensed. At any hour men might gallop up with the report that the scheme had successfully been carried into effect. Today, tomorrow, or the day after, she might be making a triumphal progress to London, where she would be housed in the royal palace. In fancy she pictured the nobles and the burgesses in festal attire, awaiting her at the gates of the city, while the bells pealed jubilantly. She did not know, poor thing, that the bells were already pealing jubilantly to celebrate Elizabeth's deliverance. In one or two days more her long martyrdom would be ended; England and Scotland would be united under her sovereignty, and all Britain would be restored to the bosom of the Church Universal.

No physician can prescribe a better remedy than hope for an exhausted body or an outwearied spirit. Now that Mary, always credulous and full of hope, felt her triumph to be so near, she seemed completely transformed. She was refreshed and rejuvenated. Though of late years she had continually suffered from fatigue and exhaustion, so that she could scarcely walk any distance without bringing on pain in the side, and was a martyr to rheumatism, she was able once more to swing herself into the saddle. Astonished at this rapid change for the better, at the very time when the conspiracy had been blown upon she wrote to her "good Morgan" as follows: "I thank God that He hath not yet set me so low, but that I am able to handle my crossbow for killing of a deer and to gallop after the hounds on horseback."

Being in this cheerful mood of restored health, she welcomed the invitation of the morose Sir Amyas (unaware, she thought, stupid Puritan that he was, how soon his jailership would come to an end!) to participate on August 8 in a stag-hunt organized by Sir Walter Aston in his park of Tixall. The weather was unsettled for a week, and it was not until the 16 that Mary, in hunting costume, was able to ride forth, attended by her court chamberlain, her two secretaries, her physician, and Paulet himself, who remained unusually friendly. Paulet, however, was accompanied by a sufficient force. A glorious morning, sunshiny and warm, the fields steaming after the recent rain. Mary spurred her horse, to win the full enjoyment of recovered energies. For weeks, for months, she had not felt so young. During all these gloomy years of imprisonment she had not been so cheerful as on this lovely forenoon. Everything looked beautiful to her, all was going well. When hope springs up in the heart, a sense of benediction falls upon the soul.

The cavalcade trotted through the gates of Tixall Park. Now, however, Mary's pulses began to beat furiously. In front of the castle was waiting a troop of armed horsemen. Were they her friends, Babington and his associates? Had the undertaking hinted at in the correspondence been successfully carried out? But, strangely enough, only one of the waiting horsemen detached himself from the group. Slowly and solemnly he rode up to the queen, bowed, and raised his hat. It was Sir Thomas Gorges, gentleman-pensioner of Queen Elizabeth. Next moment, Mary Stuart's joy and excitement were dissipated, for Sir Thomas told her in bald words that Babington's conspiracy had been discovered, and that he was charged to arrest her two secretaries.

Mary was struck dumb. Any words she uttered might betray her. Perhaps she did not immediately grasp the full extent of the danger, but the cruel truth was soon disclosed to her when she noticed that Sir Amyas Paulet made no move to ride back with her to Chartley. She grasped, at length, the meaning of this invitation to a hunting-party. She had been lured away from her house that her rooms might be searched in her absence. No doubt her private papers would be examined. The authorities would raid the diplomatic chancellery over which she had presided almost as openly as if she had still been a sovereign ruler instead of a prisoner in a strange land. She was given plenty of time to think over her blunders and her follies, being detained for seventeen days at Tixall without being allowed to write or to receive letters. She knew that her most intimate secrets must have become known to Cecil and Walsingham, that her hopes had been dashed to the ground. She had been dragged a stage lower, from the position of prisoner to that of accused criminal.

The woman who returned from Tixall to Chartley was in a very different mood from the one who, seventeen days earlier, had joyously set forth from Chartley for Tixall. She did not ride through the gateway at a lively gallop, javelin in hand, surrounded by trusty friends and adherents, but slowly, mute, accompanied only by guardians and enemies, a weary, disappointed, ageing woman, with nothing but misery in prospect. Was she surprised to find that her coffers and drawers had been broken open, and that the documents they contained had been removed? Was it not natural that the few members of the Chartley household who remained loyal to her should welcome her back with tears of affliction? She knew that all was over. But an unexpected incident, a strange call upon her services, helped her through her first despair. Downstairs in the servants' quarters was a woman in the throes of labour, the wife of Curle, her secretary, who had been taken to London that he might bear witness against her and help to destroy her. Mistress Curle was alone in her extremity, with no doctor to help her and no priest to minister to her. The queen, therefore, rising to the occasion in the everlasting sisterhood of women and of misfortune, did what she could to help, and (as the Church permits to the lay in such an extremity) herself baptized the new-born infant.

For a few days longer Mary Stuart was detained at Chartley. Then came orders to remove her to a safer hold. Fotheringay Castle was chosen for her new prison, this being the last of the many. Her wanderings were over, and soon her life would be over as well.

But Mary's sufferings during the last months of her life, tragic though they were, were slight in comparison with the abominable tortures inflicted upon the unhappy young men who had ventured all on behalf of the prisoned queen. For the most part historians are affected with a class bias, describing at great length, and often enough exclusively, the distresses of those who sit in the seats of the mighty, the triumphs and tragedies of the rulers of the earth. They ignore the deeds of cruelty done in dark places, the torments inflicted upon sufferers of little note—as if persons of high rank felt more acutely than their "inferiors." Babington and a number of his confederates (who mentions their names today, although the name and the sad destinies of Queen Mary have been immortalized on countless stages and in numberless books?) endured in three hours of hideous torture more than Mary Stuart had to endure in the twenty years of her misfortune. Traitors in the England of those days were sentenced to be "hanged, drawn, and quartered"; and this gruesome penalty was inflicted on Babington and the others with the full approval of Cecil, Walsingham, and Queen Elizabeth. After a preliminary hanging the offender was taken down from the gallows while still alive, his sexual organs were cut off, he was disembowelled, and was then quartered by the executioner. Among the seven who were thus executed on the twentieth day of September—Babington, regarded as the ringleader, Ballard, a Jesuit, Savage, and four others—were two who were little more than boys and whose only offence had been that they had given bread to their friend Babington to aid him in his flight. Even the London mob, not as a rule squeamish, had had its fill of horrors, and murmured at the long-drawn-out barbarity of the execution. Next day, therefore, when "justice" was wreaked upon seven more of the offenders, the horrible procedure was shortened. Once again, however, a place of execution became drenched with blood for the sake of this woman whose magical power it was to lure more and ever more youths to destruction. For the last time! The Dance of Death that had begun with Chastelard had now drawn to a close. No one else, except Mary herself, would perish on behalf of her dream of power and greatness.

CHAPTER TWENTY-TWO

Elizabeth against Elizabeth

(AUGUST 1586 TO FEBRUARY 1587)

ELIZABETH'S ministers of State thus achieved their end. Mary Stuart innocently entered the trap, gave her "consent," made herself "guilty." Without stirring a finger, Elizabeth could let matters take their course, so that a legal decision would sweep her dangerous rival out of her path for ever. The struggle which had lasted for a quarter of a century was over. Elizabeth was victorious, and could rejoice as merrily as her subjects, who, in the streets of London and elsewhere, were noisily celebrating the rescue of their sovereign and the triumph of the Protestant cause. But in every fulfilment, bitter is mingled with sweet in the cup. Now, when Elizabeth could strike, she hesitated. It had been far, far easier to entice a heedless prisoner into the snare than it was to slay her when the trap had closed on her. If Elizabeth had wanted to rid herself of the inconvenient captive by force, she had had ample opportunities ere this. Fifteen years earlier, parliament had requested that Queen Mary should be dealt with by the axe. In 1570, John Knox wrote to Cecil warning him "that, if he thrust not at the root, the branches, which appeared to be broken, would bud more quickly than men could believe, and with greater force than would be wished," adding emphatically, "God grant you wisdom" and signing "John Knox, with his one foot in the grave."

Always when thus urged to take sharp measures, Elizabeth answered: "I cannot slay the dove which, pursued by a falcon, has flown to me for help." Now, however, what choice was left her, when the Babington conspiracy (Walsingham's plot!) convinced her that the choice lay between her own life or Mary's? Nevertheless, Elizabeth continued to shrink from a decision, for she knew what immense possibilities, moving in ever-widening circles, were involved. It is hard for us of a later day to understand how new-fangled, how revolutionary, was the thought of executing Mary Queen of Scotland and the Isles—a notion at which the hierarchy of the western world shuddered. To send an anointed queen to the scaffold was a plain demonstration to the hitherto servile people of Europe that even a monarch was subject to doom at the hands of the executioner, and could not be regarded as sacrosanct. Thus Elizabeth's decision implied, not merely the doom of a fellow-creature, but the doom of an idea. For centuries the slaughtering of this idea would work havoc among the kings of this world. The execution of Queen Mary would be a precedent for the execution of King Charles I, her grandson; and the execution of King Charles, in its turn, would be a precedent for the execution of Louis XVI and of Marie Antoinette. Thus does destiny work. Elizabeth, taking long views, and having a strong sense of responsibility, perceived the far-reaching implications of her decision. She hesitated, vacillated, and procrastinated. Once more there became active in her, perhaps more active than ever, the struggle between reason and feeling, the war of Elizabeth against Elizabeth. It is always a moving spectacle when we contemplate a fellow human-being wrestling with conscience.

Oppressed by this bipolarity of purpose, Elizabeth tried to evade the inevitable. Again and again she refused to decide; again and again decision was forced upon her. Thus, once more, at the last moment, she tried to shuffle responsibility off upon Mary. She wrote the latter a letter (indubitably penned, though it has not come down to us) in which she asked Mary to make her a confidential communication, as from one queen to another. Mary was to avow participation in the conspiracy, and submit to Elizabeth's personal judgment, instead of being tried in open court.

This proposal was the only way out of the difficulty, short of public trial and execution. It would spare Mary the humiliations that were otherwise unavoidable. From Elizabeth's standpoint, it would provide an infallible safeguard if this dangerous pretender to her throne consented to make an avowal in her own handwriting. It would give Elizabeth a firm moral hold on Mary. Thenceforward Mary, disarmed by her concession, could go on living quietly in obscurity, and Elizabeth would be tranquil in the fierce light that beats upon a throne. Each member of the pair would be assigned a separate role. No longer would Elizabeth Tudor and Mary Stuart stand as foes and equals on the stage of history, for Mary would have become a penitent on her knees before one who had graciously pardoned her and granted her her life.

But Mary no longer wished to be saved. The strongest of her instincts was pride, and she would rather kneel to lay her head on the block than kneel before a protectress, would rather tell a preposterous falsehood than make a plain confession, would rather perish than humble herself. She was therefore deaf to this offer, which implied debasement as well as salvation. She knew that as a sovereign ruler she had played and lost. Only one power was left to her on earth, that of putting her adversary Elizabeth in the wrong. Since she could no longer do her enemy direct harm, she would use the sole weapon that remained to her, would relentlessly manifest Elizabeth's culpability to the world by dying a glorious death.

Mary rejected the proffered hand. Elizabeth, egged on by Cecil and Walsingham, was forced to adopt a course she loathed. To give the proposed trial a legal justification, the crown lawyers were summoned, and crown lawyers are wont to find good legal grounds for whatever the wearer of the crown wishes to do. Busily they sought for precedents, showing that, ere this, kings and queens had been tried before the courts; that the accusation of Mary was not a manifest breach with tradition, not an entirely new thing in the world. The examples they were able to discover were not very impressive: Cajetanus, an obscure tetrarch, who had been put to death fifteen hundred years before; Licinius, Constantine's brother-in-law, equally unknown; finally Conradin of Hohenstaufen and Joanna of Naples—these were the only sovereigns who could be shown to have lost their lives through a decision of a law-court. In their servility, the crown lawyers went so far as to declare that the court of nobles Elizabeth proposed to appoint was superfluous. They held it would suffice, since Mary Stuart's crime had been committed in Staffordshire, to bring her before a common jury of that county. This democratic suggestion did not suit Elizabeth at all. She wanted to observe the forms. One who was the leading living descendant of the House of Stuart and (herself apart) also of the House of Tudor was to be done away with in right royal fashion, with pomp and circumstance, with the respect and the reverence due to a woman who had been a reigning sovereign. She must not be shuffled out of the way by the verdict of a few farmers and burgesses. Elizabeth angrily declared: "That would be a strange sort of procedure to take against a princess. I deem it right to avoid such absurdities, and to entrust the examination of so important a matter to a sufficient number of the noblest persons and judges in this land. For we princesses stand on the world's stage in full sight of the world." A royal trial, a royal execution, a royal burial were Mary Stuart's right, and therefore Elizabeth selected forty-six commissioners from among the noblest and most distinguished in her realm.

Mary Stuart, however, had no inclination to allow herself to be examined or sentenced by even the most blue-blooded subjects of her sister-queen. When, on October 11, 1586, Mary being ill in bed at the time, Paulet introduced Sir Walter Mildmay and Barker, the notary, into her bedchamber, to deliver Queen Elizabeth's letter, which announced the decision to bring her to trial before the commissioners, Mary burst forth indignantly: "Doth not your mistress know that I am a queen by birth? Or thinketh she that I will so far prejudice my rank and station, the blood whereof I am descended, the son who is to succeed me, and the majesty of other princes, as to yield obedience to her commands? My mind is not yet so far dejected, neither will sink nor faint under this mine adversity."

But, by an eternal law, character is destiny, and neither good fortune nor bad can wholly change it. Mary's merits and defects remained the same throughout life. Always, in moments of grave peril, she could react with outstanding dignity; but always, in the end, she would show herself too indifferent, too inert, to defend herself resolutely and persistently against prolonged pressure. Just as, at the time of the York Conference, she had abandoned the strong position of her claim to inviolable sovereignty, and had thus dropped the only weapon Elizabeth feared, so was it now. Early on the morning of October 14, Mary declared her willingness to appear before the commissioners—she thereby admitted the jurisdiction of Queen Elizabeth's court.

On this fourteenth day of October 1586, a great spectacle was staged in the hall of Fotheringay Castle. At one end of the big room had been set up a dais, with a canopy and a chair of State surmounted with the arms of England, after the manner of a throne, to symbolize the invisible presence of England's queen, as supreme authority. To right and to left were ranged in order of precedence the various commissioners; before them was a table for the use of the prosecuting counsel, the presiding judge, other lawyers, and minute-takers. Mary Stuart entered, supported on one side by her physician, Bourgoigne, and on the other by Andrew Melville, her master of the household. As usual throughout the years of her imprisonment, she was dressed in black. On entering, she looked contemptuously round the assembly and said, with scorn: "How many lawyers are here assembled, and not one of them to represent me." Then she made her way to the chair that had been placed for her, not beneath the royal canopy, but a few steps from the empty throne. The "overlordship," the suzerainty of England over Scotland, which the northern land had persistently repudiated, was symbolized here by the loftier position of Elizabeth's throne. Mary would not let this pass without protest. "I am a queen by birth, and have been the consort of a king of France. My place should be there," she said, glancing at the vacant seat beneath the canopy.

The proceedings were formally opened. Just as at York and at Westminster, so now, the most primitive legal considerations were disregarded. As at the conferences, many years before, the principal witnesses, Bothwell's servants, had been executed with suspicious haste, so on this occasion had Babington and his associates been jostled out of the world before Mary's trial began. Nothing but their alleged confessions, extorted under fear of imminent death, were laid before the court. By a further amazing breach of justice, even the incriminating letters upon which so much stress was laid, the missives from Mary Stuart to Babington and from Babington to Mary Stuart, were not read aloud from the reputed originals, but from transcripts. Mary Stuart protested against this use of Phelippes's decipherments.

"Nay," she said, "bring me my own handwrit; anything to suit a purpose may be put in what you do call copies. Also, it is an easy matter to counterfeit ciphers and characters, if others have got the alphabet used for such correspondence." Then she went on to hint at Walsingham's plan for her destruction and that of her son.

Legally, the Queen of Scots had ground for a vigorous defence along the line here indicated, and had she been represented by counsel, much stress would have been laid upon the matter. But Mary stood alone before the judges, ignorant of English law, unaware of what incriminating material could be produced against her, and, to her disaster, she made the mistake she had made at York and Westminster. She did not confine herself to protests against certain suspicious circumstances in the accusation, but denied the charges against her in block, thus trying to refute much that was irrefutable. She began by denying all knowledge of Babington, but was compelled, on the second day of the trial, under stress of the proofs put in, to admit that she was acquainted with him by correspondence. This mistaken repudiation, which she was forced to withdraw, weakened her moral position, and it was too late to try a return to the old standpoint, to demand "as a queen" the right of being believed on the strength of her royal word. It was of no avail for her to exclaim: "I came to this land relying upon the friendship and the pledges of the Queen of England, who had sent me a ring in token that I could so rely." For Mary's judges were not trying her that right, which is eternal and inviolable, should prevail, but simply that they might secure peace at long last for their own queen and their own country. The verdict had been settled before the hearing; and when, on the twenty-fifth of the month, the commissioners reassembled in the Star Chamber at Westminster, only one of them, Lord Zouche, was bold enough to declare himself unsatisfied that the Scottish queen "had compassed, practised, or imagined" the death of Elizabeth. Thus the verdict was robbed of the charm of unanimity, but all the other commissioners subserviently decided as they had been told. Promptly a scrivener set to work, writing fair on parchment the court's decision that "the aforesaid Mary Stuart, a pretender to the crown of this kingdom of England, had approved and devised various plans for the purpose of injuring, destroying, or slaying the royal person of our sovereign lady the Queen of England." Parliament had already decreed that punishment for such plots against Elizabeth's life was to be death.

It had been incumbent on the assembled nobles to utter the verdict and pass sentence. The verdict had been "guilty," and the sentence one of death. Elizabeth, however, the Queen of England, was the incorporation of the highest powers in the realm, and could exercise the humane, the generous right of clemency. With her it ultimately rested whether the death-sentence should be carried out or should be annulled. Once more a choice she hated was forced upon her. What would she do? Again Elizabeth was marshalled against Elizabeth. As in the tragedies of the ancient Greek playwrights the chorus was ranged to right and to left of a conscience-stricken principal, uttering strophe and antistrophe, so now did Elizabeth hear voices both within and without, some urging her to be inflexible, and others imploring her to be forgiving. Above them all looked down unseen the supreme judge of human actions, History, whose voice is silent while the actors still live, and who utters the verdict only when the curtain has fallen on them for ever. The right wing of the chorus was loud and inexorable in clamouring "Death, Death, Death." The Lord High Treasurer, the Privy Council, Elizabeth's closest friends (such as Leicester), the lords, and the commons—one and all considered that the execution of Mary Stuart was the only way of securing tranquillity for the realm and peace of mind and safety for its queen. Both Houses of Parliament adopted an address to the Queen's most Gracious Majesty praying that sentence of death be executed forthwith against Mary. "We cannot find that there is any possible means to provide for Your Majesty's safety but by the just and speedy execution of the said queen, the neglecting whereof may procure the heavy displeasure and punishment of Almighty God."

To Elizabeth this insistence was welcome. She wanted the world at large to know that she personally had no desire to make an end of Mary Stuart, but that the English nation urged upon her the necessity of carrying out the sentence. The louder, the plainer the condemnatory voices, the better. Then she would be given a chance of performing a great aria of clemency and humaneness upon the world-stage; and, ever a play-actress, she made the most of her opportunity. She fervently acknowledged receipt of the exhortation of parliament, humbly thanking Almighty God that by His will she had been delivered from deadly peril. Thereafter, speaking in louder tones, she addressed the wider world and the tribunal of history, wishing to disclaim responsibility for Mary Stuart's fate.

"Although mine own life hath been in such deadly peril, I avow that nothing hath distressed me more than that one of mine own sex, of equal rank and birth, and so nearly akin to me by blood, should have been guilty of so great a crime. So far am I from being moved by malice that, immediately after the disclosure of certain traitorous proceedings against myself, I wrote to her privately to the effect that if she would make avowal of her guilt to me in a private letter everything could be settled quietly. I did not write to her thiswise in order to lure her into a trap, since I already was fully informed as to anything she could admit to me. But now, when matters have gone so far, even now, if she would openly admit her penitence, and if no one any longer were in her name to push her cause against me, I would willingly pardon her, were no more at stake than my own life, and not the safety and welfare of my realm. It is for your sake and that of my people that I wish to go on living." Then comes a frank admission that her hesitation is determined by her dread of the verdict of history. "For we princes stand, as it were, upon a stage, exposed to the prying glances of the world. The slightest speck upon our raiment is noticed, any weakness of ours is quickly recorded, so that we must be sedulous more than others that our actions shall always be just and honourable." For this reason she begged parliament to excuse her for not coming to an immediate decision, seeing that "it is my wont, even in matters of far less moment, to deliberate long before coming to a final decision."

Was this rigmarole truth or falsehood? Both; for, to repeat, Elizabeth was bipolar. She wanted to be freed from her adversary, but at the same time desired to pose before the world as magnanimous and clement. Twelve days later she sent to Cecil to inquire whether it would not be possible to spare Mary Stuart's life while safeguarding her own. Once more the Privy Council and parliament assured Queen Elizabeth that there was no other way out of the difficulty than Queen Mary's execution. Now let us hear Elizabeth once more. This time her words have the unmistakable ring of truth. "I am this day more in conflict with myself than ever before in my life, as to whether I shall speak or be silent. Were I to speak and to complain, I should play the hypocrite; were I to remain silent, all your pains would have been lost. It may seem strange to you that I should complain, but I must avow it hath always been my innermost wish to find some other way of achieving your safety and mine own welfare than the one that is proposed. . . . Since, however, it hath now been determined that my safety cannot be secured in any other way than by her death, I am profoundly mournful that I, who have pardoned so many rebels and have passed over so many acts of treason in silence, should be compelled to show cruelty towards so highly placed a princess." Reading between the lines, we can see that she is only asking to be over-persuaded. But, ambiguous as ever, she cannot utter a clear Yes or a plain No, for she concludes with the words: "I beg you to content yourselves for the nonce with an answer which is no answer. I do not withstand your opinion, I understand your reason, and I beg you to accept my gratitude, to excuse my inward doubts, and not to take it amiss that I send you an answer which is no answer."

The voices on the right have spoken. They have clamoured Death, Death, Death. But the voices on the left, the voices accordant with the best promptings of her heart, were also speaking loudly. The King of France sent a special envoy to talk of the common interests of monarchs. He reminded Elizabeth that by defending Mary's inviolability she would be defending her own; he exhorted her not to forget that the first rule for one who wished to reign well and happily must be to avoid bloodshed. He reminded her that the right of hospitality was sacred among all nations. Elizabeth must not sin against God by touching the head of an anointed queen. Since Elizabeth, playing the game of shilly-shally as usual, would reply only with half-assurances and ambiguous utterances, the tone of the foreign envoys grew louder. What had at first been no more than request became imperious warnings, and then open threats. Elizabeth, however, trained by nearly three decades on the throne in the intricacies of political life, had fine hearing. When addressed in this emotional way, she listened for only one thing, to learn whether, in the folds of their togas, the diplomatists had hidden commissions to break off relations and declare war. She was quick to perceive that behind the loud and blustering words there was no clash of arms, that neither Henry III nor Philip II was prepared to draw the sword and to let slip the dogs of war as soon as the axe fell upon Mary Stuart's neck.

Thus she was content to shrug her shoulders at the diplomatic stage-thunder of France and Spain. She had, doubtless, to show more caution in thrusting aside another objection, that of Scotland. For if any one on earth should regard it as a sacred duty to prevent the execution of a queen of Scotland in a strange land, it was James VI, since the blood which was to be shed ran in his own veins, since the woman whose life was to be taken was she who had given him life, his mother. Not that James was likely to be stirred by filial affection. Having become Elizabeth's pensioner and ally, it seemed to him that the mother who denied his royal title, who had invoked maledictions upon him, and had tried to sell his heritage to foreign monarchs was nothing but an obstacle in his path. Directly he heard of the discovery of the Babington conspiracy, he sent congratulations to Queen Elizabeth; and when the French ambassador, seeking him out engaged in his favourite occupation of the chase, begged him to use his influence on his mother's behalf, young James replied angrily "qu'il fallait qu'elle but la boisson qu'elle avait brassée"—that she must drink the potion she had brewed. He declared that he recked little "how closely she might be prisoned, and whether all her base servants were hanged." The best thing would be that in future she should confine her attention to praying to God. It was no affair of his; and, in actual fact, the hard-hearted son refused for some time even to send an embassy to London. Not until his mother had been condemned to death, and nationalist feeling blazed up over Scotland because the queen of a foreign land was about to slay their own anointed monarch, did the young man realize how poor a figure he would cut if he remained inactive. For form's sake, at least, he must do something. He would not, indeed, go so far as the Scottish parliament demanded, and declare his intention to make war on

England should the execution take place. Still, he sat down at his writing-desk, penned energetic, menacing dispatches to Walsingham and sent an embassy to London.

Of course Elizabeth had expected this protest. Here, likewise, she did not take it at its face-value, but listened for the fundamental tone. The deputies of James VI consisted of two groups. The official ones, those who stood in the public eye, made reiterated and loud demands for the annulment of the death-sentence. They rattled their swords, breathed threatenings and slaughter, and those among them who were Scottish nobles displayed the fervour of genuine patriotism. They did not suspect that, while they were voicing these menaces in the royal reception-room, behind the scenes another agent, a confidential representative of James VI, had been admitted to Queen Elizabeth's private apartments, to negotiate with her, on the quiet, about a very different matter, which was far more important to the King of Scotland than his mother's life, namely his recognition as heir to the English throne. We learn from the French ambassador, who was well informed as to what was going on, that this secret envoy of James VI had been commissioned to tell Elizabeth that, if James was uttering loud threats, this was done only "for his honour and reputation." Elizabeth should not take his violence "in ill part." Thus Elizabeth was plainly told what was probably no news to her, namely that James VI, far from being outraged at the prospect of his mother's execution, was prepared "to digest it" if only there were held out to him the enticement of a pledge or a half-pledge of his succession to the throne. The negotiations that now went on were of a most unsavoury character. Mary Stuart's chief enemy and her only son drew near together, being both moved by the same dark purpose, for both secretly wished Mary Stuart to be swept out of their path, provided only that the world should not know with what feelings they were animated. They wanted her dead, but had, before the public eye, to behave as if their most heartfelt wish were to protect her. In reality Elizabeth was not trying to preserve her "sister's" life, nor James VI his mother's, each of them being only concerned to keep up a good appearance "on the world-stage." James had long since shown plainly enough that he would make no difficulties for Elizabeth though the worst should happen, thus giving her a free hand for the execution of his mother. Before Elizabeth sent Mary to her death, Mary's son had sacrificed her.

Elizabeth now knew that neither France nor Spain nor Scotland, nor anyone else in the wide world, would trouble her in earnest should she decide that "the matter must come to an end." There was only one person who, perhaps, might still save Mary Stuart—Mary Stuart herself. She need merely sue for pardon, and it is probable that Elizabeth would have been satisfied with this triumph. At the bottom of her heart she was waiting for such an appeal, which would salve her sore conscience. Everything possible was done during these last weeks to break Mary's pride. As soon as sentence had been passed, Elizabeth told Sir Amyas Paulet to inform the prisoner of what had happened, whereupon this arid and sober-minded official, who was all the more repulsive for his impeccability, took the opportunity of affronting the condemned, who for him was nothing more, now, than "une femme morte sans nulle dignité." He clapped his hat on his head and sat down in her presence, showing the stupid malevolence of one who takes delight in another's misfortune; he ordered his servants to tear down her canopy of State which was decorated with the arms of Scotland. Her attendants refused to obey the jailer's orders, and when Paulet made his own menials do the dirty work, Mary hung up a crucifix where the arms of Scotland had been, in order to show that a higher power than Scotland was watching over her. To every dictatorial affront she was ready to reply with a moving gesture. "They threatened to slay me if I do not ask for pardon," she wrote to her friends, "but I reply that if they have already determined upon my death, they may consummate their injustice when they please." Let Elizabeth murder her; so much the worse for Elizabeth! Better a death which would humble her adversary before the tribunal of history, than acceptance of a feigned clemency which would invest Elizabeth with the halo of magnanimity. Instead of protesting against the death-sentence or begging for grace, as a sincere Christian she meekly thanked God for all His mercies. But to Elizabeth she replied proudly as one queen to another:

"Now since I have been on your part informed of the sentence of your last meeting of parliament, Lord Buckhurst and Master Robert Beale having admonished me to prepare for the end of my long and weary pilgrimage, I beg to return you thanks on my part for these happy tidings, and to entreat you to vouchsafe to me certain points for the discharge of my corpse. . . . As a last request, which I have thought for many reasons I ought to ask of you alone, I beg that you will accord this ultimate grace for which I should not like to be indebted to any other, since I have no hope of finding aught but cruelty from the puritans, who are at this time, God knows wherefore! the first in authority and the most bitter against me. . . .

"Then, Madam, for the sake of that Jesus to whose name all powers bow, I require you to ordain, that when my enemies have slaked their black thirst for my innocent blood, you will permit my poor desolated servants altogether to carry away my corpse, to bury it in holy ground, with the other queens of France, my predecessors, especially near the late Queen, my mother. . . . Refuse me not this my last request, that you will permit free sepulchre to this body when the soul is separated, which when united could never obtain liberty to live in repose, such as you would procure for yourself,—against which repose, before God I speak, I never aimed a blow; but God will let you see the truth of all after my death.

"And because I dread the tyranny of these to whose power you have abandoned me, I entreat you not to permit that execution to be done on me without your own knowledge, not for fear of the torments, which I am most ready to suffer, but on account of the reports which will be raised concerning my death unprotected, and without other witnesses than those who would inflict it, who, I am persuaded, would be of very different quality from those parties whom I require (being my servants) to stay spectators and witnesses of my end, in the face of our Sacrament, of my Saviour, and in obedience to His Church. And after all is over, that they together may carry away my poor corpse (as secretly as you please), and speedily withdraw, without taking with them any of my goods, except those which in dying I may leave to them, which are little enough for their long and good services.

"I ask these things, in the name of Jesus Christ, and in respect of our consanguinity, and for the sake of King Henry VII, your grandfather and mine, and by the honour of the dignity we both have held, and of our sex common. Therefore do I implore you to grant these my requests. . . .

"Your sister and cousin,
"Prisoner wrongfully, Marie (Royne)."

Strangely, and contrary to all expectations, were the roles reversed during the last days of this long-enduring struggle. After Mary Stuart was informed of the death-sentence, her self-confidence returned. Her heart pulsed unperturbed; but Elizabeth's hand trembled when she signed the death-warrant. Mary Stuart was less afraid to die than Elizabeth Tudor was to kill. Mary had long been tired of her earthly pilgrimage, and yearned for eternal rest. She spent her hours in serious preparation for the end. She made her will, dividing her worldly goods among her domestic staff; she wrote letters to her colleagues, or those who had been her colleagues when she was still on the throne; no longer to incite them into sending armies and equipping for war, but in order to assure them that she was ready to die in the Catholic faith and for the Catholic faith. This restless heart had at length found peace. Fear and hope, "the worst enemies of man," as Goethe calls them, could no longer trouble her spirit. Like her sister in misfortune, Marie Antoinette, it was under the shadow of imminent death that Mary Queen of Scotland and the Isles realized her true task. The sense of historical responsibility completely dispelled her previous indifference. She gave no thought to the possibilities of pardon, but wanted only to die an impressive death, to triumph in the last moment. She knew that nothing but a dramatic and heroic end could make the world forgive the tragic errors of her life, and that nothing more could be vouchsafed to her than a worthy exit.

An extraordinary contrast to the dignity and composure of the doomed woman in Fotheringay Castle was shown by the uncertainty, the tantrums, the perplexity, the wrathful outbursts of Elizabeth in London. Mary Stuart's mind was composed and tranquil, whereas Elizabeth Tudor was still wrestling for a decision. Never had the Queen of England suffered so much at the hands of her rival the Queen of Scotland as when the latter defencelessly awaited an unjust doom. Elizabeth was unable to sleep; she passed day after day in gloomy silence; her spirit was obsessed with the intolerable problem as to whether she should have the death-sentence carried out. She tried to thrust aside the thought as Sisyphus rolled his stone uphill, but always it rolled back again to crush her. Vainly did her ministers of State address her; she could listen only to the voice of her own conscience. Rejecting one proposal after another, she was continually asking for new ones. Cecil found her "as changeable as the weather"; at one time she was for death, at another for pardon; again and again she asked her friends whether there was not some alternative, although at the bottom of her heart she knew there could be no such thing. If only what was to happen could happen without her knowledge, without her express order, be done for her instead of by her! She feverishly struggled to evade responsibility, perpetually weighing and re-weighing the advantages and disadvantages of so conspicuous a deed. To the despair of her advisers, she put off her decision with ambiguous, irritable, nervous, and unintelligible phrases, always non-committal. "With weariness to talk, Her Majesty left off all till a time I know not when," complained Cecil, who, cold and reasonable, could not understand the distress of Elizabeth's tortured soul. Though she had put a harsh jailer in charge of Mary Stuart, she was herself in thrall to a yet harsher one, the most cruel on earth, her conscience. This struggle of Elizabeth against Elizabeth, this inability to decide whether she should listen to the voice of reason or to the voice of humanity, went on for three months, four months, five months, nearly half a year. Her nerves being thus overwrought, it was but natural that the final decision, when it came, should take the form of an explosion.

On Wednesday, February 1, 1587, William Davison, Queen Elizabeth's private secretary (Walsingham, by luck or cunning, was indisposed during these days), in the gardens at Greenwich, was unexpectedly informed by Admiral Howard that Her Majesty needed his services on the instant, and that he was to bring her Mary Stuart's death-warrant for signature. Davison procured the document, which Cecil had written with his own hand, and conveyed it with a number of other papers to the queen. But, strangely enough, Elizabeth, the great play-actress, now seemed in no hurry to sign. She counterfeited indifference, talked to Davison about other matters, looked out of the window, and remarked what a bright and beautiful winter morning it was. Then she asked the secretary casually (had she really forgotten she had sent for him to bring the death-warrant?) what those papers were on the table. Davison replied, "instruments for Your Majesty's signature," and among them one which Lord Howard had specially charged him to bring. Elizabeth picked them up and signed them in rapid succession without looking at them, including, of course, Mary Stuart's death-warrant. This was according to plan, so that she could pretend, afterwards, that she had signed the fatal deed unsuspectingly among other papers of minor importance. But then came one of her weathercock changes. Her next remark showed that she knew perfectly well what she had been about, for she assured Davison that she had delayed so long in signing the warrant only in order to show clearly that her assent was most unwilling. Still, now it had been signed, he must take it to Cecil, that the Great Seal might be put to it. "Do it secretly," she added, "for it may prove dangerous to me were it to be known before the execution actually takes place." When the warrant had been sealed, it was to be carried into effect by the proper parties. The orders were clear, leaving Davison in no doubt that Her Majesty's mind was made up. The fact that the queen had long thought the affair over in all its details was shown by her further instructions to Davison. The execution was to take place in the great hall of Fotheringay Castle, for neither the front court nor the inner court was suitable. She reiterated her demand for secrecy as to the signing of the warrant. But having been able to make up her mind at last seemed to have relieved the strain. This put her in a merry mood. She chuckled as she told Davison that, when Walsingham learned what she had done, "the grief thereof will go near to kill him outright."

Davison believed, as well he might, that his instructions were ended. He bowed and made for the door. Elizabeth, however, could never decide unhesitatingly, and those who thought she had done so were apt to find themselves mistaken. She called Davison back from the door, her merriment having passed, and her real or feigned resolution having been dissipated. Uneasily the queen paced up and down the room. Was there not another way? After all, the "Members of the Association" had sworn to kill anyone who should attempt her assassination. Since Sir Amyas Paulet and his companion Sir Drue Drury at Fotheringay were members of the "Association," was it not their unquestioned duty to do the deed, and to relieve her, the queen, from the odium of a public execution? Let Walsingham write to the pair of them in that sense.

The worthy Davison became uneasy. It was plain to him the queen wished the deed done without herself having part or lot in it. One may well suppose that the secretary regretted having had no witnesses to this important conversation. Still, what could he do? His orders were plain. He therefore went first to Cecil; the Great Seal was affixed to the warrant; then he went on to Walsingham, who forthwith composed a letter to Sir Amyas Paulet in the sense desired. Her Majesty, said Walsingham, "doth note in you both a lack of that care and zeal of her service that she looketh for at your hands. . . . In that you have not in all this time of yourselves (without other provocation) found out some way to shorten the life of that queen, considering the great peril she is subject unto hourly, so long as the said queen shall live." Especially the recipients of the letter should bear in mind that they had "good warrant and ground" for the satisfaction of their consciences towards God and the discharge of their credit and reputation towards the world, "in the oath of association which you both have so solemnly taken and vowed, especially the matter wherewith she stands in charge being so clearly and manifestly proved against her." The letter went on to say that Elizabeth "taketh it most unkindly towards her, that men professing that love towards her that you do, should in any kind of thought, for lack of the discharge of your duties, cast the burthen upon her, knowing as you do her indisposition to shed blood, especially of one of that sex and quality, and so near to her in blood as the said queen is."

This letter can hardly have reached Sir Amyas Paulet, and certainly the answer from Fotheringay could not have got back to London, when a change of wind set in at Greenwich. Next morning, Thursday, a messenger knocked at Davison's door with a note from the queen. "If the secretary has not yet taken the warrant to the chancellor for the affixing of the Great Seal, let him wait until Her Majesty has had a further talk with him." Davison hastened to the queen and told her that, as ordered, he had already had the death-warrant sealed. Elizabeth made her discontent plain, showing this by the expression of her countenance; but did not blame Davison in so many words, and, above all, refrained from ordering him to bring back the signed and sealed death-warrant. She complained once more of the fresh burdens that were continually being laid upon her shoulders. Restlessly she wandered up and down the room. Davison stood to his guns, humbly waiting for decisive orders. Suddenly Elizabeth quitted the room, without saying another word.

It was a Shakespearian scene that Elizabeth was playing before an audience of one. We cannot but think of Richard III complaining that his adversary Buckingham is alive without giving clear orders for the murder. The same injured look of King Richard III, when his vassals understand him and yet pretend not to understand, had been flashed by Elizabeth at the unhappy Davison. He felt that he was on slippery ground and tried to find securer footing. He did not wish to stand alone in a position of such overwhelming responsibility. Seeking out Sir Christopher Hatton, a close friend of the queen who had been one of the commissioners at Fotheringay, Davison explained that he, the secretary, was in a ticklish position. Elizabeth had commanded him to have the Great Seal affixed to the death-warrant, after she had signed it; but her demeanour that morning made it obvious that she was in a mood to repudiate her orders. Hatton knew Elizabeth's whimsies too well not to understand, but he, likewise, was disinclined to speak in candid terms to poor Davison. The comedy of trying to shift responsibility was carried a stage further. Elizabeth had thrown the ball to Davison; Davison passed it on to Hatton; Hatton, in his turn, brought Cecil into the game. The Lord High Treasurer was no less disinclined than the others had been to shoulder full responsibility, but he summoned a meeting of the Privy Council for the next day. All Elizabeth's intimates and closest confidants were present, Leicester, Hatton, and ten other men of rank who had had ample experience of the queen's untrustworthiness. At the council, for the first time the matter was discussed in plain English. They were agreed that Queen Elizabeth, for the sake of her moral prestige, wished to avoid any appearance of having commanded the execution of Mary Stuart. She wanted to present herself before the world as "astonished" by an accomplished fact. It was, therefore, the duty of her loyal lieges to play up to her and, in apparent defiance of the queen's will, do what she really wanted and would not expressly command. Of course this was to take an enormous responsibility, and therefore the weight of her genuine or simulated anger must not fall upon one individual. Cecil's proposal was that they should jointly order the execution and jointly accept responsibility for it. Lord Kent and Lord Shrewsbury were instructed to see to the carrying out of the death-sentence, and Beale, clerk of the Council, was sent with the necessary orders to Fotheringay. Thus the possible blame would fall upon all the members of the Privy Council who had been present at this meeting, and by their transgression of the limits of their powers—a transgression which Elizabeth secretly desired—they would remove the "burthen" from the queen.

One of Elizabeth's most conspicuous characteristics was her curiosity. She always wanted to know, and to know forthwith, everything that was going on in her palace and throughout her realm. Yet on this occasion, strangely enough, she asked neither Davison nor Cecil nor anyone else what had been done with the death-warrant she had signed. For three whole days she seemed to have utterly forgotten a matter upon which her mind had been concentrated for months past. She did not ask once more whether the document had been sealed, and in whose hands it then was. As if she had drunk of the waters of Lethe, this momentous affair seemed to have vanished from her memory. When next morning, Sunday, Sir Amyas Paulet's answer to her proposal that he and Drury should murder Mary arrived, she never inquired where the signed and sealed death-warrant might be. Paulet's answer was by no means to the queen's taste. He instantly perceived how ungrateful a task was being assigned to him. He was to make an end of Mary Stuart, and for what reward? The queen would then have him accused of the murder and hand him over to justice. Sir Amyas Paulet did not expect gratitude from any member of the House of Tudor, and had no inclination to be made a scapegoat of. Lest he might seem disobedient, the shrewd puritan appealed to a yet higher authority than the queen's, namely to God. He wrapped his refusal in the cloak of morality. His reply was, of course, to Sir Francis Walsingham, and not to Queen Elizabeth direct.

"Your letter of yesterday coming to my hand this present day at five in the afternoon, I would not fail, according to your directions, to return my answer with all possible speed, which shall deliver unto you with great grief and bitterness of mind, in that I am so unhappy to have lived to see this unhappy day, in the which I am required by direction from my most gracious Sovereign to do an act which God and the law forbid it. My good living and life are at Her Majesty's disposition, and am ready to so lose them this next morrow if it shall so please her, acknowledging that I hold them as of her near and most gracious favour, and do not desire them to enjoy them, but with Her Highness's good liking. But God forbid that I should make so foul a shipwreck of my conscience, or leave so great a blot to my poor posterity, to shed blood without law or warrant. Trusting that Her Majesty, of her accustomed clemency, will take this my dutiful answer in good part (and the rather by your good mediation), as proceeding from one who will never be inferior to any Christian subject living in duty, honour, love, and obedience towards his sovereign. And thus I commit you to the mercy of the Almighty."

But Elizabeth was by no means inclined to take in good part this dutiful answer of her trusty Paulet, whom shortly before she had so enthusiastically praised on account of his "spotless actions, wise orders, and safe regards." Angrily she tramped up and down the room, shouting that she could not stomach those "dainty and precise fellows" who would promise everything and perform nothing. Paulet was a perjurer. He had signed the Bond of Association undertaking to serve the queen at risk of his own life. "But I can do without him," she screamed. "I have Wingfield, who will not draw back." With real or pretended wrath she stormed at the unhappy Davison (Walsingham was better advised in being laid up at the moment!), who, with lamentable simplicity, assured her that the legal method was best. "Wiser men than you," said Elizabeth contemptuously, "hold different opinions." It was time that the matter was settled once for all, and a scandal to everyone concerned that she had not been freed from the "burthen" of responsibility.

Davison held his tongue. He might have replied to his royal mistress that steps to make an end to the matter once for all had already been taken. He knew, however, that nothing he could say would be more distasteful to the queen than an honest assurance of what she already knew and pretended not to know—that the messenger carrying the signed and sealed death-warrant was on his way to Fotheringay, accompanied by a thickset and burly man who was to translate words into blood, commands into performance—the London executioner.

CHAPTER TWENTY-THREE

"En Ma Fin Est Mon Commencement"

(FEBRUARY 8, 1587)

"EN MA fin est mon commencement." Such was the device, not then comprehensible, which, years before, Mary had stitched into one of her embroideries. Her foreboding was to be realized. Her tragic death was the true beginning of her fame; it only would compensate in the eyes of posterity for the offences of her youth, would transfigure her crimes and follies. For weeks the condemned woman had been circumspectly and resolutely preparing for this last ordeal. Twice, as a young queen, she had looked on while a nobleman perished beneath the executioner's axe, and had thus learned that heroism on the scaffold is the only way of compensating for so cruel a death. Mary Stuart knew that the contemporary world and posterity would scrutinize her behaviour closely when, an anointed queen, she perished by a public execution; and that to show the white feather in this decisive moment would be treason to her royal reputation. Thus, during the weeks of waiting, she concentrated her energies. Creature of impulse though she had always been, for this last hour of her life she tranquilly made ready—with the result that there might have been written of her what Andrew Marvell wrote of her grandson Charles I on the like occasion: "She nothing common did or mean, upon that memorable scene."

She gave no sign of terror or astonishment when, on Tuesday, February 7, 1587, her servants told her that Shrewsbury, Kent, and Beale had arrived from London, that they were accompanied by the High Sheriff of Northampton, and that they and Sir Drue Drury had news to communicate to her. She summoned her ladies and most of the members of her domestic staff. Then the visitors were admitted. She wanted to be surrounded by friendly witnesses, who would declare that she had been stalwart to the last, that she, daughter of

James V of Scotland and Mary of Guise, she, in whose veins flowed the blood of the Tudors, the Valois, and the Stuarts, could be steadfast in this terrible emergency. Shrewsbury, under whose care she had lived for the greater part of her long imprisonment, bent his knee and bowed his grey head. His voice trembled as he announced that Queen Elizabeth had found it necessary to yield to the urgent petition of her subjects and to command that the death-penalty should be carried into effect. Then he read the death-warrant, to which Mary listened without a sign of emotion. Having crossed herself, she said: "In the name of God, these tidings are welcome, and I bless and pray Him that the end of all my bitter sufferings is at hand. I could receive no better news, and thank the Almighty for His grace in allowing me to die for the honour of His name and of His Church, the ancient Catholic and Romaine religion." She made no further protest—except insofar as a protest was implied in her placing her hand on a Bible which lay on the table near her, and swearing: "I have never either desired the death of the queen, or endeavoured to bring it about, or that of any other person."

Herself a queen, she no longer wished to defend herself against the injustice perpetrated against her by another queen, but was ready, as a Christian woman, to accept the afflictions imposed on her by God's will, and perhaps welcomed her martyrdom gladly as the last triumph He might vouchsafe her in this life. She made only two requests: that her chaplain should assist her to the last with ghostly consolation; and that the sentence should not be executed the very next morning, that she might have more time to prepare herself for death. Both petitions were rejected. The Earl of Kent, a fanatical Protestant, answered vehemently that she needed no priest of the Popish faith, but he would see to it that she should have the ministrations of a cleric of the Reformed Church, who would instruct her in the True Religion. Of course, at this supreme hour when Mary Stuart wished to avow before the eyes of the Catholic world her faith in the creed in which she had been brought up, she would hold no commerce with a heretic. Less cruel than the refusal of the consolations of her religion to a dying woman, was the rejection of her plea for a postponement of the execution. Once the matter had been decided, the less time between the announcement and the act of doom the better. The few hours that remained to her would be so busily occupied that little opportunity was left for the intrusion of fear or unrest. One of God's gifts to mortals is that, for the dying, time is always too short.

Mary allotted the minutes of her remaining hours with far more thoughtfulness and circumspection than had been her wont in ordinary life. As a great princess, she wished to die a great death; and, with the immaculate sense for style which had always characterized her, with her native artistry and her inborn talent for seemly behaviour on solemn occasions, Mary prepared for her exit from life as one prepares for a festival, a triumph, a grand ceremony. Nothing was to be improvised, nothing was to be left to chance. Every effect was to be calculated; all was to be regal, splendid, and imposing. The details were to be as carefully thought out as the words of one of those heroic sagas that depict the exemplary death of a martyr. She ordered her evening repast for a somewhat earlier hour than usual, wanting time in which to write a few necessary letters, and to compose her mind for the solemn occasion. The meal was to symbolize the Last Supper. Having herself eaten, she summoned the members of her domestic staff and, having drunk to their welfare, enjoined them to remain faithful to the Catholic religion and to live at peace one with another. As in a scene from the *Lives of the Saints,* she asked each of them for forgiveness for any wrong she might have done to them. Then she gave to each a memento, distributing among them the rings and other jewels, the lace, and whatever valuables were left to her. On their knees, silent or sobbing, they accepted the gifts; and the queen, against her will, was herself moved to tears by their signs of devotion.

At length she retired to her private apartments, where wax candles had been lighted on the writing-table. She had still much to do before the morning: to read her will once more, to make arrangements for the hour of doom, and to write the last letters. The first of these was to Préau, her chaplain, begging him to pray for her throughout the night. He was sequestered in another part of the castle, the Earl of Kent, who was pitiless, having forbidden him to leave his room lest he should administer to Mary Stuart the "papistical" extreme unction. There were sentinels in all the corridors, and it does not seem that this letter can have been conveyed to the chaplain. Perhaps Kent did not know that the prisoner had a gold and jewelled ciborium containing a consecrated wafer sent her by the Pope, with a unique dispensation to administer the Eucharist to herself, if denied the attendance of a priest! Next the queen wrote to her relatives, Henry III and the Duke of Guise. It is an honour to her that, during this last dreadful night, she had tender thoughts for others. She knew that at her death the cutting-off of her widow's pension would leave her domestics unprovided for. Consequently she begged the King of France to make it his business to see that none of them should suffer want, to distribute her legacies, and to have Masses read "for a Christian queen, who dies as a Catholic, and has been despoiled of all her worldly goods." She had previously written to Philip II and to the Pope. There was only one of the rulers of this world to whom it might still have been expedient to write—Elizabeth. But to her Mary Stuart had no further words to say. She would ask Elizabeth for nothing, nor thank her for anything. Only by a proud silence could she still put her longtime adversary to shame; by that, and by a dignified death.

It was long after midnight when Mary went to bed. She had done all that she could during the brief span of life that was allotted her. Only a few hours more, and her soul would leave her weary frame. In a corner of the bedroom the maids were kneeling, praying silently, for they did not wish to disturb the queen's slumbers. Mary could not sleep. Her eyes were wide open in the darkness. Still, she could rest her limbs for a while, so that refreshed in mind and body she would have strength to meet Death, who was stronger than herself.

Mary had robed herself for many festal occasions, coronations, baptisms, weddings, chivalric sports, war and the chase, receptions, dances, and tourneys—always splendidly, fully aware of the power which beauty wields on earth. But never did she dress more carefully than for the greatest hour of her life, which was to be her last. She had thought out every detail of her attire on this unprecedented occasion weeks in advance, as if wishing, in a final display of vanity, to show the world how perfectly a queen could present herself on the scaffold. For two hours the tire-women were at work. She would not go to the block clad as a sinner, in drab array. She chose a robe of State for this last formal appearance—black velvet, stamped with gold, and a black stomacher. The dress had a train so long that Andrew Melville, her master of the household, carried it as she walked. She wore two rosaries and a number of scapularies. After her wig had been adjusted, a wired white veil reaching to her feet was clipped to it. The shoes were of white Spanish leather, soft leather which would not creak when she mounted the scaffold. She took out of a drawer the kerchief with which her eyes were to be bound; it was made of the finest lawn with a gold fringe, probably embroidered by her own hands. Each article of her apparel had been most purposively selected, every detail, down to her underclothing, being combined to form a harmony, and with full knowledge that on the scaffold she would be partially disrobed before the eyes of strange men. The petticoat and camisole were of crimson velvet, and she had scarlet sleeves to match, that, when her neck was severed, the spurting blood should not contrast too crudely with her underwear and her arms. Never had a woman condemned to death made herself ready for execution with more artistry and dignity.

At eight o'clock in the morning there came a knock at the door. Mary Stuart did not answer, for she was kneeling at her prie-dieu, reading aloud the prayers for the dying. Not until her devotions were finished did she rise, and at the second knock the door was opened. The Sheriff of Northampton, carrying his white wand of office (soon to be broken), entered and, with a profound reverence, said: "Madam, the lords have sent me to you." "Yes, let us go," replied the queen, as Bourgoigne, her French physician, stepped to her side.

Now began her final progress. Supported to right and to left by two of her servants, walking slowly because her legs were swollen with rheumatism, she went out through the door. She was triply armed with the weapons of the faith, that no sudden access of fear might overwhelm her. Besides the Agnus Dei hung round her neck, and the rosaries, she carried in one hand an ivory crucifix. The world was to see how a queen could die in the Catholic faith and for the Catholic faith. It was to forget the crimes and follies of her youth, and that she was now to suffer death as accessory before the fact to an intended murder. For all time to come she wished to be regarded as a martyr to the Catholic cause, a victim of her heretical enemies.

Only as far as the doorway leading out of the corridor was she accompanied by her own servitors. Paulet's men-at-arms, acting under orders, barred the way to her staff. They might serve her while she was still in her own chamber, but not in the last minutes before her death. Down the great staircase, therefore, she was assisted by two of Paulet's troopers. None but enemies were to join in the crime of leading an anointed queen to the block. On the last step, in front of the entrance to the hall where the execution was to take place, was kneeling Andrew Melville, her master of the household. To him, as one of the Scottish gentry, would be entrusted the duty of acquainting her son that the execution had taken place. The queen lifted him from his knees and embraced him. His presence was welcome to her, for it strengthened her in her forced composure. When Melville said: "It will be the sorrowfullest message that ever I carried when I shall report that my queen and mistress is dead," Mary replied: "Not so. Today, good Melville, thou seest the end of Mary Stuart's miseries, and that should rejoice thee. I pray thee carry a message from me that I die a true woman to my religion, like a true Queen of Scotland and France. But God forgive them that have long desired my end and thirsted for my blood, as the hart does for the water-brooks. Commend me to my dearest and most sweet son. Tell him I have done nothing to prejudice him in his realm, nor to disparage his dignity." Then, turning to the Earls of Shrewsbury and Kent, she asked them "to permit her poor distressed servants to be present about her at her death, that their eyes and heart may see and witness how patiently their queen and mistress will endure her execution, and so make relation, when they come into their country, that she died a true constant Catholic to her religion." To this the Earl of Kent objected. The women would make a scene. "Besides, if such an access might be allowed, they would not stick to put some superstitious popery in practice, if it were but dipping their handkerchiefs in Your Grace's blood, whereon it were very unmeet for us to give allowance."

"My lords," rejoined Mary, "I will give my word that, although then I shall be dead, they will do nothing of the kind. I hope your mistress, being a maiden queen, will vouchsafe in the regard of womanhood that I shall have some of mine own people about me at my death. I know Her Majesty hath not given you any such strait charge or commission, but that you might grant a request of far greater courtesy than this is, if I were a woman of far meaner calling than the Queen of Scots." Seeing that the Earl of Kent looked stubborn, she burst into tears, and said: "I am cousin to your queen, and descended from the blood royal of Henry VII, and a married Queen of France, and an anointed Queen of Scotland."

The two earls consulted together, and at length agreed that she might be accompanied to the scaffold by "six of her best beloved men and women." Thereupon "of her men she chose Melville, Bourgoigne, the physician, Gourion, the surgeon, and Gervais, the apothecary; and of her women, those two, Jane Kennedy and Elizabeth Curle, which did lie in her chamber." With Melville carrying her train, she walked behind the sheriff and Shrewsbury and Kent into the great hall of Fotheringay Castle.

Throughout the night carpenters had been at work in this hall. The tables and chairs had been removed. At one end a scaffold had been erected, two feet high and twelve feet broad, "with rails round about, hanged and covered with black, with a low stool, a long fair cushion, and a block covered also with black." The cushion was in front of the block; on it the queen was to kneel in order to receive the fatal stroke. To right and to left were seats for the Earls of Shrewsbury and Kent, as representatives of Queen Elizabeth. Against the farther wall stood two men, masked and clad in black velvet, with white aprons, grim and silent, the executioner and his assistant. Spectators thronged the rest of the hall. Across the floor had been run a barrier, guarded by Paulet and his soldiers. Behind it were two hundred of the nobility and gentry who had assembled in haste from the neighbourhood to witness so unique a spectacle as the execution of a queen. Outside the castle-gates hundreds upon hundreds of the common folk were thronging, allured by the news; but none of them would be admitted to the castle. Only the blue-bloods might see the shedding of the blood royal.

With an unmoved countenance Mary entered the hall. A queen since she was but a few days old, she had early learned to demean herself royally, and this exalted art did not forsake her in the supreme moment. Head erect, she mounted the two steps to the scaffold. Thus proudly, when a girl of fifteen, she had ascended the throne of France;

thus proudly, the steps leading to the altar at Rheims. Thus proudly would she have mounted the throne of England if other stars had presided over her destiny. With mingled pride and humility she had kneeled beside a King of France, and later beside a King of Scotland, to receive priestly benediction; with mingled pride and humility she now bowed her head to receive the benediction of death. She listened unmoved while Beale read the death-warrant aloud to her. So calm was her expression, friendly and almost joyful, that even Richard Wigmore, Cecil's secret agent, declared in his report to his master that she listened to the document "with so merry and cheerful a countenance as if it had been a pardon from Her Majesty."

But a hard trial still awaited her. Mary Stuart wished this ultimate hour to be a triumph, in which she could disclose herself to the world as a pillar of the faith, as a splendid flame of Catholic martyrdom. The Protestant lords were no less determined that the last gesture of her life should not be an impressive avowal of Catholicism, and they therefore did their utmost to diminish Mary Stuart's dignity by acts of petty spite. Several times on the way from her bedchamber to the hall of execution, the queen looked round to see whether her confessor was not among those present, that, if only by a sign from him, she could be assured of blessing and absolution. Vainly, however! Father Préau was prisoned in his room. Now, when she had made up her mind to suffer the execution without ghostly counsel, there appeared on the scaffold the Dean of Peterborough, Dr. Fletcher, a fanatical champion of the Reformed creed, who, to the final moment of her life, was to embody for her the war of religions which had troubled her youth and wrecked her career. The magnates in charge of the execution had thrice been sufficiently informed that Mary, a devout Catholic, would rather die without priestly aid than accept the ministrations of a heretic. But just as Queen Mary wished, on the scaffold, to make the most of her own religion, so did the Protestants wish to bring theirs to the front; it was their God who was to be honoured on this occasion, not hers. Under the pretext of care for her salvation, the dean began an evangelical exhortation, which Mary, in her impatience, several times tried to cut short. Again and again she interrupted Dr. Fletcher by assuring him that she persisted, that she was "settled," in the ancient Catholic and Romaine religion, in defence whereof, by God's grace, she was that day to spend her blood. But Fletcher was a paltry creature, with scant respect for the will of a dying woman, and inflated by vanity. Having carefully prepared his sermon, he was delighted with the chance of delivering it before so distinguished a congregation. He went on with his oration until Mary found no other means for deafening her ears than to throw herself on her knees, crucifix in one hand and missal in the other, to pray aloud in Latin, that she might drown the unctuous outpourings of the dean. The two religions, instead of joining forces to pray on behalf of the victim, were still at grips upon the scaffold, hatred being always stronger than reverence for distress. Shrewsbury and Kent, and with them most of those assembled, prayed aloud in English, while Mary and her servitors prayed aloud in Latin. As soon as Fletcher's oration came to an end, and when the silence had healed up again, Mary rose, kneeled down once more, and prayed in English for Christ's afflicted Church, for a surcease of her troubles, for her son, and for the Queen's Majesty. Pressing the crucifix to her breast, she desired the saints to make intercession for her to the Saviour of the world, Jesus Christ. Again the Earl of Kent, likewise a Protestant fanatic, interfered with her devotions, urging her to lay aside these "popish trumperies." But the dying woman was by now far beyond earthly contentions. She uttered no sound, made no sign, in answer; her voice pealed through the hall saying that she forgave her enemies with all her heart, those who had long sought her blood, and begged God to lead them to the truth.

Silence was restored. Mary knew that the end was near. For the last time she kissed the crucifix and crossed herself, saying: "Even as Thy arms, O Jesu Christ, were spread here upon the cross, so receive me into the arms of mercy, and forgive me all my sins. Amen."

That was a cruel and violent age, but it was not therefore wholly unspiritual. In many of its customs it remained more keenly aware of its own inhumanity than we are aware of our own inhumanity today. At every execution, however barbarous the method, there was a moment of human greatness amid the horror. Before the executioner stretched forth his hand to slay or to torture, he asked the victim's pardon for the wrong he was about to commit. The two masked men,

Bulle, the executioner, and his assistant, kneeled in front of Mary and begged forgiveness since it was their duty to put her to death. She answered: "I forgive you with all my heart. For I hope this death shall give an end to my troubles." The two black-robed men rose to their feet once more and made ready for their work.

Simultaneously, Jane Kennedy and Elizabeth Curle began to disrobe Mary. She helped them by removing from her neck the chain with the Agnus Dei. She made these preparations firmly and, as Wigmore reported, "with such speed as if she had longed to be gone out of the world." When the black gown had been removed, her red velvet underclothing shone forth, and, thus robed, with her long scarlet sleeves to match, she looked like a flame of blood, splendid and unforgettable. Now came the farewells. The queen embraced her assistants and exhorted them not to weep too loudly: "Ne cry vous, j'ay preye pur vous." Then, kneeling on the cushion which had been spread for her, she intoned the Latin psalm: "In te, domine, confido, ne confundar in aeternum."

Little remained to be done. She laid her head on the block, which she embraced with both arms, as one in love with death. To the end Mary Stuart maintained her royal dignity. With neither sign nor word did she show any fear. The daughter of the Stuarts, of the Tudors, and of the Guises made ready to die worthily. But what help is human dignity, what help is acquired or inherited poise, against the horror which necessarily surrounds murder? On no one (however much the books and reports may lie about the matter) can the execution of a human being produce a romantic and touching impression. Always death by the executioner's axe must be a horrible spectacle of slaughter. The first blow fell awry, striking the back of the head instead of severing the neck. A hollow groan escaped from the mouth of the victim. At the second stroke, the axe sank deep into the neck, and the blood spurted out copiously. Not until a third blow had been given was the head detached from the trunk. Now came a further touch of horror. When Bulle wished to lift the head by the hair and show it to those assembled, he gripped only the wig, and the head dropped on to the ground. It rolled like a ball across the scaffold; and when the executioner stooped once more to seize it, the onlookers could discern that it was that of an old woman with close-cropped and grizzled hair. For a moment, the spectators were overcome by their feelings, so that all held their breath in silence. At length, however, when the executioner lifted up the head and shouted: "God save the queen!" the Dean of Peterborough summoned up courage to say: "Amen! Amen! So perish all the queen's enemies." The Earl of Kent came up to the dead body and, with lowered voice, said: "Such end happen to all the queen's and Gospel's enemies!"

Pallid, where not stained with blood, was the white-haired head as it confronted the noblemen who, had her fate been different, would have been her most loyal servants and zealous subjects. For nigh on a quarter of an hour the lips continued to twitch convulsively. To lessen the horror of the spectacle, a pall was hastily drawn over the headless trunk and the gorgon-like head. Then, while amid a paralysed silence some underlings were carrying away the gloomy burden, a trifling incident revived the general consternation. As the executioner and his assistant were raising the decapitated trunk, which was to be borne into a neighbouring room to be embalmed, something stirred beneath the clothing. Unnoticed, Mary's Skye terrier had crept beneath her petticoat. Now the little beast sprang forth "embrued in her blood." Afterwards, "it would not depart from the dead corpse, but came and lay between her head and shoulders." By force it was taken away and sent to be washed. "The executioners were discharged with money for their fees, not having any one thing that belonged at her." Then, "everyone was commanded forth of the hall, saving the sheriff and his men, who carried her up into a great chamber and made ready for the surgeon to embalm her, and there she was embalmed."

CHAPTER TWENTY-FOUR

Aftermath

(1587-1603)

IN THE Greek drama a long and gloomy tragedy was always followed by a short, rollicking farce. Such an epilogue was not wanting in the drama of Mary Stuart. She was sent to the block on the morning of February 8, 1587. Next morning all London heard of the execution. A wave of intense jubilation spread through the capital and the country. Had not the usually acute ears of the Queen of England been suddenly deafened, Elizabeth must have known from the pealing of the church bells that a festival not in the calendar was being celebrated by her subjects, and what was the occasion of that tumultuous rejoicing. But she carefully refrained from asking, wrapping herself more and more closely in the mantle of ignorance. She was waiting to be officially informed of the execution of her rival, and to be seized with "astonishment" at the news. The gloomy task of acquainting the "unsuspecting" monarch of the execution of her "dear sister" had been allotted to Cecil. He did not like the job. During the many years he had held high office under Protector Somerset, Edward VI, Mary Tudor, and Queen Elizabeth, he had been through stormy times and, especially under his present mistress, had had to endure frequent storms of indignation, some genuine and some feigned. On the present occasion, therefore, the calm and serious-minded man equipped himself with an armour of indifference before he entered the royal reception-room to acquaint the queen officially with the fact that Mary had been executed. But Elizabeth's fury, this time, was unexampled. What? Mary Stuart had been put to death without her knowledge and without her express command? Impossible! Inconceivable! Never had she contemplated so cruel a measure, as long as no foreign invader set foot upon English soil. Her counsellors had cheated and betrayed her, were a pack of rascals. Her prestige, her honour, had been irrevocably tarnished before the world through this perfidious and underhand deed. Her poor, unhappy sister had been the victim of a disastrous error, a scandalous plot! Elizabeth sobbed, screamed, and stamped on the floor in her frenzy. She railed like a fish-wife at the grey-haired statesman who, in conjunction with other members of her council, had dared, without her express commission, to act upon the death-warrant she had signed.

Never for a moment had Cecil and his friends expected anything else than that Elizabeth would repudiate the action they had taken as "illegal," as a "gross usurpation of power by subordinate authorities." Believing their "usurpation of authority" would be welcome to her, they had decided to relieve Queen Elizabeth of the "burthen" of responsibility. They had expected, however, that this attitude of repudiation would be assumed by the Queen only when she was playing to the gallery, and that, under the rose, in her private audience-chamber, she would thank them for so promptly clearing her rival out of her path. But, in the depths of her mind, Elizabeth had so carefully rehearsed her simulated wrath, that, despite herself, it took possession of her and became genuine. Thus the storm that burst over Cecil's bowed head was not mere stage-thunder, but the discharge of furious indignation, a hurricane of invectives, a cloud-burst of abuse. Not content with berating Cecil, Elizabeth was almost ready to slap her most faithful adviser's face. She reviled him so unmercifully that he, now well up in years (he was fifty-five), tendered his resignation and, in punishment for his alleged excess of zeal, was actually forbidden the court for some time.

It became clear that Walsingham, who had been the prime mover in the matter, had been guided by a shrewd instinct when he fell sick, or appeared to do so, during the decisive days. For the vials of the royal wrath were emptied upon the head of his henchman, the unhappy Davison. Davison was selected as scapegoat, as the butt who was to demonstrate Elizabeth's innocence. Never, insisted Elizabeth, had she told the secretary to convey the death-warrant to Cecil and to have the Great Seal affixed thereto. He had acted on his own initiative, against her will, and, by thus exceeding his instructions, had wrought immeasurable harm. By the queen's command this "unfaithful servant," whose offence was that he had been too faithful, was haled before the Star Chamber. A decision of that august court was to proclaim to Europe that the execution of Mary Stuart had been exclusively the work of the rascal Davison, and that Elizabeth had been completely innocent in the matter. It need hardly be said that the privy councillors who had sworn to shoulder the responsibility jointly with Cecil hastened to leave their comrade, and Davison as well, in the lurch. All that concerned them was to save their own ministerial positions and sinecures amid this royal storm. Davison, who had no witnesses to confirm his story of Queen Elizabeth's orders, was sentenced to pay a fine of £10,000. Since his whole worldly wealth amounted to nothing like this sum, he was cast into jail. On the quiet, subsequently, he was granted a pension, but never while Elizabeth lived was he allowed to appear at court; his career was at an end, and thenceforward he was a broken man. It is always dangerous for courtiers to fail to understand the secret wishes of their sovereign. At times, however, it is still more disastrous when they understand these secret wishes too well.

The pretty tale of Queen Elizabeth's innocence and ignorance as regards this matter of the execution of Mary Stuart was too obvious a fabrication to impose upon her contemporaries. Perhaps there was only one person who really came to believe in this fable of the imagination, and that, strangely enough, was Elizabeth herself. One of the most remarkable capacities of persons of hysterical disposition is, not only their ability to be splendid liars, but to be imposed upon by their own falsehoods. For them the truth is what they want to be true, what they believe is what they wish to believe, so that their testimony may often be the most honourable of lies, and therefore the most dangerous. Hysteria apart, we have a tendency to self-justification and self-exculpation, and Elizabeth, presumably, felt perfectly sincere when she assured all and sundry that she had neither commanded nor desired the execution of Mary. As already said, she was bipolar in the matter. In part, she had never willed the death of Mary, and now that the death had taken place, this part, her remembrance that she had not wanted it, gradually became supreme over her remembrance that also she had desired her rival's death. Her outburst of wrath on receipt of the news, which she wished to be true but did not wish to hear, was not exclusively theatrical, but also—since her whole nature was double-faced—a genuine and honest anger; the outcome of an inability to forgive herself for having allowed her better instincts to be overpowered; and also a perfectly genuine anger against Cecil for having allowed himself to be persuaded to the execution, without instigating steps that would have relieved her of responsibility. So powerful was Elizabeth's autosuggestion to the effect that the execution had taken place in defiance of her will, so well did she succeed in deceiving herself, that again and again, thereafter, we hear the tone of genuine conviction in her asseverations. She was not merely humbugging when she put on mourning to receive the French ambassador, and assured him that she had not been so greatly moved by the death of her father or by that of her sister as by the death of Mary Queen of Scots; but she was "a poor, weak woman, environed by foes." Had not the members of the Privy Council who had played her this sorry trick been long in her service, she would have sent them to the block. She had signed the death-warrant only in order to pacify her subjects, but had never intended to have it carried into effect unless her realm were invaded by foreign armies.

In her holograph letter to James VI of Scotland, Queen Elizabeth persisted in the half-truth and half-falsehood that she had never really desired the execution of Mary Stuart. She reiterated her profound distress that the execution had been carried out "without her knowledge and consent." She called God to witness that she was "innocent in this matter," and declared that she "had never thought to put the queene your mother to death"; although her advisers were perpetually dinning into her ears that it was incumbent on her to do so. To forestall the natural objection that she was simply making a scapegoat of Davison, she proudly declared that no power on earth could induce her to shift on to another's shoulders the blame for anything she had herself commanded.

James VI, on his side, was not particularly eager to learn the truth. All he wanted was to avert from himself the suspicion of not having done enough to defend his mother. Of course it would not do for him to accept Elizabeth's assurances without demur; he, likewise, must maintain the semblance of surprise and indignation. He therefore made a great gesture, solemnly declaring that such a deed must not be left unavenged. Elizabeth's envoys were forbidden to set foot on Scottish soil, and King James's own messengers took over their dispatches from them in the town of Berwick. The world was to see that James VI showed his teeth to the murderers of his mother. But the cabinet in London had long since mixed the jam that was necessary to make the angry son swallow the unpalatable powder which was the news of his mother's execution. Simultaneously with Elizabeth's letter intended for public consumption, there was dispatched to Edinburgh a private diplomatic missive in which Walsingham informed the Scottish secretary of State that James would be successor to the throne of England, so that the whole dark affair would redound to the general good. The effect was all that could be wished. James had not a word more to say of an open breach with England. He was no longer troubled at the thought that his mother's corpse was still lying in some out-of-the-way corner of a churchyard. He made no protest because one of her last wishes, to the effect that her remains should be laid to rest in French soil, was being flatly disregarded. As if by magic, he was suddenly convinced of Queen Elizabeth's innocence, and gladly accepted the official version that the execution had been a "mistake." "Ye purge youre self of ane unhappy fact," he wrote to the Queen of England and, as her contented pensioner, expressed the hope that her "honourable conduct would become known to the world." A golden wind of promise rapidly appeased the storm of his wrath. Thenceforward peace and harmony prevailed between an undutiful son and the woman who had passed a death-sentence on his mother.

Morality and policy take divergent paths. We judge an event quite differently according as we consider it from the standpoint of humanity or from that of temporal advantage. Morally, the execution of Mary Stuart was utterly unjustifiable. Contrary to international law, in peace-time, the queen of one country had imprisoned the queen of another, had woven a snare for her, and had perfidiously encompassed her death. Just as little, however, can we deny that, from a purely political outlook, England was right in ridding the world of Mary Stuart. For, alas, what is decisive in politics is not the abstract right of what is done, but whether it is or is not advantageous in its results.

Now, as regards the execution of Mary Stuart, the results, politically speaking, provide full justification, since the murder brought England not unrest, but rest. Cecil and Walsingham had rightly estimated the positive forces that were at work in one direction and another. They knew that foreign States are always inclined to sing small when faced by a really strong government, and are ready to overlook the deeds of violence and even the crimes committed by such a government. They had been right in their supposition that the world would not be greatly disturbed by this execution. The alarums and excursions in France and Scotland, the threats of vengeance, soon quieted down. Henry III refrained from breaking off diplomatic relations with England, as he had threatened to do. He never proposed to send a soldier across the Channel on behalf of Mary Stuart when she was alive, and he was not likely to take up arms in her cause now that she was dead. Of course he had a Requiem Mass read in Notre Dame, and the court poets wrote a few elegies; but therewith, as far as France was concerned, the affair of Mary Stuart was over and done with.

Some threats were mouthed in the Scottish parliament; James VI put on mourning, but he continued to ride the horses which had been presented him by Queen Elizabeth, used the hounds she had sent him in his favourite sport of the chase, and remained the most friendly neighbour England had ever known. Only Philip the Procrastinator of Spain at length set to work seriously upon the equipment of his Invincible Armada, but he stood alone, and against him was ranged Elizabeth's good fortune, which was part of her greatness, as it is part of that of all famous rulers. The Armada was scattered by storms quite as much as by the resistance of the English fleet, and therewith the carefully planned onslaught of the Counter-Reformation collapsed. Elizabeth was victorious, and with the death of Mary Stuart her chief danger had been removed. The period of the defensive was over. English warships could now move to the attack, could navigate all the oceans, and begin the foundation of a worldwide empire. The wealth of England steadily increased; a new art grew during the last years of Elizabeth's life. Never was the queen more admired, never more loved and honoured, than after the basest act of her life. Again and again do we find that the great edifices of State are built out of blocks of harshness and injustice; always their foundations are cemented with blood. In political life it is only the vanquished who are wrong, and history strides over them with iron-shod heels.

The son of Mary Stuart was not spared a great test of his patience. He did not, as he had hoped, mount the English throne forthwith; the payment for his cowardly inertia was long delayed. He had to do what is the hardest thing for an ambitious man—to wait, to wait, to wait. For sixteen years, almost as long a time as that during which his mother had been prisoned by Elizabeth, he was inactive at Edinburgh, waiting until at length the sceptre fell from the old woman's shrivelled hand. Moodily he passed his days at one or other of his Scottish castles, riding often to the chase, writing treatises upon religious and political questions; but his chief occupation was to wait for a dead woman's shoes, to expect tidings from London. She survived with remarkable persistence until well on into her seventieth year. It seemed as if the blood of her rival must have been transfused into Elizabeth's arteries, rejuvenating her. She became stronger, more self-assured, healthier, after Mary's death. No longer did she suffer from obstinate sleeplessness. The fierce torments of an uneasy conscience that had plagued her during the months and years of indecision were assuaged now that she and her country had at length found repose. No mortal was left to threaten her position as ruler, and she devoted the remainder of her passionate energy to a struggle against Death, who must in the end rob her of her crown. When she was approaching seventy, tenacious and unyielding, the thought of dying became a horror to her. She wandered about her palaces, would not keep her bed, and moved aimlessly from room to room. Why should she vacate the position for which she had fought so long and so ruthlessly?

At length the knell sounded. Grim Death came to lay her low. Still, she lived on for days with the rattle in her throat, her restless old heart beating feebly. Beneath the windows, his horse ready saddled, an envoy of the impatient Scottish heir was awaiting a pre-arranged sign. One of Elizabeth's ladies had promised, as soon as the queen breathed her last, to lower a ring to the messenger. Long was the vigil. The Virgin Queen, who had rejected so many wooers, was reluctant to accept the embrace of Death. On March 24, 1603, a casement opened, a woman's hand was protruded, a ring was dropped. The courier mounted his horse and galloped away, to reach Edinburgh in two and a half days—a ride that became famous, for the distance is hard upon four hundred miles. He counted upon a high guerdon for his pains, for he was the bringer of good tidings. James VI of Scotland would mount the English throne as James I. In the person of Mary Stuart's son, the two kingdoms of Britain were to be united, and the long struggle between those of the same blood and speech who live on either side of the border was to come to an end. History often walks by dark and devious paths, but in the end historical necessity comes into its own.

James I settled down contentedly at Whitehall, where his mother had so often dreamed of residing. At long last he was free from monetary cares, and his ambition was satisfied; he thought more of comfort than of immortal fame. He often went out hunting; was glad to visit the theatre, there extending his patronage over a certain Shakespeare and other noted playwrights—this being one of the few good things to be recorded of the first Stuart monarch of a united Britain. A weakling, lethargic and dull-witted, devoid of Elizabeth's intellectual brilliancy, lacking the courage and the passion of his mother, he was a humdrum ruler over the joint heritage of the two queens who had so long been at feud. The union of the crowns, which each of them had so eagerly coveted, fell into his hands like an over-ripe fruit. Now, when England and Scotland were one, the time had come to forget that a Queen of Scotland and a Queen of England had troubled one another's lives with poisonous enmity. No longer could it be said that one of them had been right and the other wrong, since death had reduced the pair of them to the same level. Those who had so long fiercely opposed one another could now rest side by side. James I had his mother's mortal remains brought south from Peterborough to be interred, with great pomp and ceremony, in the British pantheon at Westminster Abbey. A marble statue of Mary Stuart was erected over her tomb, hard by the marble statue over the tomb of Elizabeth Tudor. The old quarrel was finished; neither woman would dispute the other's right to a place in the Abbey. The foes who during their lifetime had never set eyes on one another were to rest for evermore side by side as sisters in the untroubled sleep of immortality.

Index

Lightning Source UK Ltd.
Milton Keynes UK
UKOW01f1417070916

282404UK00001B/8/P

9 784871 878586